T0370535

Pro Oracle Database 23ai Administration

Manage and Safeguard Your Organization's Data

Fifth Edition

Michelle Malcher
Darl Kuhn

Apress®

Pro Oracle Database 23ai Administration: Manage and Safeguard Your Organization's Data

Michelle Malcher
Huntley, IL, USA

Darl Kuhn
Morrison, CO, USA

ISBN-13 (pbk): 979-8-8688-1037-4
https://doi.org/10.1007/979-8-8688-1038-1

ISBN-13 (electronic): 979-8-8688-1038-1

Managing Director, Apress Media LLC: Welmoed Spahr
Acquisitions Editor: Shaul Elson
Development Editor: Laura Berendson
Coordinating Editor: Gryffin Winkler
Copyeditor: Kim Burton

Cover designed by eStudioCalamar

Photo by Rodion Kutsaiev on Unsplash

Distributed to the book trade worldwide by Apress Media, LLC, 1 New York Plaza, New York, NY 10004, U.S.A. Phone 1-800-SPRINGER, fax (201) 348-4505, e-mail orders-ny@springer-sbm.com, or visit www. springeronline.com. Apress Media, LLC is a California LLC and the sole member (owner) is Springer Science + Business Media Finance Inc (SSBM Finance Inc). SSBM Finance Inc is a **Delaware** corporation.

For information on translations, please e-mail booktranslations@springernature.com; for reprint, paperback, or audio rights, please e-mail bookpermissions@springernature.com.

Apress titles may be purchased in bulk for academic, corporate, or promotional use. eBook versions and licenses are also available for most titles. For more information, reference our Print and eBook Bulk Sales web page at http://www.apress.com/bulk-sales.

Any source code or other supplementary material referenced by the author in this book is available to readers on GitHub (https://github.com/Apress). For more detailed information, please visit https://www. apress.com/gp/services/source-code.

If disposing of this product, please recycle the paper

*This book is dedicated to my beautiful daughters,
whom I enjoy laughing with every day!
—Michelle Malcher*

Table of Contents

About the Authors

 **Michelle Malcher** is a director of product management at Oracle. Her deep technical expertise, from database to security, as well as her senior-level contributions as a speaker, author, Oracle ACE director, and customer advisory board participant, have aided many corporations in architecture and risk assessment, purchasing and installation, and ongoing systems oversight. She was a founding board member for FUEL, the Palo Alto Networks User community, and a past president and long-time volunteer for the Independent Oracle User Group (IOUG). She has built teams for database security and data services and enjoys sharing knowledge about data intelligence and providing secure and standardized database environments.

 **Darl Kuhn** is an Oracle DBA consultant at RMCI. He handles all facets of database administration, from design and development to production support. He also teaches advanced database courses at the University of Denver. Darl does volunteer DBA work for the Rocky Mountain Oracle User Group. He has a graduate degree from Colorado State University and lives near Spanish Peaks, Colorado, with his wife, Heidi, and daughters, Brandi and Lisa.

About the Technical Reviewer

 **Jon Heller** is an expert SQL and PL/SQL programmer with more than 20 years of Oracle experience. He has worked as a database developer, analyst, and administrator and is the author of *Pro Oracle SQL Development* (Apress, 2023). In his spare time, he is active on Stack Overflow where he is a top user in the Oracle and PL/SQL tags. He enjoys creating open-source software, has a master's degree in computer science from North Carolina State University, and lives in Iowa with his wife and two sons.

Acknowledgments

When writing another book, it is amazing to be part of the fun of discussing data and talking about new features of database technologies, especially how new technologies are transforming companies.

I got to work with an amazing team and am thankful for their influence, guidance, and encouragement. I appreciate each of these awesome database and data people who are passionate about what they do, and I enjoy bringing along others by teaching, mentoring, and supporting others. What an opportunity to be in this career and work with others who understand how important data is! Thank you!

—Michelle Malcher

Introduction

The cloud, automation, and artificial intelligence are all buzzwords for the direction of where technology and data are headed. The interesting thing about these areas is that data still plays a very important role in all of them. Obviously, this is good for database administrators and any other guardians of data.

With these new environments and Oracle's Autonomous Database in the cloud, the question is being asked if DBAs are needed. In fact, that question has been raised for the past 15 or so years. The self-driving, tuning, and provisioning of databases is the future of the environment. However, there are still tasks that DBAs will be performing; they are also the go-to people for migrations to the cloud and data management.

Why write a book about Oracle 23ai database administration? I asked this same question in the previous edition of this book. This is still easy to answer: tasks are changing, but understanding the database is critical. Even with automated processes, issues might need troubleshooting, and automation needs to be implemented. Applications need database objects designed, created, maintained, and tuned for performance.

23ai provides some really cool ways to look at data. It is not just about relational tables and objects, but new data types and shapes of data are extremely important for application development, machine learning, and data connections. Data strategies are critical skills to have. This book is not just about the transitioning role of the DBA but about the administration skills that are still relevant in the database environment. Understanding how the database works internally helps with all of these areas.

Data is being integrated, migrated, and maintained in several databases. The structures of these environments are what it takes to create consistent, reliable, and always accessible data. Database design, development, and administration skills are needed for these systems and support applications.

This book explains the tasks needed to create Oracle 23ai on-premises and in the cloud and provides administration for the environment. It provides an inside look at the Oracle database, hardware, storage, and servers required to run Oracle. Some of the tasks presented should be done through automated processes, but DBAs need to be able to work through issues and troubleshoot any problems.

INTRODUCTION

There was careful consideration for including the content in this book to ensure it provided the right topics to give DBAs the tools they need to succeed.

Many of these topics are the same if the database is on-premises or in the cloud. Understanding the difference and how the DBAs can support migrations to the cloud are also included. Databases in the cloud serve many purposes in the enterprise. DBAs are the perfect resource to assist in migrations and ensure the data is secure and integrated into the cloud environment.

There are many examples, tips, and notes to provide any DBA of Oracle databases with the tools they need to design, implement, and administer Oracle 23ai database environments. The book also covers the tools Oracle 23ai and ways to leverage data and gain valuable insights that the business seeks through the information.

Although Oracle employs me, the views expressed in this book do not represent those of my employer. These are the thoughts and experiences that I have gained using the Oracle database over the years of industry experience. The opinions are mine, and they will allow you to use this technology in awesome ways at your company.

—Michelle Malcher

CHAPTER 1

Installing the Oracle Binaries

When you install an application on your laptop or computer, you plan to use it yourself. Even if you are just playing around with some development, you might quickly install a tool or database to check things out and learn about the application. However, that is not the case when you install enterprise-level database systems, which are normally used by an entire company (or they actually run the business), so there is quite a bit of planning and consistency that needs to happen for reliable installations of the Oracle Database.

It is the job of the database administrator (DBA) to plan and perform these installations and make it so that the management of the environment is consistent across the enterprise for a team of DBAs. If the binaries were installed differently each time or didn't follow the same directories or parameters, it would be a difficult environment to support and maintain. Some of the database environments and standards stem from earlier versions of the Oracle Database. These standards need to be considered, but with a new major release of the Oracle Database, there are opportunities to update and simplify the environment and installations.

The DBA needs to review the prerequisites, configurations, and options as part of the plan for installation. Installation is a task that every DBA should understand and be proficient at, even with more automation available in Oracle 23ai. The plan needs to include existing environments and a repeatable process for large environments. The DBA needs to set up the installs to be able to provision databases on demand and consistently.

DBA tasks are changing, and in cloud environments, the DBA tasks might be preparing self-service databases or not even needing to install the Oracle binaries. Another team member might be responsible for ensuring the database is installed, but patching and maintenance are required, so the DBA needs to understand the installation. This chapter dives into the options and configurations of past and current versions so you can gain the needed knowledge for the database environment.

1

© Michelle Malcher, Darl Kuhn 2024
M. Malcher and D. Kuhn, *Pro Oracle Database 23ai Administration*,
https://doi.org/10.1007/979-8-8688-1038-1_1

The Oracle Universal Installer (OUI) is a typical way to install the software and database. However, it doesn't lend itself to repeatability and automation. Running the graphical installer is a manual process in which you are presented with options on multiple screens. Even if you know which options to select, you may inadvertently click an undesired choice. The good news with Oracle 23ai is that it is easy to clean up the installation and start over, but the bad news is that you must start over. Once you get the installation through this manual process, you can save the response file, which is a text file that assigns the values to variables for a repeatable process and consistent installation of the software on other servers.

Tip   This chapter covers only installing the Oracle software. Chapter 2 covers creating a database. Using Oracle on the cloud is discussed later in this chapter and in Chapter 2.

Understanding the OFA

There are several prerequisites for the server, users, groups, and parameters that need to be set up for the installation, and a big decision that needs to be made is where the data is going to be persisted. The disks can be configured with file systems, raw disks, and Automatic Storage Management (ASM). If you work in an environment with several older Oracle databases, they are probably configured using the Optimal Flexible Architecture (OFA) standard. This is not just for the data files but also the software files and is a widely employed standard for specifying consistent directory structures and file-naming conventions when installing and creating Oracle databases.

The OFA is a standard that the DBA almost always customizes to fit the unique requirements of their environment. For example, a directory of /u01 might be the standard. But the base directory might be configured based on /oracle01 or some other naming convention that the server and storage teams might implement. Even though the directory names might be customized, the overall structure needs to be consistent with the environment, and the OFA standard is available for that.

The OFA standard provides ways to understand where log files are available consistently. If standards are followed, then security, migrations, and automation will be easier to implement because of the consistency across the environments. The consistent locations of the log files allow the files to be used by other tools and be secure.

The ORACLE_BASE directory in 23ai provides a way to have the ORACLE_HOME directories be read-only and have the writable files in the ORACLE_BASE. Read-only ORACLE_HOME directories separate the installation and configuration, which is important for the cloud and securing the environment. Different operating system (OS) users and groups own different directories. Also, GRID_HOME is the software for Real Application Clusters (RAC) and ASM, which would be in a different directory from the Oracle Database software. Depending on how big the enterprise is, each can be owned and maintained by other groups, once again providing a secure environment starting with the software and configuration. This simplifies patching as one image can be used for a mass rollout and can distribute a patch to many servers, which reduces downtime for patching and updating the Oracle software.

Understanding this structure is critical because most shops implement a form of the OFA standard. This structure also supports multiple ORACLE_HOMEs for different versions, patching, and other isolation, including Oracle Grid Infrastructure. You can always query the database in a SQLPlus session for the log destination files so you can see the structure with show parameter dump_dest. Using show parameter works for the recovery files too. The directories and files for the recovery area are located in db_recovery_file_dest, but you only need to remember db_recovery for show parameter db_recovery. Figure 1-1 shows the directory and filenames used with the OFA standard. Not all the directories and files found in an Oracle environment appear in this figure (there is not enough room). However, the critical and most frequently used directories and files are displayed.

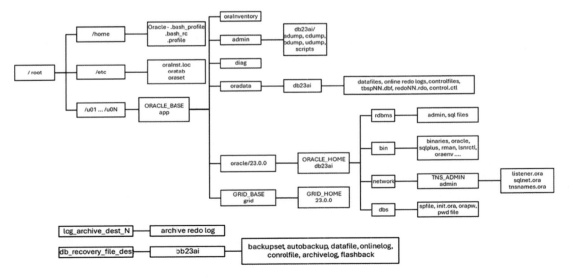

Figure 1-1. *OFA standard*

The OFA standard includes several directories that you should be familiar with.

- Oracle inventory directory (oraInventory)

- Oracle base directory (ORACLE_BASE)

- Oracle home directory (ORACLE_HOME)

- Oracle grid directory (GRID_HOME)

- Oracle network files directory (TNS_ADMIN)

- Fast Recovery Area (FRA)

Whether using file systems or ASM, these structures exist, especially for the software directories. The database files are found in these directories and are discussed in the following sections.

Oracle Inventory Directory

The Oracle inventory directory stores the inventory of Oracle software installed on the server. This directory is required and shared among all Oracle software installations on a server. When you first install Oracle, the installer checks whether there is an existing OFA directory structure in the format /u[01-09]/app. If such a directory exists, the installer creates an Oracle inventory directory, such as the following.

```
/u01/app/oraInventory
```

Figure 1-2 shows the GUI installation screen where you give the directory for the Oracle inventory.

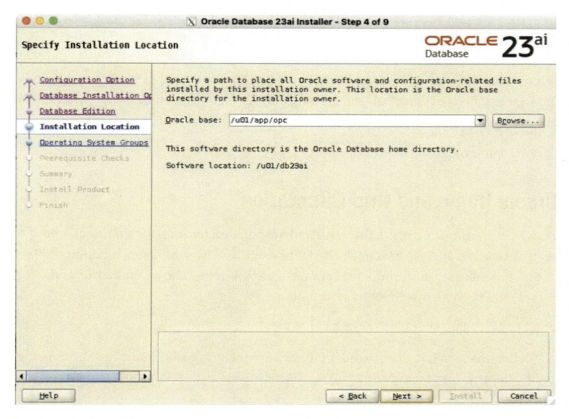

Figure 1-2. *Oracle inventory directory for installation*

If the ORACLE_BASE variable is defined for the Oracle OS user, then the installer creates the directory for the location of the Oracle inventory, as follows.

ORACLE_BASE/../oraInventory

For example, if ORACLE_BASE is defined as /ora01/app/oracle, then the installer defines the location of the Oracle inventory as follows.

/ora01/app/oraInventory

Oracle Base Directory

The Oracle base directory is the topmost directory for the Oracle software installation. You can install one or more versions of the Oracle software beneath this directory. The OFA standard for the Oracle base directory is as follows.

/<mount_point>/app/<software_owner>

5

Typical names for the mount point include /u01, /ora01, /oracle, and /oracle01. You can name the mount point according to whatever your standard is for your environment. A short, recognizable mount-point name such as /ora01 is preferred. The software owner is typically named oracle or grid. This is the OS user you use to install the Oracle software (binaries). The following is an example of a fully formed Oracle base directory path.

```
/ora01/app/oracle
```

Oracle Home and Grid Directories

The Oracle home directory defines software installation location for a particular product, such as Oracle Database 23ai or Oracle Database 19c. You must install different products or different releases of a product in separate Oracle homes. The recommended OFA-compliant Oracle home directory is as follows.

```
ORACLE_BASE/app/<version>/<install_name>
```

In the previous line of code, possible versions include 23.1.0.1 and 19.1.0.1. Possible install_name values include db23ai_01, db01, devdb1, test2, and prod1. Here is an example of an Oracle home name for a 23ai database.

```
/u01/app/oracle/23.1.0.1/db01
```

The Oracle grid home is the installation location of the grid software for the listener (Oracle network files), RAC, and ASM. Where you can have multiple Oracle homes for the database on a server, there can be only one grid home per server. Here is an example of the Oracle grid home.

```
/u01/app/grid/23.1.0.1
```

Note   Some DBAs dislike the db1 string on the end of the ORACLE_HOME and see no need for it. It is not required for the installation and can be kept as simple as /u01/app/oracle/ora23ai or /u01/app/oracle/23.1.0.1.

Oracle Network Files Directory

Some Oracle utilities use the value INS_ADMIN to locate network configuration files. This directory is defined as ORACLE_HOME/network/admin. It typically contains tnsnames. ora, listener.ora, and sqlnet.ora Oracle Net files. The listener.ora files are now typically with the Oracle grid installation and not in the database home. The listeners are normally maintained by the system that manages the grid, cluster, and ASM software. The tnsnames provide ways to connect to other databases, so these files are part of the centralized directory or database network files.

Fast Recovery Area Directory

Backup and recovery are important to any data you have in your enterprise and are important tasks for a DBA. Plenty of time is spent on recovery and backup procedures later in the book. But the initial backup and recovery plan should be included here as part of your installation and database creation. The Fast Recovery Area (FRA) is set up to have the control files, backup files, archive log files, image copies, and flashback. The FRA can be just a directory on your server or a disk group in ASM, but it is a critical directory for secure backups to recover from. Figure 1-3 shows this directory as part of the installation screen and is found in the db_recovery_ file_dest parameter for the database.

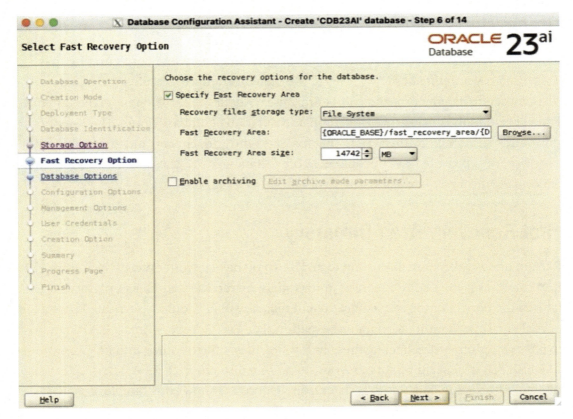

Figure 1-3. *Oracle Fast Recovery Area directory*

More on OFA is included in the appendix of the *Oracle Database Installation Guide*, and as you can see, the directories are part of the initial installation and planning. The Oracle installation creates other subdirectories; the values can be found in the database parameters.

Installing Oracle

Suppose you are new on the job, and your manager asks you how long it will take to install a new set of Oracle Database 23ai software on a server. You reply that it should take less than an hour. Your boss is incredulous and states that previous DBAs always estimated at least a day to install the Oracle binaries on a new server. The installation process has been greatly simplified over the years, and even removing and cleaning up installations is easier in case something goes wrong. Most of the time is spent setting up the users and groups and planning the installation. Even the prerequisites can be fixed as part of the installation process. You also do not need to do a manual GUI installation. You can run the RPM version of the binaries to get them installed and use the assistants to create a database after the binaries are installed.

When you are handed a new server and are given the task of installing the Oracle binaries, this usually refers to downloading and installing the software required before you can create an Oracle database. This process involves several steps.

1. Create the appropriate OS groups. In Oracle Database 23ai, there are several OS groups that you can form and use to manage the level of granularity of the SYSDBA permissions. Minimally, you must create an OS dba group and the OS oracle user. Also recommended is an oinstall group for the binary directories and a grid user for the Oracle grid installation since this is maintained separately from the database.

2. Ensure that the OS is configured adequately for an Oracle database. A prerequisite checklist is part of the installation for parameters and space, and these are listed as part of the installation guide.

3. Obtain the database installation software from Oracle. Or you can simply do a yum install of the rpm on the Linux server (`yum -y install oracle-database-ee-23ai`).

4. Unzip the grid software in the Oracle grid home, and unzip the database installation software in the Oracle database home.

5. Install the grid software first by running `./gridSetup.sh`.

6. Install the database software by running `./runInstaller`.

7. Save the response file to perform other installations and run the Oracle silent installer.

8. Troubleshoot any issues.

9. Apply any additional patches.

Note   Oracle Database software can be freely downloaded from the website (`oracle.com/downloads`). However, patch downloads require a purchased license and a My Oracle Support (MOS) account.

Step 1: Create the OS Groups and Users

If you work in a company with a system administrator (SA), then steps 1 and 2 are usually performed by the SA. If you don't have an SA, you must perform these steps yourself (this is often the case in small companies, where you may be required to perform many different job functions). Even if you have root access, you should not install Oracle as root. The grid software should be installed and owned by the grid user, and the database software as oracle. You need root to create the oracle and grid users and the groups as needed.

In the old days, a typical Oracle installation would contain one OS group (dba) and one OS user (oracle). You can still install the Oracle software using this minimalistic approach. If there is just one DBA in your company and you don't need a more granular division of privileges among team members, then this method works well with one user and one group.

However, there are multiple OS groups that Oracle recommends you create, and you can add different OS users and assign them to groups on an as-needed basis, depending on their job function. When an OS user is assigned to a group, that assignment provides the user with specific database privileges. Table 1-1 shows the OS groups and how each group maps to corresponding database privileges. For example, if you have a user who is responsible only for monitoring a database and who only needs privileges to start up and shut down the database, then that user would be assigned the oper group (which ensures that subsequent connections to the database can be done with sysoper privileges).

Table 1-1. *Mapping of OS Groups to Privileges*

OS Group	Database	System Authorized Operations	Where Referenced Privilege
oinstall	none	OS privileges to install and upgrade Oracle binaries	inst_group variable in oraInst.loc file, also in the response file
dba	sysdba	All database privileges: start up, shut down, alter database, create and drop database, toggle archivelog mode, backup and recover database	DBA_GROUP variable in response file or when prompted by OUI graphical installer

(*continued*)

Table 1-1. (*continued*)

OS Group	Database	System Authorized Operations	Where Referenced Privilege
oper	sysoper	Start up, shut down, alter database, toggle archivelog mode	OPER_GROUP variable in response file or when prompted by OUI graphical installer
racdba	sysdba for RAC	Real Application Cluster administrator	RACDBA_GROUP in response file or when prompted by OUI graphical installer
asmdba	sysdba for asm	Administrative privileges to Oracle ASM instances	OSASM_GROUP in response file or when prompted by OUI graphical installer
asmoper	sysoper for asm	Start up and shut down of Oracle ASM instance	Prompted by OUI graphical installer
asmadmin	sysasm	Mounting and dismounting of disk groups and other storage administration	Prompted by OUI graphical installer
backupdba	sysbackup	Privilege allowing user to start up, shut down and perform all backup and recovery operations	BACKUPDBA_GROUP in response file or when prompted by OUI graphical installer
dgdba	Sysdg	Privileges related to managing Data Guard environments	DGDBA_GROUP variable in response file or when prompted by OUI graphical
kmdba	Syskm	Privileged related to encryption and key management	KMDBA_GROUP variable in response file or when prompted by OUI graphical installer

Table 1-1 contains recommended group names. You don't have to use the exact names of the groups listed, and you can adjust them per your requirements. You might have a group of development DBAs, so you can have dbadev group for the Oracle binaries in the development databases. Each group would have permissions to manipulate only its set of binaries.

Once you decide which groups you need, you need access to the root user to run the groupadd command or request the users be added to the created groups depending on your user security policies. For root, add the OS groups that you need, as shown in the following examples.

```
$ groupadd oinstall
$ groupadd dba
$ groupadd oper
```

If you don't have access to the root account, you need to get your SA to run the commands, but you can verify that each group was added successfully by inspecting the contents of the /etc/group file. The following are typical entries created in the /etc/group file.

```
$ cat /etc/group
oinstall:x:500:
dba:x:501:
oper:x:502:
```

Now, create the Oracle OS user. The following example explicitly sets the group ID to 500, establishes the primary group as oinstall, and assigns the dba groups to the newly created oracle user.

```
$ useradd -u 500 -g oinstall -G dba,oper oracle
```

Note   Depending on your OEL release, OEL 9 has higher UIDs in the 1,000 to 60,000 range.

You can verify the user account information by viewing the /etc/passwd file.

```
$ cat /etc/passwd
oracle:x:500:500::/home/oracle/:/bin/bash
```

Step 2: Ensure That the OS Is Adequately Configured

The tasks associated with this step vary somewhat for each database release and OS. You must refer to the Oracle installation manual for the database release and OS vendor to get the exact requirements. Another excellent tool here is the pre-installation checklist and the installer itself, as it does a verification and helps fix issues as part of the installation.

Another reason why this step varies is because, depending on your environment, greater values and more memory in the parameters might be needed. These are only the minimum values to install and run Oracle databases. For example, for the minimum RAM, you need 1 GB for the database and 8 GB for the Oracle Grid Infrastructure, but you might have a much larger database that requires more.

For Oracle 23ai, Linux 8.4 is required, and there is a pre-installation RPM for Oracle Linux that configures the operating system for the Oracle Database and grid installations. Oracle 23ai binaries require at least 4.2 GB for Grid Infrastructure and 8.3 GB for database installations. For enhanced performance, it is recommended to disable Transparent HugePages and use standard HugePages.

Here are some typical OS components to verify.

- Memory and swap space

- System architecture

- Free disk space

- Operating system version and kernel

- Operating system software (required packages and patches); run `oracle-database-preinstall-23ai` to install all required packages

Run the following command to confirm the memory size on a Linux server.

```
$ grep MemTotal /proc/meminfo
```

To verify the amount of memory and swap space, run the following.

```
$ free -t
```

Verify the amount of space in the /tmp directory.

```
$ df -h /tmp
```

Display the amount of free disk space.

```
$ df -h
```

Verify the OS version.

```
$ cat /proc/version
```

Verify the kernel information.

```
$ uname -r
```

Determine whether the required packages are installed.

```
$ rpm -q <package_name>
```

You should always double-check the server requirements by OS and database version in the documentation and using the pre-installation packages provided for Oracle Linux.

If you are running the OUI installer, you see a list of deficiencies; some can be fixed here, and some warnings can be ignored if doing a test installation for a development or test system, as shown in Figure 1-4.

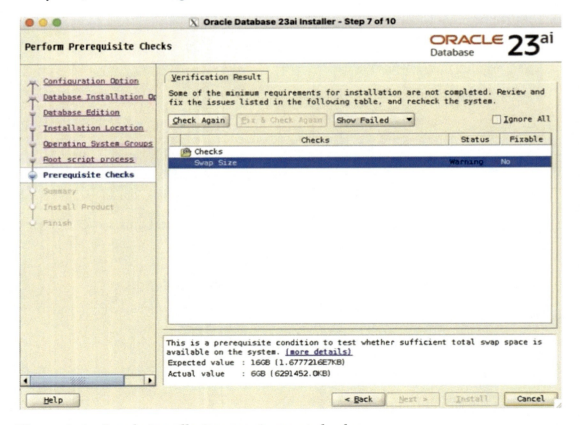

Figure 1-4. *Oracle installation requirement checks*

Step 3: Obtain the Oracle Installation Software

Usually, the easiest way to obtain the Oracle software is to download it from the Oracle website (`oracle.com/downloads`). Make sure you download the correct versions for the OS you want to install it on. If you are working with Linux systems, you can install with yum and the RPM package.

```
$ yum -y install oracle-database-server-preinstall-23ai
$ yum -y install oracle-database-ee-23ai
```

Step 4: Unzip the Files

For previous versions, it was recommended to unzip the files in a standard directory where you wanted the installation media. Starting with Oracle 18c, you should extract the binaries in the ORACLE_HOME or GRID_HOME directory. The zip file can be placed in a temporary location but extracted to ORACLE_HOME and GRID_HOME, respectively.

Of course, if you want to skip this step, you can just use the RPM image, as shown in step 3.

Installing Remotely with the Graphical Installer

Before you run the installer, you need to remotely install with the graphical interface. For the installation, you need to display the graphical output on your local computer or have a virtual type of desktop running on the virtual machine that you can remote into. Normally, in any environment, you need to connect remotely or over a bastion host without a direct connection to the server on which you are installing the database software. This remote connection is typical with virtual network computing (VNC) software or X Windows System emulation on your local computer.

The following are the steps for setting up your environment to display graphical screens on your local computer while remotely running the Oracle installer.

1. Install software on the local computer that allows X Window System emulation and secure networking. Several free tools, such as Cygwin (`http://x.cygwin.com`) for a PC or XQuartz (`www.xquartz.org`) for macOS, are available. Your company might have licensed software that you should use and install according to their policies. These run commands such as `ssh` (secure shell) and `scp` (secure copy) and provide the X emulation utilities.

2. Start an X session on the local computer using the software
    installed in step 1 and issue the startx command or the
    command needed for an X session based on your tool.

3. Log in to the remote computer from an X terminal. Use the ssh
    utility to log in.

    ```
    $ ssh -Y -l oracle <hostname>
    ```

4. Ensure that the DISPLAY variable is set correctly on the remote
    computer.

    ```
    $ echo $DISPLAY
    ```

    If your DISPLAY is set to localhost, you need to determine the
    IP address of your local computer. Use the ping or arp utility
    to determine the IP address. (If this step isn't successful, VPN
    connections might require a different IP address setting.)

    ```
    $ export DISPLAY=129.151.31.147:0.0
    ```

If DISPLAY and the connection are all configured properly, you can walk through the
graphical installer steps.

Step 5: Run the Installer for Grid

The Oracle Grid Infrastructure needs to be installed before the database software uses
ASM for the database. The file system can be used for the database without using ASM,
but there are several advantages to using ASM, and you need to just present raw disks
such as /dev/sdx for the installation. The installation handles the disk groups.

As the grid user in the Oracle grid home, you run the following.

```
# cd /u01/grid23ai
# ./gridSetup.sh
```

This is the graphical mode of OUI and requires X Windows System software or
a VNC connection. With the Oracle Cloud environment, you can easily configure a
Linux Desktop interface to run the installation on a compute node in the Oracle Cloud
Infrastructure. You'll learn more about this later in the book. If you do not have X
Windows for the graphical interface, you can run in silent mode with a response file.

We prefer the silent install after going through the graphical version at least once for the latest version of the database to understand the changes and new features of the installation.

The response file is located in ORACLE_HOME (where you unzipped the file) in the install/response directories. You need to edit this file to provide it with the values for the variables. Here is the grid home.

```
$ cd /u01/grid23ai/install/response
$ vi gridsetup.rsp
```

Here is an example of the values to provide for the following variables.

```
INVENTORY_LOCATION=/u01/app/oraInventory
oracle.install.option=HA_CONFIG (Configure Grid Infrastructure for stand
alone server)
ORACLE_BASE=/u01/app/
Groups for
oracle.install.asm.OSDBA=asmdba
oracle.install.asm.OSPER=asmoper
oracle.install.asm.OSASM=asmadmin
oracle.install.asm.SYSASMPassword=******
oracle.install.asm.diskGroup.name=DATA
oracle.install.asm.diskGroup.redundancy=EXTERNAL
oracle.install.asm.diskGroup.diskDiscoveryString=/dev/sdx
oracle.install.asm.monitorPassword=********
oracle.install.crs.rootconfig.configMethod=SUDO
```

With the newest version of the software, it might be beneficial to run through the graphical installation once manually and save the response file for assistance with the variables for future installations.

Also, a few commands require root permissions. Typically, an SA grants sudo to enable the oracle or grid user to run these commands. Using sudo allows the installation to continue without bugging your SA or logging into another window to run the commands. This is the oracle.install.crs.rootconfigMethod=SUDO variable in the response file.

The following are some of the steps for the graphical installation. Figure 1-5 shows the configuration options for the Oracle Grid Infrastructure installation.

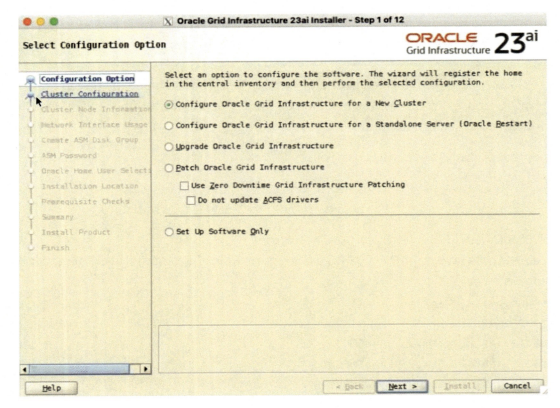

Figure 1-5. *Oracle Grid installation*

Figure 1-6 shows the ASM disk groups and the discovery path of the raw devices.

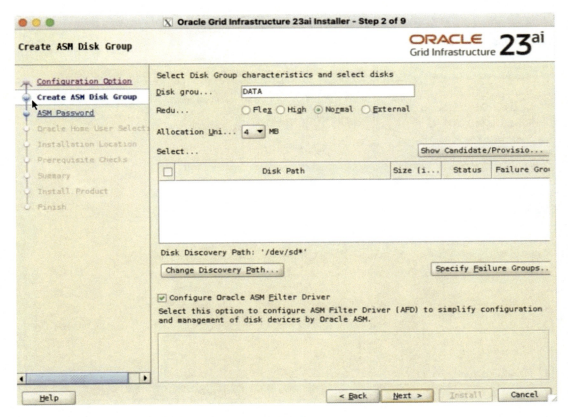

Figure 1-6. *Oracle Grid installation ASM disks*

After a few more steps of entering passwords and OS groups, you have the directories of the Oracle base and software location. The oraInventory for the grid has been provided by default based on where the run installation script was executed. This is the same as the database install with the same oraInventory.

The next step of the Grid Infrastructure installation is the root script execution configuration, as shown in Figure 1-7.

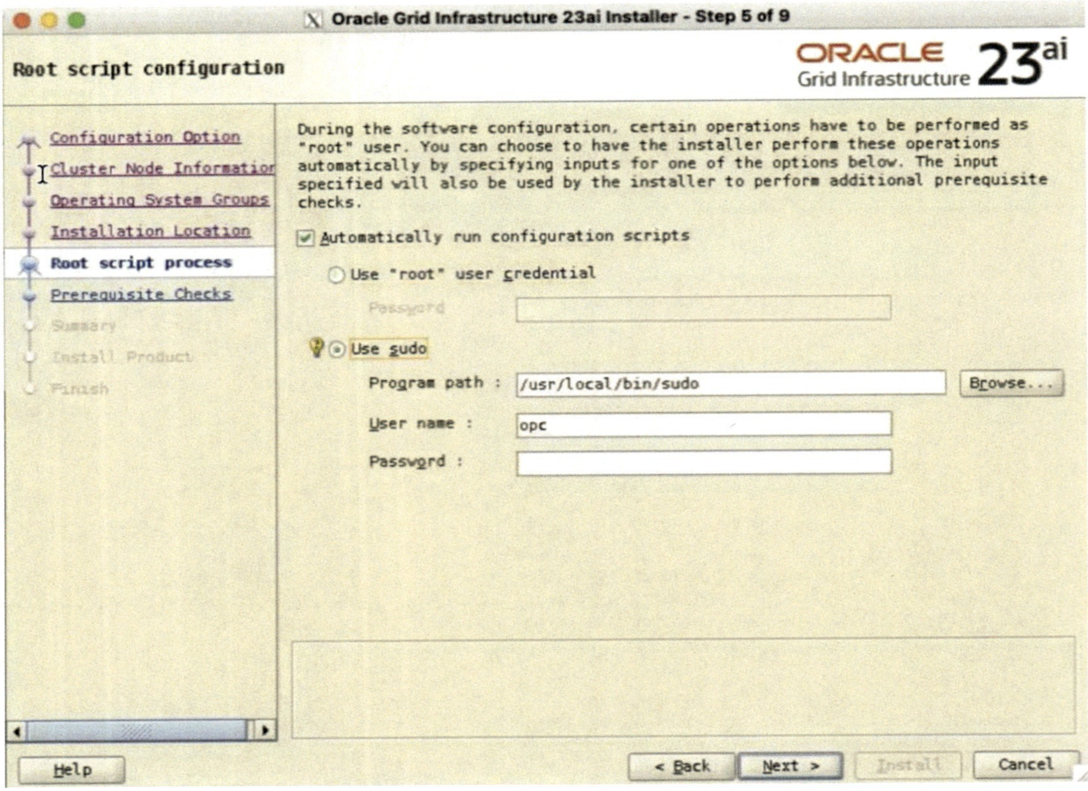

Figure 1-7. *Root script execution*

Step 6: Run the Installer for Database

The `./runInstaller` command is executed for the database installation and provides similar screens to walk through with groups and configurations. The database response file can be found and edited, as shown in the example.

The following is the database home.

```
$ cd /u01/db23ai/install/response
$ vi db_install.rsp
```

Here is an example of the values to provide for the following variables.

```
oracle.install.option=INSTALL_DB_SWONLY
UNIX_GROUP_NAME=oinstall
INVENTORY_LOCATION=/u01/app/oraInventory
ORACLE_HOME=/u01/app/oracle/db23ai
oracle.install.db.InstallEdition=EE
##Groups - can all be dba if not needed for the environment
oracle.install.db.OSDBA_GROUP=dba
oracle.install.db.OSOPER_GROUP=oper
oracle.install.db.OSBACKUPDBA_GROUP=backupdba
oracle.install.db.OSDGDBA_GROUP=dgdba
oracle.install.db.OSKMDBA_GROUP=kmdba
oracle.install.db.OSRACDBA_GROUP=racdba
oracle.install.db.rootconfig.configMethod=SUDO
```

Just as with the grid installation, it might be beneficial to manually run through the graphical installation for the database once and save the response file for assistance with the variables for future installations.

If you are only installing the software, there are just a few more screens with prerequisite checks and the same root script execution, as shown in Figure 1-7. Figure 1-8 shows the choice to create and configure a single database instance, which is also beneficial to run through once to keep the response file handy for the silent installation. With just the software-only installation, the database creation assistant is used to create the database, which is covered in a later chapter.

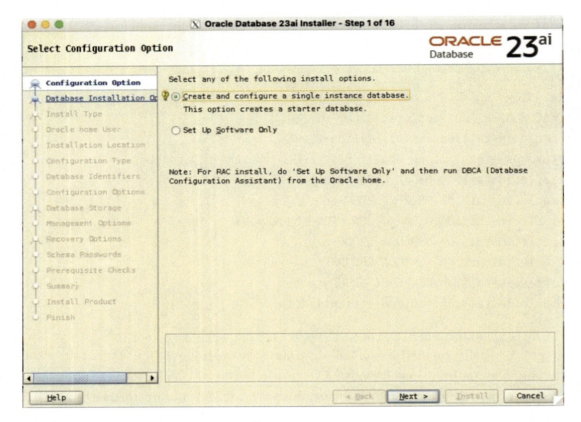

Figure 1-8. *Oracle Database installation step 1*

Step 7: Save the Response File for Additional Installations

The last step before the installation starts using the GUI installer is to save the response file. The arrow in Figure 1-9 points to the button to save the response file. After reviewing everything that was configured by walking through the installation screens, click this button before clicking the Install button.

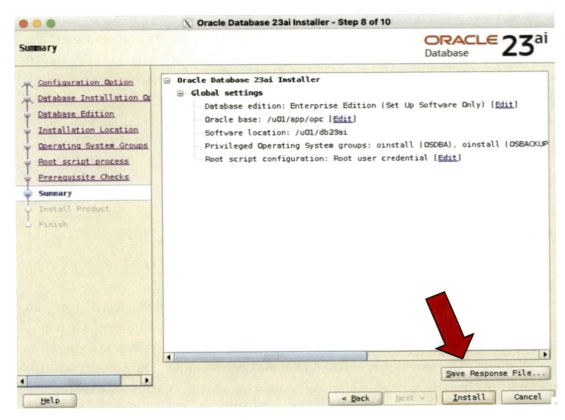

Figure 1-9. *Saving the response file*

Step 8: Troubleshoot Any Issues

If you encounter an error using a response file, 90 percent of the time, it's due to an issue with how you set the variables in the file. Inspect those variables carefully and ensure that they're set correctly. Also, if you don't fully specify the command-line path to the response file, you receive an error like the following.

```
OUI-10203: The specified response file ... is not found.
```

Here is another common error when the path or name of the response file is incorrectly specified.

```
OUI-10202: No response file is specified for this session.
```

Also, provide the correct command-line syntax when running a response file. If you incorrectly specify or misspell an option, you may receive a misleading error message, such as `DISPLAY not set`. You don't need to have your `DISPLAY` variable set when using a response file. This message is confusing because, in this scenario, the error is caused by an incorrectly specified command-line option and has nothing to do with the `DISPLAY` variable. Check all options entered from the command line and ensure that you haven't misspelled an option.

Problems can also occur when you specify an `ORACLE_HOME` and the silent installation "thinks" the given home already exists.

```
Check complete: Failed <<<<
Recommendation: Choose a new Oracle Home for installing this product.
```

Check your `inventory.xml` file (in the `oraInventory/ContentsXML` directory), and make sure there isn't a conflict with an existing Oracle home name.

There are log files that are generated with the installation and the files that are part of the inventory. The `/tmp` directory has log files based on the timestamp of when the installation was performed. Make sure that all log files are examined when trying to troubleshoot; even system logs are useful if there were processes or memory issues hit during the installation. When troubleshooting issues with Oracle installations, remember that the installer uses two key files to keep track of the installed software: `oraInst.loc` and `inventory.xml`.

Other typical errors are permissions and proper configuration of the OS groups. There might even been a prerequisite that was a warning that caused a failure. With the graphical interface you can even proceed if a prerequisite fails, which prevents those types of failures and troubleshooting.

Step 9: Apply Any Additional Patches

The Oracle software is available in the base releases. However, if additional releases, patch sets, and security patches are available, they should all be applied before rolling out a new set of Oracle binaries. Installations should be the same as the other environments with patches and with a possible exception of security patching.

Patching is not necessarily part of the installation. Knowing the details of applying patches is important to get to the latest version of the software before releasing it for use. Right after installing the binaries is a good time to make sure everything has been updated and is ready for the database to be created.

Installing in the Cloud

Oracle 18c was the first database released in the Oracle Cloud Infrastructure (OCI), and the server on-premises version became available several months later. Of course, you can use the supported versions of the Oracle Database back to 12c, depending on the virtual machine shape that is chosen. Oracle provides different options for databases in the cloud, such as when installing on a compute instance in the OCI environment. In your OCI tenancy, you create a compute instance, upload the software to your virtual machine, set up a VNC connection to install the software and run through the same steps. Now, this is an over-simplification because there are additional storage and network configurations that are needed. But you would need to do that with a virtual machine in your data center as well to make it available for your use.

Besides the virtual machine, you can install a database in your tenancy using the database cloud service, now called Oracle Base Database. You create the DB system by choosing a virtual machine shape, storage, virtual cloud network, version of the database, database name, and administrator password. The service then creates the virtual machine, installs the database software, creates the database, and even configures backups. If you want to know what the DBA needs to do at this point, there is plenty! This is about getting a database up and running as quickly and easily as possible. After that, there are plenty of tasks that DBA needs to do to manage the environment and, most importantly, manage the data!

Figure 1-10 shows the first screen for the Oracle Base Database. DB systems are created on virtual machines, but you can also have dedicated infrastructure in OCI using the Oracle Exadata Database Service on Dedicated Infrastructure. With that comes more responsibility to manage the dedicated infrastructure, similar to Exadata being in your environment. The Oracle Base Database is on shared infrastructure in OCI.

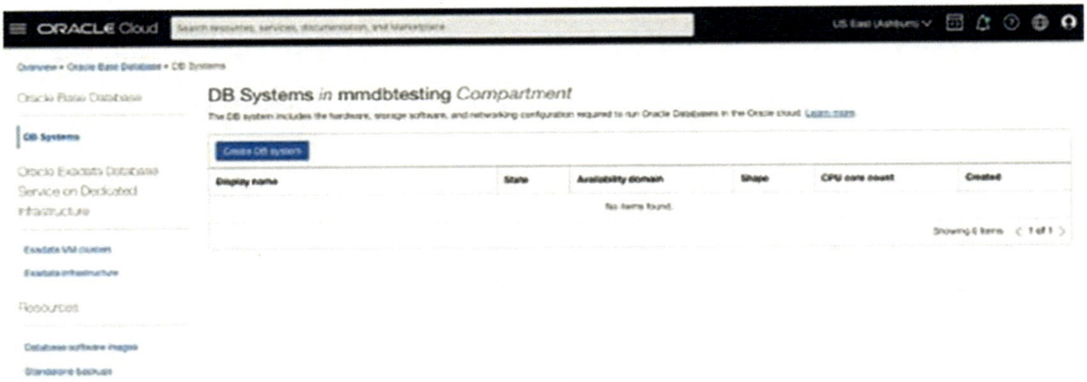

Figure 1-10.   *Using the Oracle Base Database service in OCI*

As you can see, the software installation steps are handled for most of the OCI Oracle Database services. In Figure 1-11, you see other possible database creations including Autonomous Database, dedicated infrastructure, Oracle Base Database (either on virtual machines or on bare-metal machines), and Exadata options.

Figure 1-11.   *Oracle Database on OCI*

Your company might have a database as a service based in your data center. Once you install Oracle Database, you can configure the database to do a silent installation and set up the database creation. The Oracle Cloud environment provides this, but instead of being in your data center, the servers and services are on the OCI. Even in the cloud environments, there is more than enough for a DBA to manage the database environment, ensuring that the data is managed correctly and the application development is available. Later chapters get more into these details, including more on the Oracle Cloud. But now that you understand what is behind the software installation, you can understand what is accomplished by the cloud environment or the database service.

Oracle databases are available in other clouds as well. AWS and Microsoft Azure provide Oracle Database services to install the different versions of the Oracle Database. There are reasons to have a database in multiple cloud environments, and connections are available between the cloud environments and your on-premises database to utilize the data.

As an Oracle DBA, it is becoming increasingly important to understand cloud options for the database. You can get a trial cloud account at all the major cloud vendors to try it and set up a compute instance with a database. In Oracle's cloud, OCI, you can try Oracle Autonomous Database and explore how easy it has become to install and run a database. Besides a trial account in OCI, you can get an Always Free Autonomous Database. It is a great option to have your database in the cloud and try out the features of Autonomous Database, test statements, and even write applications with Oracle's low-code APEX. It is after it is running that is the fun part, and diving into other aspects of administration and data management keeps you busy as a DBA.

CHAPTER 2

Creating a Database

An Oracle database can be created when installing the Oracle software; however, Chapter 1 discusses how to install the Oracle software first. This makes sense when configuring new environments and setting up new versions of the database. Even if you created a starter database with the installation of the software, chances are you will be creating more databases in the same Oracle home and will need to understand the different ways to create a database.

Here are a few standard ways you can create Oracle databases.

- Use the Database Configuration Assistant (DBCA) utility

- Run a `CREATE DATABASE` statement from SQL*Plus

- Clone a database from an existing database

Oracle provides creation and upgrade assistants in the `assistants` directory of `ORACLE_HOME`. These are used to create, configure, and upgrade databases. The database creation utility is DBCA, which has an intuitive interface similar to the installation software. The DBCA utility also allows you to create a database in silent mode. You update the response file with the correct variables, and the response file in silent mode is an efficient way to create the databases consistently and repeatedly. As described in Chapter 1, DBCA depends on X software and the appropriate setting for the OS `DISPLAY` variable, just like the Oracle software installation.

The SQL*Plus approach is simple and inherently scriptable. However, it does not allow the new features to be adopted quickly in the databases being created because you probably use a standard script from a previous version. With the new 23ai database release, you should run through the DBCA utility first, as it creates the response file and a database script for you to use the new features and implement new 23ai databases quickly in other environments with a SQL*Plus approach or the silent installer.

© Michelle Malcher, Darl Kuhn 2024
M. Malcher and D. Kuhn, *Pro Oracle Database 23ai Administration*,
https://doi.org/10.1007/979-8-8688-1038-1_2

Using the Database Configuration Assistant

If you are running the DBCA utility right after the Oracle software installation, many environment variables are already set, and the prerequisite steps are already completed. But if you decide to take lunch or a coffee break first, validate the `ORACLE_ HOME` and `DISPLAY` variables and then run the configuration assistant.

```
$ echo $ORACLE_HOME
$ echo $DISPLAY
$ dbca
```

There are two creation modes for creating a database in DBCA. One is the typical configuration, and the second is the advanced one. As you might already guess, the typical configuration does not require much information. You must provide a database name, storage, and password, as shown in Figure 2-1.

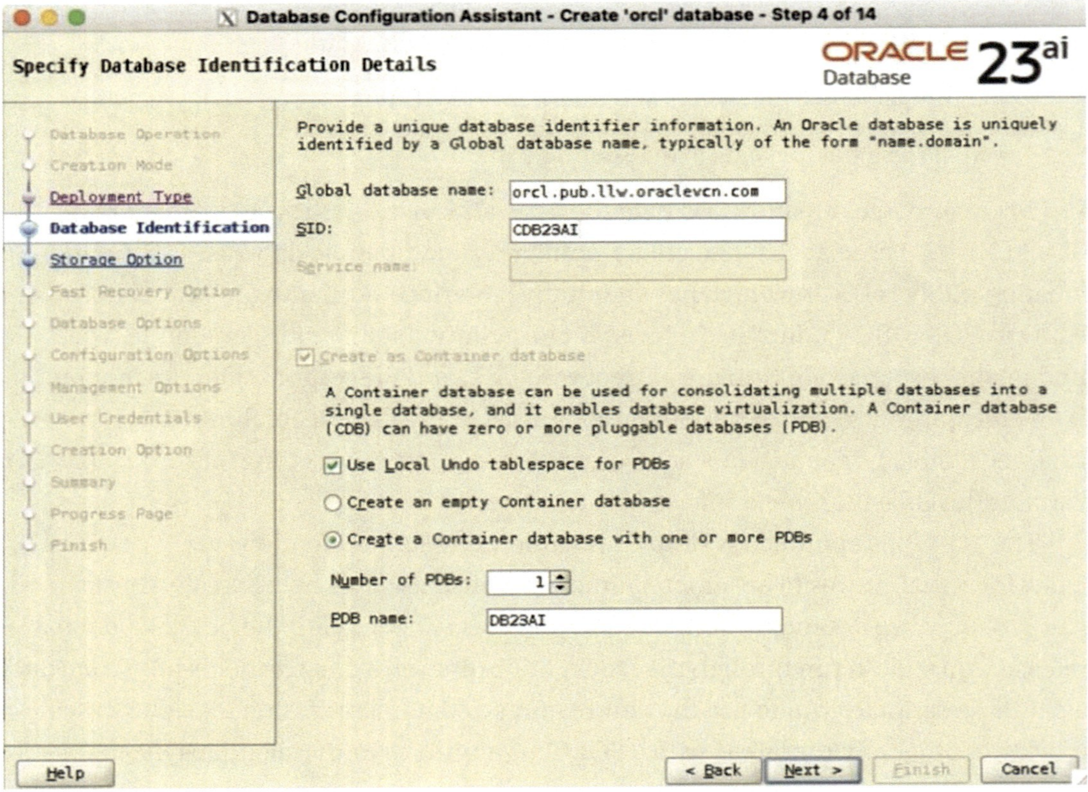

Figure 2-1. *DBCA creation mode*

In the typical configuration mode, the next screen summarizes the database to be created. Oracle 23ai creates a container database (CDB), and you need to provide a pluggable database (PDB) name. The container and pluggable databases are multitenant, which differs from previous releases. In 19c and prior releases, you could still create a non-CDB database, but this option is no longer available in 23ai and has been removed since 21c. This slightly changes how DBAs manage the databases and can even break up the tasks into system DBAs and application DBAs more than previously. This is covered in later chapters, but it is important to know that you are creating a CDB with a PDB for database creation. The CDB is the root database for most system functions, and the PDB contains application and user schemas and objects. This might seem like a big shift in managing the database, but it does separate the system and application parts of the database. The shared resources and processes are part of the CDB, and the PDB has users, tablespaces, and objects. There is also a separation of duties with permissions and settings at the PDB level instead of just at the CDB level. Again, how to start and stop the databases, backup, and recovery, and the differences for these tasks at the CDB and PDB levels are covered later. Figure 2-2 shows the summary of the database creation. Don't forget to create a response file here to make sure you can use it later in other database creations.

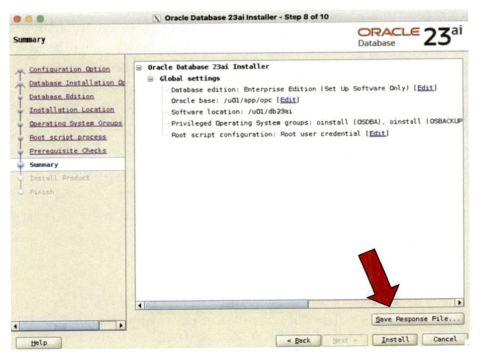

Figure 2-2. *DBCA summary*

The advanced creation mode allows the configuration of templates and parameters. You can then save a new template for future database creation with DBCA. After looking at the templates, the database name needs to be entered, and here, you can create more than one pluggable database (PDB) and decide if you want a local UNDO tablespace for the PDBs instead of a shared one in the CDB.

The storage options depend on whether you installed the grid infrastructure and created an ASM instance. This is similar to the LISTENER database because the grid infrastructure creates one listener for the server, but you can create a new listener as part of the database creation. However, we recommend creating the listener in the grid infrastructure, so when you have multiple ORACLE_HOMEs, you are not tracking down which listener is running where. It is all managed in the grid home, even if you have multiple listeners.

Another important security option to consider with the database is the Database Vault option. This sets up a Database Vault owner and manager. This allows the security of users to be provisioned by other users, such as a security administrator instead of the DBA with SYSDBA privileges. This also allows realms to be configured so that DBAs can do their normal work in the database but not have access to sensitive data. The Database Vault can be enabled later and is an additional option to the database, even though it is available as part of the installation. There are several considerations for managing the administration with Oracle Database Vault, and a team of security and database administrators would be a reason for enabling it. If you are the only database administrator, it will not provide a separation of duties and will make for more steps to do database administration. Oracle is configured with security in mind, and additional options are available for another level of security. If you are in the Oracle cloud, the database services would include many security options.

Just as you can install in the database using the DBCA utility in silent mode with a response file, you can do that when creating databases. To create a database using DBCA in silent mode, perform the following steps. The response file is in the $ORACLE_HOME/assistants/dbca directory and is a dbca.rsp file.

1. Locate the dbca.rsp file.

2. Make a copy of the dbca.rsp file.

3. Modify the copy of the dbca.rsp file for your environment.

4. Run the DBCA utility in silent mode.

First, navigate to where you copied the Oracle Database installation software, and use the `find` command to locate `dbca.rsp` (you can also use a wildcard to see all the response files, `*.rsp`).

```
$ cd $ORACLE_HOME
$ find . -name dbca.rsp
./assistants/dbca/dbca.rsp
```

Copy the file so that you're not modifying the original. (This way, you'll always have a good, original file.)

```
$ cp dbca.rsp mydb.rsp
```

Now, edit the `mydb.rsp` file. Minimally, you must modify the following parameters, as shown in the example.

```
[CREATEDATABASE]
gdbName=db23ai.oraclevcn.com
sid=db23ai
templateName=ENERAL_PURPOSE
sysPassword=PassFunwith23ai
systemPassword=PassFunwith23ai
datafileDestination=/u01/app/oracle/oradata
storageType=FS
```

Before you create the database, make sure you generate database creation scripts and save them as a database template. This allows you to use these scripts to build another database just like it after modifying the name. The scripts are in the admin directory of the database name, and instead of going through all the screenshots of the graphical installer, let's look at the variables and creation scripts to provide more details on options and allow you to see how you can use these files to automate and consistently create new databases.

Next, run the dbca utility in silent mode using a response file.

```
$ dbca -silent -createDatabase -responseFile /u01/db23ai/assistants/dbca/
mydb.rsp
$ cd $ORACLE_BASE/admin/mmfalcon23ai/scripts
$ ls
cloneDBCreation.sql
```

```
CloneRmanRestore.sql
init.ora
initmmfalcon23aiTempOMF.ora
initmmfalcon23aiTemp.ora
lockAccount.sql
mkDir.sql
mmfalcon23ai.sh
mmfalcon23ai.sql
PDBCreation.sql
plug_mm23aipdb.sql
postDBCreation.sql
postPDBCreation_mm23aipdb.sql
postScripts.sql
rmanRestoreDatafiles.sql
tempControl.ctl
```

Setting OS Variables

Now that the database is created, let's look at some of the environment variables and parameters that have been set and how to set ORACLE_HOME when managing the database.

The OS variables or environment variables get set to ensure the correct path is set for the binaries used for the database. Since the listener and ASM are in the grid home and you can have more than one Oracle home, these environment variables are even more important to be set as part of managing the database and processes on the database server or using SQL*Plus with a direct connection to the database from the server. You can remotely connect through the client tools and other management tools to the server that is not on the database server. Then this would not be as important, but if you wanted to create another database, this is where to start, and automating processes on other servers is also where you should start.

The following are the OS variables.

- ORACLE_HOME

- ORACLE_SID

- ASM_HOME

- LD_LIBRARY_PATH

- PATH

The `ORACLE_HOME` variable defines the starting point directory for the default location for the initialization file, which is $ORACLE_HOME/dbs. The `ORACLE_HOME` variable is also important because it defines the starting point directory for locating the Oracle binary files such as `sqlplus`, `dbca`, `netca`, `rman`, and so on because they are in the `ORACLE_HOME/` bin directory.

The `ORACLE_SID` variable defines the default name of the database you created or the new one you are attempting to create. `ORACLE_SID` is also used as the default name for the parameter file, which is `init(ORACLE_SID>.ora` or `spfile(ORACLE_ SID>.ora`.

The `ASM_HOME` or grid home has the listener and the disk groups defined.

The `LD_LIBRARY_PATH` variable is important because it specifies where to search for libraries on Linux/Unix boxes. The value of this variable is typically set to include `ORACLE_HOME/lib`.

The `PATH` variable specifies which directories are looked in by default when you type a command from the OS prompt. In almost all situations, `ORACLE_HOME/bin` (the location of the Oracle binaries) must be included in your `PATH` variable.

You can take several different approaches to setting the prior variables. You can do a manual hard-coded approach and export the variable; the value is always an option but not the most practical and can't be repeated easily. Think about how often you might have to log in to the database. Another way to set these variables is by placing the `export` or `setenv` command into a Linux/Unix startup file, such as `.bash_profile`, `.bashrc`, or `.profile`. However, there could be multiple databases and home directories on the server. You would have a default value always set up, but switching between would be manual and not very maintainable.

A better method for setting OS variables is a script that uses a file containing the names of all Oracle databases on a server and their associated Oracle homes. This approach is flexible, maintainable, and can be used across all database servers. For instance, if a database's `ORACLE_HOME` changes, like after an upgrade, you have to modify only one file on the server and not hunt down where the `ORACLE_HOME` variable may be hard-coded into scripts.

Understanding oratab

Oracle's approach relies on two files: `oratab` and `oraenv`.

You can think of the entries in the `oratab` file as a registry of what databases are installed on a box and their corresponding Oracle home directories. The `oratab` file is automatically created for you when you install the Oracle software. On a Linux box, `oratab` is usually placed in the `/etc/` directory. On Solaris servers, the `oratab` file is placed in the `/var/opt/oracle` directory. The `oratab` file is automatically created with the installation of the Oracle software and is automatically updated by assistants such as DBCA. It can be manually changed and updated if it isn't updated.

The `oratab` file is used for the following purposes.

- Automating the sourcing of required OS variables

- Automating the start and stop of Oracle databases on the server

The oratab file has three columns with this format.

```
<database_sid>:<oracle_home_dir>:Y|N
```

The Y or N indicates whether you want to restart automatically on a reboot of the box; Y indicates yes, and N indicates no. Automating the startup and shutdown of your database is covered in Chapter 20. Oracle srvctl also has management policies set for automatic restarting databases that don't use oratab.

Comments in the oratab file start with a pound sign (#). Here is a typical oratab file entry.

```
+ASM:/u01/grid23ai:N
db23ai:/u01/db23ai:N
```

The name of the database is db23ai with the ASM instance being +ASM. The path of each database's ORACLE_HOME directory is next on the line separated from the database name by a colon [:]. Several Oracle-supplied utilities use the oratab file.

- oraenv uses oratab to set the OS variables.

- dbstart uses it to start the database automatically on server reboots if Y.

- dbshut uses it to stop the database automatically on server reboots if Y.

The oraenv tool is discussed in the following section.

Using oraenv

If you don't properly set the required OS variables for an Oracle environment, utilities such as SQL*Plus, Oracle Recovery Manager (RMAN), and Data Pump will not work correctly. The oraenv script automatically sets required variables such as ORACLE_HOME and ORACLE_SID on an Oracle database server. (If you are in a C shell environment, there is a corresponding coraenv utility).

The oraenv utility is located in the ORACLE_HOME/bin directory, and you run it manually.

```
$ . oraenv
```

Note that the syntax to run this from the command line requires a space between the dot (.) and the oraenv tool. You are prompted for ORACLE_SID, and if the ORACLE_SID is not in the oratab file, it prompts for the ORACLE_HOME values.

```
ORACLE_SID = [orcl] ?
ORACLE_HOME = [/u01/db23ai] ?
```

Taking Another Approach to oraenv

Many DBAs use other scripts similar to oraenv and based on the oratab file.

Here is an example of a script named oraset that reads the oratab file, sets the OS variables, and presents a menu of choices.

```
#!/bin/bash
# Sets Oracle environment variables.
# Setup: 1. Put oraset file in /etc (Linux), in /var/opt/oracle (Solaris)
#        2. Ensure /etc or /var/opt/oracle is in $PATH
# Usage: batch mode: . oraset <SID>
#        menu mode: . oraset
#=============================================================================
if [ -f /etc/oratab ]; then
OTAB=/etc/oratab
elif [ -f /var/opt/oracle/oratab ]; then
OTAB=/var/opt/oracle/oratab
else
echo 'oratab file not found.'
exit
```

```
fi
#
if [ -z $1 ]; then
SIDLIST=$(egrep -v '#|\*' ${OTAB} | cut -f1 -d:)
# PS3 indicates the prompt to be used for the Bash select command.
PS3='SID? '
select sid in ${SIDLIST}; do
if [ -n $sid ]; then
HOLD_SID=$sid

break
fi
done
else
if egrep -v '#|\*' ${OTAB} | grep -w "${1}:">/dev/null; then
HOLD_SID=$1
else
echo "SID: $1 not found in $OTAB"
fi
shift
fi
#
export ORACLE_SID=$HOLD_SID
export ORACLE_HOME=$(egrep -v '#|\*' $OTAB|grep -w $ORACLE_SID.
|cut -f2 -d:)
export ORACLE_BASE=${ORACLE_HOME%%/product*}
export TNS_ADMIN=$ORACLE_HOME/network/admin
export ADR_BASE=$ORACLE_BASE/diag
export PATH=$ORACLE_HOME/bin:/usr/ccs/bin:/opt/SENSsshc/bin/\
:/bin:/usr/bin:.:/var/opt/oracle:/usr/sbin
export LD_LIBRARY_PATH=/usr/lib:$ORACLE_HOME/lib
```

You can run the oraset script from the command line or a start file such as .profile, .bash_profile, or .bashrc. To run oraset from the command line, place the oraset file in a standard location such as /etc and run it as follows.

```
$ . /etc/oraset
```

The syntax to run this from the command line requires a space between the dot (.) and the rest of the command. The script returns a menu like the following.

1. db23ai

2. mm23aidb

3. SID?

In this example, you can now enter 1 or 2 to set the OS variables required for whichever database you want to use. This allows you to set up OS variables interactively, regardless of the number of database installations on the server.

Creating a Database

Let's look at how to create a database from a script. As recommended, you can use the scripts created from the DBCA installation as a model for creating new databases and configuring the scripts for the new version of the database. The scripts from 23ai are the best way to use the latest and greatest version, eliminate deprecated parameters, and implement new features.

You need to set the environment variables as discussed in the previous section. Even if the database server does not have a database yet installed, ORACLE_HOME and GRID_HOME need to be set as the software has already been installed, as done in Chapter 1 for this information.

Looking at the script file that is found in $ORACLE_BASE/admin/$ORACLE_SID/ scripts, you see the .sh script. This script orchestrates the creation of the database, including making the needed directories for the database.

```
$ cd $ORACLE_BASE/admin/$ORACLE_SID/scripts
$ cat mmfalcon23ai.sh
#!/bin/sh
DB_HOME=$ORACLE_HOME
ASM_HOME=/u01/grid23ai
ORACLE_HOME=$ASM_HOME; export ORACLE_HOME
ORACLE_SID=+ASM; export ORACLE_SID
PERL5LIB=$ORACLE_HOME/rdbms/admin:$PERL5LIB; export PER5LIB
/u01/grid23ai/bin/sqlplus /nolog @/u01/apporacle/admin/mmfalcon23ai/
scripts/
mkDir.sql
```

```
ORACLE_HOME=$DB_HOME; export ORACLE_HOME
OLD_UMASK=`umask`
umask 0027
mkdir -p /u01/app/oracle
mkdir -p /u01/app/oracle/admin/mmfalcon23ai/adump
mkdir -p /u01/app/oracle/admin/mmfalcon23ai/dpdump
mkdir -p /u01/app/oracle/admin/mmfalcon23ai/pfile
mkdir -p /u01/app/oracle/admin/mmfalcon23ai/scripts
mkdir -p /u01/app/oracle/audit
umask ${OLD_UMASK}
PERL5LIB=$ORACLE_HOME/rdbms/admin:$PERL5LIB; export PERL5LI
ORACLE_SID=mmfalcon23ai; export ORACLE_SID
PATH=$ORACLE_HOME/bin:$ORACLE_HOME/perl/bin:$PATH; export PATH
Echo You should Add this entry in the /etc/oratab: mmfalcon23ai:/u01/
db23ai:Y /u01/db23/bin/sqlplus /nolog @/u01/app/oracle/admin/mmfalcon23ai/
scripts/ mmfalcon23ai.sql
```

To use this script for the new database, you would replace the name mmfalcon23ai with the new database, which must be done throughout all the scripts. Ideally, in a large environment, you can set up variables to pass in and create the scripts for new databases. This can be part of a process to provide a way to create and provision databases on demand. But you should first understand what the scripts are doing to make sure the environment can be configured and set up properly for the databases.

Because ASM is used to manage the database files, ORACLE_SID is first set up to log in to the +ASM instance and verify that it is available. Directories are created for the alert log and other logs, Data Pump, init.ora and spfile files, and then scripts we are looking at.

Then ORACLE_HOME is switched to the database home to log into SQL*Plus and run through the SQL statements to create the database. Before the SQL statements run, when running these scripts manually, the database name and home directory need to be manually added to /etc/oratab.

```
$ cat mmfalcon23ai.sql
set verify off
ACCEPT sysPassword CHAR PROMPT 'Enter new password for SYS: ' HIDE
ACCEPT systemPassword CHAR PROMPT 'Enter new password for SYSTEM: ' HIDE
ACCEPT pdbAdminPassword CHAR PROMPT 'Enter new password for
```

```
PDBADMIN: ' HIDE
host /u01/db23ai/bin/srvctl add database -d mmfalcon23ai -o /u01/db23ai -n
mmfalcon -m oraclevcn.com -a "DATA"
host /u01/db23ai/bin/srvctl disable database -d mmfalcon23ai
host /u01/db23ai/bin/orapwd file=/u01/db23ai/dbs/orapwmmfalcon23ai force=y
format=12
host /u01/grid23/bin/setasmgidwrap o=/u01/db23ai/bin/oracle
@/u01/app/oracle/admin/mmfalcon23ai/scripts/CloneRmanRestore.sql
@/u01/app/oracle/admin/mmfalcon23ai/scripts/cloneDBCreation.sql
@/u01/app/oracle/admin/mmfalcon23ai/scripts/postScripts.sql
@/u01/app/oracle/admin/mmfalcon23ai/scripts/lockAccount.sql @/u01/app/
oracle/admin/mmfalcon23ai/scripts/postDBCreation.sql @/u01/app/oracle/
admin/mmfalcon23ai/scripts/plug_mm23aipdb.sql @/u01/app/oracle/admin/
mmfalcon23ai/scripts/postPDBCreation_mm23aipdb.sql
```

As you can start to see, there are quite a few steps behind the creation of the database: creating directories, setting up initialization parameter files, running the create database script and post scripts that take care of the catalog, and setting up the environment so that the database can be started and used.

This script starts off asking for passwords for the SYSDBA, SYSTEM, and PDBADMIN that are needed for the administration of this environment. A password file is set up based on these passwords, which, as the OS user on the database, allows connection as sysdba to the database—again, looking back to the OS groups and roles that were created and privileges granted for the groups to perform different tasks in the environment.

The srvctl utility allows you to add, modify, and delete databases and listeners with the commands. The command is part of the scripted creation of databases, so this task becomes part of the steps and not a manual task that is done afterward.

The SQL statement to create the database is not enough, as you can see with all the pre-creation and post-creation steps. However, many of these steps would need the ORACLE_SID variable set to make sure it applies to the new databases. The main details and configuration of the database are part of DBCreate.sql.

Creating a Database Using a SQL Statement

Before looking at the SQL statement to create the database, remember all the scripts and processes done as part of the DBCA. So, there are steps to manually create the database using a SQL statement. These can be made into a script based on the scripts that were provided. Before running the CREATE DATABASE statement, work through these steps.

1. Set the OS variables.

2. Configure the initialization file.

3. Create the required directories.

4. Create the database.

5. Create a data dictionary.

The sample init.ora file from the software installation should be the starting point for the new release of the database. There are parameters that are deprecated and parameters that might not need to be set or have default values that have improved, so you should start with the sample init.ora file for that release. Many of these values change over time with the database.

Here is an init.ora example.

```
db_name="mmdb23ai"
db_domain="oraclevcn.com"
db_block_size=8192
compatible=23.0.0
enable_pluggable_database=true
sga_target=8192m
pga_aggregate_target=1572m
processes=320
control_files=(/u01/app/oracle/oradata/mmdb23ai/control01.ctl,/u02/app/
oracle/oradata/mmdb23ai/control02.ctl)
open_cursors=500
undo_tablespace=UNDOTBS1
remote_login_passwordfile=EXCLUSIVE
```

The file needs to be named properly init<SID>.ora (pfile), and before you run the create database, it should be used to create an spfile, spfile<SID>.ora. The spfile is used to modify the contents with an ALTER SYSTEM statement, and more dynamic parameters can be set without downtime.

Set the environment variables, create the init.ora file, and then create the directories for the data files and log files. Verify that the correct group and user own these directories.

```
$ mkdir -p /u01/app/oracle/oradata/mmdb23ai
$ mkdir -p /u02/app/oracle/oradata/mmdb23ai
$ mkdir -p /u01/logs/mmdb23ai
$ mkdir -p /u02/logs/mmdb23ai
$ chown -R oracle:dba /u01
$ chown -R oracle:dba /u02
```

Now, you are ready to run the CREATE DATABASE statement. The STARTUP NOMOUNT statement reads the initialization file and instantiates the background processes and memory areas used by Oracle. At this point, you have an Oracle instance but not yet a database.

Here is an example.

```
$ ORACLE_SID=mmdb23ai
$ export ORACLE_SID
$ sqlplus /nolog
SQL> CONNECT SYS AS SYSDBA
```

Here is an example connected to an idle instance.

```
SQL> CREATE SPFILE FROM PFILE;
SQL> STARTUP NOMOUNT

SQL> CREATE DATABASE mmdb23ai
USER SYS IDENTIFIED BY sys_password
USER SYTEM IDENTIFIED BY system_password
LOGFILE GROUP 1'('/u01/logs/mmdb3c/redo01a.log', '/u02/logs/mmdb23ai/
redo01b.log' SIZE 200M BLOCKSIZE 512,
GROUP 2 ('/u01/logs/mmdb23ai/redo02a.log', '/u02/logs/mmdb23ai/redo02b.log'
SIZE 200M BLOCKSIZE 512,
```

```
GROUP 3 ('/u01/logs/mmdb23ai/redo03a.log', '/u02/logs/mmdb23ai/redo03b.log'
SIZE 200M BLOCKSIZE 512,
MAXLOGHISTORY 1
MAXLOGFILES 16
MAXLOGMEMBERS 3
MAXDATAFILES 1024
CHARACTER SET AL32UTF8
NATIONAL CHARACTER SET AL16UTF16
EXTENT MANAGEMENT LOCAL
DATAFILE '/u01/app/oracle/oradata/mmdb23ai/system01.dbf' SIZE 700M REUSE
AUTOEXTEND ON NEXT 10240K MAXSIZE UNLIMITED
SYSAUX DATAFILE '/u01/app/oracle/oradata/mmdb23ai/sysaux01.dbf' SIZE 550M
REUSE AUTOEXTEND ON NEXT 10240K MAXSIZE UNLIMITED
DEFAULT TABLESPACE deftbs
DATAFILE '/u01/app/oracle/oradata/mmdb23ai/deftbs01.dbf' SIZE 500M REUSE
AUTOEXTEND ON MAXSIZE UNLIMITED
DEFAULT TEMPORARY TABLESPACE temp1
TEMPFILE '/u01/app/oracle/oradata/mmdb23ai/temp01.dbf' SIZE 20M REUSE
AUTOEXTEND ON NEXT 640K MASIZE UNLIMITED
UNDO TABLESPACE undotbs1
DATAFILE '/u01/app/oracle/oradata/mmdb23ai/undotbs01.dbf' SIZE 200M REUSE
AUTOEXTEND ON NEXT 5120K MAXSIZE UNLIMITED
ENABLE PLUGGABLE DATABASE
SEED
FILE_NAME_CONVERT = ('/u01/app/oracle/oradata/mmdb23ai/', '/u01/app/oracle/
oradata/pdbseed/')
SYSTEM DATAFILES SIZE 125M AUTOEXTEND ON NEXT 10M MAXSIZE UNLIMITED
SYSAUX DATAFILES SIZE 100M
USER_DATA TABLESPACE user1
DATAFILE '/u01/app/oracle/oradata/pdbseed/user01.dbf' SIZE 200M REUSE
AUTOEXTEND ON MAXSIZE UNLIMITED
LOCAL UNDO ON;
```

You can also use ASM with a CREATE DATABASE statement instead of file system directories. This would require that you have the +ASM instance running and available. The database files are created in the ASM disk group, and the naming is simplified because you don't have to create the directories and include them specifically in the statements. You can also use Oracle Managed Files so that the Oracle Database manages where the files are created based on a destination parameter. This also simplifies the statements and reduces errors in typing or passing in the full paths of the directories. To use Oracle Managed Files, set `DB_CREATE_FILE_DEST` to the directory for the data files in the `init.ora` file. This can be used for both ASM and file system directories.

Set the parameter in `init.ora`.

```
DB_CREATE_FILE_DEST='/u01/app/oracle/orada'a'
```

Or set the parameter using Oracle ASM.

```
DB_CREATE_FILE_DEST= +data
```

The `CREATE DATABASE` script would then be simplified to the following.

```
CREATE DATABASE mmdb23ai
USER SYS INDETIFIED BY sys_password
USER SYSTEM IDENTIFIED BY system_password
EXTENT MANAGEMENT LOCAL
DEFAULT TABLESPACE users
DEFAULT TEMPORY TABLESPACE temp
UNDO TABLESPACE undotbs1
ENABLE PLUGGABLE DATABASE
SEED
SYSTEM DATAFILES SIZE 125M AUTOEXTEND ON NEXT 10M MAXSIZE UNLIMITED
SYSAUX DATAFILES SIZE 100M;
```

So, why didn't I use the simplified example? Well, there is now the understanding of what is happening on the back end when defining where the files are being placed and where all the pieces fit for the database. Oracle Managed Files also provides an easier way to meet the standard by setting the parameter to tell the database the standard to use and keep it consistent.

If there are any issues creating the database, they are tracked in the alert log.

```
SQL> show parameter dump_dest
background_dump_dest/u01/mmdb23ai/rdbms/log
```

After the database is created in SQL*Plus, you can instantiate the data dictionary by running scripts that were created when you installed the Oracle binaries. These scripts must be run as SYS and in the container database (CDB). The question mark (?) is a SQL*Plus variable for ORACLE_HOME.

```
SQL> show user
USER is "SYS"
SQL> @?/rdbms/admin/catcdb.sql
```

You are prompted for parameter 1, which is the temporary log file directory, and parameter 2, which is the log filename for the output of these scripts.

```
Enter value for 1: /tmp
Enter value for 2: create_cdb.log
```

The database has been created, and the data dictionary has been implemented. The log file should be reviewed for any issues or failures. If there are any issues, the best place for researching and troubleshooting would be MyOracleSupport (MOS) because these scripts come directly from Oracle for this release. Issues such as running out of space or faulty permissions are ones that you should address, but if the planning and pre-steps were completed ahead of creation, these types of issues should not be showing up here.

Database vs. Instance

Although DBAs often use the terms *database* and *instance* synonymously, these two terms refer to very different architectural components. In Oracle, the term *database* denotes the physical files that make up a database: the data files, online redo log files, and control files. The term *instance* denotes the background processes and memory structures.

For example, you can create an instance without having a database present. You saw this when opening SQL*Plus and executing the startup nomount. This created an instance without having a database present. In this state, you have background processes and memory structures without any associated data files, online redo logs, or control files. The database files are not created until you issue the CREATE DATABASE statement.

Another important point is that an instance can be associated with only one database. In contrast, a database can be associated with many different instances (as with Oracle Real Application Clusters (RAC)). An instance can mount and open a database one time only. Each time you stop and start a database, a new instance is associated with it. Previously created background processes and memory structures are never associated with a database.

To demonstrate this concept, close a database with the ALTER DATABASE CLOSE statement. (It's best to use the database we just created since it is not in production yet.)

```
SQL> alter database close;
```

If you attempt to restart the database, you receive an error.

```
SQL> alter database open;
ERROR at line 1.
ORA-16196: database has been previously opened and closed
```

This is because an instance can only ever mount and open one database. You must stop and start a new instance before you can mount and open the database.

Stopping and Starting the Database

After clarifying the terms *database* vs. *instance*, it makes sense to talk about starting and stopping databases. In a 24/7 environment, this is not something that DBAs do often. But there are steps when configuring and setting up the databases initially, along with some maintenance that might be necessary.

You understand the importance of setting the environment variables for the OS user to perform these steps. You also need access to a privileged OS account in the correct OS group or a privileged database user account. Connecting as a privileged user allows you to perform administrative tasks, such as starting, stopping, and creating databases. You can use OS authentication or a password file to connect to your database as a privileged user.

Understanding OS Authentication

OS authentication means that if you can log in to a database server via an authorized OS account, you can connect to your database without requiring an additional password. A simple example demonstrates this concept. First, the id command displays the OS groups to which the oracle user belongs.

```
$ id
uid=500(oracle) gid=506(oinstall) groups=506(oinstall),507(dba),508(oper)
```

Next, a connection to the database is made with SYSDBA privileges, purposely using a bad (invalid) username and password.

```
$ sqlplus bad/notgood as sysdba
```

It is connected to the following.

```
Oracle Database 23ai Enterprise Edition Release 23.0.0.0
```

You can now verify that the connection as SYS was established.

```
SQL> show user
USER is "SYS"
```

How can it connect to the database with an incorrect username and password? Actually, it is not a bad thing (as you might initially think). The prior connection works because Oracle ignores the username/password provided, as the user was first verified via OS authentication. In that example, the Oracle OS user belongs to the dba OS group and can make a local connection to the database with SYSDBA privileges without providing a correct username and password.

See Table 1-1 in Chapter 1 for a complete description of OS groups and the mapping to corresponding database privileges. Typical groups include dba and oper, corresponding to sysdba and sysoper database privileges, respectively. The sysdba and sysoper privileges allow you to perform administrative tasks, such as starting and stopping your database.

Starting the Database

Starting and stopping your database are tasks that you perform frequently. To start/stop your database, connect with a sysdba- or sysoper-privileged user account, and issue the startup and shutdown statements. The following example uses OS authentication to connect to the database.

```
$ sqlplus / as sysdba
```

After you connect as a privileged account, you can start your database, as follows.

```
SOL> startup;
```

For the prior command to work, you need either an `spfile` or `init.ora` file in the ORACLE_HOME/dbs directory. You can also start up with a different `spfile` by providing a parameter with pfile= and the filename.

Note   Stopping and restarting the database in quick succession is known colloquially in the DBA world as *bouncing* your database.

When your instance starts successfully, you should see messages from Oracle indicating that the system global area (SGA) has been allocated. The database is mounted and then opened.

```
ORACLE instance started.
Total System Global Area 313159680 bytes
Fixed Size 2259912 bytes
Variable Size 230687800 bytes
Database Buffers 75497472 bytes
Redo Buffers 4714496 bytes
Database mounted.
Database opened.
```

From the prior output, the database startup operation goes through three distinct phases in opening an Oracle database.

- Starting the instance

- Mounting the database

- Opening the database

You can step through these one at a time when you start your database. First, start the Oracle instance (background processes and memory structures).

```
SQL> startup nomount;
```

Next, mount the database. At this point, Oracle reads the control files.

```
SQL> alter database mount;
```

Finally, open the data files and online redo log files.

```
SQL> alter database open;
```

Figure 2-3 represents the startup process.

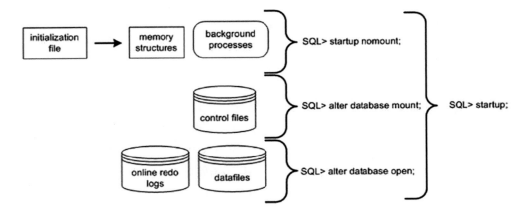

Figure 2-3. *Database startup process*

When you start up a database without any parameters, Oracle automatically steps through the three startup phases (nomount, mount open). In most cases, you issue a STARTUP statement without parameters to start your database. Table 2-1 describes the meanings of parameters that you can use with the database STARTUP statement.

Table 2-1. *Startup Parameters*

Parameter	Meaning
FORCE	Forces the instance to start after a startup or shutdown problem
RESTRICT	Only allows users with the RESTRICTED SESSION privilege to connect to the database
PFILE	Specifies the client parameter file to be used when starting the instance
QUIET	Suppresses the display of SGA information when starting the instance
NOMOUNT	Stars background processes and allocates memory; doesn't read control files
MOUNT	Starts background processes, allocates memory, reads control files
OPEN	Starts background processes, allocates memory, reads control files, and opens online redo logs and data files
OPEN RECOVER	Attempts media recovery before opening the database
OPEN READ ONLY	Opens the database in read-only mode
UPGRADE	Used when upgrading a database
DOWNGRADE	Used when downgrading a database

We discussed using restart with the database and the srvctl utility. If restart is being used, then parameters are still valid but under the startoption of the command as follows.

```
$ srvctl start database -db db_unique_name -startoption
```

Stopping the Database

Normally, you use the SHUTDOWN IMMEDIATE statement to stop a database. The IMMEDIATE parameter instructs Oracle to halt database activity and roll back any open transactions. Without the IMMEDIATE, the shutdown process waits for any open and active sessions to log out before shutting down, which could take a very long time, and chances are there are reasons for needing the database to be brought down sooner.

```
SOL> shutdown immediate;
Database closed.
Database dismounted.
ORACLE instance shut down.
```

Table 2-2 defines the parameters available with the SHUTDOWN statement. In most cases, SHUTDOWN IMMEDIATE is an acceptable method of shutting down your database. If you issue the SHUTDOWN command with no parameters, it is equivalent to issuing SHUTDOWN NORMAL.

Table 2-2. *Shutdown Parameters*

Parameter	Meaning
NORMAL	Wait for users to log out of active sessions before shutting down.
TRANSACTIONAL	Wait for transactions to finish, and then terminate the session.
TRANSACTIONAL LOCAL	Perform a transactional shutdown for local instance only.
IMMEDIATE	Terminate active sessions immediately. Open transactions are rolled back.
ABORT	Terminate the instance immediately. Transactions are terminated and are not rolled back. Used as a last-resort situation.

You should rarely need to use the SHUTDOWN ABORT statement. Usually, SHUTDOWN IMMEDIATE is sufficient. If other methods are not working, then use SHUTDOWN ABORT, but remember on startup after an ABORT command, the database will need to recover media files. It might take a significant amount of time to run through the files.

Again, the srvctl utility is used when the restart is being used.

```
$ srvctl stop database -db db_unique_name -stopoption immediate
```

Before stopping any database, confirm that ORACLE_SID is set correctly, and when logged into SQL*Plus, you can verify the database with a quick query before stopping the wrong database.

```
SOL> select name from v$database;
```

Also, when this is a container database, this closes the pluggable databases.

Tip   If you experience any issues with starting or stopping your database, look in the alert log for details. The alert log usually has a pertinent message regarding any problems.

Configuring the LISTENER

The ASM instance and listener were installed and configured when installing the grid infrastructure. When you use the tools such as the DBCA, the database is registered with the listener. Why is the listener important? Because you need to make the database accessible to remote client connections. You do this by configuring the Oracle listener. Appropriately named, the listener is the process on the database server that "listens" for connection requests from remote clients. If you don't have a listener started on the database server, then you can't connect from a remote client.

The listener can be included as part of the database home or part of the grid home. Including the listener in the grid home makes sense since there is normally only one home for the grid infrastructure, and there can be multiple database homes. This is one place to manage and maintain the listener. It also allows patching with the grid environment.

There are methods for setting up the listener. One is with the grid infrastructure or database installation. This sets up the directories and files needed for the listener. Another way is using the Oracle Net Configuration Assistant (netca). You can also manually modify the listener.ora file or copy one from another server and modify it for the correct databases, but this might cause some frustration if something is not perfectly typed as needed and the listener fails to start.

Using the Net Configuration Assistant

The netca utility assists you with all aspects of implementing a listener. You can run the netca tool in either graphical or silent mode (sound familiar?). Using netca in graphical mode is easy and intuitive. To use the netca in graphical mode, ensure the proper X software is installed, so this is useful for installations and the assistant tools. Check that your DISPLAY variable is set and that you have the GRID_HOME set.

```
$ xhost +
$ echo
$ DISPLAY :0.0
```

You can now run the netca utility.

```
$ netca
```

Next, you are guided through several screens from which you can choose options such as the name of the listener, desired port, and so on. You can configure more than one listener on a server for listening on different ports.

You can also run the netca utility in silent mode with a response file. Again, this allows you to script the process and ensure repeatability when creating and implementing listeners. First, find the default listener response file within the directory structure that contains the Oracle install media.

```
$ find . -name "netca.rsp"
./assistants/netca/netca.rsp
```

The main variable here is the listener name, which is fine to keep the default LISTENER and LISTENER_PROTOCOLS values, but you can change the port if needed.

You can start the listener background process with the lsnrctl utility.

```
$ lsnrctl start
```

You should see informational messages such as the following.

```
Listening Endpoints Summary...
(DESCRIPTION=(ADDRESS=(PROTOCOL=tcp)(HOST=mmfalcon)(PORT=1521))) Services
Summary...
Service "mmdb23ai" has 1 instance(s).
```

You can verify the services for which a listener is listening via this.

```
$ lsnrctl services
```

You can check the status of the listener with the following query.

```
$ lsnrctl status
```

For a complete listing of listener commands, issue this command.

```
$ lsnrctl help
```

Tip   Use the Linux/Unix ps -ef | grep tns command to view any listener processes running on a server.

Connecting to a Database Through the Network

Once the listener has been configured and started, you can test remote connectivity from a SQL*Plus client, as follows.

```
$ sqlplus user/pass@'server:port/service_name'
```

In the next line of code, the user and password are system/PassFun23ai, connecting the mmfalcon server, port 1521, to a database named mmdb23ai.

```
$ sqlplus system/PassFun23ai@'mmfalcon:1521/mmdb23ai'
```

This example demonstrates what is known as the *easy connect* naming method of connecting to a database. It's easy because it doesn't rely on setup files or utilities. You only need to know username, password, server, port, and service name (SID).

Another common connection method is local naming. This method relies on connection information in the ORACLE_HOME/network/admin/tnsnames.ora file. In this example, the tnsnames.ora file is edited, and the following Transparent Network Substrate (TNS) (Oracle's network architecture) entry is added.

```
mmdb23ai =
(DESCRIPTION =
(ADDRESS = (PROTOCOL = TCP)(HOST = mmfalcon)(PORT = 1521))
(CONNECT_DATA = (SERVICE_NAME = mmdb23ai)))
```

Now, you establish a connection from the OS command line by referencing the mmdb23ai TNS information in the tnsnames.ora file.

```
$ sqlplus system/PassFun23ai@mmdb23ai
```

This connection method is local because it relies on a local client copy of the tnsnames.ora file to determine the Oracle Net connection details. By default, SQL*Plus inspects the directory defined by the TNS_ADMIN variable for a file named tnsnames.ora. If not found, the directory defined by ORACLE_H0ME/network/admin is searched. If the tnsnames.ora file is found, and if it contains the alias specified in the SQL*Plus connection string (in this example, mmdb23ai), then the connection details are derived from the entry in the tnsnames.ora file.

Tip   You can use the netca utility to create a tnsnames.ora file. Start the utility and choose the Local Net Service Name Configuration option. You are prompted for input, such as the SID, hostname, and port.

Creating a Password File

Creating a password file is optional. There are some good reasons for requiring a password file.

- You want to assign non-sys users sys* privileges (sysdba, sysoper, sysbackup, and so on).

- You want to connect remotely to your database via Oracle Net with sys* privileges.

- You want to set up Oracle Data Guard need the password files on the standby servers.

An Oracle feature or utility requires the use of a password file. Perform the following steps to implement a password file.

1. Create the password file with the orapwd utility.

2. Set the initialization parameter REMOTE_LOGIN_PASSWORDFILE to EXCLUSIVE.

3. In a Linux/Unix environment, use the orapwd utility to create a password file as follows.

```
$ cd $ORACLE_HOME/dbs
        $ orapwd file=orapw<ORACLE_SID> password=<sys password>
```

In a Linux/Unix environment, the password file is usually stored in ORACLE_HOME/dbs; in Windows, it's typically placed in the ORACLE_HOME\database directory.

The filename format you specify in the previous command may vary by OS. For instance, in Windows, the format is PWD<ORACLE_SID>.ora.

To enable the password file, set the initialization parameter REMOTE_ LOGIN_ PASSWORDFILE to EXCLUSIVE (this is the default value). If the parameter is not set to EXCLUSIVE, you'll have to modify your parameter file.

```
SQL> alter system set remote_login_passwordfile='EXCLUSIVE' scope=spfile;
```

You need to stop and start the instance to instantiate the prior setting.

You can add users to the password file via the GRANT <any SYS privilege> statement. You want to be careful with these privileges and using the password file for secure configurations. Only the accounts needing these privileges should be granted access to the password file. The following example grants SYSDBA privileges to the mmalcher user (and thus adds mmalcher to the password file).

```
SQL> grant sysdba to mmalcher;
Grant succeeded.
```

Enabling a password file allows you to connect to your database remotely with SYS*-level privileges via an Oracle Net connection. This example shows the syntax for a remote connection with SYSDBA-level privileges.

```
$ sqlplus <username>/<password>@<database connection string> as sysdba
```

This allows you to do remote maintenance with sys* privileges (sysdba, sysoper, sysbackup, and so on) that would otherwise require you to log in to the database server physically. You can verify which users have sys* privileges by querying the V$PWFILE_USERS view.

```
SQL> select * from v$pwfile_users;
```

Here is some sample output.

```
USERNAMESYSDBSYSOP SYSAS SYSBA SYSDG SYSKMCON_ID
SYSTRUETRUE FALSE FALSE FALSE FALSE0
```

The concept of a privileged user is also important to RMAN backup and recovery. Like SQL*Plus, RMAN uses OS authentication and password files to allow privileged users to connect to the database. Only a privileged account can back up, restore, and recover a database.

How Many Database Instances on One Server?

How many databases should you put on one server when planning the environment and creating new databases?

This question has no simple answer because it is more than just allocating storage and memory. The correct answer is that it depends, and workloads and applications influence this. One extreme is having only one database instance running on each server. Since you can have multiple Oracle homes and even more than one database can share a home, you can have a couple of database instances running on a server if there is enough memory and CPUs to divide up the resources for the multiple instances. However, this is the advantage of the multitenant database. This technology allows you to house several pluggable databases within one container database. The pluggable databases share the instance, background processes, undo, and Oracle binaries but function as completely separate databases. Each pluggable database has its own set of tablespaces (including SYSTEM) that are not visible to any other pluggable database within the container database. This allows you to securely implement an isolated database that is sharing resources with other databases. Figure 2-4 depicts this architecture and shows one CDB on the server. You can also have multiple container databases created on one server.

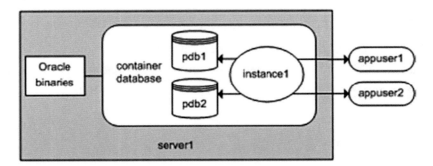

Figure 2-4. *One container database with multiple pluggable databases*

Planning database workloads and understanding the resources available on the server allows one or more databases to be created.

Understanding Oracle Architecture

This chapter introduced concepts such as database (data files, online redo log files, control files), instance (background processes and memory structures), parameter file, and listener. Now is a good time to present an Oracle architecture diagram showing the various files and processes constituting a database and instance. Some concepts depicted in Figure 2-5 have already been covered; for example, database vs. instance. Other aspects of Figure 2-5 are covered in future chapters. However, it is appropriate to include a high-level diagram to visually represent the concepts already discussed and created with the database to lay the foundation for understanding upcoming topics.

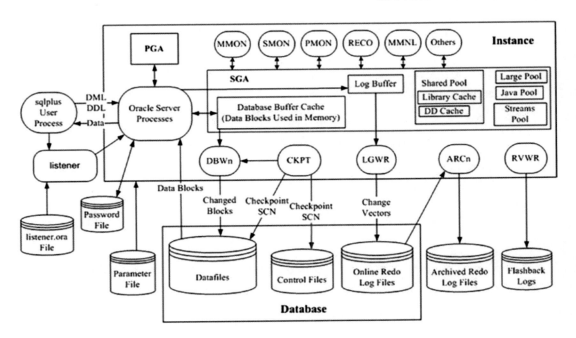

Figure 2-5. *Oracle database architecture*

There are several aspects to note about Figure 2-5. Communication with the database is initiated through a sqlplus user process. Typically, the user process connects to the database over the network. This requires that you configure and start a listener process. The listener process hands off incoming connection requests to an Oracle server process, which handles all subsequent communication with the client process. A password file is required if a remote connection is initiated as a sys user. A password file is also required for local sys connections that do not use OS authentication.

The instance consists of memory structures and background processes. When the instance starts, it reads the parameter file, which helps establish the size of the memory processes and other characteristics of the instance. When starting a database, the instance goes through three phases: nomount (instance started), mount (control files opened), and open (data files and online redo logs opened).

The number of background processes varies by database version. You can view the names and descriptions of the processes via this query.

```
SQL> select name, description from v$bgprocess;
```

This returns a long list of processes, including multiple database and log writer processes. Here are a few of the major processes.

- DBWn: The database writer writes blocks from the database buffer cache to the data files.

- CKPT: The checkpoint process writes checkpoint information to the control files and data file headers.

- LGWR: The log writer writes redo information from the log buffer to the online redo logs.

- ARCn: The archiver copies the contents of online redo logs to archive redo log files.

- RVWR: The recovery writer maintains before images of blocks in the fast recovery area.

- MMON: The manageability monitor process gathers automatic workload repository statistics.

- MMNL: The manageability monitor lite process writes statistics from the active session history buffer to disk.

- SMON: The system monitor performs system-level cleanup operations, including instance recovery in the event of a failed instance, coalescing free space, and cleaning up temporary space.

- PMON: The process monitor cleans up abnormally terminated database connections and automatically registers a database instance with the listener process.

- RECO: The recoverer process automatically resolves failed distributed transactions.

The structure of the SGA varies by Oracle release. It is the major memory structure and can be automatically managed. You can view the details for each component using this query.

```
SQL> select pool, name from v$sgastat;
```

The major SGA memory structures include the following.

- SGA: The SGA is the main read/write memory area and comprises several buffers, such as the database buffer cache, redo log buffer, shared pool, large pool, Java pool, and steams pool.

- *Buffer cache*: The buffer cache stores copies of blocks read from data files.

- *Log buffer*: The log buffer stores changes to modified data blocks.

- *Shared pool*: The shared pool contains library cache information regarding recently executed SQL and PL/SQL code. The shared pool also houses the data dictionary cache, which contains structural information about the database, objects, and users.

Finally, the program global area (PGA) is a memory area separate from the SGA. The PGA is a process-specific memory area that contains session-variable information. PGA is used for sorting, grouping, and hashing.

Dropping a Database

Yes, you just created a database, but there are a few good reasons to drop a database and clean up the database and software from the server. This was not always an easy process but it has been simplified with the installer and the assistants. If you created a test database or, after installation, realized another option would be better, you can remove what was just created. Another reason would be decommissioning the server or database.

So, if you have an unused database that you need to drop, you can use the DROP DATABASE statement to accomplish this. Doing so removes all data files, control files, and online redo logs associated with the database. Before you drop a database, ensure that you are on the correct server and are connected to the correct database.

To verify the server name, use the following.

```
$ uname -a
```

To verify the database name, use the following.

```
SQL> select name from v$database;
```

After you have verified that you are in the correct database environment, issue the following SQL commands from a SYSDBA-privileged account.

```
SQL> shutdown immediate;
SQL> startup mount exclusive restrict;
SQL> drop database;
```

Exercising Caution

You should be careful when dropping a database. You are not prompted when dropping the database, and there is no undo command except for recovering the database from the last backup. Use extreme caution when dropping a database because this operation removes data files, control files, and online redo log files. This is also why, after creating a database, we create another user to minimize the times necessary to log in with sys as sysdba.

The DROP DATABASE command is useful when you have a database that needs to be removed. It may be a test database or an old database that is no longer used. The DROP DATABASE command doesn't remove old archive redo log files. You must manually remove those files with an OS command such as rm. You can also instruct RMAN to remove the archive redo log files.

You can also use the DBCA utility to delete a database. Here, you get a choice of databases to delete and a couple more screens for confirmation verifying you really want to delete the database. Figure 2-6 shows the options you have with databases, from managing to configuring to deleting.

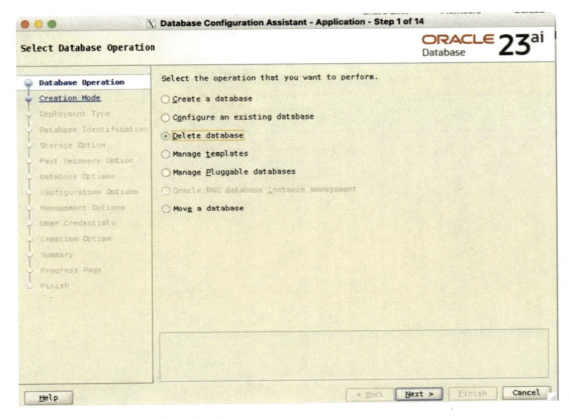

Figure 2-6. *DBCA delete database*

Figure 2-7 shows the warning you get when using DBCA. Just be a little extra cautious.

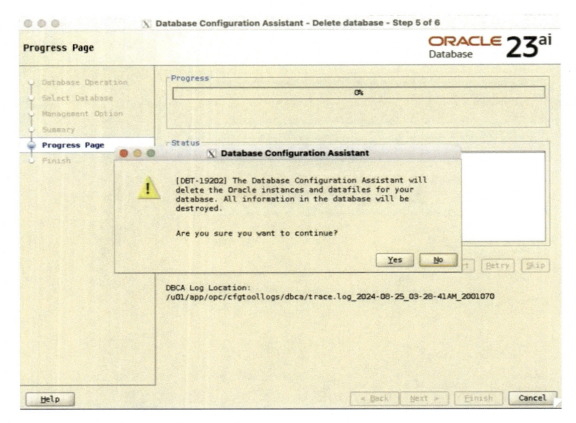

Figure 2-7. *Delete database confirmation*

If there are no more databases and you are cleaning up the old versions of the software and binaries, you can also remove those. Just like there is runInstaller, there is a deinstall. This is found in the Oracle home directory in the deinstall folder, and there is a command deinstall that removes the software and Oracle home directories. This gives you a list of databases and allows you to confirm this process.

Creating the Database in the Cloud

The previous chapter discussed installing the Oracle Base Database in the Oracle Cloud (OCI). This creates the virtual machine, computes instances, installs the database software, and creates the database. Once accomplished, you can connect to the database server and create additional databases. You also learn how to manage and maintain the Oracle Base Database on OCI in later chapters.

However, there is an additional option to create the database in OCI: create an Autonomous Database. The Oracle Autonomous Database can be created on a shared or dedicated environment. Different management tasks are needed for each of these options.

Autonomous Shared/Serverless

The Autonomous Database in a shared environment needs some information, and then, in less than five minutes, the database is up and available.

Figure 2-8 shows the basic setup for the database. A name is needed, and you have a few option types based on workload, data warehouse, transactional, JSON, or APEX for low-code applications.

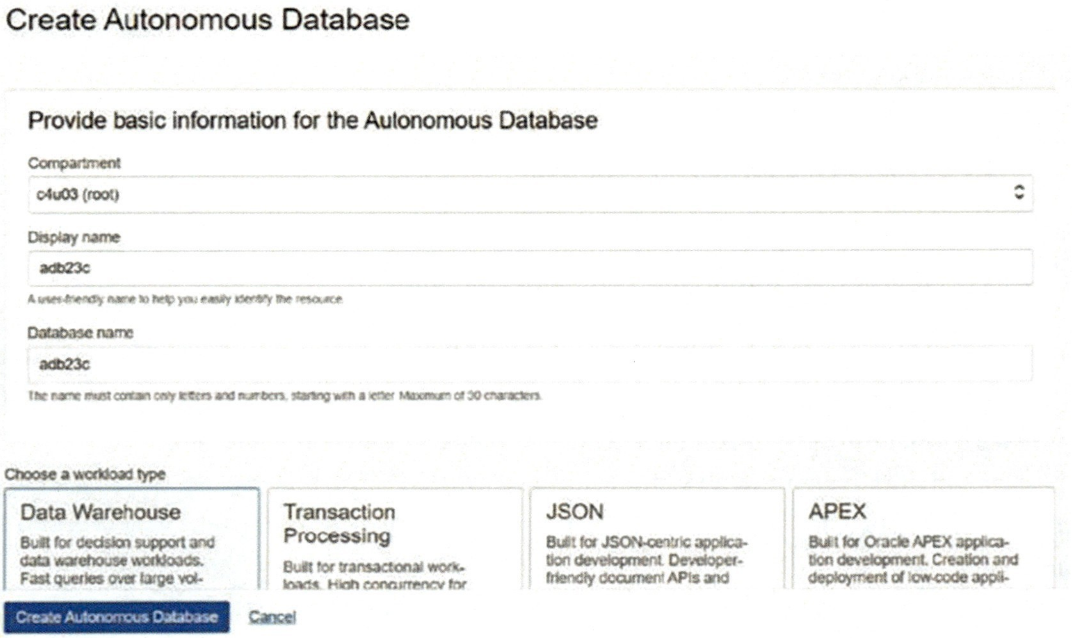

Figure 2-8. *Create Autonomous Database*

The next information that is needed is an admin password and license type. There are options on autoscaling and version of the database, but default values normally work well here.

At this point, this seems too easy. But the provisioning of the Autonomous Database in the cloud takes care of the back end, and you have a database that is easily provisioned and ready to use. Even as a DBA, some things must be done after creation, as covered in the upcoming chapters.

Autonomous Dedicated

Your company might require dedicated Exadata machines in its Oracle cloud environment. With a dedicated Autonomous Database, a little more work must be done to provide the dedicated Exadata infrastructure. Also, the DBAs can become fleet administrators, which means additional tasks in the dedicated infrastructure to set up the deployment of autonomous databases.

The fleet administrators own the container databases and the Exadata infrastructure. This should sound familiar to what was just configured with the container database set up on a database server.

These are the steps.

1. Prepare a private network for OCI.

2. Provision a cloud Exadata infrastructure.

3. Provision an autonomous container database.

4. Configure VPN connectivity in your Exadata network.

Just as groups and users are set up for a server, OCI has configured users, groups, and policies so that only privileged users can set up and manage the databases.

The network is set up with virtual cloud networks (VCNs). There are specific security policies and rules that are configured to be able to connect to the database servers and instances.

Figure 2-9 shows how to create the container databases. It is easy to navigate to this step through the Oracle Database menu from the home page. This provision the container database.

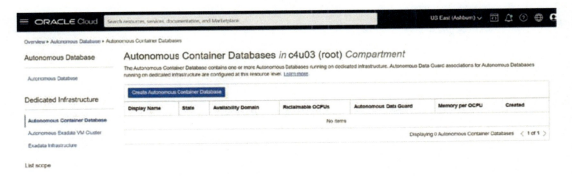

Figure 2-9. *Container database in OCI*

The last step of this database creation is to provision a VPN connection. No public IP address is assigned to the dedicated infrastructure, so to gain connectivity to the database, the best practice is to use a VPN connection. The VPN server is installed on another compute node, allowing the hostname to connect to the database with the tools.

Summary

In this chapter, you created the database and looked at different options and configurations you can use when doing this. You looked at the installed architecture and the processes running on the database server. The idea was to provide the steps to create databases efficiently through repeatable methods. The next step is to configure the environment so that you can navigate, operate, and monitor the database.

CHAPTER 3

Configuring an Efficient Environment

Now that the Oracle binaries and database have been created, let's take a small detour to set up and configure the environment to enable you to operate efficiently. Remember, a couple of commands can destroy the database, and it is extremely important to be in the correct environment. These setup steps assist with exactly that. Regardless of the functionality of graphical database administration tools, DBAs still need to perform many tasks from the OS command line and manually execute SQL statements. A DBA who takes advantage of the OS and SQL has a clear advantage over a DBA who doesn't.

In any database environment (Oracle, MySQL, etc.), an effective DBA uses advanced OS features to allow you to quickly navigate the directory, locate files, repeat commands, display system bottlenecks, and so forth. To achieve this efficiency, you must know the database's operating system.

In addition to being proficient with the OS, you must also be skillful with the SQL interface to the database. Although you can glean much diagnostic information from graphical interfaces, SQL enables you to dive deeper into the internals to do advanced troubleshooting and derive database intelligence.

This chapter lays the foundation for efficiently using the OS and SQL to manage your databases. You can use the following OS and database features to configure your environment effectively.

- OS variables

- Shell aliases

- Shell functions

- Shell scripts

- SQL scripts

© Michelle Malcher, Darl Kuhn 2024
M. Malcher and D. Kuhn, *Pro Oracle Database 23ai Administration*,
https://doi.org/10.1007/979-8-8688-1038-1_3

When you're in a stressful situation, it's paramount to have an environment where you can quickly discern where you are and what accounts you're using and tools that help you quickly identify problems. The techniques described in this chapter are like levers: they provide leverage for quickly doing large amounts of work. These tools let you focus on the issues you may face instead of verifying your location or worrying about command syntax.

This chapter begins by explaining OS techniques for enabling maximum efficiency. Later sections show how you can use these tools to display environment details automatically, navigate the file system, monitor the database proactively, and perform triage.

Tip   Consistently use one OS shell when working on your database servers. We recommend that you use the Bash shell; it contains all the most useful features from the other shells (Korn and C), plus additional features that add to its ease of use.

Customizing Your OS Command Prompt

Typically, DBAs work with multiple servers and multiple databases. In these situations, numerous terminals' sessions may be open on your screen. You can run the following commands to identify your current working environment.

```
$ hostname -a
$ id
$ whoami
$ echo $ORACLE_SID

$ pwd
```

To avoid confusion about which server you're working on, it's often desirable to configure your command prompt to display information regarding its environment, such as the machine name and database SID. In this example, the command prompt name is customized to include the hostname, user, and Oracle SID.

```
$ PS1.'[\h:\u:${ORACLE_SID}]$ '
```

The \h specifies the hostname. The \u specifies the current OS user. $ORACLE_SID contains the current setting for your Oracle instance identifier. The following is the command prompt for this example.

```
[oracle23ai:oracle:db23ai]$
```

The command prompt contains three pieces of important information about the environment: server name, OS username, and database name. When navigating multiple environments, setting the command prompt can be invaluable for keeping track of where and what environment you're in.

If you want the OS prompt automatically configured when you log in, you need to set it in a startup file. In a Bash shell environment, you typically use the .bashrc file. This file is normally located in your HOME directory. Place the following line of code in .bashrc.

```
PS1='[\h:\u:${ORACLE_SID}]$ '
```

When you place this line of code in the startup file, any time you log in to the server, your OS prompt is set automatically. In other shells, such as the Korn shell, the .profile file is the startup file.

Depending on your personal preference, you may want to modify the command prompt for your particular needs. For example, many DBAs like the current working directory displayed in the command prompt. To display the current working directory information, add the \w variable.

```
$ PS1='[\h:\u:\w:${ORACLE_SID}]$ '
```

As you can imagine, a wide variety of options are available for the information shown in the command prompt. Here is another popular format.

```
$ PS1='[\u@${ORACLE_SID}@\h:\W]$ '
```

Table 3-1 lists a few useful Bash shell variables to customize the OS command prompt.

Table 3-1. *Bash Shell Backslash-Escaped Variables for Command Prompt*

Variable	Description
\ d	Date in "weekday month day-of-month" format
\ h	hostname
\ s	Name of shell
\ t	Time in 24-hour HH:MM:SS format
\ u	Current shell
\ w	Current working directory
\ W	Base name of the current working directory (not the full path)
\ $	If the effective user identifier (UID) is 0, then displays #, otherwise, displays $

The variables available with your command prompt vary somewhat by OS and shell. For example, in a Korn shell environment, the `hostname` variable displays the server name in the OS prompt.

```
$ export PS1="[shostnames]$ "
```

If you want to include the `ORACLE_SID` variable within that string, set it as follows.

```
$ export PS1=[shostnames':"${ORACLE_SID}"]$ '
```

Try not to go overboard in terms of how much information you display in the OS prompt. Too much information limits your ability to type in and view commands on one line. As a rule of thumb, minimally, you should include the server name and database name displayed in the OS prompt. Having that information readily available saves you from thinking that you're in one environment when you're in another.

Customizing Your SQL Prompt

DBAs frequently use SQL*Plus to perform daily administrative tasks. Often, you'll work on servers that contain multiple databases. Each database contains multiple user accounts. When connected to a database, you can run the following commands to verify information: your username, database connection, and hostname.

```
SQL> show user;
SQL> select name from v$database;
```

This is useful to verify development vs. production accounts to keep them separate. Using a SQLPROMPT for a quick visual besides querying the database ensures the right environment is used for any queries, changes, and so forth.

A more efficient way to determine your username and SID is to set your SQL prompt to display that information. The following is an example.

```
SQL> SET SQLPROMPT '_USER.@_CONNECT_IDENTIFIER.> '
```

An even more efficient way to configure your SQL prompt is to have it automatically run the SET SQLPROMPT command when you log in to SQL*Plus.

Edit $ORACLE_HOME/sqlplus/admin/glogin.sql and add the previous SET SQLPROMPT command to glogin.sql.

Now, log in to SQL. Here is an example of the SQL*Plus prompt.

```
SYS@devdb23ai>
```

If you connect to a different user, this should be reflected in the prompt.

```
SQL> conn system/FunwithDB23ai
```

The SQL*Plus prompt now displays the following.

```
SYSTEM@devdb23ai
```

Setting your SQL prompt is an easy way to remind yourself which environment and user you're currently connected as. This helps prevent you from accidentally running a SQL statement in the wrong environment. The last thing you want is to think you're in a development environment and then discover that you've run a script to delete objects or stop a database while connected in a production environment.

Creating Shortcuts for Frequently Used Commands

In Linux/Unix environments, you can use two common methods to create shortcuts to other commands: create aliases for often repeated commands and use functions to form shortcuts for groups of commands. The following sections describe ways in which you can deploy these two techniques.

Using Aliases

An alias is a simple mechanism for creating a short piece of text that executes other shell commands. Here is the general syntax.

```
$ alias <alias_name>='<shell command>'
```

For instance, when faced with database problems, it's often useful to create an alias that runs a cd command that places you in the directory containing the database alert log. This example creates an alias (named bdump) that changes the current working directory to where the alert log is located.

```
$ alias bdump='cd /u01/app/oracle/diag/rdbms/db23ai/db23ai/trace'
```

Now, instead of having to type the cd command, along with a lengthy (and easily forgettable) directory path, you can simply type bdump, and they are placed in the specified directory.

```
$ bdump
$ pwd
/u01/app/oracle/diag/rdbms/db23ai/db23ai/trace
```

The prior technique allows you to navigate to the directory of interest efficiently and accurately. This is especially handy when you manage many different databases on different servers. You have to set up a standard set of aliases that allow you to navigate and work more efficiently.

To show all aliases that have been defined, use the alias command with no arguments.

```
$ alias
```

Listed next are some common examples of alias definitions you can use.

```
alias l.='ls -d .*'
alias ll='ls -l'
alias lsd='ls -altr | grep ^d'
alias sqlp='sqlplus "/ as sysdba"'
```

If you want to remove an alias definition from your current environment, use the unalias command. The following example removes the alias for lsd.

```
$ unalias lsd
```

Locating the Alert Log

The alert log directory path usually has this structure.

```
ORACLE_BASE/diag/rdbms/LOWER(<db_unique_name>)/<instance_name>/trace
```

Usually (but not always) db_unique_name is the same as instance_name. In Data Guard environments, db_unique_name is often not the same as instance_name. You can verify the directory path with this query.

```
SQL> select value from v$diag_info where name = 'Diag Trace';
```

The name of the alert log follows this format.

```
alert_<ORACLE_SID>.log
```

You can also locate the alert log from the OS (whether the database is started or not) via these OS commands.

```
$ cd $ORACLE_BASE
$ find . -name alert_<ORACLE_SID>.log
```

In the prior find command, you'll need to replace the <ORACLE_SID> value with the name of your database.

Using a Function

Like an alias, you can also use a function to form command shortcuts. A function is defined with this general syntax.

```
$ function <function_name> {
shell commands
}
```

For example, the following line of code creates a simple function (named bdump) that allows you to change the current working directory, dependent on the name of the database passed in.

```
function bdump {
if [ "$1" = "engdev" ]; then
  cd /orahome/app/oracle/diag/rdbms/engdev/ENGDEV/trace
elif [ "$1" = "stage" ]; then
  cd /orahome/app/oracle/diag/rdbms/stage/STAGE/trace
fi
echo "Changing directories to $1 Diag Trace directory"
pwd
}
```

You can now type bdump, followed by a database name at the command line, to change your working directory to the Oracle background dump directory.

```
$ bdump db23ai
Changing directories to stage Diag Trace directory
/orahome/app/oracle/diag/rdbms/db23ai/db23ai/trace
```

Using functions is usually preferable to using aliases. Functions are more powerful than aliases because of features such as the ability to operate on parameters passed in on the command line, allowing for multiple lines of code and, therefore, more complex coding.

DBAs commonly establish functions by setting them in the HOME/.bashrc file. A better way to manage functions is to create a file that stores only function code and call that file from the .bashrc file. It's also better to store special-purpose files in directories that you've created for these files. For instance, create a directory named bin under

HOME. Then, in the bin directory, create a file named dba_fcns, and place in it your function code. Now, call the dba_fcns file from the .bashrc file. Here is an example of an entry in a .bashrc file.

```
. $HOME/bin/dba_fcns
```

The following is a small sample of some of the functions you can use.

```
# show environment variables in sorted list
function envs {
if test -z "$1"
then /bin/env | /bin/sort
else /bin/env | /bin/sort | /bin/grep -i $1
fi
} # envs
#-----------------------------------------------------------#
# find largest files below this point
function flf {
find . -ls | sort -nrk7 | head -10
}
#-----------------------------------------------------------#
# find largest directories consuming space below this point
function fld {
du -S . | sort -nr | head -10
}
#-----------------------------------------------------------#
function bdump {
if [ $ORACLE_SID = "db23ai" ]; then
cd /u01/app/oracle/diag/rdbms/db23ai/db23ai/trace
elif [ $ORACLE_SID = "+ASM" ]; then
cd /u01/app/oracle/diag/asm/+asm/+ASM/trace
elif [ $ORACLE_SID = "rcat" ]; then
cd /u01/app/oracle/diag/rdbms/rcat/rcat/trace
fi
pwd
} # bdump
```

If you ever wonder whether a shortcut is an alias or a function, use the type command to verify a command's origin. This example verifies that bdump is a function.

```
$ type bdump
```

Rerunning Commands Quickly

When there are problems with a database server, you need to be able to quickly run commands from the OS prompt. You may be having a performance issue and want to run commands that navigate you to directories containing log files, or you may want to display the top-consuming processes occasionally. In these situations, you don't want to waste time retyping command sequences.

One time-saving feature of the Bash shell is its several methods for editing and rerunning previously executed commands. The following list highlights several options available for manipulating previously typed commands.

- Scrolling with the up (↑) and down (↓) arrow keys

- Using Ctrl+P and Ctrl+N

- Listing the command history

- Searching in reverse

- Setting the command editor

Each of these techniques is described briefly in the following sections.

Scrolling with the Up and Down Arrow Keys

You can use the up arrow to scroll up through your recent command history. As you scroll through previously run commands, you can rerun a desired command by pressing the Enter or Return key.

If you want to edit a command, use the Backspace key to erase characters. Use the left arrow to navigate to the desired location in the command text. After you've scrolled up through the command stack, use the down arrow to scroll back down through previously viewed commands.

Note If you're familiar with Windows, scrolling through the command stack is similar to using the DOSKEY utility.

Using Ctrl+P and Ctrl+N

The Ctrl+P keystroke (pressing the Ctrl and P keys at the same time) displays your previously entered command. If you've pressed Ctrl+P several times, you can scroll back down the command stack by pressing Ctrl+N (pressing the Ctrl and N keys at the same time).

Listing the Command History

You can use the history command to display commands the user previously entered.

```
$ history
```

Depending on how many commands have previously been executed, you may see a lengthy stack. You can limit the output to the last *n* number of commands by providing a number with the command. For example, the following query lists the last five commands that were run.

```
$ history 5
```

Here is some sample output.

```
273 cd -
274 grep -i ora alert.log
275 ssh -Y -l oracle 65.217.177.98
276 pwd
277 history 5
```

To run a previously listed command in the output, use an exclamation point (!) (sometimes called the *bang*) followed by the history number. In this example, to run the pwd command on line 276, use !.

```
$ !276
```

To run the last command you ran, use !!.

```
$ !!
```

Searching in Reverse

Press Ctrl+R, and you're presented with the Bash shell reverse-search utility.

```
$ (reverse-i-search)`':
```

From the reverse-i-search prompt, as you type each letter, the tool automatically searches through previously run commands with text similar to the string you entered. Once you're presented with the desired command match, you can rerun the command by pressing the Enter or Return key. To view all commands that match a string, press Ctrl+R repeatedly. To exit the reverse search, press Ctrl+C.

Setting the Command Editor

You can use the set - o command to make your command-line editor either vi or emacs. This example sets the command-line editor to be vi.

```
$ set -o vi
```

Now, when you press Esc+K, you're placed in a mode where you can use vi commands to search through the stack of previously entered commands.

For example, if you want to scroll up the command stack, you can use the K key. Similarly, you can scroll down using the J key. In this mode, you can use the slash (/) key and then type a string to be searched for in the entire command stack.

Tip   Before you attempt to use the command editor feature, be sure you're familiar with the vi or emacs editor.

A short example can illustrate the power of this feature. Let's say you know that you ran the ls -altr command about an hour ago. You want to run it again, but this time without the r (reverse-sort) option. To enter the command stack, press Esc+K.

```
$ Esc+K
```

You should now see the last command you executed. To search the command stack for the ls command, type /ls, and then press Enter or Return.

```
$ /ls
```

The most recently executed ls command appears at the prompt.

```
$ ls -altr
```

To remove the r option, use the right arrow key to place the prompt over the r on the screen, and press X to remove the r from the end of the command. After you've edited the command, press the Enter or Return key to execute it.

Developing Standard Scripts

If the Oracle Database environment has been around for a long time, there are probably database administration teams that have developed hundreds of scripts and utilities to help manage an environment. Many scripts are now available in tools and other DBA utilities, even if they were developed in-house. Too many scripts and utilities distract you from other important data management tasks and does not simplify the environment as the new database versions are available. It is better to use a small set of focused scripts to take advantage of the new database features and simplify the administration utilities, with each script usually less than 50 lines long. You can also look at the new database tools released with the various database versions. It loses effectiveness if you develop a script that another DBA can't understand or maintain. Also, if you need to execute a command more than a couple of times, a script should be created to execute it. If it is now a standard, regular check, or job, the script can automate the process.

These scripts are handy for jobs that automatically run or during troubleshooting since it needs to be completed quickly. Other tools also maintain databases and provide proactive alerts and monitoring of multiple databases instead of running a script against one database at a time.

This section contains several short shell functions, shell scripts, and SQL scripts to help you manage a database environment. This is by no means a complete list of scripts—rather, it provides a starting point from which you can build. Each subsection heading is the name of a script.

Note   Before you attempt to run a shell script, ensure it's executable. Use the chmod command to achieve this: chmod 750 <script> or chmod u+x <script>.

---

dba_setup

Usually, you establish a common set of OS variables and aliases in the same manner for every database server. When navigating among servers, you should set these variables and aliases consistently and repeatedly. Doing so helps you (or your team) operate efficiently in every environment. For example, it's extremely useful to set the OS prompt consistently when working with dozens of different servers. This helps you quickly identify what box you're on, which OS user you're logged in as, and so on.

One technique is to store these standard settings in a script and then have that script automatically executed when you log in to a server. We usually create a script named dba_setup to set these OS variables and aliases. You can place this script in a directory such as HOME/bin and automatically execute the script via a startup script (see the "Organizing Scripts" section later in this chapter). The following are the contents of a typical dba_setup script.

```
# set prompt
PS1='[\h:\u:${ORACLE_SID}]$ '
#
export EDITOR=vi
export VISUAL=$EDITOR
export SOLPATH=$HOME/scripts
set -o vi
#
# list directories only
alias lsd="ls -p I grep /"
# show top cpu consuming processes
alias topc="ps -e -o pcpu,pid,user,tty,args I sort -n -k 1 -r I head"
# show top memory consuming processes
alias topm="ps -e -o pmem,pid,user,tty,args | sort -n -k 1 -r | head"
#
alias sqlp='sqlplus "/ as sysdba"'
```

conn.bsh

You need to be alerted if there are issues with connecting to databases. This script checks to see if a connection can be established to the database. If a connection can't be established, an email is sent. Place this script in a directory such as HOME/bin. Make sure you modify the script to contain the correct username, password, and email address for your environment.

You must also establish the required OS variables, such as ORACLE_SID and ORACLE_HOME. You can either hard-code those variables into the script or call a script that sources the variables for you. Like the previous script, this script calls a script (named oraset) that sets the OS variables (see Chapter 2).

The script requires that the ORACLE_SID be passed to it; the following is an example.

```
$ conn.bsh DB23aiPRD
```

The following message is displayed if the script can establish a connection to the database.

```
success
db ok
```

The following are the contents of the conn.bsh script.

```
#!/bin/bash
if [ $# -ne 1 ]; then
echo "Usage: $0 SID"
exit 1
fi
# either hard code OS variables or source them from a script.
# see Chapter 2 for details on oraset script to source OS variables
. /etc/oraset $1
#
echo "select 'success', sysdate;" | sqlplus -s dbmonitor/Monitor23aiPass@$1
| grep success

  if [[ $? -ne 0 ]]; then
echo "problem with $1" | mailx -s "db problem" dbdgrp@gmail.com
else
echo "db ok"
```

```
fi
#
exit 0
```

This script is usually automated via a utility such as cron. Here is a typical cron entry.

```
# Check to connect to db.
23 * * * * /home/oracle/bin/conn.bsh db23aiprod 1>/home/oracle/bin/log/
conn.log 2>&1
```

This cron entry runs the script once per hour. Depending on your availability requirements, you may want to run a script such as this more frequently.

filesp.bsh

Use the following script to check for an operating mount point filling up. Keep in mind that larger file systems thresholds will be lower, depending on some trending of the workloads. The idea is not to create noise because a 10 TB file system still has 1 TB free, but it gives you enough time to react and resize file systems and add disk as needed. Place the script in a directory such as HOME/bin. You need to modify the script so that the mntlist variable contains a list of mount points on your database server. Because this script isn't running any Oracle utilities, there is no reason to set the Oracle-related OS variables (as with the previous shell scripts).

```
#!/bin/bash
mntlist="/u01 /u02 /ora01 /ora02 /ora03"
for ml in $mntlist
do
echo $ml
usedSpc=$(df -h $ml | awk '{print $5}' | grep -v capacity | cut -d
"%" -f1 -)
BOX=$(uname -a | awk '{print $2}')
#

case $usedSpc in
[0-9])
arcStat="relax, lots of disk space: $usedSpc"
;;
```

```
[1-7][0-9])
arcStat="disk space okay: $usedSpc"
;;
[8][0-9])
arcStat="space getting low: $usedSpc"
echo $arcStat | mailx -s "space on: $BOX" dbagrp@gmail.com
;;
[9][0-9])
arcStat="warning, running out of space: $usedSpc"
echo $arcStat | mailx -s "space on: $BOX" dbagrp@gmail.com
;;
[1][0][0])
arcStat="update resume, no space left: $usedSpc"
echo $arcStat | mailx -s "space on: $BOX" dbagrp@gmail.com
;;
*)
arcStat="huh?: $usedSpc"
esac
#
BOX=$(uname -a | awk '{print $2}')
echo $arcStat
#
done
#
exit 0
```

You can run this script manually from the command line as follows.

```
$ filesp.bsh
```

Here is the output for this database server.

```
/01
disk space okay: 79
/02
disk space okay: 64
/ora01
space getting low: 84
```

```
/ora02
disk space okay: 41
/ora03
relax, lots of disk space: 9
```

This is the type of script you should run on an automated basis from a scheduling utility such as cron. Here is a typical cron entry.

```
# Filesystem check
7 * * * * /orahome/bin/filesp.bsh 1>/orahome/bin/log/filesp.log 2>&1
```

Remember that the shell script used in this section (filesp.bsh) may require modification for your environment. The shell script depends on the output of the df -h command, which varies by OS and version. For instance, the output of df -h on a Solaris box appears as follows.

```
$ df -h
Filesystem    size    used    avail    capacity    Mounted on
/ora01        50G     42G     8.2G     84%         /ora01
/ora02        50G     20G     30G      41%         /ora02
/ora03        50G     4.5G    46G       9%         /ora03
/u01          30G     24G     6.5G     79%         /u01
/u02          30G     19G     11G      64%         /u02
```

This line in the shell script selectively reports on the "capacity" in the output of the df -h command.

```
usedSpc=$(df -h $ml | awk '{print $5}' | grep -v capacity | cut -d "%" -f1 -)
```

For your environment, you'll have to modify the prior line to correctly extract the remaining information related to disk space per mount point. For example, say you're on a Linux box and issue a df -h command, and you observe the following output.

```
Filesystem Size Used Avail Use% Mounted on
/dev/mapper/VolGroup00-LogVol00 222G 162G 49G 77% /
```

There's only one mount point, and the disk space percentage is associated with the Use% column. Therefore, to extract the pertinent information, you'll need to modify the code associated with usedSpc within the shell script; the following is an example.

```
df -h / | grep % | grep -v Use | awk '{print $4}' | cut -d "%" -f1 -
```

The shell script thus needs to have the following lines modified, as shown.

```
mntlist="/"
for ml in $mntlist
do
echo $ml
usedSpc=$(df -h / | grep % | grep -v Use | awk '{print $4}' |
cut -d "%" -f1 -)
```

top.sql

The following script lists the top CPU-consuming SQL processes. It's useful for identifying problem SQL statements. Place this script in a directory such as HOME/scripts.

```
select * from(
select
sql_text
,buffer_gets
,disk_reads
,sorts
,cpu_time/1000000 cpu_sec
,executions
,rows_processed
,sql_id
from v$sqlstats
order by cpu_time DESC)
fetch first 10 rows only;
```

This is how you execute this script.

```
SQL> @top
```

The following is a snippet of the output, showing a SQL statement that is consuming a large amount of database resources.

```
INSERT INTO "REP_MV"."GEM_COMPANY_MV"
SELECT CASE GROUPING_ID(trim(upper(nvl(ad.organization_name,u.company))))
```

```
WHEN O THEN
trim(upper(nvl(ad.organization_name,u.company)))
11004839      20937562    136    21823.59    17    12926019    6zd4xujra2kc
```

lock.sql

This script displays sessions with locks on tables preventing other sessions from completing work. The script shows details about the blocking and waiting sessions. This script is still beneficial to check on users or processes being blocked by other sessions. However, 23ai has a new feature based on priority to abort low priority sessions that are blocking other sessions. You should place this script in a directory such as HOME/scripts. The following are the contents of lock.sql.

```
SET LINES 83 PAGES 30
COL blkg_user FORM a10
COL blkg_machine FORM a10
COL blkg_sid FORM 99999999
COL wait_user FORM a10
COL wait_machine FORM a10
COL wait_sid FORM 9999999
COL obj_own FORM a10
COL obj_name FORM a10
--
SELECT
s1.username blkg_user
,s1.machine blkg_machine
,s1.sid blkg_sid
,s1.serial# blkg_serialnum
,s1.sid || ',' || s1.serial# kill_string
,s2.username wait_user
,s2.machine wait_machine
,s2.sid wait_sid
,s2.serial# wait_serialnum
,lo.object_id blkd_obj_id
,do.owner obj_own
,do.object_name obj_name
```

```
FROM v$lock l1
,v$session s1
,v$lock l2
,v$session s2
,v$locked_object lo
,dba_objects do
WHERE s1.sid = l1.sid
AND s2.sid = l2.sid
AND l1.id1 = l2.id1
AND s1.sid = lo.session_id
AND lo.object_id = do.object_id
AND l1.block = 1
AND l2.request > 0;
```

The lock.sql script is useful for determining what session has a lock on an object and showing the blocked session. You can run this script from SQL*Plus as follows.

```
SQL> @lock.sql
```

The following is a partial output (truncated so it fits on one page).

```
BLKG_USER BLKG_MACHI BLKG_SID BLKG_SERIALNUM
--------- ---------- -------- --------------
KILL_STRING
-------------------------------------------------------
WAIT_USER WAIT_MACHI WAIT_SID WAIT_SERIALNUM BLKD_OBJ_ID OBJ_OWN OBJ_NAME
--------- ---------- -------- -------------- ----------- ------- --------
MV_MAINT    speed  24       11
24,11
MV_MAINT    speed  87        7    19095 MV_MAINT INV
```

When running lock.sql from the root container, you must change DBA_OBJECTS to CDB_OBJECTS for the script to properly report locks throughout the entire database. You should also consider adding the NAME and CON_ID to the query to view the container where the lock occurs. Here's a snippet of the modified query (you'll need to replace the ... with columns you want to report on).

```
SELECT
u.con id_
u.name
,s1.usernameblkg_user
...
,do.object_name obj_name
FROM v$lock l1
,v$session s1
,v$lock l2
,v$session s2
,v$locked_object lo
,cdb_objects do
,v$containers u
WHERE s1.sid = l1.sid
AND s2.sid = l2.sid
AND l1.id1 = l2.id1
AND s1.sid = lo.session_id
AND lo.object_id = do.object_id
AND l1.block = 1
AND l2.request > 0
AND do.con_id = u.con_id;
```

users.sql

This script displays when users were created and whether their account is locked. The script is useful when you're troubleshooting connectivity issues. Place the script in a directory such as HOME/scripts. Here is a typical users.sql script for displaying user account information.

```
SELECT
username
,account_status
,lock_date
,created
FROM dba_users
ORDER BY username;
```

You can execute this script from SQL*Plus as follows.

```
SQL> @users.sql
```

Here is some sample output.

```
USERNAME    ACCOUNT_ST    LOCK_DATE    CREATED
-------     ---------     ---------    -------
SYS         OPEN          23-OCT-22
SYSBACKUP   OPEN          23-OCT-22
SYSDG       OPEN          23-OCT-22
```

Now with 23ai, you need to update `users.sql` for the multitenant database environment to get the users in the container and pluggable databases and run from the root container. Change `DBA_USERS` to `CDB_USERS` and add the `NAME` and `CON_ID` columns to report on all users in all pluggable databases.

```
SELECT
c.name

,u.username
,u.account_status
,u.lock_date
,u.created
FROM cdb_users u
,v$containers c
WHERE u.con_id = c.con_id
ORDER BY c.name, u.username;
```

Organizing Scripts

When you have a set of scripts and utilities, you should organize them so they're consistently implemented for each database server. They should become part of your steps after you install the Oracle binaries. These scripts cannot only be consistently deployed as part of this process but can also be used to test the installation and setup of databases. The following steps implement the preceding DBA utilities for each database server in your environment.

1. Create OS directories in which to store the scripts.

2. Copy your scripts and utilities to the directories created in step 1.

3. Configure your startup file to initialize the environment.

These steps are covered in the following sections.

Step 1: Create Directories

Create a standard set of directories on each database server to store your custom scripts. A directory beneath the `oracle` user's `HOME directory` is usually a good location. We generally create the following three directories.

- `HOME/bin`: Standard location for shell scripts that are run in an automated fashion (such as from `cron`)

- `HOME/bin/log`: Standard location for log files generated from the scheduled shell scripts

- `HOME/scripts`: Standard location for storing SQL scripts

You can use the `mkdir` command to create the previous directories.

```
$ mkdir -p $HOME/bin/log
$ mkdir $HOME/scripts
```

It doesn't matter where you place the scripts or what you name the directories; if you have a standard location, you always find the same files in the same locations when you navigate from server to server. In other words, it doesn't matter what the standard is, only that you have a standard.

Step 2: Copy Files to Directories

Place your utilities and scripts in the appropriate directories. Copy the following files to the `HOME/bin` directory.

```
dba_setup
dba_fcns
conn.bsh
filesp.bsh
```

Place the following SQL scripts in the HOME/scripts directory.

```
login.sql
top.sql
lock.sql
users.sql
```

Step 3: Configure the Startup File

Place the following code in the .bashrc file or the equivalent startup file for your shell (.profile for the Korn shell). It is an example of how to configure the .bashrc file.

```
# Source global definitions
if [ -f /etc/bashrc ]; then
. /etc/bashrc
fi
#
#source oracle OS variables
./etc/oraset <default_database>
#
#User specific aliases and functions
.$HOME/bin/dba_setup
.$HOME/bin/dba_fcns
```

When you log in to an environment, you have full access to all the OS variables, aliases, and functions established in the dba_setup and dba_fcns files. If you don't want to log off and back in, run the file manually, using the dot (.) command. This command executes the lines contained within a file. The following example runs the .bashrc file.

```
$ . $HOME/.bashrc
```

The dot instructs the shell to source the script. Sourcing tells the shell process to which you're currently logged in to inherit any variables set with an export command in an executed script. If you don't use the dot notation, then the variables set within the script are visible only in the context of the subshell spawned when the script is executed.

Note   In the Bash shell, the source command is equivalent to the dot (.) command.

Automating Scripts

Having these scripts in your arsenal allows quickly resolving issues and performing tasks. It also provides a standard process for running these things against the database instead of running different SQL or tasks. It is a first step to automating the work against the database.

The objective is to have a database to provide information and perform the needed tasks to address these issues. It might seem that talking about these scripts in this chapter makes no sense now; however, having these scripts can provide the basis for the automation. Understanding what needs to be monitored assists in setting up a proactive environment that does not require a DBA to run scripts manually at all hours of the day and night.

Most of these scripts fit nicely with an Oracle Enterprise Management tool as they can be inserted into scheduled jobs and run at different levels of permissions. The scripts are also good to deploy for the initial testing of the database environments when provisioned by a more automated response file or cloud control. These tests can validate that the creation steps are still properly set up and working with each version. Scripts can be scheduled and standardized for alert receivers, track alerts, and enable and disable blackouts for patching and maintenance windows. It's definitely a tool to explore and use to manage the environment.

Automation makes it easier to manage a very large database environment. Standardizing the scripts and environment setup allows a team of DBAs to work together to manage the enterprise database systems. These are just a few of the scripts for some quick checks; other checks and monitoring can be automated, even for the performance and scaling of the database. That is examined later with Autonomous Database but also looks at how to leverage what Autonomous Database does to script and do the same with the on-premises databases.

That was our little detour to configure an efficient environment. This is especially important for DBAs who manage multiple databases on multiple servers. Regular maintenance and troubleshooting activities require you to log in directly to the database server. To promote efficiency and sanity, you should develop a standard set of OS tools and SQL scripts that help you maintain multiple environments. You can use standard features of the OS to assist with navigating, repeating commands, showing system bottlenecks, quickly finding critical files, and so on.

With just a small amount of setup, you can ensure that your OS prompt always shows information such as the host and database. Anything that needs to be run against the database a few times is a perfect candidate for automation. Now let's dive into other database administration tasks.

Leveraging Tools

Along with having SQL Developer as a tool to manage databases, run queries, and load data, other user tools make tasks easier. There are also Visual Studio Code (VS Code) extensions for SQL Developer and Oracle Developer Tools, allowing developers and DBAs to edit SQL and PL/SQL, debug, explore your database schema, and view data. This is not just for on-premises databases but also in the cloud and Oracle Autonomous Databases.

If you are already using VS Code, you will find this extremely beneficial to add the extension for Oracle Developer Tools. If you are not using VS Code, it is a tool that allows you to work in other programming languages, manage databases, work with your data, and edit markdown files. This is just a list that we use it for. It is useful for editing these scripts that were just provided and connecting to the databases.

Also, SQLcl is a command-line interface that offers easier editing and working with SQL without needing SQLPlus. You have SQLPlus commands part of SQLcl and new ones with help with REST APIs and DDL. You have a describe command on an object, but in SQLcl you can easily generate the DDL statement for the object.

```
hsolo@mmdb23ai> ddl hsolo.inventory
CREATE TABLE "INVENTORY" (
"INV_ID" NUMBER,
"INV_COUNT" NUMBER,
"INV_STATUS" VARCHAR2(10))
TABLESPACE "USERS";
```

SQLcl can also modify the formatting of the DDL with a set DDL. This also allows you to change all the constraints and other object information as part of the DDL statement. The simple Command line with SQLcl makes it worth looking at the free tools with the Oracle Database available for download.

CHAPTER 4

Tablespaces and Data Files

Tablespaces are not just for tables. A tablespace is a logical container that allows you to manage groups of data files, the physical files on disk that consume space. Once a tablespace is created, you can create database objects (tables and indexes) within tablespaces, resulting in space allocated on disk in the associated data files.

A tablespace is logical because it is visible only through data dictionary views, such as DBA_TABLESPACES. You manage tablespaces through SQL*Plus or graphical tools such as SQL Developer or Enterprise Manager. Both types of tools are useful in managing the tablespaces and data files. Tablespaces only exist while the database is up and running while data files are persisted on storage systems.

Data files can also be viewed through data dictionary views, such as DBA_DATA_FILES, and have a physical presence as they can be viewed outside the database through OS utilities, such as the command ls to list the files. As mentioned, the data files persist and are visible whether the database is open or closed.

Oracle databases typically contain several tablespaces. A tablespace can have one or more data files, but a data file can be associated with only one tablespace. In other words, a data file can't be shared between two (or more) tablespaces.

Objects like tables and indexes are owned by users and created within tablespaces. An object is logically instantiated as a *segment*. A segment consists of the extent of space within the tablespace. An extent consists of a set of database blocks. It is important to know that you can get to a block for recovery, but you don't have to recover a complete database; you can recover at the block level, which allows higher availability and recoverability of databases.

© Michelle Malcher, Darl Kuhn 2024
M. Malcher and D. Kuhn, *Pro Oracle Database 23ai Administration*,
https://doi.org/10.1007/979-8-8688-1038-1_4

Figure 4-1 shows the relationship between these logical and physical constructs used to manage space within an Oracle database. With Oracle 23ai, there is less focus on segment, extent, and block management as advancements in storage and how Oracle manages files do not require the extent management that they did in years past. But it is important to understand these relationships and logical storage structures.

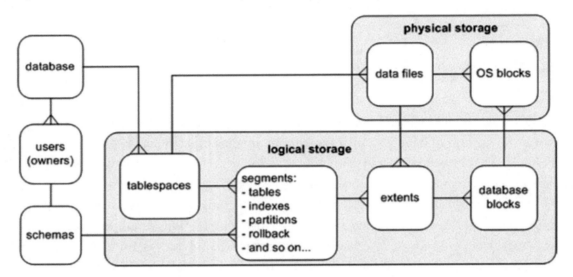

Figure 4-1. *Relationship between logical storage objects and physical storage*

As you saw when we created the database in Chapter 2, typically, five tablespaces are created when you execute the CREATE DATABASE statement.

- SYSTEM

- SYSAUX

- UNDO

- TEMP

- USERS

These tablespaces are created in the container database and pluggable database. Since Oracle 23ai is created only with a container database, you can decide if you want the UNDO tablespace created in the pluggable databases or just use the CDB UNDO tablespace. This is discussed later in the chapter, but it's good to know that these tablespaces are created in the CDB and the PDB.

These five tablespaces are the minimal set of storage containers you need to operate a database. The USERS tablespace, of course, can have a different name and is needed to keep user-owned objects separate from the SYSTEM objects. DATA is the name of the user objects in Autonomous Databases. The only required names for tablespaces are SYSTEM and SYSAUX. Even the UNDO and TEMP tablespaces can also be named differently, normally with a number or maybe an application or PDB prefix. PDBs have the user and data tablespaces associated with them, and optionally, PDBs can have their own UNDO and TEMP tablespaces. Choosing separate UNDO and TEMP tablespaces for each PDB is part of the configuration and creation of the PDB. As you open a database, you should create additional tablespaces for storing application data. This chapter discusses the purpose of the standard set of tablespaces, the need for additional tablespaces, and how to manage these critical database storage containers. The chapter focuses on the most common and critical tasks associated with creating and maintaining tablespaces and data files, progressing to more advanced topics such as moving and renaming data files.

Understanding the First Five

The SYSTEM tablespace provides storage for the Oracle data dictionary objects. This tablespace is where all objects owned by the SYS user are stored. There should not be any user-defined objects in the SYSTEM tablespace; this is reserved for SYS and a couple of other Oracle data dictionary owners.

The SYSAUX (system auxiliary) tablespace is created when you create the database. This auxiliary tablespace is a data repository for Oracle Database tools such as SQL Plan Management, Enterprise Manager, Automatic Workload Repository, Logical Standby, and so on. Audit logs are collected in the SYSAUX tablespace by default but should be configured to use another tablespace created for audit records. Some of these other tools can be configured to use additional tablespaces depending on retention and separation rules and keep the data outside the default system tablespaces.

The UNDO tablespace stores the information required to undo the effects of a transaction (insert, update, delete, or merge). This information is required if a transaction is purposely rolled back (via a ROLLBACK statement). The undo information is also used by Oracle to recover from unexpected instance crashes and to provide read consistency for SQL statements. Some database features, such as Flashback Query, also use the undo information. With all this information in the UNDO tablespace, you can see why it would make sense to separate the undo information into each PDB. The CDB has an UNDO tablespace, and each PDB should have an UNDO tablespace for all the application transactions in the PDB.

Some Oracle SQL statements require a sort area in memory or disk. For example, the results of a query may need to be sorted before being returned to the user. Oracle first uses memory to sort the query results, and the TEMP tablespace is used when there is no longer sufficient memory. Extra temporary storage may also be required when creating or rebuilding indexes. A later chapter discusses large object processing, which also needs extra temporary storage and hash operations. The space is used only for transient data for the session, and no permanent objects can be stored in a TEMP tablespace. If temporary objects are needed for a process outside of one session, the object should be stored in a permanent user tablespace. When you create a database, you typically create the TEMP tablespace and specify it as the default temporary tablespace for any users you create. Multiple temporary tablespaces with different names can be assigned to different groups of users or applications to avoid conflicts between temp space usage or one application stealing all the temp space for their use.

The USERS tablespace is not absolutely required but is often used as a default permanent tablespace for table and index data for users. As shown in Chapter 2, you create a default permanent tablespace for users when you create your database. This means that when a user attempts to create a table or index, if no tablespace is specified during object creation, the object is created in the default permanent tablespace by default.

Need for More Tablespaces

Although you could put every database user's data in the USERS tablespace for logical separation, backup, and recovery, additional tablespaces should be created for the applications and ad hoc users or developers.

DBAs used to separate table and index data for performance reasons and management of the data files. The thinking was that separating table data from index data on different files possibly different disks would reduce input/output (I/O) contention. This is because the data files for each tablespace could be placed on different disks with separate controllers.

With modern storage configurations, which have multiple layers of abstraction between the application and the underlying physical storage devices, it is debatable whether you can realize any performance gains by creating multiple separate tablespaces. Also, with Automatic Storage Management (ASM), hot spot areas on disk with I/O contention can be rebalanced and shifted around to reduce the contention.

There are still valid reasons for creating multiple tablespaces for table and index data.

- Backup and recovery requirements may be different for the tables and indexes.

- The indexes may have storage requirements different from those of the table data.

- Simplify management of objects by logically grouping tables and indexes separately.

In addition to separate tablespaces, you can sometimes create separate tablespaces for objects of different sizes. For instance, if an application has very large tables, you can create an APP_DATA_LARGE tablespace that has a large extent size and a separate APP_DATA_SMALL tablespace that has a smaller extent size. This concept also extends to binary large object (LOB) data types. You may want to separate a LOB column in its own tablespace because you want to manage the LOB tablespace storage characteristics differently from those of the regular table tablespaces.

Partitions are another possibility for different types of storage for an archiving type of storage vs. current information in the new partitions. Remember, segments and extents were managed more closely for performance in previous versions, but with automatic segment space management (ASSM) extent size is allocated and based on information of the objects stored. Even if not setting the large and smaller extents manually and using ASSM, the grouping of the objects in this way assists in the management of the objects as well as the automated space management.

Default storage settings make sense and help simplify storage management. Unless you are willing to continually help choose the right tablespace and modify objects to adjust settings, default values are the way to go. Make a plan easy to follow with minimal tablespace and space management. If needed, there are configurations you can adjust for extreme performance issues.

Container Tablespaces

With 23ai, it might make even more sense to create tablespaces by applications in the PDBs. You already have most of the system information in the SYSTEM and SYSAUX tablespaces in the CDB, and with current storage technologies, the separation of data files by the application might make the most sense to reduce the management of additional tablespaces; the application can use the PDB application containers for this separation of tablespaces. Figure 4-2 shows the different tablespaces in CDBs and PDBs.

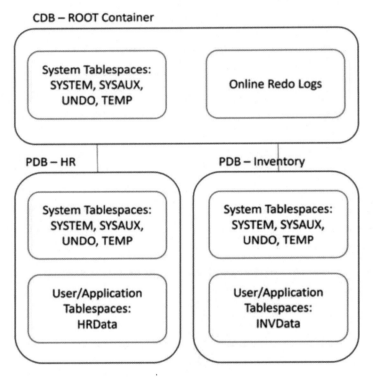

Figure 4-2. *Tablespaces in CDBs and PDBs*

As mentioned, an application container is a pluggable container designed for grouping application objects. It is optional but can store data and metadata for one or more applications. This allows the PDBs part of the application container to easily share data in central tables. Think of an application container functioning like a CDB within a CDB for grouping common objects for the applications.

In Figure 4-2, you see the separation of the HR PDB and the Inventory PDB, each with a tablespace for those applications, named HRData and INVData. This is instead of separating them by object types, tables, and indexes. Even if there is only one PDB, you can separate the application data using HRData and INVData in one PDB. The following are some reasons to consider creating separate tablespaces for each application using the database.

- Applications may have different availability requirements. Separate tablespaces let you take tablespaces offline for one application without affecting another application.

- Applications may have different backup and recovery requirements. Separate tablespaces let tablespaces be backed up and recovered independently. Separate PDBs could be the solution for this instead of more tablespaces.

- You may have some data that is purely read-only. Separate tablespaces let you put a tablespace that contains only read-only data into read-only mode.

- You may have security settings such as encrypting the tablespace and other tablespaces without encryption.

Creating Tablespaces

You use the CREATE TABLESPACE statement to create tablespaces. In most scenarios, you need to use only a few of the features available, namely, locally managed extent allocation and ASSM. The following code snippet demonstrates creating a tablespace that employs the most common features.

```
SQL> create tablespace tools
datafile '/u01/oradata/mmdb23ai/tools01.dbf'
size 100M
autoextend on next 100M maxsize unlimited
extent management local
uniform size 128K
segment space management auto;
```

You need to modify this script for your environment. For example, the directory path or ASM, data file size, and uniform extent size should be changed per environment requirements. In previous releases, there were several storage parameters, such as NEXT, PCTINCREASE, MINEXTENTS, MAXEXTENTS, and DEFAULT. These parameters must be set until locally managed tablespaces with EXTENT MANAGEMENT LOCAL, which uses a bitmap in the data file to efficiently determine whether an extent is in use.

A locally managed tablespace with uniform extents must be minimally sized for at least five database blocks per extent. As you add data to objects in tablespaces, Oracle automatically allocates more extents to an associated tablespace data file to accommodate the growth. You can give it a size or specify an AUTOALLOCATE clause, especially when you think objects in one tablespace have varying sizes. Again, this removes the need to have the different tablespaces—LARGE, SMALL, and so on.

The SEGMENT SPACE MANAGEMENT AUTO clause instructs Oracle to manage the space within the block. When you use this clause, there is no need to specify parameters. Using AUTO vastly reduces the number of parameters you need to configure and manage.

When a data file fills up, you can instruct Oracle to increase the size of the data file automatically with the AUTOEXTEND feature. Using AUTOEXTEND allows processes to run without needing DBA intervention when getting close to running out of space. MAXSIZE is optional, but it does not allow the tablespace to grow beyond that size so that the mount point disk doesn't fill up.

However, you must monitor tablespace growth and plan for additional storage space. This includes watching for processes that might load a large amount of data. Manually adding space might limit having a runaway SQL process that accidentally grows a tablespace until it has consumed all the space on a mount point. But a large load process one month over another might be rolled back if it fails on additional space requirements. Using the parameter RESUMABLE_TIMEOUT in the database, you can set a time to be able to respond to tablespace issues. If you inadvertently fill up a mount point that contains a control file of the Oracle binaries, you can hang or freeze your database so no other transactions can occur. Using ASM also helps here to be able to add another disk to the disk group to avoid filling up a mount point, and when used with RESUMABLE_TIMEOUT, it provides the time to manage. Monitoring and planning for storage and growth are still the best methods for managing tablespace sizing to proactively add the needed space.

The CREATE TABLESPACE command becomes even easier using ASM, allowing DBAs to plan on overall growth and additional storage space monitoring. It takes the disk group's defaults and parameters set to use ASM. ASM administration is covered in a later chapter, but here is a quick example.

```
SQL> create tablespace HRDATA;
```

For security, tablespaces can be transparently encrypted. Transparent means that the application does not need to change to use the encrypted tablespaces. This allows data at rest in the data files to be encrypted. When the database is open, the tablespaces are decrypted using the encryption key in the database wallet to be able to see the data through queries. Encryption makes it so that the data files cannot be viewed in plain text, which is the same for backups of the data files. As already stated, there are many options for creating tablespaces, and this security option does require the management of the encryption key, which can be centrally located or locally with the database. The create tablespace command is simple enough.

```
SOL> create tablespace HRDATA encryption using 'AES256' default storage
(encrypt);
```

If you ever need to verify the SQL required to re-create an existing tablespace, you can do so with the DBMS_METADATA package. First, set the LONG variable to a large value.

```
SOL> set long 1000000
```

Next, use the DBMS_METADATA package to display the CREATE TABLESPACE data definition language (DDL) for all tablespaces within the database.

```
SOL> select dbms_metadata.get_ddl('TABLESPACE',tablespace_name) from dba_
tablespaces;
```

Tip   You can also use Data Pump to extract the DDL from database objects. See Chapter 13 for more information.

Creating a Bigfile Tablespace

The bigfile feature allows you to create a tablespace with a very large data file assigned to it. The advantage of using the bigfile feature is the potential to create very large files. With an 8 KB block size, you can create a data file as large as 32 TB. With a 32 KB block size, you can create a data file up to 128 TB.

Use the BIGFILE clause to create a bigfile tablespace.

```
SOL> create bigfile tablespace inv_big_data
datafile '/u01/dbfile/db23ai/inv_big_data01.dbf'
size 1og
autoextend on next 1ooM maxsize unlimited
extent management local
uniform size 128k
segment space management auto;
```

As long as you have plenty of space associated with the filesystem supporting the bigfile tablespace data file, you can store massive amounts of data in a tablespace.

One potential disadvantage of using a bigfile tablespace is that if, for any reason, you run out of space on a filesystem that supports the data file associated with the bigfile, you can't expand the size of the tablespace (unless you can add space to the filesystem). You can't add more data files to a bigfile tablespace if placed on separate mount points. A bigfile tablespace allows only one data file to be associated with it.

You can make the bigfile tablespace the default type for a database using the ALTER DATABASE SET DEFAULT BIGFILE TABLESPACE statement. However, it is not recommended that you do that. You could potentially create a tablespace, not knowing it was a bigfile tablespace, and when you discovered that you needed more space, you would not know that you could not add another data file on a different mount point for this tablespace. Using ASM is less of an issue because a new disk can be dynamically added to a DISKGROUP for this tablespace.

Shrink Bigfile Tablespace

Data is dynamic, and some applications clear out tables and insert new data. Large deletes and new inserts might allow unused space to grow over time, and reorganization of the data and tables might be required to reclaim this unused free space in tablespaces. In 23ai, a new feature allows you to reclaim this space with a SHRINK_TABLESPACE procedure.

You can first analyze what will be performed with the command and then run the command to execute the shrink and reclaim the space.

```
SOL> exec dbms_space.SHRINK_TABLESPACE('USERS',
SHRINK_MODE => DBMS_SPACE.TS_MODE_ANALYZE);

SQL> exec dbms_space.SHRINK_TABLESPACE('USERS');
```

Renaming a Tablespace

Sometimes, you need to rename a tablespace. You may want to do this because a tablespace was initially erroneously named, or you may want the tablespace name to better conform to your database naming standards. Use the ALTER TABLESPACE statement to rename a tablespace. This example renames a tablespace from TOOLS to

TOOLS_DEV:
```
SOL> alter tablespace tools rename to tools_dev;
```

When you rename a tablespace, Oracle updates the name of the tablespace in the data dictionary, control files, and data file headers. Remember that renaming a tablespace doesn't rename any associated data files.

Note   You can't rename the SYSTEM tablespace or the SYSAUX tablespace.

Changing the Write Mode

In environments such as data warehouses, you may need to load data into tables and then never modify the data again. To enforce that no objects in a tablespace can be modified, you can alter the tablespace to be read-only. To do this, use the ALTER TABLESPACE statement.

```
SOL> alter tablespace inv_mgmt_rep read only;
```

One advantage of a read-only tablespace is that you must back it up only once. You should be able to restore the data files from a read-only tablespace no matter how long since the backup was made.

If you need to modify the tablespace out of read-only mode, do so as follows.

```
SOL> alter tablespace inv_mgmt_rep read write;
```

Make sure you re-enable backups of a tablespace after you place it in read/write mode.

Note   You can't make a tablespace that contains active rollback segments read-only. For this reason, the SYSTEM tablespace can't be made read-only because it contains the SYSTEM rollback segment.

Be aware that individual tables can be modified to be read-only. This allows you to control the read-only at a much more granular level (than at the tablespace level); the following is an example.

```
SOL> alter table my_tab read only;
```

While in read-only mode, you can't issue any insert, update, or delete statements against the table. Making individual tables read/write can be advantageous when you're doing maintenance (such as a data migration), and you want to ensure that users don't update the data.

This example modifies a table back to read/write mode.

```
SOL> alter table my_tab read write;
```

Dropping a Tablespace

If you have a tablespace that is unused, it is best to drop it so it does not clutter your database, consume unnecessary resources, and potentially confuse DBAs who are not familiar with the database. Before dropping a tablespace, it is a good practice to first take it offline.

```
SOL> alter tablespace inv_data offline;
```

You may want to wait to see if anybody screams that an application is broken because it can no longer write to a table or index in the tablespace to be dropped. Depending on the reason for dropping a tablespace, objects can be moved to another tablespace first before dropping. When you are sure the tablespace is not required, drop it and delete its data files.

```
SOL> drop tablespace inv_data including contents and datafiles;
```

> **Tip**   You can drop a tablespace whether it is online or offline. The exception to this is the SYSTEM and SYSAUX tablespaces, which cannot be dropped. Taking a tablespace offline before you drop it is always a good idea. By doing so, you can better determine whether an application uses any objects in the tablespace. If you attempt to query a table in an offline tablespace, you receive this error: ORA-00376: file can't be read at this time.

Dropping a tablespace using INCLUDING CONTENTS AND DATAFILES permanently removes the tablespace and any of its data files. Ensure the tablespace does not contain any data you want to keep before you drop it.

If you attempt to drop a tablespace containing a primary key referenced by a foreign key associated with a table in a tablespace different from the one you are trying to drop, you receive this error.

ORA-02449: unique/primary keys in table referenced by foreign keys

Run this query first to determine whether any foreign key constraints are affected.

```
SOL> select p.owner,
p.table_name,
p.constraint_name
f.table_name referencing_table,
f.constraint_name foreign_key_name,
f.status fk_status
from dba_constraints p,
dba_constraints f,
dba_tables t
where p.constraint_name = f.r_constraint_name
andf.constraint_type = 'R'
andp.table_name = t.table_name
andt.tablespace_name = UPPER('&tablespace_name')
order by 1,2,3,4,5;
```

If there are referenced constraints, you need to first drop the constraints or use the CASCADE CONSTRAINTS clause of the DROP TABLESPACE statement. This statement uses CASCADE CONSTRAINTS to drop any affected constraints automatically.

```
SQL> drop tablespace inv_data including contents and datafiles cascade
constraints;
```

This statement drops any referential integrity constraints from tables outside the tablespace being dropped that reference tables within the dropped tablespace.

If you drop a tablespace with required objects in a production system, the results can be catastrophic. You must perform some sort of recovery to get the tablespace and its objects back. Needless to say, be careful when dropping a tablespace.

Using Oracle Managed Files

The Oracle Managed File (OMF) feature automates many aspects of tablespace management, such as file placement, naming, and sizing. This simplifies the level of file management and the CREATE TABLESPACE commands. You control OMF by setting the following initialization parameters.

```
DB_CREATE_FILE_DEST
DB_CREATE_ONLINE_LOG_DEST_N
DB_RECOVERY_FILE_DEST
```

If you set these parameters before you create the database, Oracle uses them to place the data files, control files, and online redo logs. You can also enable OMF after your database has been created. Oracle uses the values of the initialization parameters for the locations of any newly added files. Oracle also determines the name of the newly added file. These parameters are set as input into DBCA to create a database.

The advantage of using OMF is that creating tablespaces is simplified. For example, the CREATE TABLESPACE statement does not need to specify anything other than the tablespace name. First, enable the OMF feature by setting the DB_CREATE_FILE_DEST parameter.

```
SQL> alter system set db_create_file_dest='/u01';
```

Now, issue the CREATE TABLESPACE statement.

```
SQL> create tablespace inv1;
```

This statement creates a tablespace named INV1, with a default data file size of 100 MB. Remember that you can override the default size of 100 MB by specifying a size.

```
SQL> create tablespace inv2 datafile size 20m;
```

To view the details of the associated data files, query the V$DATAFILE view and note that Oracle has created subdirectories beneath the /u01 directory and named the file with the OMF format.

```
SQL> select name from v$datafile where name like '%inv%';
NAME
------------------------------------------------------------
/u01/mmdb32c/datafile/o1_mf_inv1_8b5163q6_.dbf /u01/mmdb23ai/datafile/
o1_mf_inv2_8b5lflfc_.dbf
```

One limitation of OMF is that you're limited to one directory for placing data files. If you want to add data files to a different directory, you can alter the location dynamically.

```
SQL> alter system set db_create_file_dest='/u02';
```

Displaying the Tablespace Size

DBAs often use monitoring scripts to alert them when they need to increase the space allocated to a tablespace. Remember you have to check tablespace in both the CDB and all the PDBs, keeping in mind that the PDBs each need to be monitored because they are more dynamic and growing. The following script displays the percentage of free space left in a tablespace and data file.

```
SET PAGESIZE 100 LINES 132 ECHO OFF VERIFY OFF FEEDB OFF SPACE 1 TRIMSP ON
COMPUTE SUM OF a_byt t_byt f_byt ON REPORT
BREAK ON REPORT ON tablespace_name ON pf
COL tablespace_name FOR A17   TRU HEAD    'Tablespace|Name'
COL file_name          FOR A40   TRU HEAD    'Filename'
COL a_byt      FOR 9,990.999   HEAD    'Allocated|GB'
COL t_byt      FOR 9,990.999   HEAD    'Current|Used GB'
COL f_byt      FOR 9,990.999   HEAD    'Current|Free GB'
COL pct_free       FOR 990.0   HEAD    'File %|Free'
COL pf             FOR 990.0   HEAD    'Tbsp %|Free'
```

```
COL seq NOPRINT
DEFINE b_div=1073741824
--
SELECT 1 seq, b.tablespace_name, nvl(x.fs,0)/y.ap*100 pf, b.file_name
file_name,
b.bytes/&&b_div a_byt, NVL((b.bytes-SUM(f.bytes))/&&b_div,b.bytes/&&b_div)
t_byt,
NVL(SUM(f.bytes)/&&b_div,0) f_byt, NVL(SUM(f.bytes)/b.bytes*100,0) pct_free
FROM dba_free_space f, dba_data_files b
,(SELECT y.tablespace_name, SUM(y.bytes) fs
FROM dba_free_space y GROUP BY y.tablespace_name) x
,(SELECT x.tablespace_name, SUM(x.bytes) ap
FROM dba_data_files x GROUP BY x.tablespace_name) y
WHERE f.file_id(+) = b.file_id
ANDx.tablespace_name(+) = y.tablespace_name
andy.tablespace_name = b.tablespace_name
ANDf.tablespace_name(+) = b.tablespace_name
GROUP BY b.tablespace_name, nvl(x.fs,0)/y.ap*100, b.file_name, b.bytes
UNION ALL
SELECT 2 seq, tablespace_name,
j.bf/k.bb*100 pf, b.name file_name, b.bytes/&&b_div a_byt,
a.bytes_used/&&b_div t_byt, a.bytes_free/&&b_div f_byt,
a.bytes_free/b.bytes*100 pct_free
FROM v$temp_space_header a, v$tempfile b
,(SELECT SUM(bytes_free) bf FROM v$temp_space_header) j
,(SELECT SUM(bytes) bb FROM v$tempfile) k
WHERE a.file_id = b.file#
ORDER BY 1,2,4,3;
```

UNION ALL returns all the rows from the queries and does not marry the two sets from the queries. They are independent of each other.

If you don't have any monitoring in place, you are alerted via the SQL statement that is attempting to perform an insert or update operation that the tablespace requires more space but isn't able to allocate more. An ORA-01653 error is thrown at that point, indicating the object can't extend.

After you determine that a tablespace needs more space, you need to either increase the size of a data file or add a data file to the tablespace. After you run into a space problem, you may need to increase the maximum size of the data files or add data files to the tablespace. If you don't have any space available for new data files, you need to add more storage to the server or add more disk groups to ASM. Scripts help give you an idea about space being used, and to monitor the environment, it is useful to have tools such as Oracle Enterprise Manager and get alerts.

Displaying Oracle Error Messages and Actions

You can use the oerr utility to quickly display the cause of an error and simple instructions on what actions to take; the following is an example.

```
$ oerr ora 01653
```

Here is the output for this example.

```
01653, 00000, "unable to extend table %s.%s by %s in tablespace %s"
// *Cause: Failed to allocate an extent of the required number of
// blocks for a table segment in the tablespace indicated.
// *Action: Use ALTER TABLESPACE ADD DATAFILE statement to add one or more
// files to the tablespace indicated.
```

The oerr utility's output gives you a fast and easy way to triage problems. Google is a good second option if the information provided isn't enough.

Altering Tablespace Size

When not using AUTOEXTEND and determining which data file you want to resize, first make sure you have enough disk space to increase the size of the data file on the mount point on which the data file exists.

```
$ df -h | sort
```

Use the ALTER DATABASE DATAFILE ... RESIZE command to increase the data file's size. This example resizes the data file to 100 GB.

```
SQL> alter database datafile '/u01/oradata/db23ai/users01.dbf' resize 100g;
```

If you don't have space on an existing mount point to increase the size of a data file, then you must add a data file. To add a data file to an existing tablespace, use the ALTER TABLESPACE ... ADD DATAFILE statement.

```
SQL> alter tablespace users
add datafile '/u02/oradata/db18c/users02.dbf' size 100m;
```

With bigfile tablespaces, you can use the ALTER TABLESPACE statement to resize the data file. This works because only one data file can be associated with a bigfile tablespace.

```
SQL> alter tablespace inv_big_data resize 1P;
```

To add space to a temporary tablespace, first query the V $TEMPFILE view to verify the current size and location of temporary data files.

```
SQL> select name, bytes from v$tempfile;
```

Then, use the TEMPFILE option of the ALTER DATABASE statement.

```
SQL> alter database tempfile '/u01/oradata/db23ai/temp01.dbf' resize 500m;
```

You can also add a file to a temporary tablespace via the ALTER TABLESPACE statement.

```
SQL> alter tablespace temp add tempfile '/u01/oradata/db23ai/temp02.dbf'
size 5000m;
```

Additional Data File Operations

Occasionally, you may need to move or rename a data file. For example, you may need to move data files because of changes in the storage devices or because the files were created in the wrong location or with a nonstandard name.

The ALTER DATBASE MOVE DATAFILE command allows you to rename or move data files without any downtime. Here is an example.

```
SQL> alter database move datafile
'/u01/oradata/db23ai/hrdata01.dbf' to
'/u02/oradata/db23ai/hrdata01.dbf';
```

You can also specify the data file number from v$datafile when renaming or moving a data file.

```
SQL> alter database move datafile 2 to '/u02/oradata/db23ai/sysaux.dbf';
```

You can use the KEEP option if you are moving a data file and want to keep a copy of the original file.

```
SQL> alter database move datafile 4 to '/u02/oradata/db23ai/users01.
dbf' keep;
```

You can specify the REUSE clause to overwrite an existing file. Oracle does not allow you to overwrite or reuse a data file that is currently being used by the database, which is a good thing.

```
SQL> alter database move datafile 4 to '/u01/oradata/db23ai/users01.
dbf' reuse;
```

Move SYSTEM and UNDO

To move the SYSTEM tablespace, you need to take the tablespace offline, and because it is SYSTEM, you can take it offline only while the database is closed and not open.

```
SQL> conn / as sysdba
SQL> shutdown immediate;
SQL> startup mount;
```

Because the database is in mount mode, the data files are not open for use, and therefore, the data files do not need to be taken offline. The next step is to manually move the files via the Linux mv command.

```
$ mv /u01/oradata/db23ai/system01.dbf /u02/oradata/db23ai/system01.dbf
$ mv /u01/oradata/db23ai/undotbs01.dbf /u02/oradata/db23ai/undotbs01.dbf
```

You must move the files before you update the control file. The ALTER DATABASE RENAME FILE command expects the file to be in the renamed location. If the file is not there, an error is thrown: ORA-27037: unable to obtain file status.

Now, you can update the control file to know the new filename.

```
SQL> alter database rename file '/u01/oradata/db23ai/system01.dbf', '/u01/
oradata/db23ai/undotbs01.dbf'
to
'/u02/oradata/db23ai/system01.dbf', '/u02/oradata/db23ai/undotbs01.dbf';
  Next is to open the database:
SQL> alter database open;
```

Using ASM for Tablespaces

Using ASM to manage the physical disk and storage allocation simplifies the management of the tablespaces and data files. Adding storage means adding disks to a disk group and allows additional space to be dynamically available to the tablespaces. With storage hardware advances, there are also ways to add disks to mount points. It depends on how the databases and environments are managed and configured if ASM is part of the environment.

There are plenty of advantages to using ASM, including shared storage, ease of disk management, data file repairs, and verifications specific to the database. As part of the grid infrastructure, the +ASM instance is created and provides a way to share storage for several databases, rebalances workloads, and provides higher availability for the database storage.

The parameters for using a default storage space have already been discussed. Instead of naming mount points that can change as databases grow or move, the database using +ASM can use a disk group without worrying about names for mount points. A disk group called oradata is created to be used for database storage. The parameters for file destinations are set using the following command.

```
SQL> alter system set DB_CREATE_FILE_DEST = '+oradata';
```

To create the tablespace, use the following command.

```
SQL> create tablespace hrdata;
```

This creates a tablespace named HRDATA on the oradata disk group. +ASM generates the filenames, and to create aliases by default, a template for the filenames in +ASM is used. If a template is used, the DB_CREATE_FILE_DEST parameter will point to that template along with the disk group.

```
SQL> alter system set DB_CREATE_FILE_DEST = '+oradata(datatemplate)';
```

The data files and tablespace views are still available to see what tablespaces are created and the data files that are part of the database. The view v$datafile and dba_data_files show the files starting with the disk group +oradata. The dba_tablespaces view still shows the HRDATA tablespace as with non-ASM databases. There are also additional views that show the files in the disk groups. To see the ASM disks in the disk group view, v$asm_disk should be queried. The files in the disk group are seen in the v$asm_file and v$asm_alias views.

From v$asm_file, the number, type, and space information are available, and v$asm_alias brings in the data filename.

```
SQL> select asmfile.file_number, aliasfile.name, asmfile.type
from v$asm_file asmfile, v$asm_alias aliasfile
where asnfile.group_number=aliasfile.group_number and asmfile.file_
number=aliasfile.file_number
```

The Oracle cloud uses the ASM and ASM Cluster File System (ACFS) to present the storage. It simplifies and automates storage management. There is no need for another volume or file manager tool. Again, there are advantages to using the storage management tools with Oracle Database. There are plenty of reference materials to show how to create disk groups, add or drop disks, perform maintenance, and manage the ASM storage and file systems.

ASM is becoming a standard installation for the Oracle Base Database Service in the Oracle Cloud, and the overhead of managing an ASM instance simplifies adding storage and creating tablespaces. There are benefits to having the disk configured for Oracle databases, and throughout the rest of the book, you see examples for managing ASM and disk groups and filesystems.

As a DBA, you must manage tablespaces and data files proficiently. In any environment, you must add, rename, relocate, and drop these storage containers. These are ideal tests to be done when creating a database or in a test environment to practice the commands and restore data files. The commands, errors, and issues can be logged for future reference in a high-pressure situation for data file corruption and recovery.

Oracle requires three types of files for a database to operate: data files, control files, and online redo log files. Data files are in both CDBs and PDBs. Control files and online redo files are part of the CDB and managed there, which is discussed in the next chapter.

CHAPTER 5

Managing Control Files, Online Redo Logs, and Archivelogs

An Oracle database consists of three types of mandatory files: data files, control files, and online redo logs. In Chapter 4, the focus was on tablespaces and data files. This chapter looks at managing control files and online redo logs and implementing archivelogs. The first part of the chapter discusses typical control file maintenance tasks, such as adding, moving, and removing control files. Next, let's examine the DBA activities related to online redo log files, such as renaming, adding, dropping, and relocating these critical files. Finally, the architecture aspects of enabling and implementing archiving are covered.

Managing Control Files

A control file is a small binary file that stores the following types of information.

- Database name
- Names and locations of data files
- Names and locations of online redo log files
- Current online redo log sequence number
- Checkpoint information
- Names and locations of RMAN backup files

119

You can query much of the information stored in the control file from data dictionary views. This example displays the types of information stored in the control file querying v$controlfile_record_section.

```
SQL> select distinct type from v$controlfile_record_section;
```

Here is a partial listing of the output.

```
TYPE
----------------------------
FILENAME
TABLESPACE
RMAN CONFIGURATION
BACKUP CORRUPTION
PROXY COPY
FLASHBACK LOG
REMOVABLE RECOVERY FILES
AUXILIARY DATAFILE COPY
DATAFILE
```

You can view database-related information stored in the control file via the v$database view. The v$ views are based on x$ tables or views, and the v$database is based on an x$ table, which is just a read of the control file.

```
SQL> select name, open_mode, created, current_scn from v$database;
```

Here is the output for this example.

```
NAME       OPEN_MODE             CREATED    CURRENT_SCN
---------  --------------------  ---------  -----------
db23ai     READ WRITE            28-SEP-12  2573820
```

Every Oracle database must have at least one control file. When you start your database in nomount mode, the instance is aware of the location of the control files from the CONTROL_FILES initialization parameter in the spfile or init.ora file. When you issue a STARTUP NOMOUNT command, Oracle reads the parameter file, starts the background processes, and allocates memory structures.

```
-- locations of control files are known to the instance
SQL> startup nomount;
```

At this point, the control files have not been touched by any processes. When you alter your database into mount mode, the control files are read and opened for use.

```
-- control files opened
SOL> alter database mount;
```

If any of the control files listed in the CONTROL_FILES initialization parameter are not available, then you cannot mount your database.

When you successfully mount your database, the instance is aware of the locations of the data files and online redo logs but has not yet opened them. After you change your database to open mode, the data files and online redo logs are opened.

```
-- datafiles and online redo logs opened
SOL> alter database open;
```

Note   Keep in mind that when you issue the STARTUP command (with no options), the previously described three phases are automatically performed in this order: nomount, mount, open. When you issue a SHUTDOWN command, the phases are reversed: close the database, unmount the control file, and stop the instance.

The control file is created when the database is created. You should create at least two control files when you create your database (to avoid a single point of failure). Control files keep track of important information for the database, such as detailed data files and online redo logs, log sequence numbers, and checkpoint information. Losing a control file requires you to recover the control file for the database, and not having a control file, as well as not having a backup, makes it difficult to recover. Previously, you should have multiple control files stored on separate storage devices controlled by separate controllers. But because of storage devices, it might be difficult to know if it is a separate device, so it is important to have fault-tolerant devices with mirroring. The control file is an important part of the database and must be available or quickly restored.

Control files can also be on ASM disk groups. This allows one control file in the +ORADATA disk group and another file in the +FRA disk group. Managing the control files and details inside remains the same as on the file system, except the control files only use ASM disk groups.

After the database has been opened, Oracle frequently writes information to the control files, such as when you make any physical modifications (e.g., creating a tablespace or adding/removing/resizing a data file). Oracle writes to all control files specified by the CONTROL_FILES initialization parameter. An error is thrown if Oracle cannot write to one of the control files.

ORA-00210: cannot open the specified control file

If one of your control files becomes unavailable, shut down your database and resolve the issue before restarting. Chapter 13 dives into using RMAN and how to use RMAN to restore a control file. Fixing the problem may mean resolving a storage-device failure or modifying the CONTROL_FILES initialization parameter to remove the control file entry for the control file that is not available.

Displaying the Contents of a Control File

You can use the ALTER SESSION statement to display the physical contents of the control file; the following is an example.

```
SQL> oradebug setmypid
SQL> oradebug unlimit
SQL> alter session set events 'immediate trace name controlf level 9';
SQL> oradebug tracefile_name
```

The prior line of code displays the following name of the trace file.

```
/u01/app/oracle/diag/rdbms/mmfalcon23ai/mmfalcon23ai/trace/mmfalcon23ai_
ora_313212.trc
```

The trace file is written to the $ADR_HOME/trace directory. You can also view the trace directory name via this query.

```
SQL> select value from v$diag_info where name='Diag Trace';
```

The command works in both CDBs and PDBs, but it displays the file for the CDB. Control files are part of the CDB, and they are for each PDB.

Figure 5-1 shows a partial listing of the contents of the trace file. You can inspect the contents of the control file when troubleshooting or when trying to better understand Oracle internals.

```
┣ The following are current System-scope REDO Log Archival related
-- parameters and can be included in the database initialization file.
--
-- LOG_ARCHIVE_DEST=''
-- LOG_ARCHIVE_DUPLEX_DEST=''
--
-- LOG_ARCHIVE_FORMAT=%t_%s_%r.dbf
--
-- DB_UNIQUE_NAME="DB23AI"
--
-- LOG_ARCHIVE_CONFIG='SEND, RECEIVE, NODG_CONFIG'
-- LOG_ARCHIVE_MAX_PROCESSES=4
-- STANDBY_FILE_MANAGEMENT=MANUAL
-- FAL_CLIENT=''
-- FAL_SERVER=''
--
-- LOG_ARCHIVE_DEST_1='LOCATION=/u01/db23ai/dbs/arch'
-- LOG_ARCHIVE_DEST_1='MANDATORY REOPEN=300 NODELAY'
-- LOG_ARCHIVE_DEST_1='ARCH NOAFFIRM SYNC'
-- LOG_ARCHIVE_DEST_1='NOREGISTER'
-- LOG_ARCHIVE_DEST_1='NOALTERNATE'
-- LOG_ARCHIVE_DEST_1='NODEPENDENCY'
-- LOG_ARCHIVE_DEST_1='NOMAX_FAILURE NOQUOTA_SIZE NOQUOTA_USED NODB_UNIQUE_NAME'
-- LOG_ARCHIVE_DEST_1='VALID_FOR=(PRIMARY_ROLE,ONLINE_LOGFILES)'
-- LOG_ARCHIVE_DEST_STATE_1=ENABLE


-- Below are two sets of SQL statements, each of which creates a new
-- control file and uses it to open the database. The first set opens
-- the database with the NORESETLOGS option and should be used only if
-- the current versions of all online logs are available. The second
-- set opens the database with the RESETLOGS option and should be used
-- if online logs are unavailable.
-- The appropriate set of statements can be copied from the trace into
-- a script file, edited as necessary, and executed when there is a
-- need to re-create the control file.
--
--      Set #1. NORESETLOGS case
```

Figure 5-1. *Partial contents of a control file*

Viewing Names and Locations of Control Files

If your database is in a nomount state, a mounted state, or an open state, you can view the names and locations of the control files as follows.

```
SQL> show parameter control_files
```

You can also view control file locations and name information by querying the V$CONTROLFILE view. This query works while your database is mounted or open.

```
SQL> select name from v$controlfile;
```

If there is some reason that you cannot start your database and you need to know the names and locations of the control files, you can inspect the contents of the initialization parameter file to see where they are located. If you use an `spfile`, even though it is a binary file, you can still open it with a text editor. The safest approach is to make a copy of the `spfile` and inspect its contents with an OS editor to get the values even when the database is unavailable.

```
$ cp $ORACLE_HOME/dbs/spfilemmfalcon23ai.ora $ORACLE_HOME/dbs/
spfilemmfalcon23ai.copy
```

You can also use the `strings` command to search for values in binary files:

```
$ strings spfilemmfalcon23ai.ora | grep -i control_files
```

If you are using a text-based initialization file, you can view the file directly with an OS editor, or you can use the `grep` command.

```
$ grep -i control_files $ORACLE_HOME/dbs/initmmfalcon23ai.ora
```

Adding a Control File

Adding a control file means copying an existing control file and making your database aware of the copy by modifying your `CONTROL_FILES` parameter. This task must be done while your database is shut down. This procedure works only when you have a good existing control file that can be copied. Adding a control file isn't the same as creating or restoring a control file. Since this requires downtime, it is best to make sure you have two or three copies of the control file for redundancy on highly available storage.

If your database uses only one control file and that control file becomes damaged, you need to either restore a control file from a backup and perform a recovery or re-create the control file. If you are using two or more control files and one becomes damaged, you can use the remaining good control file(s) to quickly get your database into an operating state.

The following is the basic procedure for adding a control file if a database is using only one control file.

1. Alter the initialization file's CONTROL_FILES parameter to include the new location and name of the control file.

2. Shut down your database.

3. Use an OS command to copy an existing control file to the new location and name.

4. Restart your database.

Depending on whether you use an spfile or an init.ora file, the previous steps vary slightly. Since you can easily edit the init.ora file, let's look at the spfile change.

Note   We normally use the spfile file because of the dynamic parameters and use the init.ora file only as a backup. If we make changes to the spfile or use a scheduled job, we copy the spfile file to an init.ora file for backup.

```
SQL> create pfile from spfile;
```

Or you can specify the filename like in the following.

```
SQL> create pfile='/tmp/initdb23ai.ora' from spfile;
```

You can quickly determine whether you are using an spfile with the following SQL statement.

```
SQL> show parameter spfile
NAME     TYPE         VALUE
-------  -----------  -----------------------------------------------------------
spfile   string       +DATA/MMFALCON23AI/PARAMETERFILE/spfile.297.1124711601
```

When you have determined that you are using an `spfile`, use the following steps to add a control file.

1. Determine the `CONTROL_FILES` parameter's current value.

    ```
    SQL> show parameter control_files
    NAME              TYPE        VALUE
    ----------------  ---------   ----------------------------------------
    control_files     string      +DATA/MMFALCON23AI/CONTROLFILE/current.
                                  287.1124711513
    ```

2. Alter your `CONTROL_FILES` parameter to include the new control file that you want to add, but limit the scope of the operation to the `spfile` because this cannot be modified in memory. Make sure you include any control files listed in step 1.

    ```
    SQL> alter system set control_files= '+DATA/MMFALCON23AI/
    CONTROLFILE/current.287.1124711513', '+FRA/MMALCON23ai/
    CONTROLFILE/current.287.1124711513' scope=spfile;
    ```

3. Shut down your database.

    ```
    SQL> shutdown immediate;
    ```

4. Copy an existing control file to the new location with the same name. In this example, a new control file named `current.287.1124711513` is created using `cp` in ASM to copy from one disk group to another.

    ```
    asmcmd> cp +DATA/MMFALCON23AI/CONTROLFILE/current.287.1124711513
    +FRA/MMFALCON23AI/CONTROLFILE
    ```

    If using the file system, a simple OS `cp` command allows you to copy the control file to another directory.

5. Start up your database.

    ```
    SQL> startup;
    ```

You can verify that the new control file is being used by displaying the CONTROL_FILES parameter.

```
SQL> show parameter control_files
NAME               TYPE            VALUE
---------------    -----------     -----------------------------------
control_files      string              +DATA/MMFALCON23AI/CONTROLFILE/
current.287.1124711513, +FRA/MMFALCON23AI/CONTROLFILE/
current.287.1124711513
```

Moving a Control File

You may occasionally need to move a control file from one location to another. For example, if new storage is added to the database server, you may want to move an existing control file to a newly available location. Of course, this is a great reason to be using ASM and saves you some of the downtime and management of storage.

The procedure for moving a control file is similar to adding a control file. The only difference is that instead of copying one of the existing files, you rename and move the control file. This example shows how to move a control file when you are using an spfile.

1. Determine the CONTROL_FILES parameter's current value:

```
SQL> show parameter control_files
NAME               TYPE       VALUE
---------------    -------    ------------------------------------------
control_files      string     /u01/oradata/mmdb23ai/control01.ctl,
/u02/oradata/mmdb23ai/control02.ctl
```

2. Alter your CONTROL_FILES parameter to reflect that you are moving a control file from /u02 to /u03 and leave the control file in /u01 as is.

   Alter the spfile to reflect the new location for the control file. You have to specify SCOPE=SPFILE because the CONTROL_FILES parameter cannot be modified in memory:

```
SQL> alter system set control_files='/u01/oradata/mmdb23ai/
control01.ctl', '/u03/oradata/mmdb23ai/control02.ctl' scope=spfile;
```

3. Shut down your database.

    ```
    SQL> shutdown immediate;
    ```

4. At the OS prompt, move the control file to the new location. This
    example uses the OS mv command.

    ```
    $ mv /u02/oradata/mmdb23ai/control02.ctl /u03/oradata/
    mmdb23ai/control02.ctl
    ```

5. Start up your database.

    ```
    SQL> startup;
    ```

    You can verify that the new control file is being used by displaying
    the CONTROL_FILES parameter.

    ```
    SQL> show parameter control_files
    NAME             TYPE     VALUE
    ---------------  -------- -----------------------------------------
    control_files    string   /u01/oradata/mmdb23ai/control01.ctl,
    /u03/oradata/mmdb23ai/control02.ctl
    ```

Removing a Control File

You may run into a situation in which you experience a media failure with a storage
device that contains one of your multiplexed control files.

```
ORA-00205: error in identifying control file, check alert log for more info
```

In this scenario, you still have at least one good control file. To remove a control file,
follow these steps.

1. Identify which control file has experienced a media failure by
    inspecting the alert.log for information: ORA-00210: cannot
    open the specified control file ORA-00202: control file: '/u01/
    oradata/mmdb23/control02.ctl'.

2. Remove the unavailable control file name from the `CONTROL_FILES` parameter using `scope=spfile` as you did with adding and moving a control file.

3. If this leaves only one control file, you should also add another, as explained in the "Adding a Control File" section earlier in this chapter.

4. Stop and start your database.

    ```
    SQL> shutdown immediate;
    SQL> startup;
    ```

Online Redo Logs

Online redo logs store a record of transactions in your database. These logs serve the following purposes.

- Provide a mechanism for recording changes to the database so that you have a method of recovering transactions in the event of a media failure.

- Ensure that in the event of total instance failure, committed transactions can be recovered (crash recovery) even if committed data changes have not yet been written to the data files.

- Allow administrators to inspect historical database transactions.

- Allow other Oracle tools, such as GoldenGate or Data Guard, to replicate data.

You must have at least two online redo log groups in your database. Each online redo log group must contain at least one online redo log member. The member is the physical file that exists on disk. You can create multiple members in each redo log group, which is known as *multiplexing* your online redo log group.

Tip   Just like the control files are multiplexed, the online redo log groups should also take advantage of highly available storage or be on separate physical devices with separate controllers. Flash is another option for redo logs and can improve performance.

The log-writer log buffer (in the SGA) writes to online redo log files (on disk). The redo record has a system change number (SCN) assigned to identify the transaction redo information. There are committed and uncommitted records written to the redo logs. The log writer flushes the contents of the redo log buffer when any of the following are true.

- A COMMIT is issued.

- A log switch occurs.

- Three seconds go by.

- The redo buffer is one-third full.

Since this is a database process, the container database (CDB) manages the redo logs. PDBs do not have their own redo logs, which means that planning for space and sizing the redo logs is at the CDB level and includes all the PDB transactions.

The online redo log group that the log writer is actively writing to is the current online redo log group. The log writer writes simultaneously to all members of a redo log group. The log writer must successfully write to only one member for the database to continue operating. The database ceases operating if the log writer cannot write successfully to at least one member of the current group.

When the current online redo log group fills up, a log switch occurs, and the log writer starts writing to the next online redo log group. A log sequence number is assigned to each redo log when a switch occurs for archiving. The log writer writes to the online redo log groups in a round-robin fashion. Because you have a finite number of online redo log groups, the contents of each online redo log group are eventually overwritten. To save the history of the transaction information for recovery purposes, you must place the database in archivelog mode.

When your database is in archivelog mode after every log switch, the archiver background process copies the contents of the online redo log file to an archived redo log file. In the event of a failure, the archived redo log files allow you to restore the complete history of transactions since your last database backup.

Figure 5-2 displays a typical setup for the online redo log files. This figure shows three online redo log groups, each containing two members. The database is in archivelog mode. In the figure, group 2 has recently been filled with transactions, a log switch has occurred, and the log writer is now writing to group 3. The archiver process is copying the contents of group 2 to an archived redo log file. Another log switch occurs when group 3 fills up, and the log writer begins writing to group 1. At the same time, the archive process copies the contents of group 3 to archive log sequence 3 (and so forth).

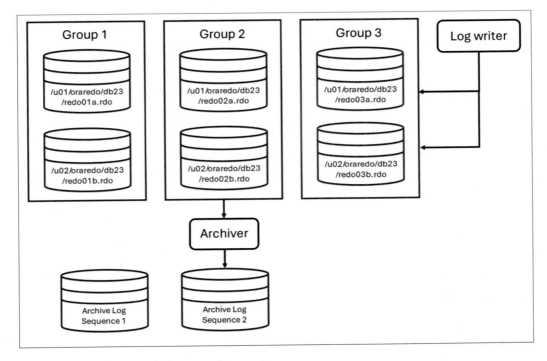

Figure 5-2. *Online redo log configuration*

The online redo log files are not intended to be backed up. These files contain only the most recent redo transaction information generated by the database. When you enable archiving, the archived redo log files protect your database transaction history.

The contents of the current online redo log files are not archived until a log switch occurs. This means if you lose all members of the current online redo log file, you lose transactions. Listed next are serval mechanisms of log files.

- Multiplex the groups.

- Consider setting the ARCHIVE_LAG_TARGET initialization parameter to ensure the online redo logs are switched regularly.

- If possible, never allow two members of the same group to share the same physical disk.

- Ensure that OS file permissions are set appropriately (restrictive, that only the owner of the Oracle binaries has permission to write and read).

- Use physical storage devices that are redundant.

- Appropriately size the log files, so that they switch and are archived at regular intervals and not waiting for archive processing.

Since the logs are written out to archivelogs and require fast writes, flash drives are a way to improve the performance of redo logs. If flash is not available, the options are to place the redo logs on physical disks and, based on the previous list to minimize failures. Hard drive disks might not provide faster writes, which does not make them the ideal choice for redo logs.

The online redo logs are not the files that are being backed up. They write to the archive logs, and RMAN backs up these files. If you did back up the online redo log files, it would be meaningless to restore them. The online redo log files contain the latest redo generated by the database. You would not want to overwrite them from a backup with old redo information. The redo log files and other data files should be excluded from other system backups (nondatabase).

Displaying Online Redo Log Information

Use the V$LOG and V$LOGFILE views to display information about the online redo log groups and corresponding members.

```
COL group# FORM 99999
COL thread# FORM 99999
COL grp_status FORM a10
COL member FORM a30
COL mem_status FORM a10
COL mbytes FORM 999999
--
SELECT
a.group#
,a.thread#
,a.status grp_status
,b.member member
,b.status mem_status
,a.bytes/1024/1024 mbytes
FROM v$log a,
```

```
v$logfile b
WHERE a.group# = b.group#
ORDER BY a.group#, b.member;
```

Here is some sample output.

GROUP#	THREAD#	GRP_STATUS	MEMBER	MEM_STATUS	MBYTES
1	1	INACTIVE	/u01/redo/db23/redo01a.rdo		500
1	1	INACTIVE	/u02/redo/db23/redo01b.rdo		500
2	1	CURRENT	/u01/redo/db23/redo02a.rdo		500
2	1	CURRENT	/u02/redo/db23/redo02b.rdo		500

The V$LOG and V$LOGFILE views are particularly helpful when diagnosing online redo log issues. You can query these views while the database is mounted or open.

The STATUS column of the V$LOG view is especially useful when working with online redo log groups.

- CURRENT: This is the log group currently being written to by the log writer.

- ACTIVE: This log group is required for crash recovery and may or may not have been archived.

- CLEARING: This log group is being cleared out by an ALTER DATABASE CLEAR LOGFILE command.

- CLEARING_CURRENT: This current log group is being cleared of a closed thread.

- INACTIVE: This log group is not required for crash recovery and may or may not have been archived.

- UNUSED: This log group has never been written to; it was recently created.

The STATUS in V$LOG refers to the log group, and V$LOGFILE reports on the status of the physical online redo log file member.

Determining the Optimal Size of Redo Logs

The redo logs need to be written out to the archive logs for backup and recovery purposes, so switching redo logs is important. The object is to try to size the online redo logs so that they switch anywhere from two to six times per hour, and also make sure there are no waits on the writing out the archive logs. The V$LOG_HISTORY contains a history of how frequently the online redo logs have switched. Execute this query to view the number of log switches per hour.

```
SOL> select count(*), to_char(first_time, 'YYYY:MM:DD:HH24') first_time
From v$log_history
group by first_time
order by 2;
```

Note   The group by clause in using an alias is a 23ai new feature in SQL.

Here is part of the output.

```
COUNT(*)FIRST_TIME
---------- -------------
1 2023:01:16:23
3 2023:01:17:03
28 2023:01:17:04
23 2023:01:17:05
68 2023:01:17:06
84 2023:01:17:07
15 2023:01:17:08
```

The previous output shows that a great deal of log switch activity occurred from approximately 4 a.m. to 7 a.m. This could be because of a nightly batch job or users in different time zones updating data. The size of the online redo logs should be increased for this database. You should try to size the online redo logs to accommodate peak traction loads on the database.

As stated, a general rule of thumb is that you should size your online redo log files so that they switch approximately two to six times per hour. You do not want them switching too often because there is overhead with the log switch; however, leaving transaction information in the redo log without archiving creates issues with recovery. If a disaster causes a media failure in your current online redo log, you can lose those transactions that haven't been archived. If a disaster causes a media failure in your current online redo log, you can lose those transactions that haven't been archived.

Oracle initiates a checkpoint as part of a log switch. During a checkpoint, the database-writer background process writes modified (also called *dirty*) blocks to disk, which is resource-intensive. Checkpoint messages in the alert log are also a way of looking at how fast logs are switching or if there are waits associated with archiving.

Tip   Use the ARCHIVE_LAG_TARGET initialization parameter to set a maximum amount of time (in seconds) between log switches. A typical setting for this parameter is 1,800 seconds (30 minutes). A value of 0 (default) disables this feature. This parameter is commonly used in Oracle Data Guard environments to force log switches after the specified amount of time elapses.

You can also query the OPTIMAL_LOGFILE_SIZE column from the V$INSTANCE_ RECOVERY view to determine whether your online redo log files have been sized correctly.

```
SOL> select optimal_logfile_size from v$instance_recovery; OPTIMAL_
LOGFILE_SIZE
--------------------
842
```

The column reports the redo log file size (in megabytes) that is considered optimal based on the initialization parameter setting of FAST_START_MTTR_TARGET. Oracle recommends that you configure all online redo logs to be at least the value of OPTIMAL_ LOGFILE_SIZE. However, when sizing your online redo logs, you must consider information about your environment (such as the frequency of the switches).

Determining the Optimal Number of Redo Log Groups

Oracle requires at least two redo log groups to function. But, having just two groups sometimes isn't enough. To understand why this is so, remember that every time a log switch occurs, it initiates a checkpoint. As part of a checkpoint, the database writer writes all modified (dirty) blocks from the SGA to the data files on disk. Also, recall that the online redo logs are written in a round-robin fashion and that, eventually, the information in a given log is overwritten. Before the log writer can overwrite information in an online redo log, all modified blocks in the SGA associated with the redo log must first be written to a data file. If not all modified blocks have been written to the data files, you will see the following message in the alert.log file.

```
Thread 1 cannot allocate new log, sequence <sequence number> Checkpoint not
complete
```

Another way to explain this issue is that Oracle must store any information required to perform a crash recovery in the online redo logs. To help you visualize this, see Figure 5-3.

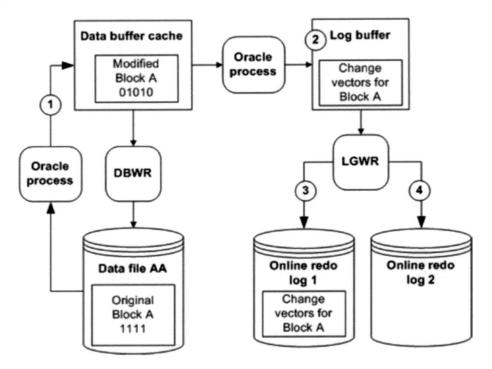

Figure 5-3. *Redo protected until the modified (dirty) buffer is written to disk*

At time 1, Block A is read from Data File AA into the buffer cache and modified. At time 2, the redo change-vector information (how the block changed) is written to the log buffer. At time 3, the log-writer process writes the Block A change-vector information to online redo log 1. At time 4, a log switch occurs, and online redo log 2 becomes the current online redo log.

Suppose that online redo log 2 fills up quickly and another log switch occurs, at which point the log writer attempts to write to online redo log 1. The log writer cannot overwrite information in online redo log 1 until the database writer writes Block A to Data File AA. Until Block A is written to Data File AA, Oracle needs information in the online redo logs to recover this block in the event of a power failure or shutdown abort. Before Oracle overwrites information in the online redo logs, it ensures that blocks protected by redo have been written to disk. If these modified blocks haven't been written to disk, Oracle temporarily suspends processing until this occurs. There are a few ways to resolve this issue.

- Add more redo log groups.

- Lower the value of FAST_START_MTTR_TARGET. Doing so causes the database-writer process to write older modified blocks to disk in a shorter time frame.

- Tune the database-writer process (modify DB_WRITER_PROCESSES).

If you notice that the "Checkpoint not complete" message is occurring often, several times a day, it is recommended that you add one or more log groups to resolve the issue. Adding an extra redo log gives the database writer more time to write modified blocks in the database buffer cache to the data files before the associated redo with a block is overwritten. There is little downside to adding more redo log groups. The main concern is that you could bump up against the MAXLOGFILES value when creating the database. If you need to add more groups and have exceeded the value of MAXLOGFILES, then you must re-create your control file and specify a higher value for this parameter.

If adding more redo log groups doesn't resolve the issue, you should carefully consider lowering the value of FAST_START_MTTR_TARGET. When you lower this value, you can potentially see more I/O because the database-writer process is more actively writing modified blocks to data files. Ideally, it would be nice to verify the impact of modifying FAST_START_MTTR_TARGET in a test environment before making the change in production. You can modify this parameter while your instance is up; this means you can quickly modify it back to its original setting if there are unforeseen side effects.

Finally, consider increasing the value of the DB_WRITER_PROCESSES parameter. Carefully analyze the impact of modifying this parameter in a test environment before you apply it to production. This value requires that you stop and start your database; therefore, if there are adverse effects, downtime is required to change this value back to the original setting. If the waits are on the archiving process, LOG_ARCHIVE_MAX_ PROCESSES can also be increased.

Adding Online Redo Log Groups

If you need to add an online redo log group, use the ADD LOGFILE GROUP statement. In this example, the database already contains two online redo log groups sized at 200 MB each. Another log group with two members is added, sized at 200 MB.

```
SQL> alter database add logfile group 4
('/u01/oraredo/db23/redo04a.rdo',
'/u02/oraredo/db23/redo04b.rdo') size 200M;
```

With ASM, the command is to add a group, and it creates the two files for the group on the disk group.

```
SQL> alter database add logfile group 4;
```

In this scenario, it is recommended that the log group you add be the same size and have the same number of members as the existing online redo logs. It is harder to accurately determine performance issues if the newly added group doesn't have the same physical characteristics as the existing groups. If a larger size is preferred, the new group can be added at the larger size; then, the other groups can be dropped and re-created with the larger size value to keep the size of the redo logs the same.

Resizing and Dropping Online Redo Log Groups

If you have two log groups sized at 200 MB and add a new log group sized at 500 MB, this will likely produce the "Checkpoint not complete" issue described in the previous section. This is because flushing all modified blocks from the SGA that are protected by the redo in a 500 MB log file can potentially take much longer than flushing modified blocks from the SGA that are protected by a 200 MB log file.

So, let's look at how to change the size because you cannot directly modify the size of an existing online redo log as you would a data file. To resize an online redo log, you have to first add online redo log groups that are the size you want and then drop the online redo logs that are the old size.

Using our example, first, you add new groups that are 500 MB using the ADD LOGFILE GROUP statement. After adding the log files with the new size, you can drop the old online redo logs. A log group must have an INACTIVE status before you can drop it. You can check the status of the log group, as shown next.

```
SQL> select group#, status, archived thread#, sequence# from v$log;
```

You can drop an inactive log group with the ALTER DATABASE DROP LOGFILE GROUP statement.

```
SQL> alter database drop logfile group <group #>;
```

If you attempt to drop the current online log group, Oracle returns an ORA-01623 error, stating that you cannot drop the current group. Use the ALTER SYSTEM SWITCH LOGFILE statement to switch the logs and make the next group the current group.

```
SQL> alter system switch logfile;
```

After a log switch, the log group that was previously the current group retains an active status as long as it contains the redo that Oracle requires to perform crash recovery. If you attempt to drop a log group with an active status, Oracle throws an ORA-01624 error, indicating that the log group is required for crash recovery. Issue an ALTER SYSTEM CHECKPOINT command to make the log group inactive.

```
SQL> alter system checkpoint;
```

Additionally, you cannot drop an online redo log group if doing so leaves your database with only one log group. This throws an ORA-01567 error and informs you that dropping the log group is not permitted because it would leave you with fewer than two log groups for your database.

When using ASM, the cleanup of the redo files happens automatically. However, using file systems, dropping an online redo log group does not remove the log files from the OS. You have to use an OS command to do this. Before you remove a file from the OS, ensure that it is not in use and that you do not remove a live online redo log file. For every database on the server, issue this query to view which online redo log files are in use.

```
SQL> select member from v$logfile;
```

Before you physically remove a log file, switch the online redo logs enough times that all online redo log groups have recently been switched; doing so causes the OS to write to the file and thus give it a new timestamp. For example, if you have three groups, make sure you perform at least three log switches.

```
SQL> alter system switch logfile;
SQL> /
SQL> /
```

Tip   Practice adding and removing redo logs before turning over a new database to production.

Controlling the Generation of Redo

For some applications, you may know beforehand that you can easily re-create the data. An example might be a data warehouse environment where you perform direct path inserts or use SQL*Loader to load data. In these scenarios, you can turn off the generation of redo for direct path loading. You use the NOLOGGING clause to do this.

```
SQL> create tablespace inv_mgmt_data
datafile '/u01/oradata/db23ai/inv_mgmt_data01.dbf' size 100M
extent management local
segment space management auto
nologging;
```

Use the ALTER TABLESPACE statement if you have an existing tablespace and want to alter its logging mode.

```
SQL> alter tablespace inv_mgmt_data nologging;
```

You can confirm the tablespace logging mode by querying the DBA_ TABLESPACES view.

```
SQL> select tablespace_name, logging from dba_tablespaces;
```

The generation of redo logging cannot be suppressed for regular INSERT, UPDATE, and DELETE statements. For regular data manipulation language (DML) statements, the NOLOGGING clause is ignored. The NOLOGGING clause does apply, however, to the following types of DML.

- Direct path INSERT statements

- Direct path SQL*Loader

The NOLOGGING clause also applies to the following types of DDL statements.

- CREATE TABLE ... AS SELECT (NOLOGGING affects only the initial create, not subsequent regular DML statements against the table)

- ALTER TABLE ... MOVE

- ALTER TABLE ... ADD/MERGE/SPLIT/MOVE/MODIFY PARTITION

- CREATE INDEX

- ALTER INDEX ... REBUILD

- CREATE MATERIALIZED VIEW

- ALTER MATERIALIZED VIEW ... MOVE

- CREATE MATERIALIZE VIEW LOG

- ALTER MATERIALIZED VIEW LOG ... MOVE

Be aware that if the redo is not logged for a table or index and you have a media failure before the object is backed up, you cannot recover the data; you receive an ORA-01578 error, indicating logical corruption of the data.

Note   You can also override the tablespace level of logging at the object level. For example, even if a tablespace is specified as NOLOGGING, you can create a table with the LOGGING clause.

Implementing Archivelog Mode

Recall from the discussions earlier in this chapter that archive redo logs are created only if your database is in archivelog mode. If you want to preserve your database transaction history to facilitate point-in-time and other types of recovery, you need to enable that mode.

In normal operation, changes to your data generate entries in the database to redo log files. A log switch is initiated as each online redo log group fills up. When a log switch occurs, the log-writer process stops writing to the most recently filled online redo log group and starts writing to a new online redo log group. The online redo log groups are written in a round-robin fashion, meaning the contents of any given online redo log group are eventually overwritten. Archivelog mode preserves redo data for the long term by employing an archiver background process to copy the contents of a filled online redo log to an *archive redo log file*. The trail of archive redo log files is crucial to recovering the database with all the changes intact up to the precise point of failure.

Marking Architectural Decisions

When you implement archivelog mode, you also need a strategy for managing the archived log files. The archive redo logs consume disk space. If left unattended, these files eventually use up all the space allocated. If this happens, the archiver cannot write a new archive redo log file to disk, and your database stop processing transactions. At that point, you have a hung database. You then need to intervene manually by creating space for the archiver to resume work. For these reasons, there are several architectural decisions you must carefully consider before you enable archiving.

- Where to place the archive redo logs and whether to use the fast recovery area to store them

- How to name the archive redo logs

- How much space to allocate to the archive redo log location

- How often to back up the archive redo logs

- When it is okay to permanently remove archive redo logs from the disk

- How to remove archive redo logs using RMAN based on a retention policy

- Whether multiple archive redo log locations should be enabled

- When to schedule the small amount of downtime that is required

As a general rule, you should have enough space in your primary archive redo location to hold at least a day's worth of archive redo logs. This lets you back them up daily and then remove them from the disk after they have been backed up.

If you decide to use a fast recovery area (FRA) for your archive redo log locations, you must ensure that it contains sufficient space to hold the number of archive redo logs generated between backups. Keep in mind that the FRA typically contains other types of files, such as RMAN backup files, flashback logs, and so on. If you use an FRA, be aware that generating other types of files can potentially impact the space required by the archive redo log files. Some parameters can be set to manage the FRA and provide a way to resize the space for recovery for the database to continue instead of increasing space on the file system.

The parameters DB_RECOVERY_FILE_DEST and DB_RECOVERY_FILE_DEST_SIZE set the file location for the FRA and the size of the space used by the database. These can also prevent one database from filling up the space for other databases on the same server. The ASM disk group FRA can be created to manage the space using ASM. DB_ RECOVERY_FILE_DEST = +FRA allows the database to use the FRA disk group. Again, there are advantages of managing space behind the scenes in a scenario that fills up space. Using these parameters along with ASM removes specific file systems and allows more options to quickly address issues with archive logs and use the recovery areas. FRA is recommended for this since the parameters are dynamic and allow changes to occur to prevent the database from hanging. This should be included in the planning and architecting of the archive mode of the database.

You need a strategy for automating the backup and removal of archive redo log files. RMAN automates the backup and removal of archive redo log files. Later chapters discuss RMAN backups and recovery.

Setting the Archive Redo File Locations

Before you set your database mode to archiving, you should specifically instruct Oracle where you want the archive redo logs to be placed. You can set the archive redo log file destination with the following techniques.

- Set the LOG_ARCHIVE_DEST_N database initialization parameter.

- Implement FRA.

Tip   If you do not specifically set the archive redo log location via an initialization parameter or by enabling the FRA, then the archive redo logs are written to a default location. The location should be specified for production systems, not the default location.

The initialization parameters should be set for both LOG_ARCHIVE_DEST_N and LOG_ARCHIVE_FORMAT. LOG_ARCHIVE _FORMAT includes a format with information about the thread, sequence number, and database ID.

The following is the typical format.

```
log_archive_format='db23ai_%t_%s_%r.arc'
```

You can set several different locations for the archive redo log file destination. For most production systems, one archive redo log destination location is usually sufficient. You can view the value of the LOG_ARCHIVE_DEST_N parameter by running the following.

```
SOL> show parameter log_archive_dest
```

Besides the parameter, there is a view that you can query for the archive redo log locations and details.

```
SOL> select dest_name
,destination
,status
,binding
from v$archive_dest;
```

Using the FRA for Archive Log Files

The FRA is an area on disk, defined in the database initialization parameters, that can be used to store files, such as archive redo logs, RMAN backup files, flashback logs, multiplexed control files, and online redo logs. To enable the use of FRA, you must set two initialization parameters.

- DB_RECOVERY_FILE_DEST_SIZE specifies the maximum space to be used for all files that are stored in the FRA for a database.

- DB_RECOVERY_FILE_DEST specifies the base directory for the FRA.

When you create an FRA, you are not creating anything, but just telling an Oracle database which directory to use when storing files in the FRA. For example, say 200 GB of space is reserved on a mount point, and you want the base directory for the FRA to be /u01/fra. To enable the FRA, first set DB_RECOVERY_FILE_ DES_SIZE.

```
SQL> alter system set db_recovery_file_dest_size=1000G scope=both;
```

Next, set the DB_RECOVERY_FILE_DEST parameter.

```
SQL> alter system set db_recovery_file_dest='/u01/fra' scope=both;
```

Using ASM, you set the destination to one of the disk groups.

```
SQL> alter system set db_recovery_file_dest=+FRA scope=both;
```

If you have set the LOG_ARCHIVE_DEST_N parameter to be a location on disk, archive redo logs are written to LOG_ARCHIVE_DEST and not written to the FRA.

The following shows how you can verify that the archive location is using FRA: SQL> archive log list;.

Database Log Mode	Archive Mode
Automatic archival	Enabled
Archive destination	USE_DB_RECOVERY_FILE_DEST
Oldest online log sequence	73
Next log sequence to archive	75
Current log sequence	75

These parameters manage the files and directories, and you can use both the FRA and a non-FRA location by setting log_archive_dest_1 and 2 as follows.

```
SQL> alter system set log_archive_dest_1='location=/u01/oraarch/db23ai';
SQL> alter system set log_archive_dest_2='location=USE_DB_RECOVERY_
FILE_DEST';
```

Enabling Archivelog Mode

After you have set the location for your archive redo log files, you can enable it as SYS with the following.

```
SQL> shutdown immediate;
SQL> startup mount;
SQL> alter database archivelog;
SQL> alter database open;
```

You can confirm archivelog mode with this query.

```
SQL> archive log list;
```

You can also confirm it.

```
SQL> select log_mode from v$database;
LOG_MODE
ARCHIVELOG
```

Disabling Archivelog Mode

Usually, you don't disable archivelog mode for a production database. However, there might be a reason for disabling it, and if you can afford the downtime, you should at least know how to turn off archivelog mode. If you do this, be sure you make a backup as soon as possible after re-enabling archiving.

To disable archiving, do the following as SYS.

```
SQL> shutdown immediate;
SQL> startup mount;
SQL> alter database noarchivelog;
SQL> alter database open;
```

You can confirm archivelog mode with either one of these queries.

```
SQL> archive log list;
SQL> select log_mode from v$database;
LOG_MODE
NOARCHIVELOG
```

Reacting to Lack of Disk Space for Archive Logs

The archiver background process writes archive redo logs to your specified location. If, for any reason, the archiver process cannot write to the archive location, your database hangs. Any users attempting to connect receive the following error.

```
ORA-00257: archiver error. Connect internal only, until freed.
```

As a production-support DBA, you never want to let your database get into that state. Sometimes, unpredictable events happen, and you must quickly deal with unforeseen issues.

Note   DBAs who support production databases have a mindset completely different from architect DBAs. Getting new ideas or learning about new technologies is a perfect time to work together and communicate what might work or not work in your environment. Set up time outside of troubleshooting with production DBAs and architects to plan and set environmental strategies.

In this situation, with the archiver error, your database is as good as down and completely unavailable. To fix the issue, you have to act quickly.

- If using the FRA, increase the space allocation for DB_RECOVERY_ FILE_DEST_SIZE.

- If using the FRA, change the destination to a different location in the parameter DB_RECOVERY_FILE_DEST.

- Use RMAN to back up and delete the archive log files.

- Remove expired files from the directory using RMAN.

- Move files to a different location as a temporary solution, which requires cleanup afterward.

- Compress old files in the archive redo log location.

The quickest and safest way to resolve the archiver error is to increase the allocation or change the directory with the DB_RECOVERY_FILE_DEST parameters. Moving files is another quick way to resolve the archiver error with an OS utility such as mv; however, for restore and recovery processes, you have to let the recovery process know about the new locations of these files. You also have to be careful not to move an archive redo log that is currently being written to. You can use the V$ARCHIVED_LOG view to verify if the file appears there; this means it has been completely archived.

Using the FRA with ASM also allows you to move the location or quickly add disk to the FRA disk group.

When the archive redo log files destination is full, you must scramble to resolve it. This is why a good deal of thought should be done about the system's architecture for a 24/7 production database. This includes monitoring the workload and properly sizing the disks and redo logs.

Writing the archive redo logs to one location is sufficient for most databases. However, if you have any disaster recovery or high availability requirements, you should write to multiple locations. Sometimes, DBAs set up a job to back up the archive redo logs every hour and copy them to an alternate location or even to an alternate server.

Backing up Archive Redo Log Files

Depending on your business requirements, you may need a strategy for backing up archive redo log files. Minimally, you should back up any archive redo logs generated during a database backup in archivelog mode. Additional strategies may include the following.

- Periodically copying archive redo logs to an alternate location and then removing them from the primary destination

- Copying the archive redo logs to tape or backup storage and then deleting them from disk

- Using two archive redo log locations

- Using Data Guard for a robust disaster recovery solution

Remember that you need all archive redo logs generated since the begin time of the last good backup to ensure that you can completely recover your database. Only after you are sure you have a good backup of your database should you consider removing archive redo logs that were generated prior to the backup. You can use RMAN to back up the archive redo logs. Additionally, you should specify an RMAN retention policy for these files and have RMAN remove the archive redo logs only after the retention policy requirements are met. (See Chapter 13 for more information on using RMAN.)

Summary

This chapter described how to configure and manage control files and online redo log files and enable archiving. Control files and online redo logs are critical database files; a normally operating database cannot function without them. These files are all managed by the container database (CDB), where the PDB has additional data files.

Up to this point, you have learned about tasks such as installing the Oracle software, creating databases; managing tablespaces, data files, control files, and online redo log files; and archiving. The next several chapters concentrate on configuring a database for application use and include topics such as creating users and database objects.

CHAPTER 6

Users and Basic Security

Security and access to the database are important. The database needs users to perform the varying tasks of the administrator, developer, applications, and users. When you create a database, a few default accounts are created. In 23ai, the accounts are just schemas, so they are not available to log in. making the database more secure and limiting the exposure of gaining access to the database through a default account.

As applications and users need access to the database, you need to create and manage new accounts. This includes choosing an appropriate authentication method, implementing password security, and allocating user privileges.

Note   Prior to Oracle Database 23ai, default accounts were installed with passwords but locked by default. The recommendation was to make sure that the accounts were locked. Now, these accounts are just schema accounts and not configured by default to be able to log into the database.

Types of Users

There are a few types of users for the Oracle Database. You already learned about a few that are needed to install the software and create the database.

Depending on the size of the environment and how many people are available to manage the environment, there might be the same person in each of these roles. However, for security policies and separation of duties for large enterprises, tasks, and access are divided into different roles to manage the security and tasks of the databases.

© Michelle Malcher, Darl Kuhn 2024
M. Malcher and D. Kuhn, *Pro Oracle Database 23ai Administration*,
https://doi.org/10.1007/979-8-8688-1038-1_6

Here is a list of typical Oracle Database users.

- Database administrators

- Security officers

- Network administrators

- Application developers

- Application administrators

- Database users

Database administration is typically performed by a group of database administrators (DBAs), who are responsible for installing and upgrading the Oracle Database server and tools. DBAs manage the storage and storage structures for the database based on application designs. Backup and recovery operations are in the hands of the DBAs, along with creating and managing objects. These are typical tasks for system DBAs, and there can be shared responsibilities of DBAs and application administrators or applications DBAs.

Security officers add users and access to the database. They are responsible for managing and monitoring access to the database and maintaining the system's security. Security policies can be implemented so that the creation of users is performed by the security team and not the DBAs.

Network administrators for the database manage the Oracle networking products such as database listeners and Oracle Net Services. This is not a typical network administrator, but they manage the encryption in transit with `sqlnet.ora` settings and `listener.ora` values, and verify that new databases are added to listeners and `tnsnames.ora` files. DBAs typically do this, but it is possible to separate this role.

Application developers design and implement database applications. They design the database objects and tune the application during development. As they work in the database, they work with the DBAs to ensure the database configurations are designed for the applications and that storage and other resources are available. With 23ai, there is even a new role called `DB_DEVELOPER_ROLE` to provide the needed access for database developers.

Application administrators might be more responsible for the design and resources for the application than actually coding and developing the application. This role can even be described as an application DBA, who helps manage all the database resources, creates objects, and verifies performance and configurations.

Database users interact with the database through applications or database tools. Direct access to the database is not necessarily typical. However, there are reasons to have database access and users for tables and data that is available. There are tools to load data and perform analytics and queries on data that database users would use. Other typical ways to get to the data are using APIs or database applications.

Most of these users have database accounts to log into the database, but they don't need to execute operating system commands. OS-level accounts for Oracle are used as the database software is installed and the database created, and normally they are limited to these administrators. Different operating system accounts can be used, but the correct access to the database files and storage is needed to perform administration tasks. Users accessing the database do not need operating system access.

Managing Default Users

When you create a database, there are default users such as SYS and SYSTEM, and the passwords are set when the database is created. The passwords can be changed and managed with security policies.

The following is the list of the administrative user accounts.

- SYS

- SYSTEM

- SYSBACKUP

- SYSDG

- SYSKM

- SYSRAC

Administrative accounts have special permissions required to administer different areas of the database. These accounts also have CREATE ANY TABLE or ALTER SESSION privileges and EXECUTE privileges on the SYS schema. It is recommended to create a different account and grant the proper roles and privileges for daily tasks and the administrator so that the SYS and SYSTEM accounts are not used.

SYSBACKUP is for Oracle Recovery Manager (RMAN) backup and recovery operations. SYSDG is for Data Guard operations with the Data Guard Broker or DGMGRL. SYSKM performs the keystore operations for Transparent Data Encryption. SYSRAC manages

Oracle Real Application Clusters, connecting the database to the clusterware using SRVCTL. SYSRAC is not available to grant to a database user and is only for the Oracle agent.

The DBA role is automatically created with the database. This role should be granted only to database administrators. In 23ai, the DB_DEVELOPER_ROLE role is the new role also created with the database to grant the permissions for a developer to connect and create objects in the application schema.

DB_DEVELOPER_ROLE has about 24 permissions granted to create application objects, develop in JavaScript and PL/SQL, verify performance, and redact data in the application. This role allows developers to create domains, jobs, and mining models and, with the resource role, create other objects like tables, views, and graphs, including JSON Duality Views. With create MLE, the developer can use the Multilingual Engine for JavaScript.

Read-Only Users

With 23ai, a user can be created as read-only, and combined with a schema grant, the user can read any of the objects in that schema.

```
SQL> create user MMREADONLY identified by "PasswOrd123!"
read only;
```

You can also alter an existing user to read-only, meaning any existing privileges granted to that user will be overridden. Even after setting a user to read only and then adding DBA will be overridden. You would have to alter a user back to read write before the user can use the other granted privileges.

```
SQL> alter user hsolo read only;
SQL> alter user hsolo read write;
```

If you were expecting to be able to change your user back to read write, remember your DBA permissions have been overridden, and you would have to have another privileged user change it back.

By default, a user is READ WRITE but to see if a user is READ ONLY, you can query DBA_USERS.

```
SQL> select username, read_only from dba_users
Where username='MMALCHER';
USERNAME        READ_ONLY
--------------- -----------

MMALCHER        NO
HSOLO           YES
```

Default Accounts as Schema-Only

Several predefined schema accounts are created automatically when the database is created. Most of these accounts in 23ai are now defined as schema-only accounts, except for the sample accounts. The accounts are locked and expired during the installation, and it is recommended to keep them as schema-only accounts. Schema-only accounts cannot log into the database. They can have objects and be granted system privileges to create objects such as tables and procedures. These schemas can be configured for client users in proxy authentication. To see if an account is schema-only, query the DBA_USERS view, and AUTHENTICATION_TYPE shows NONE if the account is schema-only.

SYS vs. SYSTEM

Oracle novices sometimes ask, "What's the difference between the SYS and SYSTEM schemas?" The SYS schema is the superuser of the database, owns all internal data dictionary objects, and is used for tasks such as creating a database, starting or stopping the instance, backing up and recovering, and adding or moving data files. These types of tasks typically require the SYSDBA or SYSOPER role. Security for these roles is often controlled through access to the OS account owner of the Oracle software. Additionally, security for these roles can be administered via a password file, which allows remote client/server access. The SYS account can be locked, which prevents unauthorized access from the server and another OS account, but the SYSDBA role needs to be granted to an authorized user first. Even though locking the SYS account prevents a shared default account from being used, some options or systems might require SYS to remain unlocked. As with other highly privileged accounts, the password should be managed appropriately and locked down.

In contrast, the SYSTEM account is not very special. It is just an account that has been granted the DBA role. Many companies lock the SYSTEM schema after database creation and never use it because it is often the first schema a hacker tries to access when attempting to break into a database.

Rather than risking an easily guessable entry point to the database, privileged users should be granted the role directly or as part of their security group. Another account might be used for automated jobs and granted the DBA role for administrative tasks. Tasks such as creating users, changing passwords, and granting database privileges are available through other APIs to manage privileges instead of having these highly privileged accounts in the database. It is normally a requirement that auditing shows which DBA logged on and when and then creates a separate privileged account for each DBA on the team (and, in turn, on database auditing). We normally have one account for regular use and a separate privileged account that was granted the privileges needed to perform tasks as the DBA.

Passwords

In 23ai, passwords must be a minimum of 12 bytes and can be up to 1,024 bytes. Password complexity is also required by default, and additional policies can be implemented based on your company policies.

Passwords are set with the installation for SYS and SYSTEM and should be modified regularly with ALTER USER. When creating a new user, you create the user with the identified clause to set the password, or you can modify the password with an ALTER USER command.

```
SQL> alter user HSOLO identified by "W3lcomeH3r3123";
```

You can also interactively change the password so that it is not shown on the screen.

```
SQL> passw HSOLO
Changing password for HSOLO
New password:
Retype new password:
Password changed
```

Creating Users

When creating a user, you need to consider the following factors.

- Username and authentication method

- Basic privileges

- Default permanent tablespace and space quotas

- Default temporary tablespace

- Common and local users

Choosing a Username and Authentication Method

A username that matches your company's security policies or standards for application names can be used. Schema accounts should be meaningful and help identify the purpose of a user.

Authentication is the method used to confirm that the user is who they say they are. Oracle supports a robust set of authentication methods.

- Database authentication (username and password stored in database)

- OS authentication

- Network authentication

- Global user authentication and authorization

- External service authentication

A simple, easy, and reliable form of authentication is through the database. In this form of authentication, the username and password are stored within the database. The password is not stored in plain text but in a secure, hashed format. When connecting to the database, the user provides a username and password. The database checks the entered username and password against information stored in the database. If there is a match, the user can connect to the database with the privileges associated with the account.

Another commonly implemented authentication method is through the OS. OS authentication means that if you can successfully log in to a server, you can connect to a local database without providing username and password. In other words, you can associate database privileges with an OS account, an associated OS group, or both. Since 19c you can centrally manage your users in Active Directory and integrate as users or global users in the database.

Examples of database and OS authentication and global users are discussed in the next two sections. If you have more sophisticated authentication requirements, you should investigate network, global, or external service authentication. See the *Oracle Database Security Guide*, which is available as part of the Oracle Database documentation, for more information regarding these methods.

Creating a User with Database Authentication

Database authentication is established with the CREATE USER SQL statement. To create users as a DBA, your account must have the CREATE USER system privilege. This example creates a user named HSOLO with the password W3lcomeHere123 and assigns the default permanent tablespace USERS, default temporary tablespace TEMP, and unlimited space quota on the USERS tablespace.

```
SQL> create user hsolo identified by W3lcomeHere123
default tablespace users
temporary tablespace temp
quota unlimited on users;
```

This creates a bare-bones schema that has no privileges to do anything in the database. To make the user useful, you must minimally grant it the CREATE SESSION system privilege.

```
SQL> grant create session to hsolo;
```

If the new schema needs to be able to create tables, you need to grant it additional privileges, such as CREATE TABLE.

```
SQL> grant create table to hsolo;
```

Roles such as the DB_DEVELOPER_ROLE role or permissions to tables and schemas can be granted.

Creating a User with OS Authentication

OS authentication assumes that database privileges can be associated with and derived from the OS if the user can log in to the OS user account. There are two types of OS authentication.

- Authentication through assigning specific OS roles to users (allows database privileges to be mapped to users)

- Authentication for regular database users via the `IDENTIFIED EXTERNALLY` clause

Authentication through OS roles is explained in Chapter 2. DBAs use this type of authentication, allowing them to connect to an OS account, such as oracle, and then connect to the database with SYSDBA privileges without specifying a username and password.

After logging in to the database server, users created with the `IDENTIFIED EXTERNALLY` clause can connect to the database without specifying a username and password.

- Users with access to the server don't have to maintain a database username and password.

- Scripts that log in to the database don't have to use hard-coded passwords if executed by OS-authenticated users.

- Another database user can't hack into a user by trying to guess the username and password connection string. The only way to log in to an OS-authenticated user is from the OS.

When using OS authentication, Oracle prefixes the value contained in the `OS_AUTHENT_PREFIX` database initialization parameter to the OS user connecting to the database. The default value for this parameter `OPS$`, but it is recommended to set it to a null string.

```
SQL> alter system set os_authent_prefix = '' scope=spfile;
```

You have to stop and start your database for this modification to take effect, so the decision to use OS authentication and the parameters settings should be made when creating the database. If you want an OS-authenticated user to be able to access the database, you still need to create the user.

```
SQL> create user jsmith identified externally;
SQL> grant create session to jsmith;
```

Now, when jsmith logs in to the database server, this user can connect to SQL*Plus as follows.

```
$ sqlplus /
```

No username or password is required because the OS has already authenticated the user.

Configuring a Centrally Managed User

A centrally managed user is considered a user in one place, such as Active Directory or another LDAP service. The user can be managed for authentication and authorizations centrally, such that a user in Active Directory has authentication managed via password or another type of key and, using security groups, has the authorizations managed. If a user changes security groups, the authorization changes, and if the user is inactive in Active Directory, the user cannot authenticate to other applications or databases.

A user can be created in the database as a global user, which means the database reaches out to Active Directory to get details about the user, first to authenticate the password and then to verify the groups for authorization. The database is configured with a user to Active Directory and the ldap.ora file is updated with the information to authenticate against the Active Directory. Once configured, a user can be created with the following syntax.

```
SQL> create user hsolodba identified globally as 'cn=hsolodba group,ou=dbat
eam,dc=example,dc=com';
```

This allows Oracle Database to recognize the user hsolodba, which is in Active Directory, as a user that can access this database. The password is the same as the one in Active Directory, and the group can be used to map to a database role for permissions.

Identity management is important for an enterprise, allowing a person to have roles and tasks based on their functions in the enterprise. As those functions may change or are no longer with the company, the account is centrally managed instead of in each database. The Oracle Cloud has an Identity Access Management (OCI IAM) that configures roles and allows users to be added. They are managed as part of the Identity Management service and not in each database.

Users can be imported into the OCI IAM so that each account does not have to be entered. Even if not importing all the enterprise users, working in this way allows consideration of which users should be migrated, and then you can verify the roles.

Common and Local Users

Each CDB and PDB has a list of valid database users. Common users have access to their various containers and are in the CDB. Local users are specific to a PDB. SYS and SYSTEM accounts are common users that Oracle creates automatically in a pluggable environment and can navigate across the system container. CDB common users can have different privileges in different PDBs.

Common users are created with the C## or c## at the start of the username. The COMMON_USER_PREFIX parameter sets the prefix, and even though you can change the prefix, this might produce name conflicts and should be handled carefully. The example creates a common user in all PDBs from the CDB.

```
SQL> create user c##dba identified by "W3lcome1234";
```

Common users must be granted privileges from within each pluggable database. In other words, granting a common user privileges while connected to the root container does not cascade to the PDBs. If you need to grant a common user a privilege that spans PDBs, create a common role and assign it to the common user.

What use is there for a common user? One situation would be the performance of common DBA maintenance activities across PDBs not requiring SYSDBA-level privileges. For example, you want to set up a DBA account that has the privileges to create users, grants, and so on, but you don't want to use an account such as SYS (which has all privileges in all databases). In this scenario, you would create a common DBA user and a DBA common role that contains the appropriate privileges. The common role would then be assigned to the common DBA.

A local user is a regular user created in a PDB. A local user is created as in the previous sections. A local username must be unique only for the PDB in which it was created. Local users can have administrative privileges only for the PDB where the local account was created. Roles are also common or local. All Oracle-supplied roles are common but can be granted to a local user.

Understanding Schemas vs. Users

A schema is a collection of database objects (such as tables and indexes). A user is an account to connect to the database with the username and password. Users can also own objects, which then the owner is the schema of the objects. You already learned about default schemas created to own database system objects.

When you connect as a user, by default, you can manipulate objects in the schema owned by the user with which you connect to the database. For example, when you attempt to describe a table, Oracle accesses the current user's schema by default. Therefore, there is no reason to preface the table name with the currently connected user (owner). Suppose the currently connected user is INV_MGMT. Consider the following DESCRIBE command.

```
SQL> describe inventory;
```

The prior statement is identical in function to the following statement.

```
SQL> desc inv_mgmt.inventory;
```

You can alter your current user's session to point at a different schema via the ALTER SESSION statement.

```
SQL> alter session set current_schema = sales;
```

This statement does not grant the current user (in this example, INV_MGMT) any extra privileges. The statement instructs Oracle to use the schema qualifier SALES for any subsequent SQL statements referencing database objects. If the appropriate privileges have been granted, the INV_MGMT user can access the SALES user's objects without having to prefix the schema name to the object name.

Just as describe and desc are identical functions, describing the ORDERS table is the same as using SALES.ORDERS.

```
SQL> desc SALES.ORDERS
```

If the alter session is set to SALES, the results are the same.

```
SQL> desc ORDERS
```

Schema-Only Accounts

As with some of the default accounts created, you can also create a schema-only account. These are designed to own the objects and not be used as accounts to log into the database and are created without a password. This is ideal for application schemas and holds all the objects, so changes to these objects can be done if granted the privilege to access these accounts. These accounts have no privilege to log in directly to the database. So even without a password, there is no possibility to log in, and an error occurs.

```
SQL> create user app1 NO AUTHENTICATION;
```

In the dba_users table, this user has an AUTHENTICATION_TYPE=NONE, and the password column is NULL. Schema-only accounts can be granted privileges to create tables and other objects; however, they cannot have administrative privileges assigned to them. Even granting CREATE SESSION to the schema-only account does not allow you to log in to this schema account directly.

```
SQL> grant create session to app1;
Grant succeeded.
SQL> connect app1
Enter password:
ERROR:
ORA-01005: null password given; logon denied
Warning: You are no longer connected to ORACLE.
```

A proxy connection can be made to perform the DDL statements in other accounts, including the schema-only accounts. The following is an example of using hsolosdba as the account when logging in to the database; the schema-only account is app1.

```
SQL> alter user app1 grant connect through hsolodba;
SQL> connect hsolodba[app1]/Pa33wordHello!
SQL> select sys_context('USERENV','SESSION_USER') as session_user,
sys_context('USERENV', 'SESSION_SCHEMA') as session_schema, sys_
context('USERENV', 'PROXY_USER') as proxy_id, user;
SESSION_USER SESSION_SCHEMA    PROXY_ID       USER
------------ --------------    -------------  ------

APP1         APP1              HSOLODBA       APP1
```

That is correct; no FROM clause is needed in 23ai. In prior versions, you needed to use FROM DUAL in the query. In 23ai, you can grant privileges to the schema, and it doesn't have to be for each object.

```
SQL> grant select any table on schema APP_SCHEMA;
```

This schema can be created without a password so that it can simply be used as an application schema for the objects in the database. Privileges can be granted to the schema for all the objects of that schema. You cannot log in as this schema account; the schema-only account is just the owner of the objects or the owner to run code and procedures. This is something to consider for application schemas, and, as explained in the upcoming "Managing Privileges" section, grants and permissions can still be handled by roles for these objects.

Assigning Default Permanent and Temporary Tablespaces

Ensuring that users have a correct default permanent tablespace and temporary tablespace helps prevent inadvertently filling up the SYSTEM or SYSAUX tablespaces, which could cause the database to become unavailable and create performance problems. The USERS tablespace is normally the default tablespace.

When maintaining a database, you should verify the default permanent and temporary tablespace settings to make certain they meet your database standards. You can look at user information by selecting from the DBA_USERS view.

```
SQL> select username, password, default_tablespace, temporary_tablespace
from dba_users;
```

Here is a small sample of the output.

USERNAME	PASSWORD	DEFAULT_TABLESPACE	TEMPORARY_TABLESPACE
JSMITH	EXTERNAL	USERS	TEMP
MDDATA		USERS	TEMP
SYSBACKUP		USERS	TEMP

All your users should be assigned a temporary tablespace that has been created as type temporary. Usually, this tablespace is named TEMP, and there could be temporary tablespaces for a PDB or just in the CDB.

If you find any users with inappropriate default tablespace settings, or you want to change to a different temporary tablespace, you can modify them with the ALTER USER statement.

```sql
SQL> alter user inv_mgmt default tablespace users temporary
tablespace temp2;
```

SYSTEM should never be assigned as a temporary tablespace, and SYSTEM and SYSAUX should not be assigned to users.

Modifying Users

Sometimes you need to modify existing users for the following types of reasons.

- Change a user's password

- Lock or unlock a user

- Change the default permanent or temporary tablespace

- Change a profile or role

- Change system or object privileges

- Modify quotas on tablespaces

Use the ALTER USER statement to modify users. Listed next are several SQL statements that modify a user. This example changes a user's password using the IDENTIFIED BY clause.

```sql
SQL> alter user inv_mgmt identified by W3lcomeHere123;
```

This example locks a user account.

```sql
SQL> alter user inv_mgmt account lock;
```

This example alters the user's quota on the USERS tablespace.

```sql
SQL> alter user inv_mgmt quota 500G on USERS;
```

> **Note**   Since ALTER USER is a highly privileged command and there are many
> reasons for using it, it might now fall into the hands of a security team to execute.
> Other commands and procedures can be written around this, and then the
> permissions are given to those to execute. Also, an Oracle Security Option, Oracle
> Database Vault, limits the ability to alter users and allows the security teams to
> perform these actions.

Dropping Users

Before you drop a user, it is recommended that you first lock the user. Locking the
user prevents others from connecting to a locked database account. This allows you to
better determine whether someone is using the account before it is dropped. Here is an
example of locking a user.

```
SQL> alter user hsolodba account lock;
```

Any user or application attempting to connect to this user now receives the
following error.

```
ORA-28000: the account is locked
```

Issue this query to view the users and lock dates in your database.

```
SQL> select username, lock_date from dba_users;
```

To unlock an account, issue this command.

```
SQL> alter user hsolodba account unlock;
```

Locking users is a handy technique for securing your database and discovering
which users are active.

Be aware that by locking a user, you are not locking access to a user's objects. For
instance, if a USER_A has select, insert, update, and delete privileges on tables owned by
USER_B, if you lock the USER_B account, USER_A can still issue DML statements against
the objects owned by USER_B. Objects are audited to see if they are being used. (More on
auditing objects in Chapter 20.)

It is worth checking to see if there is a valid backup of the objects for the user or do a quick backup. A user cannot be dropped if they still own objects in the database. This is why application objects must be put in a different schema instead of creating all objects under an individual account. If an application is being decommissioned, backups and retention policies should also be considered.

After you are sure that a user and its objects are not needed, use the DROP USER statement to remove a database account. This example drops the user hsolodba.

```
SQL> drop user hsolodba;
```

The prior command won't work if the user owns any database objects. Use the CASCADE clause to remove a user and have its objects dropped.

```
SQL> drop user hsolodba cascade;
```

The DROP USER statement may take a great deal of time to execute if the user being dropped owns a vast number of database objects. In these situations, you may want to consider dropping the user's objects before dropping the user.

Profiles

When you create users, requirements call for strong passwords and for the passwords to adhere to a set of security rules. You may want to ensure that a certain user cannot consume inordinate amounts of CPU resources. These two examples can be done in database profiles. An Oracle profile is a database object that serves two purposes.

- Enforces password security settings

- Limits system resources that a user consumes

Tip   Don't confuse a database profile with a SQL profile. A database profile is an object assigned to a user that enforces password security and constrains database resource usage. In contrast, a SQL profile is associated with a SQL statement and contains corrections to statistics to help the optimizer generate a more efficient execution plan.

Limiting Database Resource Usage

As mentioned, the password profile settings take effect when you assign the profile to a user. Unlike password settings, kernel resource profile restrictions don't take effect until you set the RESOURCE_LIMIT initialization parameter to TRUE, which is the default for your database. The following is an example.

```
SQL> alter system set resource_limit=true scope=both;
```

To view the current setting of the RESOURCE_LIMIT parameter, issue this query.

```
SQL> select name, value from v$parameter where name='resource_limit';
```

When you create a user, if you don't specify a profile, the DEFAULT profile is assigned to the user. You can modify the DEFAULT profile with the ALTER PROFILE statement. The next example modifies the DEFAULT profile to limit CPU_PER_SESSION to 240,000 (in hundreds of seconds).

```
SQL> alter profile default limit cpu_per_session 240000;
```

This limits any user with the DEFAULT profile to 2,400 seconds of CPU use. You can set various limits in a profile. The following are examples of database resource settings you can limit.

- CONNECT_TIME

- CPU_PER_SESSION

- IDLE_TIME

- LOGICAL_READS_PER_SESSION

- SESSIONS_PER_USER

You can also create a custom profile and assign it to users via the CREATE PROFILE statement. You can then assign that profile to any existing database users. The following SQL statement creates a profile that limits resources, such as the amount of CPU and individual sessions can consume.

```
create profile user_profile_limit
limit
sessions_per_user 20
cpu_per_session 240000
```

```
logical_reads_per_session 1000000
connect_time 480
idle_time 120;
```

After you create a profile, you can assign it to a user. In the next example, the user hsolo is assigned USER_PROFILE_LIMIT.

```
SQL> alter user hsolo profile user_profile_limit;
```

Managing Privileges

A database user must be granted privileges before the user can perform any tasks in the database. In Oracle, you assign privileges either by granting a specific privilege to a user or by granting the privilege to a role and then granting the role that contains the privilege to a user. There are different types of privileges: system privileges, schema, and object privileges.

Assigning Database System Privileges

Database system privileges allow you to connect to the database and create and modify objects. There are hundreds of different system privileges. You can view system privileges by querying the DBA_SYS_PRIVS view.

```
SQL> select distinct privilege from dba_sys_privs;
```

System privileges are the same in CDB and PDBs. You can grant privileges to other users or roles. To be able to grant privileges, a user needs the GRANT ANY PRIVILEGE privilege or must have been granted a system privilege with ADMIN OPTION.

Use the GRANT statement to assign a system privilege to a user. For instance, minimally, a user needs CREATE SESSION to connect to the database. You grant this system privilege, as shown next.

```
SQL> grant create session to inv_mgmt;
```

Usually, a user needs to do more than connect to the database. For instance, a user may need to create tables and other database objects. This example grants a user the CREATE TABLE and CREATE DATABASE LINK system privileges.

```
SQL> grant create table, create database link to inv_mgmt;
```

It's the same for the schema-only account.

```
SQL> grant create table, create database link to app1;
```

With all the individual privileges, it is easier to use roles. Whether or not they are provided roles such as DBA and DB_DEVELOPER_ROLE, or you can create your own role, but more on the roles in a moment.

```
SQL> grant db_developer_role to hsolo_dev;
```

If you need to take away privileges, use the REVOKE statement.

```
SQL> revoke create table from inv_mgmt;
```

Oracle has a feature that allows you to grant a system privilege to a user and also gives that user the ability to administer a privilege. You do this with the WITH ADMIN OPTION clause.

```
SQL> grant create table to inv_mgmt with admin option;
```

Granting WITH ADMIN OPTION can get quickly out of hand with managing and monitoring privileges. It is recommended to limit this use in a production environment and have security controls around roles and granting privileges.

Assigning Database Object Privileges

Database object privileges allow you to access and manipulate other users' objects. The types of database objects to which you can grant privileges include tables, views, materialized views, sequences, packages, functions, procedures, user-defined types, directories, and now with 23ai schemas. To be able to grant object privileges, one of the following must be true.

- You own the object.
- You have been granted the object with GRANT OPTION.
- You have the GRANT ANY OBJECT PRIVILEGE system privilege.

This example grants object privileges (as the object owner) to the INV_MGMT_ APP user.

```
SQL> grant insert, update, delete, select on registrations to inv_mgmt_app;
```

The GRANT ALL statement is equivalent to granting INSERT, UPDATE, DELETE, and SELECT to an object. Other privileges are included in the ALL command, such as ALTER, INDEX, REFERENCES, READ, ON COMMIT REFRESH, QUERY REWRITE, DEBUG, and FLASHBACK. The next statement is equivalent to the prior statement.

```
SQL> grant all on registrations to inv_mgmt_app;
```

You can also grant INSERT and UPDATE privileges to tables at the column level. The next example grants INSERT privileges to specific columns in the INVENTORY table.

```
SQL> grant insert (inv_id, inv_name, inv_desc) on inventory to inv_ mgmt_app;
```

If you need to take away object privileges, use the REVOKE statement. This example revokes DML privileges from the INV_MGMT_APP user.

```
SQL> revoke insert, update, delete, select on registrations from
inv_ mgmt_app;
```

Grouping and Assigning Privileges

A role is a database object that allows you to logically group system or object privileges, or both, so that you can assign those privileges in one operation to a user. You can also grant roles to other roles, but be careful with nesting too many roles as it does make it difficult to manage. Roles help you manage aspects of database security by providing a central object with privileges assigned to it. You can subsequently assign the role to multiple users or other roles.

To create a role, connect to the database as a user with the CREATE ROLE system privilege. Next, create a role and assign the system or object privileges you want to group together. This example uses the CREATE ROLE statement to create the JR_DBA role.

```
SQL> create role jr_dba;
```

The next several lines of SQL grant system privileges to the newly created role.

```
SQL> grant select any table to jr_dba;
SQL> grant create any table to jr_dba;
SQL> grant create any view to jr_dba;
SOL> grant create synonym to jr_dba;
SOL> grant create session to jr_dba;
SOL> grant create database link to jr_dba;
```

Next, grant the role to any user you want to possess those privileges.

```
SOL> grant jr_dba to jsmith;
SOL> grant jr_dba to lwalker;
```

The JSMITH and LWALKER users can now perform tasks such as creating synonyms and views. To see the users to which a role is assigned, query the DBA_ROLE_PRIVS view.

```
SOL> select grantee, granted_role from dba_role_privs order by 1;
```

To see the roles granted to your currently connected user, query from the USER_ROLE_PRIVS view.

```
SOL> select * from user_role_privs;
```

To revoke a privilege from a role, use the REVOKE command.

```
SOL> revoke create database link from jr_dba;
```

Similarly, use the REVOKE command to remove a role from a user.

```
SOL> revoke jr_dba from lwalker;
```

Note   Unlike other database objects, roles don't have owners. A role is defined by the privileges assigned to it.

Schema Privileges

New with 23ai, you can now grant a schema to a user. This means all the objects in the schema are granted. This simplifies if new objects are added or modified, grants are based on a schema. New tables and objects are accessible without specifically granting access to that table.

This simplifies the management of the grants for database objects. Normally the grants are saved before doing any changes and then added back in or maintained as part of the object itself. At the schema level, the permissions are already available for any new objects or changes.

Creating a role and granting privileges to the role is still recommended, but you can grant it to individual users, too.

```
SQL> grant select any table, insert any table, update any table, delete any
table any table on schema app1 to hsolo;
SQL> grant select any table, insert any table on schema app1 to app_
dev_role;
SQL> grant execute any procedure on schema app1 to app_user_role;
```

Schema-level privileges show up in the audit trail. Just as privileges can be granted at the schema, they can also be revoked.

Some privileges are excluded from being able to grant for a schema, which makes sense since they are administrative- and system-level privileges. The following are the excluded privileges.

- SYSDBA

- SYSOPER

- SYSASM

- SYSBACKUP

- SYSDG

- SYSKM

You can grant privileges such as create.

```
SQL> grant create any table on schema app1 to app_dev_role;
```

Being able to grant permission at the schema level simplifies granting privileges as objects change. It still makes sense to create roles with these privileges to manage the permissions for users.

PL/SQL and Roles

If you work with PL/SQL, sometimes you get this error when attempting to compile a procedure or a function.

```
PL/SQL: ORA-00942: table or view does not exist
```

What is confusing is that you can describe the table.

```
SQL> desc app_table;
```

Why doesn't the PL/SQL seem able to recognize the table? It is because PL/ SQL requires that the owner of the package, procedure, or function be explicitly granted privileges to any objects referenced in the code. The PL/SQL code owner can't have obtained the grants through a role.

When confronted with this issue, try this as the owner of the PL/SQL code.

```
SQL> set role none;
```

Now, try to run a SQL statement that accesses the table in question.

```
SQL> select count(1) from app_table;
```

If you can no longer access the table, you have been granted access through a role. To resolve the issue, explicitly grant access to any tables to the PL/SQL code owner (as the table owner).

```
SQL> connect owner/pass
SQL> grant select on app_table to proc_owner;
```

You should be able to connect as the PL/SQL code owner and successfully compile your code.

Roles provide a way to grant the needed privileges for a function or tasks for the user to perform. The roles are the best way to manage the privileges as the user maps to security groups. Role-based access to the different objects and system privileges allow simple auditing to know who has a role and verify that individual privileges are not being granted.

## CHAPTER 7

Tables and Constraints

The next logical step is to create objects in the database. Usually, the objects created for an application are tables, constraints, and indexes. A table is the basic storage container for data in a database. You create and modify the table structure via DDL statements, such as `CREATE TABLE` and `ALTER TABLE`. You access and manipulate table data via DML statements (`INSERT, UPDATE, DELETE, MERGE, SELECT`).

Tip One important difference between DDL and DML statements is that with DML statements, you must explicitly issue a COMMIT or ROLLBACK to end the transaction.

A constraint is a mechanism for enforcing that the data adheres to business rules. For example, you may have a business requirement that all customer IDs be unique within a table. In this scenario, you can use a primary key constraint to guarantee that all customer IDs that are inserted or updated in a `CUSTOMER` table are unique. Constraints inspect data as they're inserted, updated, and deleted to ensure that no business rules are violated.

This chapter deals with common techniques for creating and maintaining tables and constraints. When you create a table, it almost always needs one or more constraints defined; therefore, it makes sense to cover constraint management along with tables. The first part of the chapter focuses on common table creation and maintenance tasks. The latter part of the chapter discusses constraint management.

Understanding Table Types

Oracle Database supports a vast and robust variety of table types. These various types are described in Table 7-1.

175

© Michelle Malcher, Darl Kuhn 2024
M. Malcher and D. Kuhn, *Pro Oracle Database 23ai Administration*,
https://doi.org/10.1007/979-8-8688-1038-1_7

Table 7-1. *Oracle Table Type Descriptions*

Table Type	Description	Typical Use
Heap organized	The default table type and the most commonly used	Table type to use unless you have a specific reason to use a different type
Private temporary	Session private data, stored for the duration of a session or transaction, space allocated in temporary segments	Program needs a temporary table structure to store and sort data; table is not required after program ends; private temporary tables are dropped at the end of the session or transaction
Global temporary	A table that holds data in temporary segments	Used to temporarily store data for processing; the metadata is like a permanent table, but data in stored in temporary segments
Index organized	Data stored in a B-tree (balanced tree) index structure sorted by primary key	Table is queried mainly on primary key columns; provides fast random access
Partitioned	A logical table that consists of separate physical segments	Type used with large tables with millions of rows
External	Tables that use data stored in OS files outside the database	Lets you efficiently access data in a file outside the database (such as a CSV file)
In-memory external	Data that is not needed to load into Oracle storage and used for scanning as part of big data sets	Data that can be scanned for both RDBMS and Hadoop in-memory
Clustered	A group of tables that share the same data blocks	Used to reduce I/O for tables that are often joined on the same columns; not commonly used
Hash clustered	A table with data that is stored and retrieved using a hash function	Reduces the I/O for tables that are mostly static (not growing after initially loaded)
Nested	A table with a column with a data type that is another table	Collections; each row has a single one-dimensional array

(continued)

Table 7-1. (*continued*)

Table Type	Description	Typical Use
Object	A table with a column with a data type that is an object type	Rarely used, as other data types have become available
Column organized	A table where data is physically stored in columns instead of rows	Used by Oracle In-Memory for fast analytic queries
JSON	Native binary storage for JSON in a table, data type, or collection	Used to store JSON data to retrieve JSON using SQL; binary storage called OSAN used for JSON documents

This chapter focuses on the table types that are most often used: heap-organized, index-organized, and temporary tables. Partitioned tables are used extensively in data warehouse environments and are covered separately in Chapter 11, and external tables are covered in Chapter 15. For information on table types not covered in this book, see the *SQL Language Reference Guide* in the Oracle Database documentation.

Understanding Data Types

When creating a table, you must specify the column names and corresponding data types. As a DBA, you should understand the appropriate use of each data type. Application issues, performance, and the accuracy of data can be affected by the wrong choice of data type. For instance, if a character data type is used when a date data type should have been used, this causes needless conversions and headaches when attempting to do date math and reporting. Compounding the problem, it can be difficult to modify data types after an incorrect data type is implemented in the production environment, as this introduces a change that might break the existing code. Once you go wrong, it is extremely tough to backtrack and choose the right course. It is more likely you will end up with hack upon hack as you attempt to find ways to force the ill-chosen data type to do the job that it was never intended to do.

Oracle supports the following groups of data types.

- Character

- Numeric

- Vector

- JSON

- Boolean

- Date/time

- ROWID

- LOB/ CLOB/ BLOB

- XML

The following sections provide a brief description of each and usage recommendations.

Note   Specialized data types, anytype types, spatial types, media types, and user-defined types are not covered in this book. Oracle Database can handle any data type and workload; the documentation can provide more information on ones not included in these chapters.

Character

Use a character data type to store characters and string data. The following character data types are available in Oracle.

- VARCHAR2

- CHAR

- NVARCHAR2 and NCHAR

VARCHAR

The VARCHAR2 data type is what you should use in most scenarios to hold character/string data. A VARCHAR2 allocates space based only on the number or characters in the string. If you insert a one-character string into a column defined to be VARCHAR2(30), Oracle consumes space for only one character. The following example verifies this behavior.

```
SQL> create table varchar2_example (d varchar2(30));
SQL> insert into varchar2_example values ('a');
SQL> select dump(d) from varchar2_example;
```

Here is a snippet of the output, verifying that only 1 byte has been allocated.

```
DUMP(D)
----------------
Typ=1 Len=1
```

Note   Are VARCHAR and VARCHAR2 the same? VARCHAR is reserved for the ANSI standard and distinguishes between NULL and an empty string, and in Oracle, it can change. VARCHAR2 is an Oracle standard; it behaves the same and does not change. It does not distinguish between an empty string and NULL.

When you define a VARCHAR2 column, you must specify a length. There are two ways to do this: BYTE and CHAR. BYTE specifies the maximum length of the string in bytes, whereas CHAR specifies the maximum number of characters. For example, to specify a string that contains at most 30 bytes, you define it as follows.

```
varchar2(30 byte)
```

Many DBAs do not realize that if you do not specify BYTE or CHAR, the default length is calculated in bytes. In other words, VARCHAR2(30) is the same as VARCHAR2(30 byte). If you specify VARCHAR2(30 char), you can always store 30 characters in the string, regardless of whether some characters require more than 1 byte. As demonstrated, only the size of the column is stored, and to support multiple bytes, it is easier to adjust to a larger value for the VARCHAR2 and use the default for bytes.

CHAR

In almost every scenario, a VARCHAR2 is preferable to a CHAR. The VARCHAR2 data type is more flexible and space-efficient than CHAR. This is because a CHAR is a fixed-length character field. If you define a CHAR(30) and insert a string that consists of only one character, Oracle allocates 30 bytes of space. This can be an inefficient use of space and can be difficult to match because of the inserted spaces. If using CHAR, it does make sense to use it only if the size of the value will not change and is absolutely static in size. CHAR might have been good for a flag, but now you have the BOOLEAN data type to choose too.

```
SQL> create table char_example ( d char(30));
SQL> insert into char_example values ('a');
SQL> select dump(d) from char_example;
DUMP(D)
----------------
Typ=96 Len=30
```

NVARCHAR2 and NCHAR

The NVARCHAR2 and NCHAR data types are useful if you have a database that was created with a single-byte, fixed-width character set; but sometime later, you need to store multibyte character set data in the same database. You can use the NVARCHAR2 and NCHAR data types to support this requirement.

When the database is created you should plan for using a multibyte character set by default and be able to standardize with the use of VARCHAR2 and provide enough length to handle the multibyte characters.

Note   VARCHAR2 can be 4,000 characters by default, and if you want to store more characters, the next choice is a CLOB. You can extend this to 32,767 characters in a VARCHAR2 or NVARCHAR2 data type by setting the MAX_STRING_ SIZE = EXTENDED.

Numeric

Use a numeric data type to store data that you may need to use with mathematic functions, such as SUM, AVG, MAX, and MIN. You should never store numeric information in a character data type. When you use a VARCHAR2 to store data that is inherently numeric, you are introducing future failures into your system and inefficient queries. Eventually, you will want to report or run calculations on numeric data; if they are not a numeric data type, you will get unpredictable results.

Oracle supports three numeric data types.

- NUMBER

- BINARY_DOUBLE

- BINARY_FLOAT

For most situations, you use the NUMBER data type for any type of number data. Its syntax is NUMBER(scale, precision), where scale is the total number of digits, and precision is the number of digits to the right of the decimal point. So, with a number defined as NUMBER(5, 2), you can store values +/–999.99. That is a total of five digits, with two used for precision to the right of the decimal point. If defined as NUMBER(5), the values can be to the right or left of the decimal with a total of five digits. This value fits 2.4531, as would 55,555.

Tip   Oracle allows a maximum of 38 digits for a NUMBER data type. This is almost always sufficient for any type of numeric application.

What sometimes confuses DBAs is that you can create a table with columns defined as INT, INTEGER, REAL, DECIMAL, and so on. These data types are all implemented by Oracle with a NUMBER data type; for example, a column specified as INTEGER is implemented as a NUMBER(38).

The BINARY_DOUBLE and BINARY_FLOAT data types are used for scientific calculations. These map to the DOUBLE and FLOAT Java data types. Use the NUMBER data type for all your numeric requirements unless your application performs rocket-science calculations.

Vector

Oracle Database 23ai new feature of AI Vector Search brings along a new data type to use in your tables with other types of data or even multiple vector columns. The vector data type allows you to store vector embeddings directly in the tables. You can use different models, ones that you import into the database or other models that you can use to generate the vectors and either insert them into the table with the vector data type or load them into the table. Defining the data as vectors allows the vector search capabilities on this data and combines it with other relational data.

You can define the vector as just vector data type, which allows future type developments with models and does not put a specific format.

```
SQL> create table product (
product_id number,
product_name varchar2(80),
product_description varchar2(1000),
product_vector vector);
```

However, there are reasons for putting specific formats on the data type, maybe using constraints for a specific AI model. Then the vector can be defined using one of the following formats.

```
SQL> create table product (
product_id number,
product_name varchar2(80),
vector1 vector(3, float32),
vector2 vector(3073, *),
vector3 vector(*, float32));
```

With different AI embedding models, you create vector embeddings with various dimensions. 23ai currently allows you to use up to 64K dimensions, and current common models use about 3K dimensions or the length of the vectors.

Documents, images, and other unstructured data normally are significant in size and take up more tablespace if stored in the database. These objects are not required to be stored in the database with the vectors, and the vectors stored in the database are fairly small. Even with thousands of dimensions, the number of arrays stored as vectors is about 8 bytes.

JSON

Previous versions of Oracle had procedures to convert table data into JSON or read JSON into the database. The JSON can be put into the database tables with JSON columns. The schema or any other information about the JSON data do not need to be known, and it can be stored in the table with other data and queried using SQL. JSON is a new SQL and PL/SQL data type for JSON data and is optimized for query and DML processing.

The JSON data type uses a binary format, OSON. You can also store JSON in a different data type, VARCHAR2, with CLOB or BLOB. Then, the data is textual and unparsed character data. There are performance reasons to use the right data type, including now using the JSON data type for JSON.

Here is an example of creating a table with a JSON column.

```
SQL> create table j_order
(order_id number,
date_loaded timestamp,
po_document JSON);
```

You can also put a check constraint on JSON if inserting it into a VARCHAR2 column.

```
SQL> create table j_order
(order_id number,
date_loaded timestamp,
po_document varchar2(23767)
constraint ensure_json check (po_document is json));
```

With the support of the JSON data type, this means normal transactions, indexing, querying, and views are all simplified.

Date/Time

When capturing and reporting date-related information, you should always use a DATE or TIMESTAMP data type, not VARCHAR2. Using the correct date-related data type allows you to perform accurate Oracle date calculations, aggregations, and dependable sorting for reporting. If you use a VARCHAR2 for a field that contains date information, you are guaranteeing future reporting inconsistencies and needless conversion functions such as TO_DATE and TO_CHAR.

Oracle supports three date-related data types.

- DATE

- TIMESTAMP

- INTERVAL

The DATE data type contains a date component and a time component that is granular to the second. By default, if you do not specify a time component when inserting data, then the time value defaults to midnight (0 hour at 0 second). If you need to track time at a more granular level than the second, then use TIMESTAMP; otherwise, feel free to use DATE.

The TIMESTAMP data type contains a data component and a time component that is granular to fractions of a second. When you define a TIMESTAMP, you can specify the fractional second precision component. For instance, if you wanted five digits of fractional precision to the right of the decimal point, you would specify that as TIMESTAMP(5).

The maximum fractional precision is 9; the default is 6. If you specify 0 fractional precision, you have the equivalent of the DATE data type.

The TIMESTAMP data type comes in two additional variations: TIMESTAMP WITH TIME ZONE and TIMESTAMP WITH LOCAL TIME ZONE. These are time zone–aware data types, meaning that when the user selects the data, the time value is adjusted to the time zone of the user's session.

Oracle also provides an INTERVAL data type. This is meant to store a duration, or interval, of time. There are two types: INTERVAL YEAR TO MONTH and INTERVAL DAY TO SECOND. Use the former when precision to the year and month is required. Use the latter when you need to store interval data granular to the day and second.

INTERVAL

When choosing an interval type, let your choice be driven by the level of granularity you desire in your results. For example, you can use INTERVAL DAY TO SECOND to store intervals several years in length; it is just that you express such intervals in terms of days, perhaps of several hundreds of days. Recording the number of days represented by a year or month depends on which specific year and month are under discussion.

Similarly, if you need granularity in months, you can't back into the correct number of months based on the number of days. So, choose the type to match the granularity needed for your application.

RAW

The RAW data type allows you to store binary data in a column. This type of data is sometimes used for storing globally unique identifiers or small amounts of encrypted data. The RAW data type can have a maximum size of 32,767 bytes, and large amounts of binary data should be stored in a CLOB.

If you select data from a RAW column, SQL*Plus implicitly applies the built-in RAWTOHEX function to retrieved data. The data is displayed in hexadecimal format, which goes for inserting data into a RAW column. The built-in HEXTORAW function is implicitly applied.

This is important because if you create an index on a RAW column, the optimizer may ignore the index, as Oracle is implicitly applying functions where the RAW column is referenced in the SQL. A normal index may be of no use, whereas a function-based index using RAWTOHEX may result in a substantial performance improvement.

ROWID

When DBAs hear the word ROWID (row identifier), they often think of a pseudocolumn provided with every table row that contains the physical location of the row on disk; that is correct. However, many DBAs do not realize that Oracle supports an actual ROWID data type, meaning you can create a table with a column defined as ROWID.

There are a few practical uses for the ROWID data type. One valid application would be if you are having problems when trying to enable a referential integrity constraint and want to capture the ROWID of rows that violate a constraint. In this scenario, you could create a table with a column of the type ROWID and store it in the ROWIDs of offending records within the table. This affords you an efficient way to capture and resolve issues with the offending data.

Tip   Never be tempted to use a ROWID data type and the associated ROWID of a row within the table for the primary key value. This is because the ROWID of a row in a table can change. For example, an ALTER TABLE...MOVE command may change every ROWID within a table. Normally, the primary key values of rows within a table should never change. Using ROWID for the primary key is a mistake because the ROWIDs can change even without modifying the actual value. For this reason, instead of using ROWID for a primary key value, use a sequence-generated nonmeaningful number, such as an identity column.

LOB

Oracle supports storing large amounts of data in a column via a LOB data type. Oracle supports the following types of LOBs.

- CLOB

- NCLOB

- BLOB

- BFILE

If you have textual data that does not fit within the confines of a VARCHAR2, then you should use a CLOB to store these data. A CLOB is useful for storing large amounts of character data, such as log files. An NCLOB is similar to a CLOB but allows information encoded in the national character set of the database.

BLOBs are large amounts of binary data that usually are not meant to be human readable. Typical BLOB data include image, audio, and video files.

CLOBs, NCLOBs, and BLOBs are known as internal LOBs. This is because they are stored inside Oracle databases. These data types reside within data files associated with the database.

BFILEs are known as external LOBs. BFILE columns store a pointer to a file on the OS that is outside the database. When it is not feasible to store a large binary file within the database, then use a BFILE. BFILEs do not participate in database transactions and are not covered by Oracle security or backup and recovery. If you need those features, use a BLOB, not a BFILE.

Creating a Table

The number of table features has expanded in 23ai. There are several new SQL enhancements and a new data type with BOOLEAN, and the Oracle documentation has more than 200 pages covering CREATE and ALTER TABLE statements and table maintenance. This chapter does not cover all the details. For most situations, you typically need to use only a fraction of the table options available.

The following are general factors to consider when creating a table.

- Type of table (heap-organized, temporary, index-organized, partitioned, etc.)

- Naming conventions

- Column data types and sizes

- Constraints (primary key, foreign keys, check)

- Index requirements (see Chapter 8)

- Initial storage requirements

- Special features (virtual columns, read-only, parallel, compression, no logging, invisible columns)

- Growth requirements

- Tablespace(s) for the table and its indexes

Before you run a CREATE TABLE statement, you need to consider each item in the previous list. To that end, DBAs often use data modeling tools to help manage the creation of DDL scripts to make database objects. Data modeling tools allow you to visually define tables and relationships and the underlying database features.

Creating a Heap-Organized Table

To create a heap-organized table, use the CREATE TABLE statement and data types and lengths associated with the columns. The Oracle default table type is heap organized. The term *heap* means that the data are not stored in a specific order in the table; instead, they are a heap of data.

```
SQL> CREATE TABLE dept
(deptno NUMBER(10)
, dname VARCHAR2(14 CHAR)
, loc VARCHAR2(14 CHAR));
```

If you do not specify a tablespace, then the table is created in the default permanent tablespace of the user that creates the table. Allowing the table to be created in the default permanent tablespace is fine for a few small test tables. For anything more sophisticated, you should explicitly specify the tablespace in which you want tables created.

Usually, when you create a table, you should specify constraints, such as the primary key. The following code shows the most common features you use when creating a table. This DDL defines primary keys, foreign keys, tablespace information, and comments.

```
SQL> CREATE TABLE dep
(deptno NUMBER(10)
,dname VARCHAR2(20)
,loc VARCHAR2(20)
,CONSTRAINT dept_pk PRIMARY KEY (deptno)
USING INDEX TABLESPACE hr_index)
TABLESPACE hr_data;
SQL> COMMENT ON TABLE dept is 'Department table';
SQL> CREATE UNIQUE INDEX dept_uk1 on dept(dname)
TABLESPACE hr_index;
SQL> CREATE TABLE emp
(empno NUMBER(10)
,ename VARCHAR2(20)
,job VARCHAR2(20)
,mgr NUMBER(4)
,hiredate DATE
,sal NUMBER(7,2)
,comm NUMBER(7,2)
,deptno NUMBER(10)
,CONSTRAINT emp_pk PRIMARY KEY (empno)
USING INDEX TABLESPACE hr_index
) TABLESPACE hr_date;
SQL> COMMENT ON TABLE emp IS 'Employee table';
SQL> ALTER TABLE emp ADD CONSTRAINT emp_fk1
FOREIGN KEY (deptno)
REFERENCES dept(deptno);
SQL> CREATE INDEX emp_fk1 on emp(deptno)
TABLESPACE hr_index;
```

When creating a table, it inherits its space properties from the tablespace in which it is created and does not need to be specified. This simplifies administration and maintenance. If you have tables that require different physical space properties, then you can create separate tablespaces to hold tables with differing needs. For instance, you might create an HR_DATA_LARGE tablespace with extent sizes of 16 MB and an HR_DATA_SMALL tablespace with extent sizes of 128 KB and choose where a table is created based on its storage requirements. See Chapter 4 for an explanation of the creation of tablespaces.

Table Recommendations

Set standards for naming the database objects. This can be based on the application and simplifies maintenance.

Use the right data type for the data. If storing a date, use a DATE; if storing a number, use a NUMBER. It seems simple, but it is worth the additional step of loading the data to convert it to the correct data type instead of storing it as is. If it comes in as VARCHAR2, and should be DATE or JSON change the data type to match the data type.

Leverage the data type length and precision if business rules and application rules need to be followed.

Use a numeric primary key. You can create a surrogate key with the identity column if the data does not have a unique numeric identifier. You can use a sequence, possibly with a trigger, to generate the number for the key, or you can use an identity column that autoincrements.

Create audit-type columns such as CREATE_DT, UPDATE_DT, and CHANGE_USER, which can be automatically populated with default values or triggers.

Use check constraints when appropriate including NOT NULL.

Implementing Virtual Columns

A virtual column is based on one or more existing columns from the same table or a combination of constants, SQL functions, and user-defined PL/SQL functions or both. Virtual columns are not stored on disk; they are evaluated at runtime when the SQL query executes. Virtual columns can be indexed and have stored statistics.

```
SQL> create table inventory (
inv_id number,
inv_count number,
inv_status generated always as ( case when inv_count <= 100 then 'GETTING
LOW' when inv_count > 100 then 'OK' end)
);
```

Note   GENERATED ALWAYS is optional, but it helps to recognize the virtual column. To modify the virtual column value, you can modify the function or calculation as an ALTER TABLE statement.

The following are the advantages of implementing virtual columns.

- You can create an index on a virtual column; internally, Oracle creates a function-based index.

- You can store statistics in a virtual column that can be used by the cost-based optimizer (CBO).

- Virtual columns can be referenced in WHERE clauses.

- Virtual columns are permanently defined in the database; there is one central definition of such a column.

Implementing Invisible Columns

The main use for an invisible column is to ensure that adding a column to a table does not disrupt any existing application code. If the application code does not explicitly access the invisible column, it appears to the application as if the column does not exist.

When a column is invisible, it cannot be viewed via the following.

- DESCRIBE

- SELECT * (to access all the table's columns)

- %ROWTYPE (in PL/SQL)

However, the column can be accessed if explicitly specified in a SELECT clause or referenced directly in a DML statement (INSERT, UPDATE, DELETE, or MERGE). Invisible columns can also be indexed, just like visible columns.

A table can be created with invisible columns, or a column can be added or altered to be invisible. A column that is defined as invisible can also be altered to be visible. Here is an example of creating a table with an invisible column.

```
SQL> create table inventory
(inv_id number,
inv_desc varchar2(30),
inv_profit number invisible);
```

When creating a table with invisible columns, at least one column must be visible.

Creating Blockchain Tables

Introduced in 21c, the blockchain tables are append-only. Inserts are allowed, but deletes are prohibited or restricted based on time. The blockchain table is made tamper-resistant by special sequencing and chaining algorithms.

All participants in the blockchain network have access to the same tamper-resistant ledger. Since it is a centralized ledger model in the database, it reduces overhead and has lower latency.

Blockchain is just added to the CREATE TABLE statement, and you need to specify additional attributes that determine when a blockchain table can be dropped if it is no longer in use and a hash can be used.

```
SQL> create blockchain table ledger_employee
(employee_idnumber,
salarynumber)
NO DROP until 31 days idle
NO DELETE locked
HASHING USING
"SHA2_512" version "v1";
```

Information about blockchain tables is in the USER_BLOCKCHAIN_TABLES. You can grant permissions on the table, and even with delete permissions, you get an error message if you attempt to execute a delete statement.

```
SQL> delete from ledger_employee
Where employee_id=106;
ERROR at line 1:
ORA-05715:operation not allowed on the blockchain or immutable table
```

Making Read-Only Tables

You can place individual tables in read-only mode. Doing so prevents any INSERT, UPDATE, or DELETE statements from running against a table. An alternate way to do this is to make the tablespace read-only and use this tablespace for static tables for read-only.

There are several reasons why you may require the read-only feature at the table level.

- The data in the table is historical and should never be updated in normal circumstances.

- You are performing some maintenance on the table and want to better determine whether there is any change while it is being updated.

- You want to drop the table, but before you do, you want to better determine whether users are attempting to update the table.

Use the ALTER TABLE statement to place a table in read-only mode.

```
SQL> alter table inventory read only;
```

You can verify the status of a read-only table by issuing the following query.

```
SQL> select table_name, read_only from user_tables where read_only='YES';
```

To modify a read-only table to read/write, issue the following SQL.

```
SQL> alter table inventory read write;
```

Using an Identity Column

Let's look at an autoincrementing (identity) column with the GENERATE AS IDENTITY clause. This example creates a table with the primary key column that is automatically populated and incremented.

```
SQL> create table inventory
(inv_id number generated as identity,
inv_desc varchar2(30));
Table created.
SQL>alter table inventory add constraint inv_pk primary key (inv_id);
```

Now, you can populate the table without specifying the primary key value.

```
SQL> insert into inventory (inv_desc)
values ('Book'), ('Table');
SQL> select * from inventory;
INV_ID INV_DESC


_____ _____
1      Book
2      Table
```

When you create an identity column, Oracle automatically creates a sequence and associates the sequence with the column. You can view the sequence information in USER_SEQUENCES.

USER_TAB_COLUMNS also identifies the identity columns.

```
SQL> select table_name, identity_column
from user_tab_columns
where identity_column='YES';
```

When creating a table with an identity column (such as in the prior example), you can't directly specify a value for the identity column, such as when you try the following.

```
SQL> insert into inventory values(3, 'Chair');
ORA-32795: cannot insert into a generated always identity column
```

The following syntax can be used to create the table to avoid this error and create a table that allows those occasional inserts into an identity column.

```
SQL> create table inventory
(inv_id number generated by default on null as identity,
Inv_desc varchar2(30));
```

Because the underlying mechanism for populating an identity column is a sequence, you have some control over how the sequence is created (just like you would if you manually created a sequence). For instance, you can specify at what number to start the sequence and by how much the sequence increments each time. This example specifies that the underlying sequence starts at 30 and increments by two each time.

```
SQL> create table inventory
(inv_id number generated as identity (start with 50 increment by 2),
Inv_desc varchar2(30));
```

There are some caveats to be aware of when using autoincrementing columns.

- Only one per table is allowed.

- They must be numeric.

- They cannot have default values.

- NOT NULL and NOT DEFERRABLE constraints are implicitly applied.

- CREAT TABLE ... AS SELECT does not inherit identity column properties.

Also, remember that after inserting into a column that is autoincremented, if you issue a rollback, the transaction is rolled back, but not the autoincremented values from the sequence. This is the expected behavior of a sequence. You can roll back such an insert, but the sequence values are used and gone.

Default Parallel SQL Execution

If you work with large tables, you may want to consider creating your tables as PARALLEL. This instructs Oracle to set the degree of parallelism for queries and any subsequent INSERT, UPDATE, DELETE, MERGE, and query statements. This example creates a table with a PARALLEL clause of 2.

```
SQL> create table inventory
(inv_id number,
inv_desc varchar2(30),
create_dt date default sysdate)
parallel 2;
```

You can specify PARALLEL, NOPARALLEL, or PARALLEL n. If you do not specify n, Oracle sets the degree of parallelism based on the PARALLEL_THREADS_PER_CPU initialization parameter (PARALLEL_THREADS_PER_CPU × CPU_COUNT × INSTANCE_COUNT). The main issue is that if a table has been created with a default degree of parallelism, any subsequent queries execute with parallel threads. You may wonder why a query or a DML statement executes in parallel (without explicitly invoking a parallel operation).

Parallel query operations spawn P_0 processes, and if tables are created with a larger default parallel degree, then there is a risk of hitting the "ORA-00020 maximum number of processes" error. There is an available resource parameter PQ_TIMEOUT_ACTION that timeout inactive parallel queries. This allows high-priority parallel queries to have the needed resources to execute. There is also a simpler way to cancel the runaway SQL without manually killing the parallel processes if they get out of control by a default parallel degree of something like 64 by using the ALTER SYSTEM CANCEL SQL statement.

Parallelism can be important for performance tuning; however, it is also very complicated and can fail in many ways, causing regression in other queries. Using parallelism would not be recommended until you understand your database's configuration and how your table's degree of parallelism could affect the entire system.

Compressing Table Data

As your database grows, you may want to consider table-level compression. Compressed data can use less disk space, less memory, and reduced I/O. Queries that read compressed data potentially run faster because there are fewer blocks to process. However, CPU usage increases as the data is compressed and uncompressed as writes and reads occur, so there is a trade-off.

Four types of compression are available.

- Basic compression

- Advanced row compression

- Warehouse compression (hybrid columnar compression)

- Archive compression (hybrid columnar compression)

Basic compression is enabled with the COMPRESS or COMPRESS BASIC clause (they are synonymous). This example creates a table with basic compression.

```
SQL> create table inventory
(inv_id number,
inv_desc varchar2(300),
create_dt timestamp)
compress basic;
```

Basic compression provides compression as data are direct-path inserted into the table.

> **Note**   Basic compression requires the Oracle Enterprise Edition, but it does not
> require an extra license. Other types of compression are additional license options
> for the database. As with options of the database, evaluation needs to be done
> for the storage cost and compression ratio to provide the right cost analysis for
> this option.

Advanced row compression is enabled with the ROW STORE COMPRESS
ADVANCED clause.

```
SQL> create table inventory
(inv_id number,
inv_desc varchar2(300),
create_dt timestamp)
row store compress advanced;
```

Advanced row compression provides compression when initially inserting data into
the table and in subsequent DML operations. You can verify the compression for a table
via the following SELECT statement.

```
SQL> select table_name, compression, compress_for
from user_tables
where table_name='INVENTORY';
TABLE_NAME   COMPRESS   COMPRESS_FOR
----------   ----------   ---------------
INVENTORY    ENABLED      ADVANCED
```

You can also create a tablespace with the compression clause. Any table created in
the tablespace inherits the tablespace compression settings.

The following are some table maintenance considerations with compression.

- Columns need to be less than 255.

- Altering to allow compression does not compress the existing data.
  You must rebuild the table.

- In moving the table, you need to rebuild any associated indexes.

- Compression can be disabled via the NOCOMPRESS clause. Again, this
  does not affect the existing data.

Avoiding Redo Creation

When you are creating a table, you have the option of specifying the NOLOGGING clause. The NOLOGGING feature can greatly reduce the amount of redo generation for certain types of operations. Sometimes, when you are working with large amounts of data, it is desirable, for performance reasons, to reduce the redo generation when you initially create and insert data into a table.

Notice that we said greatly "reduce" the amount of redo and not eliminate. The downside to reducing the redo generation is that you cannot recover the data created via NOLOGGING in the event a failure occurs after the data is loaded (and before you can back up the table). If you can tolerate some risk of data loss, then use NOLOGGING, but back up the table soon after the data are loaded. If your data is critical, then do not use NOLOGGING. If your data can be easily re-created, then NOLOGGING is desirable when you are trying to improve the performance of large data loads.

The NOLOGGING feature never affects redo generation for normal DML statements (INSERT, UPDATE, and DELETE) but can significantly reduce redo generation for the following types of operations.

- SQL*Loader direct-path load

- Direct-path INSERT

- CREATE TABLE AS SELECT

- ALTER TABLE MOVE

- Creating or rebuilding an index

There are some quirks (features) when using NOLOGGING. If your database is in FORCE LOGGING mode, then redo is generated for all operations, regardless of NOLOGGING. Likewise, when you are loading a table, if the table has a referential foreign key constraint defined, then a redo is generated regardless of whether you specify NOLOGGING.

NOLOGGING can be specified at a statement level, table, or tablespace level. It is easier to specify the NOLOGGING at the table level.

You can determine the effects of NOLOGGING by measuring the amount of redo generated for an operation with logging enabled vs. operating in NOLOGGING mode. If you have a development environment that you can test in, you can monitor how often the redo logs switch while the operation is taking place. Another simple test is the timing of the job with and without logging. NOLOGGING should be faster.

Creating a Table from a Query

It is convenient to create a table based on the definition of an existing table. For instance, say you want to create a quick backup of a table before you modify the table's structure or data. Use the CREATE TABLE AS SELECT (CTAS) statement, as shown in the following example.

```
SQL> create table inventory_backup
as select * from inventory;
```

The previous statement creates an identical table, complete with data. If you do not want the data included, and you want the structure of the table replicated, then provide a WHERE clause that always evaluates to false, such as 1=2.

```
SQL> create table inventory_empty
as select * from inventory
where 1=2;
```

The CTAS technique does not create any indexes, constraints, or triggers. You must create indexes and triggers separately if you need those objects from the original table. CTAS is useful when backing up a table or troubleshooting a data problem in conjunction with a flashback query, which is discussed in a later chapter.

Enabling DDL Logging

Oracle allows you to enable the logging of DDL statements to a log file. This type of logging is switched on with the ENABLE_DDL_LOGGING parameter (the default is FALSE). You can set this at the session or system level. This feature provides an audit trail regarding which DDL statements have been issued and when they were run. Here is an example of setting this parameter at the system level.

```
SQL> alter system set enable_ddl_logging=true scope=both;
```

The file is an alert log type file, and depending on the capture, there can be multiple files, but it is a different file just for capturing the DDL statements. The file's location depends on the database version, but you can query the location path.

```
SQL> select value from v$diag_info where name='Diag Alert'; SQL> select
value from v$diag_info where name='ADR Home';
```

Within this directory is a file with the format `ddl_<SID>.log`. This file contains a log of DDL statements that have been issued after DDL logging has been enabled, and DDL logging is found in the `log.xml` file.

Modifying a Table

Altering a table is a common task. New requirements frequently mean you must rename, add, drop, or change column data types. Changing a table in development environments can be a trivial task: you do not often have large quantities of data or hundreds of users accessing a table simultaneously. However, for active production systems, you need to understand the ramifications of trying to change tables that are currently being accessed, already populated with data, or both.

Obtaining the Needed Lock

When you modify a table, you must have an exclusive lock on the table. One issue is that if a DML transaction has a lock on the table, you cannot alter it. In this situation, you receive this error.

```
ORA-00054: resource busy and acquire with NOWAIT specified or
timeout expired
```

The prior error message is somewhat confusing, leading you to believe you can resolve the problem by acquiring a lock with `NOWAIT`. However, this generic message is generated when the DDL you issue cannot obtain an exclusive lock on the table. Instead of scheduling an outage for a maintenance window or trying over and over again with the statement, you can use the `DDL_LOCK_TIMEOUT` parameter.

Setting the `DDL_LOCK_TIMEOUT` parameter repeatedly attempts to run a DDL statement until it obtains the required lock on the table. This can be set at the system or session level, and the time is in seconds.

```
SQL> alter session set ddl_lock_timeout=100;
```

Another way to avoid waiting on transactions and perform modifications to the table is to use the `DBMS_REDEFINITION` package. This package is for online table operations and allows table changes from the column types, names, and sizes of renaming tables.

This package allows online operations without disrupting the database users for implementing other options. This is also a good way to validate new procedures and table changes before making the switch.

Renaming a Table

There are a couple of reasons for renaming a table.

- It makes the table conform to standards.

- It better determines whether the table is being used before you drop it.

This example renames a table from INVENTORY to INV.

```
SQL> rename inventory to inv;
```

Adding a Column

Use the ALTER TABLE ... ADD statement to add a column to a table. This example adds a column to the INV table.

```
SQL> alter table inv add(inv_count number);
```

Altering a Column

Occasionally, you need to alter a column to adjust its size or change its data type. Use the ALTER TABLE ... MODIFY statement to adjust the size of a column.

```
SQL> alter table inv modify inv_desc varchar2(256);
```

Making a column a larger size is easier, but if you want to decrease the size, you need to verify that there are no values in the column that are greater.

```
SQL> select max(length(inv_desc)) from inv;
```

When you change a column to NOT NULL, each column must have a valid value. First, verify that there are no null values.

```
SQL> select inv_count from inv where inv_count is null;
```

You can alter the table to have a default value, which helps with any new values and inserts, but it is just a quick UPDATE statement to change to a value, and then you can run the `alter table` statement.

```
SQL> alter table inv modify (inv_count not null);
SQL> alter table inv modify (inv_count default 0);
```

If you want to remove the default value of a column, then set it to NULL as follows.

```
SQL> alter table inv modify (inv_count default NULL);.
```

Sometimes, you need to change a table's data type; for example, a column originally incorrectly defined as a VARCHAR2 must be changed to a NUMBER. Before changing a column's data type, verify that all values for an existing column are valid numeric values. There is an Oracle function for this, VALIDATE_CONVERSION. You can use the VALIDATE_CONVERSION.

```
SQL> select validate_conversion('1000' as number);
SQL> select validate_conversion('June 24, 2023, 20:34' as date 'Month dd,
YYYY, HH24MI')
```

Or you can use ON CONVERSION ERROR syntax.

```
SQL> select to_number('1000' default null on conversion error);
```

Renaming a Column

There are reasons to rename a column.

Sometimes, requirements change, and you may want to modify the column name to better reflect what the column is used for.

If you are planning to drop a column, it does not hurt to rename the column first to better determine whether any users or applications are accessing it.

Use the ALTER TABLE ... RENAME statement to rename a column.

```
SQL> alter table inv rename column inv_count to inv_amt;
```

Dropping a Column

Tables sometimes end up having columns that are never used. This may be because the initial requirements changed or were inaccurate. If you have a table that contains an unused column, you should consider dropping it. If you leave an unused column in a table, you may run into issues with future DBAs not knowing what the column is used for, and the column can potentially consume space unnecessarily.

Before you drop a column, we recommend that you first rename it. Doing so allows you to determine whether users or applications use the column. After you are confident the column is not being used, make a backup of the table using Data Pump export, then drop the column. These strategies provide options if you drop a column and later realize it is needed.

To drop a column, use the ALTER TABLE ... DROP statement.

```
SQL> alter table inv drop (inv_desc);
```

Be aware that the DROP operation may take some time if the table from which you remove the column contains a large amount of data. This time lag may delay transactions while the table is being modified (because the ALTER TABLE statement locks the table). In scenarios such as this, you may want to mark the column unused and drop it later when you have a maintenance window.

```
SQL> alter table inv set unused (inv_desc);
```

When you mark a column unused, it no longer shows up in the table description. The SET UNUSED clause does not incur the overhead associated with dropping the column. This technique lets you quickly stop the column from being seen or used by SQL queries or applications. Any query that attempts to access an unused column receives the following error.

```
ORA-00904: ... invalid identifier
```

You can later drop any unused columns when you've scheduled some downtime for the application. Use the DROP UNUSED clause to remove any columns marked UNUSED.

```
SQL> alter table inv drop unused columns;
```

Displaying Table DDL

Sometimes, a table definition is not documented at the time of creation, maybe from a DBA or developer or directly from the application. Normally, you should maintain the database DDL code in a source control repository or a modeling tool.

If your shop does not have the DDL source code, there are a few ways that you can manually reproduce DDL.

- Query the data dictionary.

- Use Data Pump.

- Use the DBMS_METADATA package.

- Use data tools such as SQL Developer.

The Data Pump utility is an excellent method for generating the DDL used to create database objects. Using Data Pump to generate DDL is covered in Chapter 13.

The GET_DDL function of the DBMS_METADATA package is usually the quickest way to display the DDL required to create an object. This example shows how to generate the DDL for a table named INV.

```
SQL> set long 10000
SQL> select dbms_metadata.get_ddl('TABLE','INV') from dual;
```

Here is some sample output.

```
DBMS_METADATA.GET_DDL('TABLE','INV')
--------------------------------------
SQL> CREATE TABLE "MV_MAINT"."INV"
( "INV_ID" NUMBER,
"INV_DESC" VARCHAR2(30 CHAR),
"INV_COUNT" NUMBER
) SEGMENT CREATION DEFERRED
PCTFREE 10 PCTUSED 40 INITRANS 1 MAXTRANS 255
NOCOMPRESS LOGGING
TABLESPACE "USERS";
```

The following SQL statement displays all the DDL for the tables in a schema.

```
SQL> select
dbms_metadata.get_ddl('TABLE',table_name)
from user_tables;
```

If you want to display the DDL for a table owned by another user, add the SCHEMA parameter to the GET_DDL procedure.

```
SQL> select
dbms_metadata.get_ddl(object_type=>'TABLE', name=>'INV', schema=>'INV_APP')
from dual;
```

Note   You can display the DDL for almost any database object type, such as INDEX, FUNCTION, ROLE, PACKAGE, MATERIALIZED VIEW, PROFILE, CONSTRAINT, SEQUENCE, and SYNONYM.

Dropping a Table

Use the DROP TABLE statement to remove an object, such as a table, from a user. This example drops a table named INV.

```
SQL> drop table inv;
```

You should see the following confirmation.

```
Table dropped.
```

If you attempt to drop a parent table with either a primary key or a unique key referenced as a foreign key in a child table, you see an error like the following.

```
ORA-02449: unique/primary keys in table referenced by foreign keys
```

You must either drop the referenced foreign key constraint(s) or use the CASCADE CONSTRAINTS option when dropping the parent table.

```
SQL> drop table inv cascade constraints;
```

You must be the owner of the table or have the DROP ANY TABLE system privilege to drop a table. If you have the DROP ANY TABLE privilege, you can drop a table in a different schema by prepending the schema name to the table name.

```
SQL> drop table inv_mgmt.inv;
```

If you do not prepend the table name to a username, Oracle assumes you are dropping a table in your current schema.

Tip If flashback query or flashback database is enabled, keep in mind that you can flash back a table before the drop for an accidentally dropped table.

Undropping a Table

Suppose you accidentally drop a table, and you want to restore it. First, verify that the table you want to restore is in the recycle bin.

```
SQL> show recyclebin;
```

Here is some sample output.

```
ORIGINAL NAME RECYCLEBIN NAME OBJECT TYPE DROP TIME
------------- --------------- ----------- ----------------
INV BIN$0F27WtJGbXngQ4TQTwq5Hw==$0  TABLE 2022-12-08:12:56:45
```

Next, use the FLASHBACK TABLE...TO BEFORE DROP statement to recover the dropped table.

```
SQL> flashback table inv to before drop;
```

Note You cannot use the FLASHBACK TABLE...TO BEFORE DROP statement for a table created in the SYSTEM tablespace.

When you issue a DROP TABLE statement (without PURGE), the table is renamed (to one that starts with BIN$) and placed in the recycle bin. The recycle bin is a mechanism that allows you to view some of the metadata associated with a dropped object. You can view complete metadata regarding renamed objects by querying DBA_ SEGMENTS.

```
SQL> select
owner
,segment_name
,segment_type
,tablespace_name
from dba_segments
where segment_name like 'BIN$%';
```

The FLASHBACK TABLE statement simply renames the table to its original name. By default, the RECYCLEBIN feature is enabled. You can change the default by setting the RECYCLEBIN initialization parameter to OFF.

We recommend that you not disable the RECYCLEBIN feature. It is safer to leave this feature enabled and purge the RECYCLEBIN to remove objects that you want permanently deleted. This means the space associated with a dropped table is not released until you purge your RECYCLEBIN. If you want to purge the entire contents of the currently connected user's recycle bin, use the PURGE RECYCLEBIN statement.

```
SQL> purge recyclebin;
```

If you want to purge the recycle bin for all database users, do the following as a SYSDBA-privileged user or user with the PURGE DBA_RECYCLEBIN role.

```
SQL> purge dba_recyclebin;
```

If you want to bypass the RECYCLEBIN feature and permanently drop a table, use the PURGE option of the DROP TABLE statement.

```
SQL> drop table inv purge;
```

You cannot use the FLASHBACK TABLE statement to retrieve a table dropped with the PURGE option. All the space used by the table is released, and any associated indexes and triggers are also dropped.

Removing Data from a Table

You can use either the DELETE statement or the TRUNCATE statement to remove records from a table. A DELETE statement is a way to change the data or, in this case, remove it, which is logged and can be rolled back or committed.

However, a TRUNCATE command has no way to roll back. TRUNCATE is considered changing a table or a DDL statement, even changing the previous size of the table, and it is almost like the table was just created. There are additional permissions that are needed to truncate a table instead of a delete.

You can't truncate a table that has a primary key defined that is referenced by an enabled foreign key constraint in a child table, even if there are no rows in that table. Because a TRUNCATE statement is DDL, you can't truncate two separate tables as one transaction. Compare this behavior with that of DELETE. Oracle allows you to use the DELETE statement to remove rows from a parent table while the constraints that reference a child table are enabled. This is because DELETE generates undo, is read consistently, and can be rolled back.

Note Another way to remove data from a table is to drop and re-create the table. However, this means you must re-create any indexes, constraints, grants, and triggers that belong to the table. Additionally, when you drop a table, it is unavailable until you re-create it and reissue any required grants. Usually, dropping and re-creating a table is acceptable only in a development or test environment.

Moving a Table

Moving a table means rebuilding its current tables or building it in a different tablespace. You may want to move a table because its current tablespace has disk space storage issues or because you want to lower the table's high-water mark.

Use the ALTER TABLE ... MOVE statement to move a table from one tablespace to another. This example moves the INVENTORY table to the USERS tablespace.

```
SQL> alter table inventory move tablespace users;
```

You can verify that the table has been moved by querying USER_TABLES.

```
SQL> select table_name, tablespace_name from user_tables
where table_name='INVENTORY';
TABLE_NAME                            TABLESPACE_NAME
-----------------------------------   ----------------------------
INVENTORY                             USERS
```

Note   The ALTER TABLE ... MOVE statement does not allow DML to execute while running. There are some restrictions, but there is an ALTER TABLE ... MOVE ONLINE statement that does not restrict access to the table or use the DBMS REDEFINITION package.

When you move a table, all its indexes are rendered unusable. This is because a table's index includes the ROWID as part of the structure. The ROWID table contains information about the physical location. Given that the ROWID of a table changes when the table moves from one tablespace to another (because the table rows are now physically located in different data files), any indexes on the table contain incorrect information. To rebuild the index, use the ALTER INDEX ... REBUILD command.

Oracle ROWID

Every row in every table has an address. The address of a row is determined from a combination of the following.

- Data file number
- Block number
- Location of the row within the block
- Object number

You can display the address of a row in a table by querying the ROWID pseudocolumn, as shown in the following example.

```
SQL> select rowid, emp_id from emp;
```

Here is some sample output.

```
ROWID              EMP_ID
------------------ ----------
AAAFJAAAFAAAAJfAAA 1
```

The ROWID pseudocolumn value is not physically stored in the database. Oracle calculates its value when you query it. The ROWID contents are displayed as base-64 values that can contain the characters A–Z, a–z, 0–9, +, and /. You can translate the ROWID value into meaningful information via the DMBS_ROWID package. For instance, to display the relative file number in which a row is stored, issue the following statement.

```
SQL> select dbms_rowid.rowid_relative_fno(rowid), emp_id from emp;
```

Here is some sample output.

```
DBMS_ROWID.ROWID_RELATIVE_FNO(ROWID)EMP_ID
51
```

You can use the ROWID value in a SQL statement's SELECT and WHERE clauses. In most cases, the ROWID uniquely identifies a row. However, it is possible to have rows in different tables stored in the same cluster and, therefore, contain rows with the same ROWID.

Creating a Global Temporary Table

Use the CREATE GLOBAL TEMPORARY TABLE statement to create a table that stores data only provisionally. You can specify that the temporary table retains the data for a session or until a transaction commits. Use ON COMMIT PRESERVE ROWS to specify that the data be deleted at the end of the user's session. In this example, the rows are retained until the user explicitly deletes the data or terminates the session.

```
SQL> create global temporary table analyzed_tables
on commit preserve rows
as select * from user_tables
where lst_analyzed > sysdate - 1;
```

Specify ON COMMIT DELETE ROWS to indicate that the data should be deleted at the end of the transaction. The following example creates a temporary table named TEMP_OUTPUT and specifies that records should be deleted at the end of each committed transaction.

```
create global temporary table temp_output(
temp_row varchar2(30))
on commit delete rows;
```

Note   If you do not specify a commit method for a global temporary table, then the default is ON COMMIT DELETE ROWS.

You can create a temporary table and grant other users access to it. However, a session can only view the data it inserts into a table. In other words, if two sessions are using the same temporary table, a session cannot select any data inserted into the temporary table by a different session.

A global temporary table is useful for applications that briefly store data in a table structure. After you create a temporary table, it exists until you drop it. In other words, the definition of the temporary table is "permanent"—it is the short-lived data (in this sense, the term *temporary table* can be misleading).

You can view whether a table is temporary by querying the TEMPORARY column of DBA/ALL/USER TABLES.

```
SQL> select table_name, temporary from user_tables;
```

Temporary tables are designated with a Y in the TEMPORARY column. Regular tables contain an N in the TEMPORARY column.

When you create records in a temporary table, space is allocated in your default temporary tablespace. You can verify this by running the following SQL.

```
SQL> select username, contents, segtype from v$sort_usage;
```

If you are working with a large number of rows and need better performance for selectively retrieving rows, you may want to consider creating an index on the appropriate columns in your temporary table.

```
SQL> create index temp_index on temp_output(temp_row);
```

Use the DROP TABLE command to drop a temporary table.

```
SQL> drop table temp_output;
```

Temporary Table Redo

No redo data are generated for changes to blocks of a global temporary table. However, rollback (undo) data is generated for a transaction against a temporary table. Because the rollback data generates a redo, some redo data are associated with a transaction for a temporary table. You can verify this by turning on statistics tracing and viewing the redo size as you insert records into a temporary table.

```
SQL> set autotrace on
```

Next, insert a few records into the temporary table.

```
SQL> insert into temp_output values(1);
```

Here is a snippet of the output (showing only the redo size).

```
140 redo size
```

The redo load is less for temporary tables than normal tables because the redo generated is associated only with the rollback (undo) data for a temporary table transaction.

Additionally, the undo for temporary objects is stored in the temporary tablespace, not the undo tablespace.

Private Temporary Tables

Oracle 18c introduced private temporary tables, which are memory-based temporary tables used for the session or transaction and then dropped.

This is different from the global temporary table, as the metadata of the table is not permanent but the same as the data; in this case, the whole table is for the session and private.

There is a PRIVATE_TEMP_TABLE_PREFIX parameter for defining the prefix of the name for the table, with a default of ORA$PTT_. Also, it's important to know how the temp table will be used. You are expected to be a user schema, and the private temporary table creation fails if you are a SYS or SYSTEM user.

You need to use the prefix to create the table.

```
SQL> create private temporary table ora$ppt_work_temp_table (
idnumber,
name_descvarchar2(80),
valid_values number)
on commit preserve definition;
```

The ON COMMIT DROP DEFINITION clause is the default, which means the table is dropped when the transaction is finished.

It does make sense to use the private temporary table as dynamic in PL/SQL, where if you need an existing table in PL/SQL, the object needs to be referenced to compile, and it would be useful to use a global temporary table.

211

In PL/SQL.

```
> begin
execute immediate 'create private temporary table ora$ptt_work_temp_table
(id number, name_desc varchar2(80)) on commit drop definition';
...
execute immediate 'insert into ora$ptt_work_temp_table
values(1,'Testing')';
...
end;
/
```

Since private temporary tables are memory-based, no metadata is captured in the data dictionary, and database links cannot access the data or materialized views. While in the transaction or session, you can use the DBA/USER_ PRIVATE_TEMP_TABLES table to see the details. Already discussed was that the PL/SQL would need to include it in an execute immediate statement as with dynamic SQL.

Creating an Index-Organized Table

An index-organized table (IOT) is an efficient object when the table data is typically accessed through querying on the primary key. Use the ORGANIZATION INDEX clause to create an IOT.

```
SQL> create table prod_sku
(prod_sku_id number,
sku varchar2(256),
create_dtt timestamp(5),
constraint prod_sku_pk primary key(prod_sku_id)
) organization index
including sku
pctthreshold 30
tablespace inv_data
overflow
tablespace inv_data;
```

An IOT stores the entire contents of the table's row in a B-tree index structure. IOTs provide fast access for queries with exact matches, range searches, or both on the primary key.

All columns specified, up to, and including the column specified in the INCLUDING clause are stored in the same block as the PROD_SKU_ID primary key column. In other words, the INCLUDING clause specifies the last column to keep in the index segment. Columns listed after the column specified in the INCLUDING clause are stored in the overflow data segment. In the previous example, the CREATE_DTT column is stored in the overflow segment.

PCTTHRESHOLD specifies the percentage of space reserved in the index block for the IOT row. This value can be from 1 to 50 and defaults to 50 if no value is specified. The index block must have enough space to store the primary key.

The OVERFLOW clause describes which tablespace should be used to store overflow data segments. DBA/ALL/USER_TABLES includes an entry for the table name used when creating an IOT. Additionally, DBA/ALL/USER_INDEXES contains a record with the name of the primary key constraint specified. The INDEX_TYPE column contains a value of IOT - TOP for IOTs.

```
SQL> select index_name,table_name,index_type from user_indexes;
```

Managing Constraints

The next several sections in this chapter deal with constraints. Constraints provide a mechanism for ensuring that data conforms to certain business rules. You must be aware of what types of constraints are available and when it is appropriate to use them. Oracle offers several types of constraints.

- Primary key

- Unique key

- Foreign key

- Check

- NOT NULL

The following sections discuss implementing and managing these constraints.

Creating Primary Key Constraints

When you implement a database, most tables you create require a primary key constraint to guarantee that every record in the table can be uniquely identified. There are multiple techniques for adding a primary key constraint to a table. The first example creates the primary key inline with the column definition.

```
SQL> create table dept(
dept_id number primary key
,dept_desc varchar2(30));
```

If you select the CONSTRAINT_NAME from USER_CONSTRAINTS, note that Oracle generates a cryptic name for the constraint (such as SYS_C003682). Use the following syntax to explicitly give a name to a primary key constraint.

```
SQL> create table dept(
dept_id number constraint dept_pk primary key using index tablespace users,
dept_desc varchar2(30));
```

Note   When you create a primary key constraint, Oracle also creates a unique index with the same name as the constraint. You can control which tablespace the unique index is placed in via the USING INDEX TABLESPACE clause.

You can also specify the primary key constraint definition after defining the columns. The advantage of doing this is that you can define the constraint on multiple columns. The next example creates the primary key when the table is created, but not inline with the column definition.

```
SQL> create table dept(
dept_id number,
dept_desc varchar2(30),
constraint dept_pk primary key (dept_id)
using index tablespace users);
```

If the table has already been created and you want to add a primary key constraint, use the ALTER TABLE statement. This example places a primary key constraint on the DEPT_ID column of the DEPT table.

```
SQL> alter table dept
add constraint dept_pk primary key (dept_id)
using index tablespace users;
```

When a primary key constraint is enabled, Oracle automatically creates a unique index associated with the primary key constraint. Some DBAs prefer to first create a nonunique index on the primary key column and then define the primary key constraint.

```
SQL> create index dept_pk on dept(dept_id) tablespace users;
SQL> alter table dept add constraint dept_pk primary key (dept_id);
```

The advantage of this approach is that you can drop or disable the primary key constraint independently of the index. When working with large data sets, you may want that sort of flexibility. If you do not create the index before creating the primary key constraint, then whenever you drop or disable the primary key constraint, the index is automatically dropped.

Confused about which method to use to create a primary key? All the methods are valid and have their merits. We've used all these methods to create primary key constraints. Usually, we use the ALTER TABLE statement, which adds the constraint after the table has been created.

Enforcing Unique Key Values

In addition to creating a primary key constraint, you should create unique constraints on any combinations of columns that should always be unique within a table. For example, for the primary key for a table, it is common to use a numeric key (sometimes called a *surrogate key*) populated via a sequence. Besides the surrogate primary key, sometimes users have a column (or columns) that the business uses to uniquely identify a record (also called a *logical key*). Using both a surrogate key and a logical key does the following.

- Lets you efficiently join parent and child tables on a single numeric column

- Allows updates to logical key columns without changing the surrogate key

215

A unique key guarantees uniqueness on a table's defined column(s). There are some subtle differences between primary key and unique key constraints. For example, you can define only one primary key per table, but several unique keys exist. Also, a primary key does not allow a NULL value in any of its columns, whereas a unique key allows NULL values.

As with the primary key constraint, you can use several methods to create a unique column constraint. This method uses the UNIQUE keyword inline with the column.

```
SQL> create table dept(
dept_id number
,dept_desc varchar2(30) unique);
```

If you want to explicitly name the constraint, use the CONSTRAINT keyword.

```
SQL> create table dept(
dept_id number
,dept_desc varchar2(30) constraint dept_desc_uk1 unique);
```

As with primary keys, Oracle automatically creates an index associated with the unique key constraint. You can specify inline the tablespace information for the associated unique index.

```
SQL> create table dept(
dept_id number
,dept_desc varchar2(30) constraint dept_desc_uk1
unique using index tablespace users);
```

You can also alter a table to include a unique constraint.

```
SQL> alter table dept
add constraint dept_desc_uk1 unique (dept_desc)
using index tablespace users;
```

You can create an index on the columns of interest before you define a unique key constraint.

```
SQL> create index dept_desc_uk1 on dept(dept_desc) tablespace users;
SQL> alter table dept add constraint dept_desc_uk1 unique(dept_desc);
```

This can be helpful when working with large data sets and you want to disable or drop the unique constraint without dropping the associated index.

Tip   You can also enforce a unique key constraint with a unique index. See Chapter 8 for information on using unique indexes to enforce unique constraints.

Creating Foreign Key Constraints

Foreign key constraints ensure that a column value is contained within a defined list of values. Using a foreign key constraint is an efficient way of enforcing that data be a predefined value before an insert or update is allowed. This technique works well for the following scenarios.

- The list of values contains many entries.
- Other information about the lookup value needs to be stored.
- It is easy to select, insert, update, or delete values via SQL.

For example, suppose the EMP table is created with a DEPT_ID column. To ensure that each employee is assigned a valid department, you can create a foreign key constraint that enforces the rule that each DEPT_ID in the EMP table must exist in the DEPT table.

Tip   If the condition you want to check for consists of a small list that does not change very often, consider using a check constraint instead of a foreign key constraint. For instance, if you have a column that is always defined as containing either a 0 or a 1, a check constraint is an efficient solution.

For reference, here's how the parent table DEPT table was created for these examples.

```
SQL> create table dept(
dept_id number primary key,
dept_desc varchar2(30));
```

A foreign key must reference a column in the parent table that has a primary key or a unique key defined on it. DEPT is the parent table and has a primary key defined on DEPT_ID.

You can use several methods to create a foreign key constraint. The following example creates a foreign key constraint on the DEPT_ID column in the EMP table.

```
SQL> create table emp(
emp_id number,
name varchar2(30),
dept_id constraint emp_dept_fk references dept(dept_id));
```

Note that the DEPT_ID data type is not explicitly defined. The foreign key constraint derives the data type from the referenced DEPT_ID column of the DEPT table. You can also explicitly specify the data type when you define a column (regardless of the foreign key definition).

```
SQL> create table emp(
emp_id number,
name varchar2(30),
dept_id number constraint emp_dept_fk references dept(dept_id));
```

You can also specify the foreign key definition out of line from the column definition in the CREATE TABLE statement.

```
SQL> create table emp(
emp_id number,
name varchar2(30),
dept_id number,
constraint emp_dept_fk foreign key (dept_id) references dept(dept_id)
);
```

And, you can alter an existing table to add a foreign key constraint.

```
SQL> alter table emp
add constraint emp_dept_fk foreign key (dept_id)
references dept(dept_id);
```

Note   Unlike with primary key and unique key constraints, Oracle does not automatically add an index to foreign key columns; you must explicitly create indexes on them. See Chapter 8 for a discussion on why it is important to create indexes on foreign key columns and how to detect those that do not have associated indexes.

Checking for Specific Data Conditions

A check constraint works well for lookups when you have a short list of fairly static values, such as a column that can be either Y or N. In this situation, the list of values most likely won't change, and no information needs to be stored other than Y or N, so a check constraint is an appropriate solution. A table and a foreign key constraint are a better solution if you have a long list of values that needs to be periodically updated.

Also, a check constraint works well for a business rule that must always be enforced, and that can be written with a simple SQL expression. If you have sophisticated business logic that must be validated, the application code is more appropriate.

You can define a check constraint when you create a table. The following enforces the ST_FLG column to contain either a 0 or 1.

```
SQL> create table emp(
emp_id number,
emp_name varchar2(30),
st_flg number(1) CHECK (st_flg in (0,1))
);
```

A slightly better method is to give the check constraint a name.

```
SQL> create table emp(
emp_id number,
emp_name varchar2(30),
st_flg number(1) constraint st_flg_chk CHECK (st_flg in (0,1))
);
```

A more descriptive way to name the constraint is to embed information in the constraint name that describes the condition that was violated; for example,

```
SQL> create table emp(
emp_id number,
emp_name varchar2(30),
st_flg number(1) constraint "st_flg must be 0 or 1" check (st_flg in (0,1))
);
```

You can also alter an existing column to include a constraint. The column must not contain any values that violate the constraint being enabled.

```
SQL> alter table emp add constraint
"st_flg must be 0 or 1" check (st_flg in (0,1));
```

Note   The check constraint must evaluate to a true or unknown (NULL) value in the row being inserted or updated. You cannot use subqueries or sequences in a check constraint. Also, you can't reference the UID, USER, SYSDATE, or USERENV SQL functions or the LEVEL or ROWNUM pseudocolumns.

Enforcing NOT NULL Conditions

Another common condition to check for is whether a column is null; you use the NOT NULL constraint to do this. The NOT NULL constraint can be defined in several ways. The following shows the simplest technique.

```
SQL> create table emp(
emp_id number,
emp_name varchar2(30) not null);
```

A slightly better approach is to give the NOT NULL constraint a name that makes sense to you. Naming the constraint allows you to see what the constraint is for instead of a system-generated constraint name, which might be confused with a primary or foreign key constraint.

```
SQL> create table emp(
emp_id number,
emp_name varchar2(30) constraint emp_name_nn not null);
```

Use the ALTER TABLE command to modify a column for an existing table. For the following command to work, there must not be any NULL values in the column being defined as NOT NULL.

```
SQL> alter table emp modify(emp_name not null);
```

Note   If there are currently NULL values in a column that is being defined as NOT NULL, you must first update the table so that the column has a value in every row.

Disabling Constraints

One nice feature of Oracle is that you can disable and enable constraints without dropping and re-creating them. This means you avoid having to know the DDL statements that would be required to re-create the dropped constraints.

Occasionally, you need to disable constraints. For example, you may be trying to truncate a table but receive the following error message.

```
ORA-02266: unique/primary keys in table referenced by enabled foreign keys
```

Oracle does not allow a truncate operation on a parent table with a primary key referenced by an enabled foreign key in a child table. If you need to truncate a parent table, you must disable all the enabled foreign key constraints that reference the parent table's primary key. Run this query to determine the names of the constraints that need to be disabled.

```
SQL> col primary_key_table form a18
SQL> col primary_key_constraint form a18
SQL> col fk_child_table form a18
SQL> col fk_child_table_constraint form a18
--
SQL> select
b.table_name primary_key_table
```

```
,b.constraint_name primary_key_constraint
,a.table_name fk_child_table
,a.constraint_name fk_child_table_constraint
from dba_constraints a
,dba_constraints b
where a.r_constraint_name = b.constraint_name
and a.r_owner = b.owner
and a.constraint_type = 'R'
and b.owner = upper('&table_owner')
and b.table_name = upper('&pk_table_name');
```

For this example, there is only one foreign key dependency.

```
PRIMARY_KEY_TAB PRIMARY_KEY_CON FK_CHILD_TABLE FK_CHILD_TABLE_DEPTDEPT_
PKEMPEMP_DEPT_FK
```

Use the ALTER TABLE statement to disable constraints on a table. In this case, there is only one foreign key to disable.

```
SQL> alter table emp disable constraint emp_dept_fk;
```

You can now truncate the parent table.

```
SQL> truncate table dept;
```

Do not forget to re-enable the foreign key constraints after completing the truncate operation.

```
SQL> alter table emp enable constraint emp_dept_fk;
```

You can disable a primary key and all dependent foreign key constraints with the CASCADE option of the DISABLE clause. For example, the next line of code disables all foreign key constraints related to the primary key constraint.

```
SQL> alter table dept disable constraint dept_pk cascade;
```

This statement does not cascade through all levels of dependencies; it only disables the foreign key constraints directly dependent on DEPT_PK. Also, keep in mind that there is no ENABLE...CASCADE statement. To re-enable the constraints, you have to query the data dictionary to determine which constraints have been disabled and then re-enable them individually.

Sometimes, you run into situations when loading data in which it is convenient to disable all the foreign keys before loading the data. In these situations, the `impdb` utility imports the tables alphabetically and does not ensure that child tables are imported before parent tables. You may also want to run several Data Pump import jobs in parallel to take advantage of parallel hardware. In such scenarios, you can disable the foreign keys, perform the import, and then re-enable the foreign keys.

The following is a script that uses SQL to generate SQL to disable all foreign key constraints for a user.

```
set lines 132 trimsp on head off feed off verify off echo off pagesize 0
spo dis_dyn.sql
select 'alter table ' || a.table_name
|| ' disable constraint ' || a.constraint_name || ';'
from dba_constraints a
,dba_constraints b
where a.r_constraint_name = b.constraint_name
and a.r_owner = b.owner
and a.constraint_type = 'R'
and b.owner = upper('&table_owner');
spo off;
```

This script generates a file named `dis_dyn.sql`, which contains the SQL statements to disable all the foreign key constraints for a user.

Enabling Constraints

This section contains a few scripts to help you enable constraints that you've disabled. Listed next is a script that creates a file with the SQL statements required to re-enable any foreign key constraints for tables owned by a specified user.

```
set lines 132 trimsp on head off feed off verify off echo off pagesize 0
spo enable_dyn.sql
select 'alter table ' || a.table_name
|| ' enable constraint ' || a.constraint_name || ';'
from dba_constraints a
,dba_constraints b
where a.r_constraint_name = b.constraint_name
```

223

```
and a.r_owner = b.owner
and a.constraint_type = 'R'
and b.owner = upper('&table_owner');
spo off;
```

When enabling constraints, by default, Oracle checks to ensure that the data does not violate the constraint definition. If you are fairly certain that the data integrity is fine and that you do not need to incur the performance hit by revalidating the constraint, you can use the NOVALIDATE clause when re-enabling the constraints. Here is an example.

```
SQL> select 'alter table ' || a.table_name
|| ' modify constraint ' || a.constraint_name || ' enable novalidate;'
from dba_constraints a
,dba_constraints b
where a.r_constraint_name = b.constraint_name
and a.r_owner = b.owner
and a.constraint_type = 'R'
and b.owner = upper('&table_owner');
```

The NOVALIDATE clause instructs Oracle not to validate the constraints being enabled, but it does enforce that any new DML activities adhere to the constraint definition.

In multiuser systems, the possibility exists that another session has inserted data into the child table while the foreign key constraint was disabled. If that happens, you see the following error when you attempt to re-enable the foreign key.

```
ORA-02298: cannot validate (<owner>.<constraint>) - parent keys not found
```

In this scenario, you can use the ENABLE NOVALIDATE clause.

```
SQL> alter table emp enable novalidate constraint emp_dept_fk;
```

To clean up the rows that violate the constraint, first, ensure an EXCEPTIONS table is created in your currently connected schema. If you do not have an EXCEPTIONS table, use this script to create one.

```
SQL> @?/rdbms/admin/utlexcpt.sql
```

Next, populate the EXCEPTIONS table with the rows that violate the constraint using the EXCEPTIONS INTO clause.

```
SQL> alter table emp modify constraint emp_dept_fk validate exceptions into
exceptions;
```

This statement still throws the ORA-02298 error as long as there are rows that violate the constraint. The statement also inserts records into the EXCEPTIONS table for any bad rows. You can now use the ROW_ID column of the EXCEPTIONS table to remove any records that violate the constraint.

Here, you see that one row needs to be removed from the EMP table.

```
SQL> select * from exceptions;
```

Here is some sample output.

```
ROW_IDOWNERTABLE_NAME CONSTRAINT


AAAFKQAABAAAK8JAAB MV_MAINT EMPEMP_DEPT_FK
```

To remove the offending record, issue a DELETE statement.

```
SQL> delete from emp where rowid = 'AAAFKQAABAAAK8JAAB';
```

If the EXCEPTIONS table contains many records, you can run a query such as the following to delete by OWNER and TABLE_NAME.

```
SQL> delete from emp where rowid in
(select row_id
from exceptions
where owner=upper('&owner') and table_name = upper('&table_name'));
```

You may also run into situations where you must disable the primary key, unique key constraints, or both. For instance, you may want to perform a large data load and, for performance reasons, want to disable the primary key and unique key constraints. You do not want to incur the overhead of checking every row as it is inserted.

The same general techniques used for disabling foreign keys apply to disabling primary and unique keys. Run this query to display the primary key and unique key constraints for a user.

```
SQL> select
a.table_name
,a.constraint_name
,a.constraint_type
from dba_constraints a
where a.owner = upper('&table_owner')
and a.constraint_type in ('P','U')
order by a.table_name;
```

When the table name and constraint name are identified, use the ALTER TABLE statement to disable the constraint.

```
SQL> alter table dept disable constraint dept_pk;
```

Note   Oracle does not let you disable a primary key or unique key constraint that is referenced in an enabled foreign key constraint. You first have to disable the foreign key constraint.

CHAPTER 8

Indexes

An index is an optionally created database object used primarily to increase query performance. Indexes can also limit the amount of data that is returned in the results without retrieving all a table's data columns. This can keep results in-memory and bring back results faster. The purpose of a database index is similar to that of an index in the back of a book. A book index associates a topic with a page number. When locating information in a book, it is usually much faster to examine the index first, find the topic of interest, and identify associated page numbers. With this information, you can navigate directly to specific page numbers in the book.

If a topic appears on only a few pages within the book, then the number of pages to read is minimal. In this manner, the usefulness of the index decreases with an increase in the number of times a topic appears in a book. In other words, if a subject entry appears on every page of the book, there would be no benefit to creating an index on it. In this scenario, regardless of the presence of an index, it would be more efficient for the reader to scan every page of the book.

Besides the pages in a book, tables with many, many columns can use indexes to return only the values of the columns or allow the index to be in-memory with the columns needed for joins to improve query performance. The scan of the index might be faster than a scan of the wide table and all the columns, and the sizing of the index might allow it to be used in-memory.

Note Searching all blocks of a table is known as a *full-table scan*. Full-table scans occur when there is no available index or when the query optimizer determines a full-table scan is a more efficient access path than using an existing index.

227

© Michelle Malcher, Darl Kuhn 2024
M. Malcher and D. Kuhn, *Pro Oracle Database 23ai Administration*,
https://doi.org/10.1007/979-8-8688-1038-1_8

A database index stores the column value of interest and its row identifier (ROWID). The ROWID contains the physical location of the table row on the disk that stores the column value. With the ROWID in hand, Oracle can efficiently retrieve table data with a minimum of disk reads. In this way, indexes function as a shortcut to the table data. If there is no available index, Oracle reads each row in the table to determine whether the row contains the desired information.

In addition to improving performance, Oracle uses indexes to help enforce the primary key and unique key constraints. Additionally, Oracle can better manage certain table-locking scenarios when indexes are placed on foreign key columns.

Whereas it is possible to build a database application devoid of indexes, without or too many of them, you almost guarantee poor performance. Indexes allow excellent scalability, even with very large data sets. If indexes are important to database performance, why not place them on all tables and column combinations? The answer is short: indexes are not free. They consume disk space and system resources. As column values are modified, any corresponding indexes must also be updated. In this way, indexes use storage, I/O, CPU, and memory resources. A poor choice of indexes leads to wasted disk usage and excessive consumption of system resources. This results in a decreased database performance and a greater cost for DML statements.

Automation and proactively tuning database applications are ever-growing areas of the database. Indexes, statistics, and overall database configuration play into developing the strategies to tune. There are enhanced statistics and a collection of information about indexes being used. These tools can be utilized in index planning and design for the database tables and indexes.

For these reasons, when you design and build an Oracle database application, consideration must be given to your indexing strategy. As an application architect, you must understand the physical properties of an index, what types of indexes are available, and strategies for choosing which table and column combinations to index. A correct indexing methodology is central to achieving maximum performance for your database. SQL plans and invisible indexes can help determine the right combination of indexes.

Vector Indexes

With vectors in the Oracle Database 23ai and AI Vector Search there are new reasons for indexes and a new index type in the database. Vector indexes are specialized vectors that assist with speeding up similarity searches. Vector indexes also let you specify a target accuracy percentage value to determine the number of candidates to consider in the search. The vector indexes make vector searches faster by reducing the search scope by clustering vectors into structures on attributes. This clustering of vectors is referred to as *nearest neighbors*. A vector index can also make the search faster by reducing the vector size and the number of bits representing vector values.

To create a vector index, you need to determine the category or organization of the index. In Oracle AI Vector Search in 23ai, the following categories are supported.

- In-Memory Neighbor Graph Vector Index – Hierarchical Navigable Small World (HNSW) is the type of In-Memory Neighbor Graph vector index supported. HNSWs are layered hierarchical organizations using principles from small-world networks.

- Neighbor Partition Vector Index – Inverted File Flat (IVF) index is supported. IVF balances speed and high search quality and is a partitioned-based index.

The In-Memory Neighbor Graph Vector Index needs to leverage the new vector pool in the SGA. There is a new parameter, VECTOR_MEMORY_SIZE, that specifies the size of the vector pool and it is a dynamic parameter. The size of the vector pool can be estimated based on the size of the vector dimension type (around 4 to 8 bytes) * number of vectors * number of dimensions * 1.3. If the vector pool is not available, you can create a Neighbor Partition Vector Index.

With vector indexes, there are new parameters to set based on closest neighbors and the maximum number of neighbors a vector can have. There is also TARGET ACCURACY, which impacts the accuracy of indexes and approximate searches. Vector indexes can be globally partitioned and a degree of parallelism can be used to create the index. Here is an example of a create statement for the HNSW vector index.

```
SQL> create vector index product_hnsw_idx on products (product_vector)
ORGANIZATION INMEMORY NEIGHBOR GRAPH DISTANCE COSINE
WITH TARGET ACCURACY 95 PARAMETERS (type HNSW, neighbors 40,
efconstruction 500);
```

This index requires the vector pool, and the distance function for the index must be the same as the distance function used in the vector_distance(), or the index cannot be used. The parameters are optional, but here it is fine-tuning the maximum number of connections per vector to be 40 and the maximum number of closest vector candidates to consider at 500 for each step of the search.

```
SQL> create vector index product_ivf_idx on products (product_vectors)
ORGANIZATION NEIGHBOR PARTITIONS
DISTANCE COSINE
WITH TARGET ACCURACY 95;
```

Because ORGANIZATION is set to NEIGHBOR PARTITIONS, the vector pool is not needed, and it creates a vector index of the category IVF. WITH TARGET ACCURACY is also optional, but target accuracy influences the number of partitions to probe the search. You can also specify target accuracy in the search query, but if no target accuracy is specified, it uses what was set when the index was created.

Information regarding the vector indexes is in the ALL/DBA/USER_INDEXES views. The INDEX_TYPE is a vector, and there is INDEX_SUBTYPE of INMEMORY_NEIGHBOR_GRAPH_HNSW or NEIGHBOR_PARTITIONS_IVF. Indexes that are not vector indexes do not have a subtype. Data changes to vectors can only be performed with IVF vector indexes, and they can be rebuilt using the REBUILD_INDEX function, which is discussed later in this chapter.

Deciding When to Create an Index

There are usually two different situations in which DBAs and developers decide to create indexes.

- Proactively, when deploying an application, the DBAs and developers make an educated guess on which tables and columns to index.

- Reactively, when application performance bogs down, and users complain of poor performance. The DBAs and developers attempt to identify slow-executing SQL queries and how indexes might be a solution.

Proactively Creating Indexes

When creating a new database application, part of the process involves identifying primary, unique, and foreign keys. The columns associated with those keys are usually candidates for indexes. Here are some guidelines.

- Define a primary key constraint for each table. This automatically creates an index on the columns specified in the primary key.

- Create unique key constraints on columns that must differ from the primary key columns. Each unique key constraint automatically creates an index on the columns specified in the constraint.

- Manually create indexes on foreign key columns. This is done for better performance to avoid certain locking issues.

In other words, some of the decision process on what tables and columns to index is automatically done for you when determining the table constraints. When creating primary and unique key constraints, Oracle automatically creates indexes for you. There is some debate about whether to create indexes on foreign key columns. There might even be a debate on table constraints in general. These indexes are further discussed later in this chapter.

Constraint indexes and primary or foreign keys can be automated to run with table creation or as part of the object builds in the database. Also, if foreign keys are newly created, an index can be generated as part of the code to make sure that the indexes are created as changes are made. Instead of manually checking all constraints, indexes, and keys, DDL can be generated based on new objects and added as part of proactively creating indexes.

In addition to creating indexes related to constraints, if you have enough knowledge of the SQL contained within the application, you can create indexes related to tables and columns referenced in `SELECT,` `FROM`, and `WHERE` clauses. In our experience, DBAs and developers are not adept at proactively identifying such indexes. Rather, these indexing requirements are usually identified reactively.

Reactively Creating Indexes

Rarely do DBAs and developers accurately create the right mix of indexes when first deploying an application. That is not a bad thing or unexpected; it is hard to predict everything that occurs in a large database system, including data growth and other data uses. Furthermore, as the application matures, changes are introduced to the database (new tables, new columns, new constraints, and database upgrades that add new features, behaviors, and so on). The reality is that you must react to unforeseen situations in your database that warrant adding indexes to improve performance.

Index strategies also must be revisited for major database releases or system resource changes. For example, more memory on the server allows a table scan to perform better and maybe eliminate a need for an index. Or, an index that was beneficial because of how the optimizer calculated cost or upgrades might validate a different query plan for better performance.

Index strategies are not just about creating indexes but also about cleaning up indexes no longer in use because of better statistics and optimizer query plans without the index.

The following describes a typical process for reactively identifying poorly performing SQL statements and improving performance with indexes.

1. A poorly performing SQL statement is identified, a user complains about a specific statement, the DBA runs an automatic database diagnostic monitor (ADDM) or automatic workload repository (AWR) reports to identify resource-consuming SQL, and so on.

2. The DBA checks the table and index statistics to ensure that out-of-date statistics are not causing the optimizer to make bad choices.

3. The DBA/developer determines that the query cannot be rewritten in a way that alleviates performance issues.

4. The DBA/developer examines the SQL statement and determines which tables and columns are accessed by inspecting the SELECT, FROM, and WHERE clauses.

5. The DBA/developer performs testing and recommends creating an index based on a table and one or more columns.

Once you have identified a poorly performing SQL query, consider creating indexes for the following situations.

- Create indexes on columns used often as predicates in the WHERE clause; when multiple columns from a table are used in the WHERE clause, consider using a concatenated (multicolumn) index.

- Create a covering index (i.e., an index on all columns) in the SELECT clause.

- Create indexes on columns used in the ORDER BY and GROUP BY clauses.

- Create function-based indexes on the function in the WHERE clauses.

Oracle allows you to create an index that contains more than one column. Multicolumn indexes are known as *concatenated indexes* (also called *composite indexes*). These indexes are especially effective when you often use multiple columns in the WHERE clause when accessing a table. Concatenated indexes are, in many instances, more efficient in this situation than creating separate, single-column indexes.

Columns included in the SELECT and WHERE clauses are also potential candidates for indexes. Sometimes, a covering index in a SELECT clause results in Oracle using the index structure itself (and not the table) to satisfy the results of the query. Also, if the column values are selective enough, Oracle can use an index on columns referenced in the WHERE clause to improve query performance.

Also consider creating indexes on columns used in the ORDER BY, GROUP BY, UNION, and DISTINCT clauses. This may result in greater efficiency for queries that frequently use these SQL constructs.

It is OK to have multiple indexes per table. However, the more indexes you place on a table, the slower the DML statements. Do not fall into the trap of randomly adding indexes to a table until you stumble upon the right combination of indexed columns. Rather, verify the performance of an index before you create it in a production environment. Oracle Database has improved how it reviews index usage, and these statistics can be considered when deciding to keep indexes or if a different index is needed. SQL plans and other reporting for the index usage help determine which indexes are needed.

Keep in mind that it is possible to add an index that increases one statement's performance while hurting others' performance. You must be sure that the improved statements warrant the penalty being applied to other statements. You should only add an index when you are certain it improves performance.

Planning for Robustness

After deciding to create an index, it is prudent to make a few foundational decisions that affect maintainability and availability. Oracle provides a wide assortment of indexing features and options. As a DBA or a developer, you need to be aware of the various features and how to use them. If you choose the wrong type of index or use a feature incorrectly, there may be serious, detrimental performance implications. Later you learn about invisible indexes, which can be an easy way to hide an index from use before dropping, which can help with testing the right indexes. It is still recommended to consider these listed manageability features before creating an index.

- Type of index

- Initial space required and growth

- Temporary tablespace usage for creation

- Tablespace placement

- Naming conventions

- Columns to include

- Single-column or multicolumn (composite) indexes

- Special features, such as `PARALLEL, NOLOGGING, COMPRESSION`

- Uniqueness

- Functions that are used

- Impact on performance of `SELECT` statements

- Impact on performance of `INSERT, UPDATE`, and `DELETE` statements.

These topics are discussed in the next sections of this chapter.

Determining Which Type of Index to Use

Oracle provides a wide range of index types and features. The correct use of indexes results in a well-performing and scalable database application. Conversely, if you incorrectly or unwisely implement a feature, there may be detrimental performance implications. Table 8-1 summarizes the various Oracle index types available. At first glance, this is a long list and may be somewhat overwhelming to somebody new to Oracle. However, deciding which index type to use is not as daunting as it might initially seem. For most applications, you should simply use the default B-tree index type.

Table 8-1. *Oracle Index Type and Usage Descriptions*

Index Type	Usage
B-tree	Default index; good for columns with high cardinality, high degree of distinct values. Use a normal B-tree index unless you have a concrete reason to use a different index type or feature.
IOT	Index-organized table is efficient when most of the column values are included in the primary key. You access the index as if it were a table. The data are stored in a B-tree-like structure.
Unique	A form of B-tree index; used to enforce uniqueness in column values and normally used with primary and unique key constraints.
Reverse-key	A form of B-tree index; useful for balancing I/O in an index that has many sequential inserts. Alternative is to use scalable sequences for the primary keys and reduce the need for the reverse-key index.
Key-compressed	Good for concatenated indexes in which the leading column is often repeated; compresses leaf block entries; applies to B-tree and IOT indexes.
Descending	A form of B-tree index; used with indexes in which corresponding column values are sorted in a descending order. You cannot specify descending for a reverse-key index and is ignored with bitmap indexes.
Bitmap	Excellent in data warehouse environments with low cardinality, low degree of distinct values, columns and SQL statements using many AND or OR operators in the WHERE clause. Bitmap indexes are not appropriate for OLTP databases in which rows are frequently updated.
Bitmap join	Useful in data warehouse environments for queries that use star schema structures that join fact and dimension tables.
Function-based	Good for columns that are usually referenced through SQL functions; can be used with either a B-tree or bitmap index.

(continued)

Table 8-1. (*continued*)

Index Type	Usage
Indexed virtual column	An index defined on a virtual column of a table; useful for columns that usually have SQL functions applied to them; a viable alternative to a function-based index.
Invisible	The index is not visible to the query optimizer. However, the structure of the index is maintained as table data are modified. Useful for testing an index before making it visible to the application. Any index type can be created as invisible.
Global partitioned	Global index across all partitions in a partitioned or regular table; can be a B-tree index type and cannot be a bitmap index type.
Local partitioned	Local index based on individual partitions in a partitioned table; can be either a B-tree or bitmap index type.
Oracle Text	Provides indexing, word and theme searching. Different types of indexing used such as CONTEXT, CTXCAT, CTXRULE.
B-tree cluster	Used with clustered tables.
Hash cluster	Used with hash clusters.
Vector Indexes	Used for indexes on vectors assists in speeding up similarity searches.

In a deployment of Oracle on Exadata and with Autonomous Database, there are options to use automatic indexing and to use and implement indexing. How the indexes are chosen and why indexes are working better are part of the information you can pull from the database. So, it is not a black box to tune which index to use; it can provide details so that you can put indexes into place automatically or review and implement them when ready. Even with these deployments, it is helpful to understand the performance changes and index types.

You probably noticed several of the index types listed are just variations on the B-tree index. A reverse-key index, for example, is merely a B-tree index optimized for evenly spreading I/O when the index value is sequentially generated and inserted with similar values. This chapter focuses on the most commonly used indexes and features, and index-organized tables (IOT) were covered in Chapter 7.

Estimating the Size of an Index Before Creation

If you do not work with large databases, then you do not need to worry about estimating the amount of space an index initially consumes. However, for large databases, you absolutely need an estimate of how much space it takes to create an index. If you have a large table in a data warehouse environment, a corresponding index could easily be hundreds of gigabytes in size. In this situation, you need to ensure that the database has adequate disk space available.

The best way to predict the size of an index is to create it in a test environment with a representative set of production data. However, since it might be difficult to build a test environment complete replica of production data, a subset can be used to extrapolate the size required in production. Another way to estimate the size of an index is using the DBMS_SPACE.CREATE_INDEX_COST procedure.

For reference, here is the table creation script on which the index used in the subsequent examples is based.

```
SQL> CREATE TABLE cust
(cust_id NUMBER
, last_name VARCHAR2(30)
, first_name VARCHAR2(30)
) TABLESPACE users;
```

Next, several thousand records are inserted into the prior table. The following is a snippet of the insert statement (note that multivalue inserts are available starting in 23ai).

```
SQL> insert into cust values(7, 'ACER', 'SCOTT'),
(5, 'STARK', 'JIM'),
(3, 'GREY', 'BOB'),
(11, 'KAHN', 'BRAD'),
(21, 'DEAN', 'ANN'),
...
```

Now, suppose you want to create an index on the CUST table as follows.

```
SQL> create index cust_idx1 on cust(last_name);
```

The following is the procedure for estimating the amount of space the index initially consumes.

```
SQL> set serverout on
SQL> exec dbms_stats.gather_table_stats(user,'CUST');
SQL> variable used_bytes number
SQL> variable alloc_bytes number
SQL> exec dbms_space.create_index_cost ('create index cust_idx1 on cust
(last_name)', :used_bytes, :alloc_bytes);
SQL> print :used_bytes
```

The following is some sample output for this example.

```
USED_BYTES

19800000
SQL> print :alloc_bytes
ALLOC_BYTES
33554432
```

Statistics need to be gathered to give better results, and it depends on the number of records. Indexes continue to grow as rows are inserted into the tables, and because some tables might have multiple indexes, this is where the index space can grow quickly.

Creating Indexes and Temporary Tablespace Space

Related to space usage, sometimes DBAs forget that Oracle often requires space in either memory or disk to sort an index as it is created. If the available memory area is consumed, Oracle allocates disk space as required within the default temporary tablespace. If you are creating a large index, you may need to increase the size of your temporary tablespace.

Another approach is to create an additional temporary tablespace and then assign it to be the default temporary tablespace of the user creating the index. After the index is created, reassign the user's default temporary tablespace to the original temporary tablespace.

Creating Separate Tablespaces for Indexes

For critical applications, you must consider how much space tables and indexes consume and how fast they grow. Space consumption and object growth have a direct impact on database availability. If you run out of space, your database becomes unavailable. The best way to manage space in the database is by creating tablespaces tailored to space requirements and then creating objects in specified tablespaces that you have designed for those objects. With that in mind, we recommend that you separate tables and indexes into different tablespaces. Consider the following reasons.

- Doing so allows differing backup and recovery requirements. You may want the flexibility of backing up the indexes at a different frequency than the tables. Or, you may choose not to back up indexes because you know that you can re-create them.

- If you let the table or index inherit its storage characteristics from the tablespace, you can tailor storage attributes for objects created within the tablespace when using separate tablespaces. Tables and indexes often have different storage requirements (such as extent size and logging).

- When running maintenance reports, it is sometimes easier to manage tables and indexes when the reports have sections separated by tablespace.

If these reasons are valid for your environment, it is probably worth the extra effort to employ different tablespaces for tables and indexes. If you do not have any of the prior needs, then it is fine to put tables and indexes together in the same tablespace.

We should point out that DBAs often consider placing indexes in separate tablespaces for performance reasons. If you have the luxury of creating a storage system from scratch and can set up mount points that have their own sets of disks and controllers, you may see some I/O benefits from separating tables and indexes into different tablespaces. Nowadays, storage administrators often give you a large slice of storage in a storage area network (SAN), and there is no way to guarantee that data and indexes are stored physically on separate disks (and controllers). Thus, you typically do not gain any performance benefits by separating tables and indexes into different tablespaces. Also, when using ASM, disks can be rebalanced for performance.

Establishing Naming Standards

When you are creating and managing indexes, it is highly desirable to develop some standards regarding naming. Consider the following motives.

- Diagnosing issues is simplified when error messages contain information that indicates the table, index type, and so on.

- Reports that display index information are more easily grouped and more readable, making it easier to spot patterns and issues.

Given those initial thoughts and needs, here are some sample index-naming guidelines.

- Primary key index names should contain the table name and a suffix such as _PK.

- Unique key index names should contain the table name and a suffix such as _UKN, where N is a number.

- Indexes on foreign key columns should contain the foreign key table and a suffix such as _FKN, where N is a number.

- Indexes that are not used for constraints should contain the table name and a suffix such as _IDXN, where N is a number.

- Function-based index names should contain the table name and a suffix such as _FNXN, where N is a number.

- Bitmap index names should contain the table name and a suffix such as _BMXN, where N is a number.

Some shops use prefixes when naming indexes. For example, a primary key index would be named PK_CUST (instead of CUST_PK). All these various naming standards are valid. It does not matter what the standard is, depending on groupings and making the names clearly understandable, as long as everybody on the team is following the standards set.

Creating Indexes

As described previously, when you think about creating tables, you must think about the corresponding index architecture. Creating the appropriate indexes and using the correct index features usually result in dramatic performance improvements. Conversely, creating indexes on the wrong columns or using features in the wrong situations can cause dramatic performance degradation.

Having said that, after giving some thought to what kind of index you need, the next logical step is to create the index. Creating indexes and implementing specific features are discussed in the next several sections.

Creating B-tree Indexes

The default index type in Oracle is a B-tree index. To create a B-tree index on an existing table, use the CREATE INDEX statement. This example creates an index on the CUST table, specifying LAST_NAME as the column.

```
SQL> CREATE INDEX cust_idx1 on cust(last_name);
```

By default, Oracle creates an index in your default permanent tablespace. Sometimes, that may be the desired behavior. But you may remember some reasons for having indexes in a specific tablespace.

```
SQL> CREATE INDEX cust_idx1 on cust(last_name) TABLESPACE reporting_index
```

Because B-tree indexes are the default type and are used extensively with Oracle applications, it is worth taking some time to explain how this particular type of index works. A good way to understand the workings of an index is to show its conceptual structure, along with its relationship with a table (an index cannot exist without a table). Take a look at Figure 8-1; the top section illustrates the CUST table with some data. The table data are stored in two separate data files, and each data file contains two blocks. The bottom part of the diagram shows a balanced, treelike structure of a B-tree index named CUST_IDX1, created on a LAST_NAME of the CUST table. The index is stored in one data file and consists of four blocks.

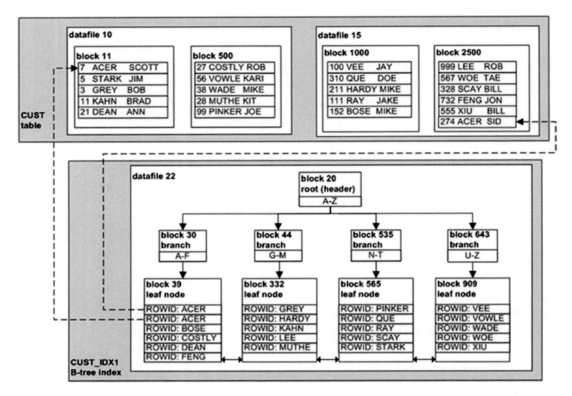

Figure 8-1. *Oracle B-tree hierarchical index structure and associated table*

The index definition is associated with a table and column(s). The index structure stores a mapping of the table's ROWID and the column data on which the index is built. A ROWID usually uniquely identifies a row within a database and contains information to physically locate a row (data file, block, and row position within block). The two dotted lines in Figure 8-1 depict how the ROWID (in the index structure) points to the physical row in the table for the column values of ACER.

The B-tree index has a hierarchical tree structure. When Oracle accesses the index, it starts with the top node, called the *root* (or *header*) block. Oracle uses this block to determine which second-level block (also called a *branch block*) to read next. The second-level block points to several third-level blocks (leaf nodes), which contain a ROWID and the name value. In this structure, it takes three I/O operations to find the ROWID. Once the ROWID is determined, Oracle uses it to read the table block that contains the ROWID.

Let's look at examples to illustrate how an index works. Consider the following query.

```
SQL> select last_name from cust where last_name = 'ACER';
```

Oracle accesses the index, first reading the root block 20; then, it determines that the branch block 30 needs to be read; and, finally, it reads the index values from the lead node block 39. Conceptually, that would be three I/O operations. In this case, Oracle does not need to read the table because the index contains sufficient information to satisfy the results of the query. You can verify the access path of a query by using the autotrace utility. The following is an example.

```
SQL> set autotrace trace explain;
SQL> select last_name from cust where last_name = 'ACER';
```

Note that only the index was accessed (and not the table) to return the data.

```
| Id | Operation          | Name      | Rows | Bytes | Cost (%CPU)| Time     |
------------------------------------------------------------------------------
|  0 | SELECT STATEMENT   |           |  1   |  6    |  1 (0)     | 00:00:01 |
|* 1 | INDEX RANGE SCAN   | CUST_IDX1 |  1   |  6    |  1 (0)     | 00:00:01 |
------------------------------------------------------------------------------
```

Also consider this query.

```
SQL> select first_name, last_name from cust where last_name = 'ACER';
```

Here, Oracle would follow the same index access path by reading blocks 20, 30, and 39. However, because the index structure does not contain the FIRST_NAME value, Oracle must also use the ROWID to read the appropriate rows in the CUST table (blocks 11 and 2500). The following is a snippet of the output from autotrace, indicating that the table has also been accessed.

```
| Id | Operation                           | Name      | Rows | Bytes |Cost
-----------------------------------------------------------------------------
|  0 |   SELECT STATEMENT                  |           |  1   |  44   |  2
|  1 |   TABLE ACCESS BY INDEX ROWID BATCHED| CUST      |  1   |  44   |  2 |
|* 2 |   INDEX RANGE SCAN                  | CUST_IDX1 |  1   |       |  1
-----------------------------------------------------------------------------
```

Also note at the bottom of Figure 8-1 the bidirectional arrows between the leaf nodes. This illustrates that the leaf nodes are connected via a doubly linked list, thus making index range scans possible. For instance, suppose you have this query.

```
SQL> select last_name from cust where last_name >= 'A' and last_name <= 'J';
```

243

To determine where to start the range scan, Oracle would read the root, block 20; then, the branch block 30; and, finally, the leaf node block 39. Because the leaf node blocks are linked, Oracle can navigate forward as needed to find all required blocks (and does not have to navigate up and down through branch blocks). This is a very efficient traversal mechanism for range scans.

Viewing Index Metadata

Oracle provides two types of views containing details about the structure of the indexes.

- INDEX_STATS
- DBA/ALL/USER_INDEXES

The INDEX_STATS view contains information regarding the HEIGHT (number of blocks from root to leaf blocks), LF_ROWS (number of index entries), and so on. The INDEX_STATS view is populated only after you analyze the structure of the index. The following is an example.

```
SQL> analyze index cust_idx1 validate structure;
```

The DBA/ALL/USER_INDEXES views contain statistics, such as BLEVEL (number of blocks from root to branch blocks; this equals HEIGHT – 1), LEAF_BLOCKS (number of leaf blocks), and so on. The DBA/ALL/USER_INDEXES views are populated automatically when the index is created and refreshed via the DBMS_STATS package.

Vector indexes are a new type, and the details for the indexes are in the DBA/ALL/USER_INDEXES views as INDEX_TYPE=VECTOR. This also means when getting the metadata DDL with DBMS_METADATA, the object is VECTOR_INDEX and not just INDEX.

Creating Concatenated Indexes

Oracle allows you to create an index that contains more than one column. Multicolumn indexes are known as concatenated indexes. These indexes are especially effective when you often use multiple columns in the WHERE clause when accessing a table.

Suppose you have the following scenario, in which two columns from the same table are used in the WHERE clause.

```
SQL> select first_name, last_name
from cust
where first_name = 'JIM'
and last_name = 'STARK';
```

Because both FIRST_NAME and LAST_NAME are often used in WHERE clauses for retrieving data, it may be efficient to create a concatenated index on the two columns.

```
SQL> create index cust_idx2 on cust(first_name, last_name);
```

Often, it is not clear whether a concatenated index is more efficient than a single-column index. For the previous SQL statement, you may wonder whether it is more efficient to create two single-column indexes on FIRST_NAME and LAST_NAME, such as this.

```
SQL> create index cust_idx3 on cust(first_name);
SQL> create index cust_idx4 on cust(last_name);
```

In this scenario, if you are consistently using the combination of columns that appear in the WHERE clause, then the optimizer most likely uses the concatenated index and not the single-column indexes. Using a concatenated index, in these situations, is usually much more efficient. You can verify that the optimizer chooses the concatenated index by generating an explain plan. The following is an example.

```
SQL> set autotrace trace explain;
```

Then, run this query.

```
SQL> select first_name, last_name
from cust
where first_name = 'JIM'
and last_name = 'STARK';
```

The following is sample output indicating that the optimizer uses the concatenated index on CUST_IDX2 to retrieve data.

```
---------------------------------------------------------------------------
| Id | Operation           | Name      | Rows | Bytes | Cost (%CPU) | Time ---- |
| 0  | SELECT STATEMENT |            | 1    | 44    | 1 (0)       | 00:00:01  |
|* 1 | INDEX RANGE SCAN | CUST_IDX2  | 1    | 44    | 1 (0)       | 00:00:01  |
---------------------------------------------------------------------------
```

The optimizer can use a concatenated index even if the leading-edge column (or columns) is not present in the WHERE clause. This ability to use an index without reference to leading-edge columns is known as the *skip-scan feature.*

A concatenated index that is used for skip scanning can, in certain situations, be more efficient than a full-table scan. However, you should try to create concatenated indexes that use the leading column. If you are consistently using only a lagging-edge column of a concatenated index, then consider creating a single-column index on the lagging column.

Creating Multiple Indexes on the Same Set of Columns

Multiple indexes can be on the same set of columns, but there must be something physically different about the index. For example, one index is created as a B-tree index, and the second as a bitmap index.

Also, there can be only one visible index for the same combination and order of columns. Any other indexes created on that same set must be declared invisible, as shown next.

```
SQL> create index cust_idx2 on cust(first_name, last_name);
SQL> create bitmap index cust_bmx1 on cust(first_name, last_name)
invisible;
```

Why would you want two indexes defined on the same set of columns? You might want to do this if you originally implemented B-tree indexes and now want to change them to bitmap—the idea is that you create the new indexes as invisible and then drop the original indexes and make the new indexes visible. In a large database environment, this would enable you to make the change quickly. See the "Implementing Invisible Indexes" section for more information.

Implementing Function-Based Indexes

Function-based indexes are created with SQL functions or expressions in their definitions. Sometimes, function-based indexes are required when queries use SQL functions. For example, consider the following query, which uses an SQL UPPER function.

```
SQL> select first_name from cust where UPPER(first_name) = 'JIM';
```

In this scenario there may be a normal B-tree index on the FIRST_NAME column, but Oracle does not use a regular index that exists on a column when a function is applied to it.

In this situation, you can create a function-based index to improve the performance of queries that use a SQL function in the WHERE clause. This example creates a function-based index.

```
SQL> create index cust_fnx1 on cust(upper(first_name));
```

Function-based indexes allow index lookups on columns referenced by functions in the WHERE clause of a SQL query. The index can be as simple as the preceding example, or it can be based on complex logic stored in a PL/SQL function.

Any user-created SQL functions must be declared deterministic before they can be used in a function-based index. *Deterministic* means that for a given set of inputs, the function always returns the same results. You must use the keyword DETERMINISTIC when creating a user-defined function that you want to use in a function-based index.

If you want to see the definition of a function-based index, select from the DBA/ALL/USER_IND_EXPRESSIONS view to display the SQL associated with the index. If you are using SQL*Plus, be sure to issue a SET LONG command first. The following is an example.

```
SQL> SET LONG 500
SQL> select index_name, column_expression from user_ind_expressions;
```

The SET LONG command in this example tells SQL*Plus to display up to 500 characters from the COLUMN_EXPRESSION column, which is of type LONG.

Creating Unique Indexes

When you create a B-tree index, you can also specify that the index is unique. Doing so ensures that non-NULL values are unique when you insert or update columns in a table.

Suppose you have identified a column (or combination of columns) in the table (outside the primary key) that is used heavily in the WHERE clause. In addition, this column (or combination of columns) has the requirement that it be unique within a table. This is a good scenario in which to use a unique index. Use the UNIQUE clause to create a unique index.

```
SQL> create unique index cust_uk1 on cust(first_name, last_name);
```

The unique index does not enforce uniqueness for NULL values inserted into the table. In other words, you can insert the value NULL into the indexed columns for multiple rows.

You must be aware of some interesting nuances regarding unique indexes, primary key constraints, and unique key constraints (see Chapter 7 for a thorough discussion of primary key constraints and unique key constraints). When you create a primary key constraint or a unique key constraint, Oracle automatically creates a unique index and a corresponding constraint that is visible in DBA/ALL/USER_CONSTRAINTS.

When you create a unique index explicitly (as in the example in this section), Oracle creates a unique index but does not add an entry for a constraint in DBA/ALL/USER_CONSTRAINTS. Why does this matter? Consider this scenario.

```
SQL> create unique index cust_uk1 on cust(first_name, last_name); SQL>
insert into cust values(500,'JOHN','DEERE'),
(501,'JOHN','DEERE');
```

Here is the corresponding error message that is thrown.

```
ERROR at line 1:
ORA-00001: unique constraint (MV_MAINT.CUST_UK1) violated
```

If you are asked to troubleshoot this issue, the first place you look is in DBA_CONSTRAINTS for a constraint named CUST_IDX1. However, there is no information.

```
SQL> select constraint_name
from dba_constraintswhere constraint_name='CUST_UK1';
```

Here is the output.

```
no rows selected
```

The no rows selected message can be confusing: the error message thrown when you insert it into the table indicates that a unique constraint has been violated, yet there is no information in the constraint-related data dictionary views. In this situation, you must look at DBA_INDEXES and DBA_IND_COLUMNS to view the details of the unique index that has been created.

```
SQL> select a.owner, a.index_name, a.uniqueness, b.column_name
from dba_indexes a, dba_ind_columns b
where a.index_name='CUST_UK1'
and a.table_owner = b.table_owner
and a.index_name = b.index_name;
```

If you want to have information related to the constraint in the DBA/ALL/USER_ CONSTRAINTS views, you can explicitly associate a constraint after the index has been created.

```
SQL> alter table cust add constraint cust_idx1 unique(first_name,
last_name);
```

In this situation, you can enable and disable the constraint independent of the index. However, because the index was created as unique, the index still enforces uniqueness regardless of whether the constraint has been disabled.

When should you explicitly create a unique index vs. creating a constraint and having Oracle automatically create the index? There are no hard-and-fast rules. We prefer creating a unique key constraint and letting Oracle automatically create the unique index because then we get information in both the DBA/ALL/USER_CONSTRAINTS and DBA/ ALL/USER_INDEXES views.

However, Oracle's documentation recommends that if you have a scenario in which you are strictly using a unique constraint to improve query performance, it is preferable to create only the unique index. This is appropriate. If you take this approach, just be aware that you may not find any information in the constraint-related data dictionary views.

Implementing Bitmap Indexes

Bitmap indexes are recommended for columns with a relatively low degree of distinct values (low cardinality). You should not use bitmap indexes in OLTP databases with high INSERT/UPDATE/DELETE activities owing to locking issues; the structure of the bitmap index results in many rows potentially being locked during DML operations, which causes locking problems for high-transaction OLTP systems.

Bitmap indexes are commonly used in data warehouse environments. A typical star schema structure consists of a large fact table and many small dimension (lookup) tables. In these scenarios, it is common to create bitmap indexes on fact table foreign key columns. The fact tables are typically inserted on a daily basis and usually are not updated or deleted from.

Listed next is a simple example that demonstrates the creation and structure of a bitmap index. First, create a LOCATIONS table.

```
SQL> create table locations(
location_id number
,region varchar2(10));
```

Now, insert the following rows into the table.

```
SQL> insert into locations values(1,'NORTH'), (2,'EAST'),
(3,'NORTH'),
(4,'WEST'),
(5,'EAST'),
(6,'NORTH'),
(7,'NORTH');
```

You use the BITMAP keyword to create a bitmap index. The next line of code creates a bitmap index on the REGION column of the LOCATIONS table.

```
SQL> create bitmap index locations_bmx1 on locations(region);
```

Bitmap indexes are effective at retrieving rows when multiple AND and OR conditions appear in the WHERE clause. For example, to perform the task find all rows with a region of EAST or WEST, a Boolean algebra OR operation is performed on the EAST and WEST bitmaps to quickly return rows 2, 4, and 5.

Bitmap indexes and bitmap join indexes are available only with the Oracle Enterprise Edition of the database. Also, you cannot create a unique bitmap index.

Creating Bitmap Join Indexes

Bitmap join indexes store the results of a join between two tables in an index. Bitmap join indexes are beneficial because they avoid joining tables to retrieve results. The syntax for a bitmap join index differs from that of a regular bitmap index in that it contains FROM and WHERE clauses. Here is the basic syntax for creating a bitmap join index.

```
SQL> create bitmap index <index_name>
on <fact_table> (<dimension_table.dimension_column>)
from <fact_table>, <dimension_table>
where <fact_table>.<foreign_key_column> = <dimension_table>.<primary_key_
column>;
```

Bitmap join indexes are appropriate in situations in which you are joining two tables, using the foreign key column (or columns) in one table relating to the primary key column (or columns) in the other table. For example, suppose you typically retrieve the FIRST_NAME and LAST_NAME from the CUST dimension table while joining to a large F_SHIPMENTS fact table. This next example creates a bitmap join index between the F_SHIPMENTS and CUST tables.

```
SQL> create bitmap index f_shipments_bmx1
on f_shipments(cust.first_name, cust.last_name)
from f_shipments, cust
where f_shipments.cust_id = cust.cust_id;
```

Now, consider a query such as this.

```
SQL> select c.first_name, c.last_name
from f_shipments s, cust c
where s.cust_id = c.cust_id
and c.first_name = 'JIM'
and c.last_name = 'STARK';
```

The optimizer can choose to use the bitmap join index, thus avoiding the expense of having to join the tables. For small amounts of data, the optimizer most likely chooses not to use the bitmap join index, but as the data in the table grows, using the bitmap join index becomes more cost-effective than full-table scans or using other indexes.

Implementing Reverse-Key Indexes

Reverse-key indexes are similar to B-tree indexes, except that the bytes of the index key are reversed when an index entry is created. For example, if the index values are 201, 202, and 203, the reverse-key index values are 102, 202, and 302.

```
Index value    Reverse-key value
------------   ------------------
201            102
202            202
203            302
```

Reverse-key indexes can perform better in scenarios in which you need a way to evenly distribute index data that would otherwise have similar values clustered together. Thus, when using a reverse-key index, you avoid having I/O concentrated in one physical disk location within the index during large inserts of sequential values. You cannot specify REVERSE for a bitmap index or an IOT.

Use the REVERSE clause to create a reverse-key index.

```
SQL> create index cust_idx1 on cust(cust_id) reverse;
```

You can verify that an index is a reverse-key by running the following query.

```
SQL> select index_name, index_type from user_indexes;
```

Instead of using reverse-key indexes to solve the incremental sequence issue here, scalable sequences are also available. You can use the scalable sequences to populate your primary key.

Scalable sequences add a prefix number, pad zeros, and then have the incrementing number.

```
SQL> create sequence seq_scale_pk
minvalue 1
maxvalue 9999999999
scale;
SQL> select seq_scale_pk.nextval;
1023760001
```

```
SQL> select seq_scale_pk.nextval;
1023760002
New connection
SQL> select seq_scale_pk.nextval;
1087420003
```

As you can see, a new session changes the prefix. If you are able to define your sequences for the primary key as scalable, this is a better way to address the issue that reverse-key indexes were addressing.

Creating Key-Compressed Indexes

Index compression is useful for indexes where one or more of the columns contains highly repetitive data. Compressed indexes, in these situations, have the following advantages.

- Reduced storage

- More rows stored in leaf blocks, which can result in less I/O when accessing a compressed index

You cannot create a key-compressed index on a bitmap index.

Suppose you have a table defined as follows.

```
SQL> create table users(
last_name varchar2(30)
,first_name varchar2(30)
,address_id number);
```

You want to create a concatenated index on the LAST_NAME and FIRST_NAME columns. You know from examining the data that there is duplication in the LAST_NAME column. The compression clause allows you only to specify how many of the left-most columns should be compressed. You cannot compress a specific indexed column without also compressing the index column before it. Use the COMPRESS N clause to create a compressed index.

```
SQL> create index users_idx1 on users(last_name, first_name) compress 2;
```

The prior line of code instructs Oracle to create a compressed index on two columns. You can verify that an index is compressed as follows.

```
SQL> select index_name, compression
from user_indexes
where index_name like 'USERS%';
```

Here is some sample output indicating that compression is enabled for the index.

```
INDEX_NAMECOMPRESS
USERS_IDX1ENABLED
```

Parallelizing Index Creation

In large database environments in which you are attempting to create an index on a table that is populated with many rows, you may be able to greatly increase the index creation speed by using the PARALLEL clause.

```
SQL> create index cust_idx1 on cust(cust_id)
parallel 2
tablespace reporting_index;
```

If you do not specify a degree of parallelism, Oracle selects a degree based on the number set in the CPU_COUNT parameter and set in the value of PARALLEL_THREADS_ PER_CPU.

You can run this query to verify the degree of parallelism associated with an index.

```
SQL> select index_name, degree from user_indexes;
```

You can also disable parallelism, as execution plans might show unwanted parallelism.

```
SQL> alter index cust_idx1 noparallel;
```

Avoiding Redo Generation When Creating an Index

You can optionally create an index with the NOLOGGING clause. Doing so has these implications.

- The redo is not generated that would be required to recover the index in the event of a media failure.

- Subsequent direct-path operations also do not generate the redo required to recover the index information in the event of a media failure.

The following is an example of creating an index with the NOLOGGING clause.

```
SQL> create index cust_idx1 on cust(cust_id)
nologging
tablespace users;
```

The main advantage of NOLOGGING is that when you create the index, a minimal amount of redo information is generated, which can have significant performance implications for a large index. The disadvantage is that if you experience a media failure soon after the index is created (or have records inserted via a direct-path operation) and you restore and recover the database from a backup that was taken prior to the index creation, you see this error when the index is accessed.

```
ORA-01578: ORACLE data block corrupted (file # 4, block # 1044)
ORA-01110: data file 4: '/u01/dbfile/O18C/users01.dbf'
ORA-26040: Data block was loaded using the NOLOGGING option
```

This error indicates that the index is logically corrupt. In this scenario, you must rebuild the index before it is usable. In most scenarios, it is acceptable to use the NOLOGGING clause when creating an index because the index can be re-created without affecting the table on which the index is based.

You can run this query to view whether an index has been created with NOLOGGING.

```
SQL> select index_name, logging from user_indexes;
```

Implementing Invisible Indexes

As discussed in creating an index on the same columns with only one visible, you have the option of making an index invisible to the optimizer. Oracle still maintains an invisible index (as DML occurs on the table) but does not make it available for use by the optimizer. You can use the OPTIMIZER_USE_INVISIBLE_INDEXES database parameter to make an invisible index visible to the optimizer.

Invisible indexes have a couple of interesting uses.

- Altering an index to be invisible before dropping it allows you to quickly recover if you later determine that the index is required.

- You may be able to add an invisible index to a third-party application without affecting existing code or support agreements.

These two scenarios are discussed in the following sections.

Making an Existing Index Invisible

Suppose you have identified an index that is not being used and are considering dropping it. In earlier releases of Oracle, you could mark the index UNUSABLE and then later drop indexes that you were certain weren't being used. If you later determined that you needed an unusable index, the only way to re-enable the index was to rebuild it. For large indexes, this could take a great amount of time and database resources.

Making an index invisible has the advantage of telling only the optimizer not to use the index. The invisible index is still maintained as the underlying table has records inserted, updated, and deleted. If you decide that you later need the index, there is no need to rebuild it; you simply make it visible again.

You can create an index as invisible or alter an existing index to be invisible The following is an example.

```
SQL> create index cust_idx2 on cust(first_name) invisible;
SQL> alter index cust_idx1 invisible;
```

You can verify the visibility of an index via this query.

```
SQL> select index_name, status, visibility from user_indexes;
```

Here is some sample output.

```
INDEX_NAME               STATUS       VISIBILITY
----------------------   -----------  ----------
CUST_IDX1                VALID        INVISIBLE
CUST_IDX2                VALID        INVISIBLE
USERS_IDX1               VALID        VISIBLE
```

Use the VISIBLE clause to make an invisible index visible to the optimizer again.

```
SQL> alter index cust_idx1 visible;
```

Note   If you have a B-tree index on a foreign key column and you decide to make it invisible, Oracle can still use the index to prevent certain locking issues. Before you drop an index on a column associated with a foreign key constraint, ensure that it is not used by Oracle to prevent locking issues. See the "Indexing Foreign Key Columns" section later in this chapter for more information.

Guaranteeing Application Behavior Is Unchanged When You Add an Index

You can also use an invisible index when you are working with third-party applications. Often, third-party vendors do not support customers adding their own indexes to an application. However, there may be a scenario in which you are certain you can increase a query's performance without affecting other queries in the application.

You can create the index as invisible and then use the OPTIMIZER USE INVISIBLE INDEXES parameter to instruct the optimizer to consider invisible indexes. This parameter can be set at the system or session level. Here is an example.

```
SQL> create index cust_idx1 on cust(cust_id) invisible;
```

Now, set the OPTIMIZER_USE_INVISIBLE_INDEXES database parameter to TRUE. This instructs the optimizer to consider invisible indexes for the currently connected session.

```
SQL> alter session set optimizer_use_invisible_indexes=true;
```

You can verify that the index is being used by setting AUTOTRACE to on and running the SELECT statement.

```
SQL> set autotrace trace explain;
SQL> select cust_id from cust where cust_id = 3;
```

The following is some sample output indicating that the optimizer chose to use the invisible index.

```
-------------------------------------------------------------------------
| Id | Operation          | Name      | Rows | Bytes | Cost (%CPU) | Time ---- |
| 0  | SELECT STATEMENT   |           | 1    | 5     | 1 (0)       | 00:00:01 |
|* 1 | INDEX RANGE SCAN   | CUST_IDX1 | 1    | 5     | 1 (0)       | 00:00:01 |
-------------------------------------------------------------------------
```

Keep in mind that an *invisible index* simply means an index the optimizer cannot see. Just like any other index, an invisible index consumes space and resources during DML statements.

Maintaining Indexes

As applications age, you invariably have to perform some maintenance activities on existing indexes. You may need to rename an index to conform to newly implemented standards, or you may need to rebuild a large index to move it to a different tablespace that better suits the index's storage requirements. The following list shows common tasks associated with index maintenance.

- Renaming an index

- Displaying the DDL for an index

- Rebuilding an index

- Setting indexes to unusable

- Monitoring an index

- Dropping an index

Each of these items is discussed in the following sections.

Renaming an Index

Sometimes, you need to rename an index. The index may have been erroneously named when it was created, or perhaps you want a name that better conforms to naming standards. Use the ALTER INDEX ... RENAME TO statement to rename an index.

```
SQL> alter index cust_idx1 rename to cust_index1;
```

You can verify that the index was renamed by querying the data dictionary.

```
SQL> select
table_name
,index_name
,index_type
,tablespace_name
,status
from user_indexes
order by table_name, index_name;
```

Displaying Code to Re-create an Index

You may be performing routine maintenance activities, such as moving an index to a different tablespace, and before you do so, you want to verify the current storage settings. You can use the DBMS_METADATA package to display the DDL required to re-create an index. Here is an example.

```
SQL> set long 10000
SQL> select dbms_metadata.get_ddl('INDEX','CUST_IDX1') from dual;
```

Here is a partial listing of the output.

```
SQL> CREATE INDEX "MV_MAINT"."CUST_IDX1" ON "MV_MAINT"."CUST" ("CUST_ID")
PCTFREE 10 INITRANS 2 MAXTRANS 255 INVISIBLE COMPUTE STATISTICS
```

To show all index DDL for a user, run this query.

```
SQL> select dbms_metadata.get_ddl('INDEX',index_name) from user_indexes;
```

You can also display the DDL for a particular user. You must provide as input to the GET_DDL function the object type, object name, and schema. The following is an example.

```
SQL> select
dbms_metadata.get_ddl(object_type=>'INDEX', name=>'CUST_IDX1',
schema=>'INV')
from dual;
```

Rebuilding an Index

There are a couple of good reasons to rebuild an index.

- Modifying storage characteristics, such as changing the tablespace

- Rebuilding an index that was previously marked unusable to make it usable again

Use the REBUILD clause to rebuild an index. This example rebuilds an index named CUST_IDX1.

```
SQL> alter index cust_idx1 rebuild;
```

Oracle attempts to acquire a lock on the table and rebuild the index. If there are any active transactions that haven't been committed, Oracle cannot obtain a lock, and the following error is thrown.

```
ORA-00054: resource busy and acquire with NOWAIT specified or
timeout expired
```

In this scenario, you can either wait until there is little activity in the database or try setting the DDL_LOCK_TIMEOUT parameter.

```
SQL> alter session set ddl_lock_timeout=15;
```

The DDL_LOCK_TIMEOUT initialization parameter instructs Oracle to repeatedly attempt to obtain a lock (for 15 seconds, in this case).

Transactions can block rebuilding indexes, but the index rebuild itself can block other transactions until the rebuild is complete. To avoid a rebuild from blocking transactions, use the key ONLINE.

```
SQL> alter index cust_idx1 rebuild online;
```

If no tablespace is specified, Oracle rebuilds the index in the tablespace in which the index currently exists. Specify a tablespace if you want the index rebuilt in a different tablespace.

```
SQL> alter index cust_idx1 rebuild tablespace reporting_index;
```

If you are working with a large index, you may want to consider using features such as NOLOGGING, PARALLEL, or both. This next example rebuilds an index in parallel while generating a minimal amount of redo.

```
SQL> alter index cust_idx1 rebuild parallel nologging;
```

Making Indexes Unusable

If you have identified an index that is no longer being used, you can mark it UNUSABLE. From that point forward, Oracle does not maintain the index, nor does the optimizer consider the index for use in SELECT statements. The advantage of marking the index UNUSABLE (rather than dropping it) is that if you later determine that the index is being used, you can alter it to a USABLE state and rebuild it without needing the DDL on hand to re-create it.

Here is an example of marking an index UNUSABLE.

```
SQL> alter index cust_idx1 unusable;
```

You can verify that it is unusable via this query.

```
SQL> select index_name, status from user_indexes;
```

The index has an UNUSABLE status.

```
INDEX_NAME            STATUS
-------------------- --------
CUST_IDX1            UNUSABLE
```

If you determine that the index is needed (before you drop it), then it must be rebuilt to become usable again.

```
SQL> alter index cust_idx1 rebuild;
```

Another common scenario for marking indexes UNUSABLE is that you are performing a large data load. When you want to maximize table-loading performance, you can mark the indexes UNUSABLE before performing the load. After you have loaded the table, you must rebuild the indexes to make them usable again.

Note   The alternative to setting an index to UNUSABLE is to drop and re-create it. This approach requires the CREATE INDEX DDL.

Dropping an Index

If you have determined that an index is not being used, then it is a good idea to drop it. Unused indexes take up space and can potentially slow down DML statements (because the index must be maintained as part of those DML operations). You can always test the performance by making an index invisible first before dropping it. Remember, there are time and resources involved in creating a large index on a widely used table, so the validation is a good setup before hours of poor performance while you rebuild an index. Use the DROP INDEX statement to drop an index.

```
SOL> drop index cust_idx1;
```

Dropping an index is a permanent DDL operation; there is no way to undo an index drop other than to re-create the index. Before you drop an index, it does not hurt to quickly capture the DDL required to re-create the index. Doing so allows you to re-create the index in the event you subsequently discover that you did need it after all.

Indexing Foreign Key Columns

Foreign key constraints ensure that when inserting into a child table, a corresponding parent table record exists. This is the mechanism for guaranteeing that data conforms to parent-child business relationship rules. Foreign keys are also known as *referential integrity constraints*.

Unlike primary key and unique key constraints, Oracle does not automatically create indexes on foreign key columns. Therefore, you must create a foreign key index manually based on the columns defined as the foreign key constraint. In most scenarios, you should create indexes on columns associated with a foreign key. Here are two good reasons.

- Oracle can often make use of an index on foreign key columns to improve the performance of queries that join a parent table and child table (using the foreign key columns).

- If no B-tree index exists on the foreign key columns, when you insert or delete a record from a child table, all rows in the parent table are locked for the duration of the statement for the update or delete. For applications that actively modify both the parent and child tables, this can cause locking and deadlock issues, but for the duration of the statement.

One could argue that if you know your application well enough and can predict that queries will not be issued, that join tables on foreign key columns, and that certain update/delete scenarios are never encountered (that result in entire tables being locked), then by all means, do not place an index on foreign key columns. In our experience, however, this is seldom the case: developers rarely think about how the "black-box database" might lock tables; some DBAs are equally unaware of common causes of locking; teams experience high turnover rates, and the DBA de jour is left holding the bag for issues of poor database performance and hung sessions. Considering the time and resources spent chasing down locking and performance issues, it does not cost that much to put an index on each foreign key column in your application. We know some purists argue against this, but we tend to avoid pain, and an unindexed foreign key column is a ticking bomb.

Having made our recommendation, we'll first cover creating a B-tree index on a foreign key column. Then, we'll show you some techniques for detecting unindexed foreign key columns.

Implementing an Index on a Foreign Key Column

Let's say you have a requirement that every record in the ADDRESS table be assigned a corresponding CUST_ID column from the CUST table. To enforce this relationship, you create the following ADDRESS table and a foreign key constraint.

```
SQL> create table address(address_id number
,cust_address varchar2(2000)
,cust_id number);
--
SQL> alter table address add constraint addr_fk1
foreign key (cust_id) references cust(cust_id);
```

Note   A foreign key column must reference a column in the parent table that
has a primary key or unique key constraint defined on it. Otherwise, you receive
the error ORA-02270: no matching unique or primary key for this
column-list.

You realize that the foreign key column is used extensively when joining the CUST
and ADDRESS tables and that an index on the foreign key column increases performance.
In this situation, you have to create an index manually. For instance, a regular B-tree
index is created on the foreign key column of CUST_ID in the ADDRESS table.

```
SQL> create index addr_fk1
on address(cust_id);
```

You do not have to name the index the same name as the foreign key (as we did in these
lines of code). It is a personal preference as to whether you do that. We feel it is easier to
maintain environments when the constraint and corresponding index have the same name.

When creating an index, if you do not specify the tablespace name, Oracle places the
index in the user's default tablespace. It is usually a good idea to explicitly specify which
tablespace the index should be placed in. The following is an example.

```
SQL> create index addr_fk1
on address(cust_id)
tablespace reporting_index;
```

Determining Whether Foreign Key Columns Are Indexed

If you are creating an application from scratch, it is fairly easy to create the code and
ensure that each foreign key constraint has a corresponding index. However, if you have
inherited a database, it is prudent to check if the foreign key columns are indexed.

You can use data dictionary views to verify if all columns of a foreign key constraint
have a corresponding index. The task is not as simple as it might first seem. For example,
the following is a query that gets you started in the right direction.

```
SQL> SELECT DISTINCT
a.ownerowner
,a.constraint_name cons_name
,a.table_nametab_name
```

```
,b.column_namecons_column
,NVL(c.column_name,'***Check index****') ind_column
FROM dba_constraints a
,dba_cons_columns b
,dba_ind_columns c
WHERE constraint_type = 'R'
AND a.owner = UPPER('&&user_name')
AND a.owner = b.owner
AND a.constraint_name = b.constraint_name
AND b.column_name = c.column_name(+)
AND b.table_name = c.table_name(+)
AND b.position = c.column_position(+)
ORDER BY tab_name, ind_column;
```

This query, while simple and easy to understand, does not correctly report on unindexed foreign keys for all situations. For example, in the case of multicolumn foreign keys, it does not matter if the constraint is defined in an order different from that of the index columns as long as the columns defined in the constraint are in the leading edge of the index. In other words, for a constraint on (COL1, COL2), an index works on either (COL1,COL2) or (COL2,COL1); the order of the same set of columns doesn't matter. Also, an index on (COL1,COL2,COL3) also works because the extra index column is OK as long as the leading columns match.

```
SQL> create index column_test_idx on table1 (col2, col1);
SQL> create index column_test_idx on table1 (col1, col2, col3);
```

Another issue is that a B-tree index protects you from locking issues, but a bitmap index does not. In this situation, the query should also check the index type.

In these scenarios, you need a more sophisticated query to detect indexing issues related to foreign key columns. The query checks the index type and finds the related tables and their indexes to show what the index columns are with the tables and indexes. The following example is a more complex query that uses the LISTAGG analytic function to compare columns (returned as a string in one row) in a foreign key constraint with corresponding indexed columns.

```
SQL> SELECT
CASE WHEN ind.index_name IS NOT NULL THEN
CASE WHEN ind.index_type IN ('BITMAP') THEN
'** Bitmp idx **'
```

```
ELSE
'indexed'
END
ELSE
'** Check idx **'
END checker
,ind.index_type
,cons.owner, cons.table_name, ind.index_name, cons.constraint_name,
cons.cols
FROM (SELECT
c.owner, c.table_name, c.constraint_name
, LISTAGG(cc.column_name, ',' ) WITHIN GROUP (ORDER BY cc.column_name) cols
FROM dba_constraints c
,dba_cons_columns cc
WHERE c.owner = cc.owner
AND c.owner = UPPER('&&schema')
AND c.constraint_name = cc.constraint_name
AND c.constraint_type = 'R'
GROUP BY c.owner, c.table_name, c.constraint_name) cons
LEFT OUTER JOIN
(SELECT
table_owner, table_name, index_name, index_type, cbr
,LISTAGG(column_name, ',' ) WITHIN GROUP (ORDER BY column_name) cols
FROM (SELECT
ic.table_owner, ic.table_name, ic.index_name
,ic.column_name, ic.column_position, i.index_type
,CONNECT_BY_ROOT(ic.column_name) cbr
FROM dba_ind_columns ic
,dba_indexes i
WHERE ic.table_owner = UPPER('&&schema')
AND ic.table_owner = i.table_owner
AND ic.table_name = i.table_name
AND ic.index_name = i.index_name
CONNECT BY PRIOR ic.column_position-1 = ic.column_position
AND PRIOR ic.index_name = ic.index_name)
```

```
GROUP BY table_owner, table_name, index_name, index_type, cbr) ind
ON cons.cols = ind.cols
AND cons.table_name = ind.table_name
AND cons.owner = ind.table_owner
ORDER BY checker, cons.owner, cons.table_name;
```

This query prompts you for a schema name and then displays all foreign key constraints that do not have corresponding indexes. This query also checks for the index type; as previously stated, bitmap indexes may exist on foreign key columns but do not prevent locking issues.

Table Locks and Foreign Keys

Let's look at a simple example that demonstrates the locking issue when foreign key columns are not indexed. First, create two tables (DEPT and EMP) and associate them with a foreign key constraint.

```
SQL> create table emp(emp_id number primary key, dept_id number); SQL>
create table dept(dept_id number primary key);
SQL> alter table emp add constraint emp_fk1 foreign key (dept_id)
references dept(dept_id);
```

Next, insert some data.

```
SQL> insert into dept values(10),
(20),
(30);
SQL> insert into emp values(1,10),
(2,20),
(3,10);
SQL> commit;
```

Open two terminal sessions. From one, delete one record from the child table (do not commit).

```
SQL> delete from emp where dept_id = 10;
```

Then, attempt to delete from the parent table some data not affected by the child table delete.

```
SQL> delete from dept where dept_id = 30;
```

The delete from the parent table hangs until the child table transaction is committed. Without a regular B-tree index on the foreign key column in the child table, any time you attempt to insert or delete in the child table, a table-wide lock is placed on the parent table; this prevents deletes or updates in the parent table until the child table transaction completes.

Now, run the prior experiment, except this time, additionally create an index on the foreign key column of the child table.

```
SQL> create index emp_fk1 on emp(dept_id);
```

You should be able to run the prior two deleted statements independently. When you have a B-tree index on the foreign key columns, if deleting from the child table, Oracle will not excessively lock all rows in the parent table.

Indexes are important tools for performance when querying the data. There are some costs involved when using and creating them, but analyzing the SQL statements and planning the storage and maintenance indexes allow faster data access.

## CHAPTER 9

Views, Duality Views, and Materialized Views

Views are used extensively in reporting applications to present data APIs and subsets of data to users. One could start to look at views as a way of managing data and presenting data sets differently for applications and users to consume the data. It is not just reading the data; the capabilities exist to modify it through the view.

Oracle Database 23ai presents a new feature, JSON Relational Duality, that allows you to present data to applications as a JSON view over the relational tables. Now, you can use the existing relational tables or a relational data model from other systems and leverage JSON duality views for different applications wanting to use JSON or viewing the more flexible data schemas you get with JSON documents. Using the same tables to view data in different formats is a powerful tool that can remove additional steps of data integration and move data out of the database system to provide the JSON documents.

Another type of view that has been part of the Oracle Database for a while now is a materialized view. Materialized views (MVs) allow storing the result set of analytics or complex queries in a table for better performance and easier access to complex aggregations.

These views and objects in the database provide the tools to simplify data access and manage the data in an Oracle Database. This chapter looks at how to implement these views and some of their main use cases.

Implementing Views

A basic view is really a SQL statement stored in the database as an object. Conceptually, when you select from a view, Oracle looks up the view definition in the data dictionary, executes the query the view is based on, and returns the results.

© Michelle Malcher, Darl Kuhn 2024
M. Malcher and D. Kuhn, *Pro Oracle Database 23ai Administration*,
https://doi.org/10.1007/979-8-8688-1038-1_9

In addition to selecting from a view, in some scenarios, it is possible to execute INSERT, UPDATE, and DELETE statements against the view, which results in modifications to the underlying table data. So, in this sense, instead of simply describing a view as a stored SQL statement, it is more accurate to conceptualize a view as a logical table built on other tables or views, or both.

The following are some common uses for views.

- Create an efficient method of storing a SQL query for reuse

- Provide an interface layer between an application and physical tables

- Hide the complexity of a SQL query from an application

- Report to a user only a subset of columns or rows, or both

You should be able to start to see how useful views are for application APIs and how they can provide the needed data sets to applications and users.

Creating a View

You can create views on tables, materialized views, or other views. To create a view, your user account must have the CREATE VIEW system privilege. If you want to create a view in another user's schema, then you must have the CREATE ANY VIEW privilege.

For reference, the view creation example in this section depends on the following base table.

```
SQL> create table sales (
sales_id number primary key
, amnt number
, state varchar2(2)
, sales_person_id number);
```

Also assume that the table has the following data initially inserted into it.

```
SQL> insert into sales values(1, 222, 'CO', 8773),
(20,827, 'FL', 9222);
```

The CREATE VIEW statement is used to create a view. The following code creates a view (or replaces it if the view already exists) that selects a subset of columns and rows from the SALES table.

```
SQL> create or replace view sales_rockies as
select sales_id, amnt, state
from sales
where state in ('CO','UT','WY','ID','AZ');
```

CREATE OR REPLACE VIEW is useful for modifying a view if it exists or creating a new one without verifying it already exists. If you don't want to overwrite existing views, use CREATE VIEW statements.

When you select from SALES_ROCKIES, it executes the view query and returns data from the SALES table as appropriate.

```
SQL> select * from sales_rockies;
```

Given the view query, it is intuitive that the output shows only the following columns and one row.

```
SALES_ID    AMNT        ST
---------- ----------- --
1           222         CO
```

What is not as apparent is that you can also issue UPDATE, INSERT, and DELETE statements against a view, which results in modification of the underlying table data. For example, the following insert statement against the view results in inserting a record in the SALES table.

```
SQL> insert into sales_rockies (
sales_id, amnt, state)
Values (2, 100, 'CO');
```

Additionally, as the owner of the table and view (or as a DBA), you can grant DML privileges to other users on the view. For instance, you can grant SELECT, INSERT, UPDATE, and DELETE privileges on the view to another user, which allows the user to select and modify data referencing the view to another user, which allows the user to select and modify data referencing the view. However, having privileges on the view does not give the user direct SQL access to the underlying tables. Any users granted privileges on the view can manipulate data through the view but not issue SQL against the object the view is based on.

If you create the view using the WITH READ ONLY clause, users cannot perform INSERT, UPDATE, or DELETE operations on the view. This is useful if you use views for reporting and never intend to be used as a mechanism for modifying the underlying table's data; then, you should always create the views with the WITH READ ONLY clause. Doing so prevents accidental modifications to the underlying tables through a view that was never intended to be used to modify data.

Updatable Join Views

The previous example had inserts and data modification on a view with one table defined in the FROM clause of the SQL query. However, this is also possible with multiple tables defined. This is known as an *updatable join view*.

For reference purposes, here are the CREATE TABLE statements for the two tables used in the examples in this section.

```
SQL> create table dept (
dept_id number primary key
, dept_name varchar2(15));
--
SQL> create table emp (
emp_id number primary key
, emp_name varchar2(15)
, dep_id number
, constraint emp_dept_fk
foreign key (dept_id) references dept(dept_id));
```

And let's seed some data for the two tables.

```
SQL> insert into dept values (1, 'HR'),
'IT'),
'SALES');
SQL> insert into emp values (10, 'John', 2),
(20, 'George', 1),
(30, 'Fred', 2),
(40, 'Craig', 1),
(50, 'Linda', 2),
(60, 'Carrie', 3);
```

Here is an example of an updatable join view based on the two prior base tables.

```
SQL> create or replace view emp_dept_v
as
select a.emp_id, a.emp_name, b.dept_name, b.dept_id
from emp a, dept b
where a.dept_id = b.dept_id;
```

Underlying tables can be updated only if the following conditions are true.

- The DML statement must modify only one underlying table.

- The view must be created without the READ ONLY clause.

- The column being updated belongs to the key-preserved table in the join view.

An underlying table in a view is key preserved if the table's primary key can also be used to uniquely identify rows returned by the view. An example with data illustrates whether an underlying table is key preserved. In this scenario, the primary key of the EMP table is the EMP_ID column; the primary key of the DEPT table is the DEPT_ID column. Here is some sample data returned by querying the view.

EMP_ID	EMP_NAME	DEPT_NAME	DEPT_ID
10	John	IT	2
20	George	HR	1
30	Fred	IT	2
40	Craig	HR	1
50	Linda	IT	2
60	Carrie	SALES	3

As you can see from the output of the view, the EMP_ID column is always unique. Therefore, the EMP table is key preserved, and its columns can be updated. In contrast, the view's output shows that it is possible for the DEPT_ID column not to be unique. Therefore, the DEPT table is not key preserved, and its columns can't be updated.

When you update the view, modifications that result in columns that map to the underlying EMP table should be allowed because the EMP table is key preserved in this view.

```
SQL> update emp_dept_v set emp_name = 'Jon' where emp_id = 10;
```

Modifying and Dropping a View

If you need to modify the SQL query on which a view is based, either drop and re-create the view or use the CREATE or REPLACE syntax, as in the previous examples.

For instance, say you add a REGION column to the SALES table.

```
SQL> alter table sales add (region varchar2(30));
SQL> create or replace view sales_rockies as
select sales_id, amnt, state, region
from sales
where state in ('CO', 'UT', 'WY', 'ID', 'AZ')
with read only;
```

The advantage of using the CREATE OR REPLACE method is that you do not have to reestablish access to the view for users with previously granted permissions. Also, you don't have to re-create the view if you do not want to include the new column in the view. However, if you remove a column that the view is using, the view compiles with errors, and you have to re-create the view without the column.

Renaming a view is also possible with the RENAME statement.

```
SQL> rename sales_rockies to sales_rockies_old;
```

You should see this message.

```
Table renamed.
```

It would make more sense if it said "View renamed," but the message in this case does not exactly match the operation.

Dropping a view makes sense if you are no longer using it.

```
SQL> drop view sales_rockies_old;
```

Keep in mind that when you drop a view, any dependent views, materialized views, and synonyms become invalid. Additionally, any grants associated with the dropped view are also removed.

JSON Relational Duality Views

You might see this as a developer topic inserted into a database administration book, but having relational tables and delivering data in different formats while maintaining data consistency and performance is too important to keep to the developers or DBAs. You can use SQL, graph syntax, PL/SQL, JavaScript, or your favorite programming language to access data from the database.

JSON Relational Duality makes it easy to maintain the JSON documents without going back and forth to the database for ID or updates against other documents to ensure data consistency maintained across the board. JSON duality views leverage the relational tables by providing JSON documents using the data you have as part of other applications or the relational tables that you use for transactions.

Also, if you have gotten into the practice of providing data services from the database through APIs or views, this is going to show you how easy it is to use JSON in the Oracle Database and provide JSON documents for applications to read, insert, and modify.

The first part of this chapter demonstrated the basic view concepts with a few examples to implement, create, and maintain views as database objects. Now, let's dive into how to create JSON duality views on some of the same types of tables.

The following are the `create table` statements for these examples.

```
SQL> create table emp (
emp_id number primary key
, emp_name varchar2(30)
, emp_email varchar2(30)
, job_profile varchar2(30));
SQL> create table managers (
Mgr_id number primary key
, manager_name varchar2(30));
SQL> create table dept (
Dept_id number primary key
, dept_name varchar2(30));
SQL> create table teams (
Team_id number primary key
, Dept_id number
, Mgr_id number
, emp_id number
```

```
, constraint fk_dept_id1 foreign key (dept_id) references dept(dept_id)
, constraint fk_mgr_id1 foreign key (mgr_id) references managers(mgr_id)
, constraint fk_emp_id1 foreign key (emp_id) references emp(emp_id));
```

Let's add some data to see the relational data and see what it looks like in JSON.

```
SQL> insert into emp values (10, 'John', 'john@company.com','Developer'),
(20, 'George','george@company.com','Recruiter'),
(30, 'Linda','linda@company.com','DBA');
3 rows created.
SQL> insert into managers values (10,'Michelle'),
(20,'Fred'),
(30,'Amanda');
3 rows created.
SQL> insert into dept values (10, 'Database'),
(20, 'Application Dev'),
(30, 'Sales1');
3 rows created.
SQL> insert into teams values (1, 10, 10, 30),
20,20,10),
30,30,20);
3 rows created.
SQL> select * from emp;
EMP_ID  EMP_NAME    EMP_EMAIL            JOB_PROFILE
------  ----------  ------------------  --------------------

10      John        john@company.com    Developer
20      George      george@company.com  Recruiter
30      Linda       linda@company.com   DBA
```

You can also simply select from the table in JSON formatting.

```
SQL> select JSON {
'emp_id' : emp_id,
'emp_name' : emp_name}
from emp;

JSON{'EMP_ID':EMP_ID,'EMP_NAME':EMP_NAME}
-----------------------------------------------------------
```

```
{"emp_id":10,"emp_name":"John"}
{"emp_id":20,"emp_name":"George"}
{"emp_id":30,"emp_name":"Linda"}
```

Now, you can create a simple duality view on the emp table.

```
SQL> create or replace JSON Duality view emp_v as
select JSON {
'emp_id' : emp_id,
'emp_name' : emp_name,
'emp_email' : emp_email,
'job_profile' : job_profile
}
from emp with (insert, update, delete);
```

Here the SQL syntax was used to create the view, and the insert, update, and delete operations allow you to perform those actions against the view. The relational table is updated as a result.

Select from the view to see the JSON format.

```
SQL> select json_serialize(data pretty) from emp_v;
JSON_SERIALIZE(DATAPRETTY)
----------------------------------------------------------------
{
  "_metadata" :
  {
  "etag" : "B17C5788DC747E44CECADD5BC2102DBB",
  "asof" : "0000000001A0B3CE"
  },
  "emp_id" : 10,
  "emp_name" : "John",
  "emp_email" : "john@company.com",
  "job_profile" : "Developer"
}
{
  "_metadata" :
  {
```

```
  "etag" : "49DA4FE10C57A01EF3F8BC540450813A",
  "asof" : "0000000001A0B3CE"
  },
  "emp_id" : 20,
  "emp_name" : "George",
  "emp_email" : "george@company.com",
  "job_profile" : "Recruiter"
}
{
  "_metadata" :
  {
  "etag" : "335B4B83F68BAF4CF98FDE74EFA634A9",
  "asof" : "0000000001A0B3CE"
  },
  "emp_id" : 30,
  "emp_name" : "Linda",
  "emp_email" : "linda@company.com",
  "job_profile" : "DBA"
}
```

Notice the emp_id is the primary key and additional fields of metadata have been added. The etag can be used for optimistic locking, and it represents the current state of the object. The asof metadata is the system change number (SCN) for consistent reads. If you update the emp, the state of the object has changed for those updated records, and the etag would then change. The etag provides the checks and validations for the updates with no optimistic locking. It really makes it easy to work with high-concurrency systems and scales very nicely.

From the select statement, you can see every row is one employee, and each employee is a JSON document in the view.

Now let's look at a duality view on multiple tables. Also, notice that this uses the graph syntax built into the Oracle Database. This is another way of querying the data. You can also build the view with SQL syntax like with emp_v.

```
SQL> create or replace json duality view emp_dept_v as
    emp @insert
    {
```

```
      emp_id: emp_id
      emp_name:emp_name
job_profile : job_profile
      teams : teams @insert @update @delete
      {team_id: team_id
      dept @update
      {dept_id : dept_id
      dept_name:dept_name}
managers @update
      {mgr_id:mgr_id
      manager_name:manager_name}
      }
      }
};
```

The JSON document is made up of different entities, and the data is shared in the
views. With the insert/update/delete, you can perform these actions on the view, and
that update or insert occurs in the relational tables that populate these views. This
eliminates managing all JSON documents to update every document with the change.
Also, having everything available in the JSON document avoids making more round-trips
to the database to fetch IDs as things change because it is based on the relational table
data. The JSON duality view has all the needed data available, including the changes,
as data is modified through the view to the tables. As you can see, some columns
are excluded from the view, and not all columns from the table are required in the
duality view.

So, what does this view look like? (The first regular SQL statement is just to return the
rows, and then it appears in pretty print so the JSON data is more readable.)

```
SQL> select * from emp_dept_v;

DATA
--------------------------------------------------------------------------
{"_metadata":{"etag":"35477E1A68C1D304B2D758BC1A2A928E","asof"
:"0000000001A07758 {"_metadata":{"etag":"AA9EF15169BED8FD8DABB10C0644912D",
"asof" :"0000000001A07758 {"_metadata":{"etag":"800216E465E7D063FA92E32D08
7C842D","asof" :"0000000001A07758
```

```
SQL> select json_serialize(data pretty) from emp_dept_v;
JSON_SERIALIZE(DATAPRETTY)

{
  "_              :
  metadata" {
    "etag" : "35477E1A68C1D304B2D758BC1A2A928E",
    "asof" : "0000000001A07602"
  },
  "emp_id" : 10,
  "emp_name" : "John",
  "job_profile" : "Developer",
  "teams" :
  [
    {
      "team_id" : 2,
      "DEPT" :
      {
      "dept_id" : 20,
      "dept_name" : "Application Dev",

   281

"MANAGERS" :
        [
          {

   281

     "mgr_id" : 20,

   281

     "manager_name" : "Fred"
        }
      ]
      }
    }
  ]
```

```
}
{
  _metadata"
  {
    "etag" : "AA9EF15169BED8FD8DABB10C0644912D",
    "asof" : "0000000001A07602"
  },
  "emp_id" : 20,
  "emp_name" : "George",
  "job_profile" : "Recruiter",
  "teams" :
  [
    {
      "team_id" : 3,
      "DEPT" :
      {
      "dept_id" : 30,
      "dept_name" : "Sales1",
      "MANAGERS" :
      [
        {
          "mgr_id" : 30,
          "manager_name" : "Amanda"
        }
      ]
      }
    }
  ]
}
{
  "_ metadata"
  { :
    "etag" : "800216E465E7D063FA92E32D087C842D",
    "asof" : "0000000001A07602"
  },
```

```
  "emp_id" : 30,
  "emp_name" : "Linda",
  "job_profile" : "DBA",
  "teams" :
  [
    {
      "team_id" : 1,
      "DEPT" :
      {
      "dept_id" : 10,
      "dept_name" : "Database",
      "MANAGERS" :
      [
        {
          "mgr_id" : 10,
          "manager_name" : "Michelle"
        }
      ]
      }
    }
  ]
}
```

Now let's insert a row into the emp_v for the new employee.

```
SQL> insert into emp_v d (data) values ('
{"emp_id" : 100,
"emp_name" : "Bob",
"emp_email" : "bob@company.com",
"job_profile" : "DBA"}');
SQL> select * from emp;
EMP_ID EMP_NAME    EMP_EMAIL            JOB_PROFILE
------ ---------- ------------------- ----------------

10     John       john@company.com    Developer
20     George     george@company.com  Recruiter
30     Linda      linda@company.com   DBA
100    Bob        bob@company.com     DBA
```

Now, let's insert a row into the emp_dept_v with a new team name.

```
SQL> insert into emp_dept_v d (data)
  values ('
  {"emp_id" : 200,
"emp_name" : "Hope",
  "job_profile" : "Intern",
  "teams": [
  {
  "team_id" : 4,
  "DEPT" :
  {"dept_id" : 30,
  "dept_name" : "Sales"
  }
  }
  ]
  }');
```

Selecting from the emp table shows another entry.

```
SQL> select * from emp;
    EMP_ID      EMP_NAME      EMP_EMAIL            JOB_PROFILE
    ----------  ------------  ------------------   ------------
    100         Bob           bob@company.com      DBA
    200         Hope                               Intern
```

Selecting from the teams table inserts the row with the department and manager.

```
SQL> select * from teams;

    TEAM_ID     DEPT_ID       MGR_ID        EMP_ID
    ----------  ------------  ----------    --------
    1           10            10            30
    2           10            20            20
    3           30            30            20
    4           30            30            200
```

Finally, the JSON duality view shows the JSON data.

```
JSON_SERIALIZE(DATAPRETTY)
-----------------------------------------------------------
      "etag" : "2D5336A00DE24B4F6A2C0F892DE77144",
      "asof" : "0000000001A0BB6A"
  },
  "emp_id" : 600,
  "emp_name" : "Hope",
  "job_profile" : "Intern",
  "teams" :
  [
    {
      "team_id" : 4,
      "DEPT" :
      {
      "dept_id" : 30,
      "dept_name" : "Sales",
      "MANAGERS" :
      [
        {
          "mgr_id" : 30,
          "manager_name" : "Amanda"
        }
      ]
      }
    }
  ]
}
```

Not all fields were inserted, but that data wasn't provided through the view. Depending on the application and how the data is being used, those areas can be handled programmatically, through triggers, or by including the data in the insert.

There are also data dictionary views that provide metadata about the duality views: DBA/ALL/USER_JSON_DUALITY_VIEWS, DBA/ALL/USER_JSON_DUALITY_VIEW_TABS, DBA/ALL/USER_JSON_DUALITY_VIEW_TAB_COLS, and DBA/ALL/USER_JSON_DUALITY_VIEW_LINKS.

```
SQL> select view_name from user_json_duality_views;
VIEW_NAME
-------------------------------------------------------------

EMP_V
EMP_DEPT_V
```

With Oracle Database 23ai, there are simplified ways to handle JSON documents. There are JSON data types, schemas, and functions to view the JSON format more easily. It is easier to use SQL or graph syntax for easier-to-read JSON. Now JSON duality views give applications ways to get and put data, read data, and modify it when necessary while sharing the same data source and avoiding costly integrations and data consistency issues.

Materialized Views

This topic fits into our data management coverage and preparing the data for reporting, other applications, and data services. Materialized views are valuable tools to use in your database environment.

An MV allows you to execute a SQL query at a point in time and store the result set in a table (either locally or in a remote database). After the MV is populated, you can rerun the MV query and store the fresh results in the underlying table. There are ways to automate refreshes as well as real-time MVs.

There are three main uses for MVs.

- Replicating data to offload query workloads to separate reporting databases

- Improving performance of queries by periodically computing and storing the results of complex aggregations of data, which lets users query point-in-time results

- Stopping the query from executing if the query rewrite does not happen

The MV can be a query based on tables, views, and other MVs. The base tables are often referred to as *master tables*. When you create an MV, Oracle internally creates a table (with the same name as the MV) and an MV object (visible in DBA/ALL/USER_ OBJECTS).

MV Terminology

There are many terms related to refreshing MVs. You should be familiar with these terms before implementing the features. Table 9-1 defines the various terms relevant to MVs.

Table 9-1. *MV Terminology*

Term	Meaning
MV SQL statement	SQL query that defines what data are stored in the underlying MV base table.
MV underlying table	Database table that has the same name as the MV and that stores the result of the MV SQL query.
Master (base) table	Table that an MV references in its FROM clause of the MV SQL statement.
Complete refresh	Process in which an MV is deleted from and completely refreshed with an MV SQL statement.
Fast refresh	Process during which only DML changes (against the base table) that have occurred since the last refresh are applied to an MV.
MV log	Database object that tracks DML changes to the MV base table. An MV log is required for fast refreshes. It can be based on the primary key, ROWID, or object ID.
Simple MV	MV based on a simple query that can be fast refresh.
Complex MV	MV based on a complex query that isn't eligible for fast refresh.
Build mode	Mode that specifies whether the MV should be immediately populated or deferred.
Refresh mode	Mode that specifies whether the MV should be refreshed on demand, on commit, or never.
Query rewrite	Feature that allows the optimizer to choose to use MVs (instead of base tables) to fulfill the requirements of a query (even though the query doesn't directly reference the MVs).
Local MV	MV that resides in the same database as the base table(s).
Remote MV	MV that resides in a database separate from that of the base table(s).
Refresh group	Set of MVs refreshed at the same consistent transactional point.

This table is a good reference as you read the rest of the chapter. The examples further explain these terms and concepts.

Just like with other objects in the database and what you saw with JSON duality views, data dictionary views are helpful when working with MVs. Table 9-2 describes the MV-related data dictionary views.

Table 9-2. *MV Data Dictionary View Definitions*

Data Dictionary View	Meaning
DBA/ALL/USER_MVIEWS	Information about MVs, such as owner, base query, last refresh time, and so on
DBA/ALL/USER_MVIEW_REFRESH_TIMES	MV last refresh times, MV names, master table, and master owner
DBA/ALL/USER_REGISTERED_MVIEWS	All registered MVs; helps identify which MVs are using which MV logs
DBA/ALL/USER_MVIEW_LOGS	MV log information
DBA/ALL/USER_BASE_TABLE_MVIEWS	Base table names and last refresh dates for tables that have MV logs
DBA/ALL/USER_MVIEW_ AGGREGATES	Aggregate functions that appear in SELECT clauses for MVs
DBA/ALL/USER_MVIEW_COMMENTS	Any comments associated with MVs
DBA/ALL/USER_MVIEW_DETAIL_PARTITION	Partition and freshness information
DBA/ALL/USER_MVIEW_DETAIL_SUBPARTITION	Subpartition and freshness information
DBA/ALL/USER_MVIEW_DETAIL_RELATIONS	Local tables and MVs that an MV is dependent on
DBA/ALL/USER_MVIEW_JOINS	Joins between two columns in the WHERE clause of an MV definition
DBA/ALL/USER_MVIEW_KEYS	Columns or expressions in the SELECT clause of an MV definition

(*continued*)

Table 9-2. (*continued*)

Data Dictionary View	Meaning
DBA/ALL/USER_TUNE_MVIEW	Result of executing the DBMS_ADVISOR. TUNE_MVIEW procedure
V$MVREFRESH	Information about MVs currently being refreshed
DBA/ALL/USER_REFRESH	Details about MVs refresh groups
DBA_RGROUP	Information about MV refresh groups
DBA_RCHILD	Children in an MV refresh group

Creating Basic Materialized Views

The following are the two most common configurations.

- Creating complete refresh MVs that are refreshed on demand

- Creating fast-refresh MVs that are refreshed on demand

It is important to understand these basic configurations. They lay the foundation for everything else you do with the MV feature.

The SALES table is the basis for the MV examples.

```
SQL> create table sales(
sales_id number primary key
, sales_amt number
, region_id number
, sales_dtt date);
SQL> insert into sales values (1,101,10,sysdate-10),
(2,511,20,sysdate-20),
(3,11,30,sysdate-30);
commit;
```

Keep in mind the performance of these queries, which are being executed thousands/millions of times a day and consuming a large amount of database resources. These examples cannot simulate that but show how to create and maintain these views.

You need both the CREATE MATERIALIZED VIEW and CREATE TABLE system privileges
to create an MV. If a user creating MVs doesn't own the base table, then SELECT access on
the base table is also required to perform an ON COMMIT REFRESH.

Suppose you wanted to create an MV that reports on daily sales. Use the CREATE
MATERIALIZED VIEW...AS SELECT statement to do this. The following statement names
the MV, specifies its attributes, and defines the SQL query it is based on.

```
SQL> create materialized view sales_daily_mv
segment creation immediate
refresh
complete
on demand
as
select sum(sales_amt) sales_amt
, trunc(sales_dtt) sales_dtt
from sales
group by sales_dtt;
Materialized view created.
```

Note   Using an alias with GROUP BY is a new 23ai feature.

Let's look at the USER_MVIEWS data dictionary to verify that the MV was created as
expected. Run this query.

```
SOL> select mview_name, refresh_method, refresh_mode
, build_mode, fast_refreshable
from user_mviews
where mview_name = 'SALES_DAILY_MV';
MVIEW_NAME    REFRESH_ REFRES BUILD_MOD FAST_REFRESHABLE
--------------- -------- ------ --------- -----------------
SALES_DAILY_MV COMPLETE DEMAND IMMEDIATE DIRLOAD_LIMITEDDML
```

If new data is inserted, this MV is refreshed on demand only. To initiate a fast refresh
of the MV, use the REFRESH procedure of the DBMS_MVIEW package. This example passes
two parameters to the REFRESH procedure: the name and the refresh method. C is for
complete, and F is for fast, and to run a fast refresh, the MV needs to have an MV log.

Now, you attempt to initiate a fast refresh of the MV using the REFRESH procedure of the DBMS_MVIEW package. This example passes two parameters to the REFRESH procedure: the name and the refresh method. The name is SALES_DAILY_MV, and the parameter is F (for fast).

```
SOL> exec dbms_mview.refresh('SALES_DAILY_MV','F');
```

Because this MV was not created in conjunction with an MV log, a fast refresh is not possible. The following error is thrown.

```
ORA-23413: table "MV_MAINT"."SALES" does not have a materialized view log
```

Instead, a complete refresh is initiated. The parameter passed in is C (for complete).

```
SOL> exec dbms_mview.refresh('SALES_DAILY_MV','C');
```

The output indicates success.

```
PL/SQL procedure successfully completed.
```

To make this MV fast refreshable, a log needs to be created. Here are the criteria for a fast refreshable MV.

1. A base table is recommended with a primary key. (rowid can be used if there is no primary key.)

2. Create an MV log on the base table.

3. Create an MV as a fast refreshable.

    ```
    SQL> create materialized view log on sales with primary key;
    SQL> create materialized view sales_rep_mv
    segment creation immediate
    refresh
    with primary key
    fast
    on demand
    as
    select
    sales_id
    ,sales_amt
    ,trunc(sales_dtt) sales_dtt
    from sales;
    ```

First, when an MV log is created, a corresponding table is also created that stores the rows in the base table that changed and how they changed (`insert`, `update`, or `delete`). The MV log table name follows the `MLOG$_<base table name>` format.

A table is also created with the `RUPD$_<base table name>` format. Oracle automatically creates this `RUPD$` table when you create a fast refreshable MV using a primary key. The table is there to support the updatable MV feature. You do not have to worry about this table unless you are dealing with updatable MVs (see the Oracle Advanced Replication Guide for more information on updatable MVs). If you're not using the updatable MV feature, you can ignore the `RUPD$` table.

Oracle creates an index with the `<base table name>_PK1` format. This index is automatically created for primary key-based MVs and based on the base table's primary key column(s). If this is a `ROWID` instead of a primary key, then the index name has the format `I_SNAP$_<table_name>` and is based on the `ROWID`. If you do not explicitly name the primary key index on the base table, then Oracle gives the MV table primary key index a system-generated name, such as `SYS_C008780`.

Now that you understand the underlying architectural components, let's look at the data in the MV.

```
SQL> select sales_amt, to_char(sales_dtt,'dd-mon-yyyy')
from sales_rep_mv
order by 2;
```

Here is some sample output.

```
SALES_AMT TO_CHAR(SALES_DTT,'D
---------- --------------------
511 10-jan-2023
101 20-jan-2023
127 30-jan-2023
```

Let's add two records to the base SALES table.

```
SQL> insert into sales values (6, 99, 20, sysdate-6), (7, 127, 30,
sysdate-7);
SQL> commit;
```

At this point, it is instructional to inspect the M$LOG table. You should see two records identifying how the data in the SALES table have changed.

```
SQL> select count(1) from mlog$_sales;
```

There are two records.

```
COUNT(1)
----------
2
```

Next, let's refresh the MV. This MV is fast refreshable, so you call the REFRESH procedure of the DBMS_MVIEW package with the F (for fast) parameter.

```
SQL> exec dbms_mview.refresh('SALES_REP_MV','F');
```

A quick inspection of the MV shows two new records.

```
SQL> select sales_amt, to_char(sales_dtt,'dd-mon-yyyy')
from sales_rep_mv
order by 2;
```

Here is some sample output.

```
SALES_AMT TO_CHAR(SALES_DTT,'D
---------- --------------------
511 10-jan-2023
101 20-jan-2023
127 23-jan-2023
99 24-jan-2023
127 30-jan-2023
```

Additionally, the count of the MLOG$ has dropped to zero. After the MV refresh is complete, those records are no longer required.

```
SQL> select count(1) from mlog$_sales;
```

Here is the output.

```
COUNT(1)
----------
0
```

You can verify the last method whereby an MV was refreshed by querying the USER_ MVIEWS view.

```
SQL> select mview_name, last_refresh_type, last_refresh_date
from user_mviews

order by 1,3;
```

Here is some sample output.

```
MVIEW_NAME               LAST_REF LAST_REFR
----------------------- -------- ----------
SALES_DAILY_MV           COMPLETE 30-JAN-23
SALES_REP_MV             FAST     30-JAN-23
```

Going Beyond the Basics

When you understand the architecture of a fast refresh, you will not have difficulty learning advanced MV concepts. If this is the first time looking at MVs, realizing that an MV's data is stored in a regular database table is important. This helps you understand architecturally what is and is not possible. For the most part, because the MV and MV log are based on tables, most features available with a regular database table can also be applied to the MV table and MV log table. For instance, the following Oracle features are readily applied to MVs.

- Storage and tablespace placement

- Indexing

- Partitioning

- Compression

- Encryption

- Logging

- Parallelism

Numerous MV features are available. Many are related to attributes you can apply to any table, such as storage, indexing, compression, and encryption. Other features are related to the type of MV created and how it is refreshed.

Creating an Unpopulated MV

When you create an MV, you can instruct Oracle whether to initially populate the MV with data. For example, if it takes several hours to build an MV, you may want to define the MV and then populate it as a separate job.

This example uses the BUILD DEFERRED clause to instruct Oracle not to initially populate the MV with the results of the query.

```
SQL> create materialized view sales_mv
tablespace users
build deferred
refresh complete on demand
as
select sales_id, sales_amt
from sales;
```

At this point, querying the MV results in zero rows returned. At some later point, you can initiate a complete refresh to populate the MV with data.

Creating an MV Refreshed on Commit

You may be required, when data are modified in the master table, to have them immediately copied to an MV. In this scenario, use the ON COMMIT clause when you create the MV. The master table must create an MV log for this technique to work.

```
SQL> create materialized view log on sales with primary key;
```

Next, an MV is created that refreshes on commit.

```
SQL> create materialized view sales_mv
refresh
on commit
as
select sales_id, sales_amt from sales;
```

As data are inserted and committed in the master table, any changes are also available in the MV that would be selected by the MV query.

The ON COMMIT refreshable MV has a few restrictions you need to be aware of.

- The master table and MV must be in the same database.

- You cannot execute a distributed transaction on the base table.

- This approach is not supported with MVs that contain object types or Oracle-supplied types.

Also consider the overhead associated with committing data simultaneously in two places; this can affect the performance of a high-transaction OLTP system. Additionally, the base table cannot commit a transaction if there is any problem with updating the MV. For example, if the tablespace in which the MV is created becomes full (and cannot allocate another extent), you see an error such as this when trying to insert it into the base table.

```
ORA-12008: error in materialized view refresh path
ORA-01653: unable to extend table MV_MAINT.SALES_MV by 16 in tablespace...
```

For these reasons, you should use this feature only when you are sure it will not affect performance or availability.

Note   You cannot specify that an MV be refreshed with both ON COMMIT and ON DEMAND. In addition, ON COMMIT is not compatible with the START WITH and NEXT clauses of the CREATE MATERIALIZED VIEW statement.

Creating a Never Refreshable MV

You may never want an MV to be refreshed. For example, you may want to guarantee that you have a snapshot of a table at a point in time for auditing purposes. Specify the NEVER REFRESH clause when you create the MV to achieve this.

```
SQL> create materialized view sales_mv
never refresh
as
select sales_id, sales_amt
from sales;
```

You receive the following error if you attempt to refresh a nonrefreshable MV.

```
ORA-23538: cannot explicitly refresh a NEVER REFRESH materialized view
```

You can alter a never-refreshable view to be refreshable. Use the ALTER MATERIALIZED VIEW statement to do this.

```
SOL> alter materialized view sales_mv refresh on demand complete;
```

You can verify the refresh mode and method with the following query.

```
SQL> select mview_name, refresh_mode, refresh_method from user_mviews;
```

Creating MVs for Query Rewrite

The query rewrite feature allows the optimizer to recognize that an MV can be used to fulfill the requirements of a query instead of using the underlying master (base) tables. If you have an environment in which users frequently write their own queries and are unaware of the available MVs, this feature can greatly help with performance. There are three prerequisites for enabling query rewrite.

- Oracle Enterprise Edition

- Setting database initialization parameter QUERY_REWRITE_ ENABLED to TRUE

- MV either created or altered with the ENABLE QUERY REWRITE clause

This example creates an MV with query rewrite enabled.

```
SQL> create materialized view sales_daily_mv
segment creation immediate
refresh
complete
on demand
enable query rewrite
as
select
sum(sales_amt) sales_amt
,trunc(sales_dtt) sales_dtt
from sales
group by trunc(sales_dtt);
```

You can verify that query rewrite is in use by examining a query's explain plan via the autotrace utility.

```
SQL> set autotrace trace explain
```

Now, suppose a user runs the following query, unaware that an MV exists that already aggregates the required data.

```
SQL> select
sum(sales_amt) sales_amt
,trunc(sales_dtt) sales_dtt
from sales
group by trunc(sales_dtt);
```

Here is a partial listing of autotrace output that verifies that query rewrite is in use.

```
-----------------------------------------------------------------------
| Id | Operation                   | Name          | Cost (%CPU)| Time     |
-----------------------------------------------------------------------
|  0 | SELECT STATEMENT            |               | 3    (0)   | 00:00:01 |
|  1 | MAT_VIEW REWRITE ACCESS FULL | SALES_DAILY_MV | 3    (0)   | 00:00:01 |
-----------------------------------------------------------------------
```

As you can see from the prior output, even though the user selected directly from the SALES table, the optimizer determined that it could more efficiently satisfy the results of the query by accessing the MV.

You can tell if query rewrite is enabled for an MV by selecting the REWRITE_ENABLED column from USER_MVIEWS.

```
SQL> select mview_name, rewrite_enabled, rewrite_capability
from user_mviews
where mview_name = 'SALES_DAILY_MV';
```

If a query is not using the query rewrite functionality, and you think it should be, use the EXPLAIN_REWRITE procedure of the DBMS_MVIEW package to diagnose issues.

Creating a Fast Refreshable MV Based on a Complex Query

In many situations, when you base an MV on a query that joins multiple tables, it is deemed complex and is available only for a complete refresh. However, in some scenarios, you can create a fast refreshable MV when you reference two tables that are joined together in the MV query.

This section describes how to use the EXPLAIN_MVIEW procedure in DBMS_MVIEW to determine whether it is possible to fast refresh a complex query. To help you completely understand the example, this section shows the SQL used to create the base tables. Let's say you have two base tables defined as follows.

```
SQL> create table region(
region_id number
,reg_desc varchar2(30)
,constraint region_pk primary key(region_id));
--
SQL> create table sales(
sales_id number
,sales_amt number
,region_id number
,sales_dtt date
,constraint sales_pk primary key(sales_id)
,constraint sales_fk1 foreign key (region_id) references
region(region_id));
```

Additionally, REGION and SALES have MV logs created on them, as shown next.

```
SQL> create materialized view log on region with primary key;
SQL> create materialized view log on sales with primary key;
```

Also, for this example, the base tables have these data inserted.

```
SQL> insert into region values(10,'East'),
(20,'West'),
(30,'South'),
(40,'North');
--
```

```
SQL> insert into sales values
(1,100,10,sysdate),
(2,200,20,sysdate-20),
(3,300,30,sysdate-30);
```

Suppose you want to create an MV that joins the REGION and SALES base tables as follows.

```
SQL> create materialized view sales_mv
as
select
 a.sales_id
,b.reg_desc
from sales a
    ,region b
where a.region_id = b.region_id;
```

Next, let's attempt to fast refresh the MV.

```
SQL> exec dbms_mview.refresh('SALES_MV','F');
```

This error is thrown.

```
ORA-12032: cannot use rowid column from materialized view log...
```

The error indicates that the MV has issues and cannot be fast refreshed. To determine whether this MV can become fast refreshable, use the output of the EXPLAIN_MVIEW procedure of the DBMS_MVIEW package. This procedure requires that you first create an MV_CAPABILITIES_TABLE. Oracle provides a script to do this. Run this script as the owner of the MV.

```
SQL> @?/rdbms/admin/utlxmv.sql
```

After you create the table, run the EXPLAIN_MVIEW procedure to populate it.

```
SQL> exec dbms_mview.explain_mview(mv=>'SALES_MV',stmt_id=>'100');
```

Now, query MV_CAPABILITIES_TABLE to see what potential issues this MV may have.

```
SQL> select capability_name, possible, msgtxt, related_text
from mv_capabilities_table
where capability_name like 'REFRESH_FAST_AFTER%'
and statement_id = '100'
order by 1;
```

Next is a partial listing of the output. The P (for possible) column contains an N (for no) for every fast refresh possibility.

```
CAPABILITY_NAME            P MSGTXT                      RELATED_TEXT
-------------------------- - ---------------------------- 
REFRESH_FAST_AFTER_INSERT N the SELECT list does not have B
                             the rowids of all the detail tables
REFRESH_FAST_AFTER_INSERT N mv log must have ROWID        MV_MAINT.REGION
REFRESH_FAST_AFTER_INSERT N mv log must have ROWID        MV_MAINT.SALES
```

MSGTXT indicates the following issues. The MV logs need to be ROWID-based, and the ROWID of the tables must appear in the SELECT clause. First, drop and re-create the MV logs with ROWID (instead of a primary key).

```
SQL> drop materialized view log on region;
SQL> drop materialized view log on sales;
--
SQL> create materialized view log on region with rowid;
SQL> create materialized view log on sales with rowid;
--
SQL> drop materialized view sales_mv;
--
SQL> create materialized view sales_mv
as
select
a.rowid sales_rowid
,b.rowid region_rowid
,a.sales_id
,b.reg_desc
from sales a
    ,region b
where a.region_id = b.region_id;
```

Next, reset the MV_CAPABILITIES_TABLE, and repopulate it via the EXPLAIN_MVIEW procedure.

```
SQL> delete from mv_capabilities_table where statement_id=100; SQL> exec
dbms_mview.explain_mview(mv=>'SALES_MV',stmt_id=>'100');
```

The output shows that it is now possible to fast refresh the MV.

```
CAPABILITY_NAME          P MSGTXT    RELATED_TEXT
------------------------------ - -------------------------

REFRESH_FAST_AFTER_ANY_DML        Y
REFRESH_FAST_AFTER_INSERT         Y

REFRESH_FAST_AFTER_ONETAB_DML     Y
```

Execute the following statement to see if the fast refresh works.

```
SQL> exec dbms_mview.refresh('SALES_MV','F');
PL/SQL procedure successfully completed.
```

The EXPLAIN_MVIEW procedure is a powerful tool that allows you to determine whether a refresh capability is possible and, if it is not possible, why it is not and how to potentially resolve the issue.

Oracle Database 23ai also supports fast refresh on ANSI join syntax for MVs. Our query in the example had the following.

```
from sales a
    ,region b
where a.region_id = b.region_id
```

But now this syntax is also valid.

```
from sales a
    join region b
on (a.region_id = b.region_id)
```

Real-Time Materialized Views

It was discussed that materialized views can be fast refreshed, but there can still be a lag. Real-time MVs can roll forward information based on the logs, which is like doing a fast refresh, but it is completing it in real time.

Real-time functionality is available if the following is true.

- QUERY_REWRITE_INTEGRITY is enforced or TRUSTED

- MV is not set to REFRESH ... ON COMMIT

- MV must be able to do a fast refresh

- **ENABLE ON QUERY COMPUTATION** is used

Now, when the MV is queried, the data winds forward of a stale state, making the data appear fresh to the statement. The changes are not persisted in the MV does a refresh.

Oracle Views

This chapter covered the database objects and views. However, these were very different views. A view lets you logically present data to an application, reporting, or other database and data management tools. So, even though views, JSON duality views, and materialized views provide different functionality and have different purposes, they expose data stored in relational tables. JSON Relational Duality gives you the data as JSON documents generated on demand and organized relationally and hierarchically. Materialized views store the snapshot of the data, provide better performance, and can be used to perform analytical queries to also store.

The simplicity of using native database commands to create various views and set up access to these views through normal database security is a great tool to provide the needed data for applications and APIs. Now, with Oracle 23ai, having JSON Relational Duality Views provides standardized, straightforward joins with all sorts of data, including JSON, to state-of-the-art analytics, machine learning, and reporting.

CHAPTER 10

Data Dictionary Fundamentals

The previous chapters in this book focused on topics such as creating a database, strategically implementing tablespaces, managing users, implementing basic security, and working with tables, indexes, and views. You have already accessed the data dictionary views in several SQL queries to do the following.

- Show what users are in the database

- Display the owners of each table and associated privileges

- Show the settings of various database parameters

- Determine which columns have foreign key constraints defined on them

- Display details about materialized view refreshes and lags

In this regard, Oracle's data dictionary is vast and robust. Almost every conceivable piece of information about the physical and logical characteristics of the database, users, objects, and dynamic performance metrics is in the data dictionary. A senior-level DBA must possess and export knowledge of the data dictionary.

It is time to dive into the inner workings of the data dictionary. Knowledge of these workings provides a foundation for understanding your environment, extracting pertinent information, and doing your job.

© Michelle Malcher, Darl Kuhn 2024
M. Malcher and D. Kuhn, *Pro Oracle Database 23ai Administration*,
https://doi.org/10.1007/979-8-8688-1038-1_10

The first few sections of this chapter cover the architecture of the data dictionary and how it is created. Also shown are the relationships between logical objects and physical structures and how they relate to specific data dictionary views. This understanding serves as a basis for writing SQL queries to extract the information needed to be a more efficient and effective DBA. New releases add new dictionary views, and some might be deprecated, so it is important to pay attention to how to use these views and learn about the changes. Finally, several examples illustrate how DBAs use the data dictionary.

Data Dictionary Architecture

If you inherit a database and are asked to maintain and manage it, typically, you inspect the contents of the data dictionary to determine the physical structure of the database and see what events are currently transacting. Besides figuring out what you inherited, these views help to automate processes and troubleshoot problems. Toward this end, Oracle provides two general categories of read-only data dictionary views.

- The contents of your database, such as users, tables, indexes, constraints, privileges, and other objects are sometimes referred to as the static CDB/DBA/ALL/USER data dictionary views. They are based on internal tables stored in the SYSTEM tablespace. The term *static*, in this sense, means that the information within these views changes only as you make changes to your database, such as adding a user, creating a table, or modifying a column.

- A real-time view of activity in the database, such as users connected to the database, SQL currently executing, memory usage, locks, and I/O statistics are based on virtual memory tables called *dynamic performance views*. Oracle continuously updates the information in these views as events take place within the database. The views are also sometimes called the V$ or GV$ views. GV$ views are global views across all nodes in the database system and normally have an additional column to let you know which node they are referring to.

The next two sections describe these types of data dictionary views further.

Static Views

Oracle refers to a subset of the data dictionary views as static and based on the physical tables maintained internally by Oracle. The term *static* can sometimes be a misnomer. For example, the DBA_SEGMENTS and DBA_EXTENTS views change dynamically as the amount of data in your database grows and shrinks. Regardless, Oracle has distinguished between static and dynamic, and it is important to understand this architectural nuance when querying the data dictionary. There are four levels of static views.

- USER

- ALL

- DBA

- CDB

The USER views contain information available to the current user. For example, the USER_TABLES view contains information about tables owned by the current user. No special privileges are required to select from the USER-level views.

At the next level are the ALL static views. The ALL views show you all object information the current user has access to. For example, the ALL_TABLES view displays all database tables on which the current user can perform any type of DML operation. No special privileges are required to query from the ALL-level views.

Next are the DBA static views. The DBA views contain metadata describing all objects in the database (regardless of ownership or access privilege). To access the DBA views, a DBA role or SELECT_CATALOG_ROLE must be granted to the current user.

The CDB-level views provide information about all pluggable databases within a container database. The CDB-level views report across all containers (root, seed, and all pluggable databases) in a CDB. For instance, if you wanted to view all users within a CDB database, you would do so from the root container by querying CDB_USERS. You notice that many static data dictionary and dynamic performance views have a new column, CON_ID. This column uniquely identifies each pluggable database within a container database. The root container has a CON_ID of 1. The seed has a CON_ID of 2. Each new pluggable database created within the CDB is assigned a unique sequential container ID.

The static views are based on internal Oracle tables, such as USER$, TAB$, and IND$. If you have access to the SYS schema, you can view underlying tables directly via SQL. For most situations, you need to access only the static views based on the underlying internal tables.

The data dictionary tables (such as USER$, TAB$, and IND$) are created during the execution of the CREATE DATABASE command. As part of creating a database, the sql.bsq file is executed, which builds these internal data dictionary tables. The sql.bsq file is generally located in the ORACLE_HOME/rdbms/admin directory; you can view it via an OS editing utility (such as vi, in Linux/Unix, or Notepad in Windows).

The static views are created when you run the catalog.sql script (usually, you run this script once the CREATE DATABASE operation succeeds). The catalog.sql script is located in the ORACLE_HOME/rdbms/admin directory. Figure 10-1 shows the process of creating the static data dictionary views.

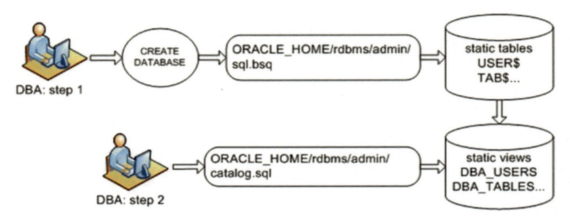

Figure 10-1. *Creating the static data dictionary views*

Dynamic Performance Views

The dynamic performance data dictionary views are colloquially called the V$ and GV$ views. Oracle constantly updates these views and reflects the current condition of the instance and database. Dynamic views are critical for diagnosing real-time performance issues.

The V$ and GV$ views are indirectly based on underlying X$ tables, which are internal memory structures that are instantiated when you start your Oracle instance. Some of the V$ views are available when the Oracle instance is started. For example, V$PARAMETER contains meaningful data after the STARTUP NOMOUNT command has been issued and does not require the database to be mounted or open. Other dynamic views (such as V$CONTROLFILE) depend on information in the control file and contain significant information only after the database has been mounted. Some V$ views (such as V$DB) provide kernel-processing information and thus have useful results only after the database has been opened.

At the top layer, the V$ views are synonyms that point to underlying SYS.V_$ views. At the next layer down, the SYS.V_$ objects are views created on top of another layer of SYS.V$ views. The SYS.V$ views are based on the SYS.GV$ views. At the bottom layer, the SYS.GV$ views are based on the X$ memory structures.

The top-level V$ synonyms and SYS.V_$ views are created when you run the catalog.sql script, which you usually do after the database is initially created.

Figure 10-2 shows the process for creating the V$ dynamic performance views.

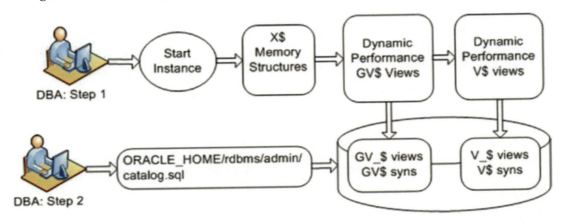

Figure 10-2. *Creating the V$ dynamic performance data dictionary views*

Accessing the V$ views through the topmost synonyms is usually adequate for dynamic performance information needs. On rare occasions, you want to query internal information that may not be available through the V$ views. In these situations, it is critical to understand the X$ underpinnings.

If you work with Oracle Real Application Clusters (RACs), you should be familiar with the GV$ global views. These views provide global dynamic performance information regarding all instances in a cluster (whereas the V$ views are instance-specific). The GV$ views contain an INST_ID column for identifying specific instances in a clustered environment.

You can display the V$ and GV$ view definitions by querying the VIEW_DEFINITION column of the V$FIXED_VIEW_DEFINITION view. For instance, this query displays the definition of the V$CONTROLFILE.

```
SQL> select view_definition from v$fixed_view_definition where view_
name='V$CONTROLFILE';
VIEW_DEFINITION
--------------------------------------------------------------------------
select STATUS , NAME, IS_RECOVERY_DEST_FILE, BLOCK_SIZE, FILE_SIZE_ BLKS,
CON_ID from GV$CONTROLFILE where inst_id = USERENV('Instance')
```

A Different View of Metadata

DBAs commonly face the following types of database issues.

- Database refusing connections because the maximum number of sessions is exceeded.

- An application is hung, apparently because of a locking issue.

- An insert into a table fails because a tablespace cannot extend.

- A PL/SQL statement is failing, with a memory error.

- A user tries to update a record, but a unique key constraint violation is thrown.

- A SQL statement has been running for hours longer than normal.

- Application users have reported that performance seems sluggish and something must be wrong with the database.

This list is a small sample of the typical issues a DBA encounters daily. A certain amount of knowledge is required to efficiently diagnose and handle these types of problems. A fundamental piece of that knowledge is understanding Oracle's physical structures and corresponding logical components.

For example, if a table cannot extend because a tablespace is full, what knowledge do you rely on to solve this problem? You need to understand that when a database is created, it contains multiple logical space containers called *tablespaces*. Each tablespace consists of one or more physical data files. Each data file consists of many OS blocks. Each table consists of a segment, and every segment contains one or more extents. As a segment needs space, it allocates additional extents within a physical data file.

Once you understand the logical and physical concepts involved, you intuitively look in data dictionary views such as DBA_TABLES, DBA_SEGMENTS, DBA_TABLESPACES, and DBA_DATA_FILES to pinpoint the issue and add space as required. In a wide variety of troubleshooting scenarios, your understanding of the relationships of various logical and physical constructs allows you to focus on querying views that help you quickly resolve the problem at hand. To that end, inspect Figure 10-3. This diagram describes the relationships between logical and physical structures in an Oracle database. The rounded rectangle shapes represent logical constructs, and the sharp-cornered rectangles are physical files.

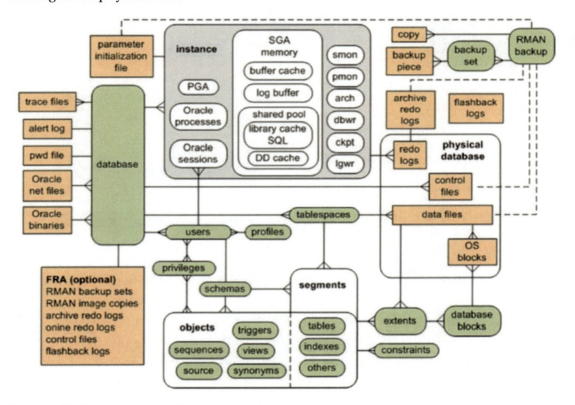

Figure 10-3. *Oracle database logical and physical structure relationships*

Logical objects are viewable from SQL only after the database has been started. In contrast, physical objects can be viewed via OS utilities even if the instance is not started.

Figure 10-3 does not show all the relationships of all logical and physical aspects of an Oracle database. Rather, it focuses on components that you are most likely to encounter daily. This base relational diagram forms a foundation for leveraging Oracle's data dictionary infrastructure.

Keep an image of Figure 10-3 open in your mind; now, add it to Figure 10-4.

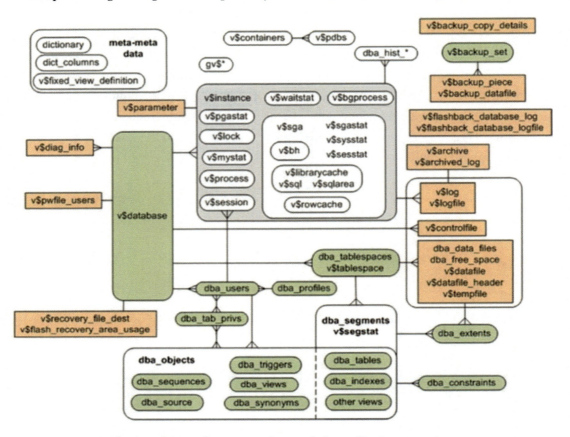

Figure 10-4. *Relationships of commonly used data dictionary views*

Voilà, these data dictionary views map very closely to almost all the logical and physical elements of an Oracle database. Figure 10-4 does not show every data dictionary view. Indeed, the figure barely scratches the surface. However, this diagram provides you with a secure foundation to build your understanding of how to leverage the data dictionary views to get the data you need to do your job.

The diagram shows the relationships between views but does not specify which columns to use when joining views together. You have to describe the tables and make an educated guess on how the views should be joined.

Use the diagram as a guide for where to start looking for information and how to write SQL queries that answer problems and expand your knowledge of Oracle's internal architecture and inner workings. This anchors your problem-solving skills on a solid foundation. Once you firmly understand the relationships of Oracle's logical and physical components and how this relates to the data dictionary, you can confidently address any database issue.

Note   There are several thousand CDB/DBA/ALL/USER static views and more than 900 V$ dynamic performance views.

A Few Creative Uses of the Data Dictionary

Every chapter of this book presents several SQL examples of leveraging the data dictionary to better understand concepts and resolve problems. It is worth showing a few offbeat examples of how DBAs leverage the data dictionary. The next few sections do just that. Keep in mind that this is just the tip of the iceberg: there are an endless number of queries and techniques that DBAs employ to extract and use data dictionary information.

Derivable Documentation

Sometimes, if you are troubleshooting an issue and are under pressure, you need to quickly extract information from the data dictionary to help resolve the problem. However, you may not know the exact name of a data dictionary view or its associated columns. If you are like me, it is impossible to keep all the data dictionary view names and column names in your head. Additionally, if you work with databases in different versions, it is sometimes difficult to keep track of which view may be available with a given release of Oracle.

CDB_OBJECTS was queried to get a count of the number of views for 23ai.

```
SOL> select count(1) from dba_objects where object_name like 'CDB%';

COUNT(1)
----------
2617
```

Books, posters, and Google searches can provide this information. But if you cannot find exactly what you are looking for, you can use the documentation in the data dictionary. You can query from four views in particular.

```
CDB_OBJECTS
DBA_OBJECTS
DICTIONARY
DICT_COLUMNS
```

If you know roughly the name of the view from which you want to select information, you can first query from DBA_OBJECTS. For instance, if you are troubleshooting an issue regarding materialized views and you cannot remember the exact names of the data dictionary views associated with materialized views, you can do the following.

```
SQL> select object_name from dba_objects where object_name like 'DBA_MV%';

OBJECT_NAME
------------------------------------------------------------
DBA_MVIEW_ANALYSIS
DBA_MVIEW_ANALYSIS
DBA_MVIEW_AGGREGATES
DBA_MVIEW_AGGREGATES
DBA_MVIEW_DETAIL_RELATIONS
DBA_MVIEW_DETAIL_RELATIONS
DBA_MVIEW_KEYS
DBA_MVIEW_KEYS
DBA_MVIEW_JOINS
...
DBA_MVREF_STATS
DBA_MVREF_STATS
38 rows selected.
```

That may be enough to get you in the ballpark or have a short list to look through. But often you need more information about each view. This is when the DICTIONARY and DICT_COLUMNS views can be invaluable. The DICTIONARY view stores the names of the data dictionary views. It has two columns.

```
SQL> desc dictionary
 Name                        Null?       Type
 -------------------- ----------  ----------------------
 TABLE_NAME                               VARCHAR2(128)
 COMMENTS                                 VARCHAR2(4000)
```

Again, let's look at the dictionary for a description of the MV data dictionary views.

```
SQL> select table_name, comments
from dictionary
where table_name like 'DBA_MV%';
TABLE_NAME              COMMENTS
------------------ --------------------------------
DBA_MVIEWS             All materialized views in the database
DBA_MVIEW_AGGREGATES Description of the materialized view aggregates
                       accessible to dba
DBA_MVIEW_ANALYSIS     Description of the materialized views
                       accessible to dba
```

In this manner, you can quickly determine which view you need to access. If you want further information about the view, you can describe it; for example,

```
SQL> desc dba_mviews
```

If that does not give you enough information regarding the column names, you can query the DICT_COLUMNS view. This view provides comments about the columns of a data dictionary view; for example,

```
SQL> select column_name, comments
from dict_columns
where table_name='DBA_MVIEWS';
```

Here is a fraction of the output.

```
COLUMN_NAME        COMMENTS

---------------- ----------------------------------------

OWNER              Owner of the materialized view
```

MVIEW_NAME	Name of the materialized view
CONTAINER_NAME	Name of the materialized view container table
QUERY	The defining query that the materialized view instantiates

This way, you can generate and view documentation for most data dictionary objects. The technique allows you to quickly identify appropriate views and columns that may help you in a troubleshooting situation.

Displaying User Information

You may find yourself in an environment with hundreds of databases on dozens of different servers. In such a scenario, you want to ensure that you do not run the wrong commands, connect to the wrong database, or both. When performing DBA tasks, it is prudent to verify that you are connected to the appropriate account and the correct database. You can run the following SQL commands to verify the currently connected user and database.

```
SQL> show user;
SQL> select * from user_users;
SQL> select name from v$database;
SQL> select instance_name, host_name from v$instance;
SQL> show pdbs;
```

An efficient way of staying aware of your environment is to set your prompt automatically, via the login.sql script, to display user and instance information. This example manually sets the SQL prompt.

```
SQL> set sqlprompt '&_USER.@&_CONNECT_IDENTIFIER.> '
```

Here is what the SQL prompt now looks like.

```
SYS@mmdb23>
```

You can also use the SYS_CONTEXT built-in SQL function to extract information from the data dictionary regarding your connected session. The following is the general syntax for this function.

```
SYS_CONTEXT('<namespace>','<parameter>',[length])
```

This example displays the user, authentication method, host, and instance.

```
SYS@mmdb23> select
sys_context('USERENV','CURRENT_USER') usr
,sys_context('USERENV','AUTHENTICATION_METHOD') auth_mth
,sys_context('USERENV','HOST') host
,sys_context('USERENV','INSTANCE_NAME') inst
from dual;
```

USERENV is a built-in Oracle namespace. More than 50 parameters are available when you use the USERENV namespace with the SYS_CONTEXT function. See the *Oracle SQL Language Reference*, which can be freely downloaded from the Technology Network area of the Oracle website (`https://docs.oracle.com/database`) for a complete list of parameters.

Determining Your Environment's Details

Sometimes, when deploying code through various development, test, beta, and production environments, it is handy to be prompted as to whether you are in the correct environment. The technique for accomplishing this requires two files: `answer_yes.sql` and `answer_no.sql`. The following is the content of `answer_yes.sql`.

```
-- answer_yes.sql
PROMPT
PROMPT Continuing...
```

The following is the content of `answer_no.sql`.

```
-- answer_no.sql
PROMPT
PROMPT Quitting and discarding changes...
ROLLBACK;
EXIT;
```

Now, you can insert the following code into the first part of your deployment script; the code prompts you as to whether you are in the right environment and if you want to continue.

```
WHENEVER SQLERROR EXIT FAILURE ROLLBACK;
WHENEVER OSERROR EXIT FAILURE ROLLBACK;
select host_name from v$instance;
select name as db_name from v$database;
SHOW user;
SET ECHO OFF;
PROMPT
ACCEPT answer PROMPT 'Correct environment? Enter yes to continue: '
@@answer_&answer..sql
```

If you type in yes, the answer_yes.sql script executes, and you continue running any other scripts you call. If you type in no, then the answer_no.sql script runs, and you exit from SQL*Plus and end up at the OS prompt. If you press the Enter key without typing, you exit and return to the OS prompt.

Displaying Table Row Counts

When you are investigating performance or space issues, it is useful to display each table's row count. To calculate row counts manually, you would write a query such as this for each table that you own.

```
SQL> select count(*) from <table_name>;
```

Manually crafting the SQL is time-consuming and error-prone. In this situation, it is more efficient to use SQL to generate the SQL required to solve the problem. This next example dynamically selects the required text based on information in the DBA_TABLES view. Create a SQL script file named tabcount_generator.sql with the following code. In SQL*Plus, run that script as a DBA-privileged user with a command like @tabcount_generator. sql. The script prompts you for a username each time, generates a new filename named tabcount_<user>.sql that contains all the necessary SELECT COUNT(*) commands for that schema, and then runs that new script and displays the table names and row counts.

```
UNDEFINE user
SPOOL tabcount_&&user..sql
SET LINESIZE 132 PAGESIZE 0 TRIMSPOOL OFF VERIFY OFF FEED OFF TERM OFF
SELECT
'SELECT RPAD(' || ''''|| table_name ||''''||',30)'
```

```
|| ',' || ' COUNT(1) FROM &&user..' || table_name || ';'
FROM dba_tables
WHERE owner = UPPER('&&user')
ORDER BY 1;
SPOOL OFF;
SET TERM ON
@@tabcount_&&user..sql
SET VERIFY ON FEED ON
```

If the username you provide to the script is INVUSER, then you can manually run the generated script as follows.

```
SQL> @tabcount_invuser.sql
```

Remember that if the table row counts are high, this script can take a long time to run (several minutes).

Developers and DBAs often use SQL to generate SQL statements. This is a useful technique when you need to apply the same SQL process (repetitively) to many different objects, such as all tables in a schema. If you do not have access to DBA-level views, you can query the USER_TABLES view; for example,

```
SPOOL tabcount.sql
SET LINESIZE 132 PAGESIZE 0 TRIMSPO OFF VERIFY OFF FEED OFF TERM OFF
SELECT
'SELECT RPAD(' || '''' || table_name || '''' ||',30)'
|| ',' || ' COUNT(*) FROM ' || table_name || ';'
FROM user_tables
ORDER BY 1;
SPOOL OFF;
SET TERM ON
@@tabcount.sql
SET VERIFY ON FEED ON
```

If you have accurate statistics, you can query the NUM_ROWS column of the CDB/DBA/ALL/USER_TABLES views. This column normally has a close row count if statistics are generated on a regular basis. The following query selects NUM_ROWS from the USER_TABLES view.

```
SQL> select table_name, num_rows from user_tables;
```

One final note: if you have partitioned tables and want to show row counts by partition, use the next few lines of SQL and PL/SQL code to generate the SQL required.

```
UNDEFINE user
SET SERVEROUT ON SIZE 1000000 VERIFY OFF
SPOOL part_count_&&user..txt
DECLARE
counter NUMBER;
sql_stmt VARCHAR2(1000);
CURSOR c1 IS
SELECT table_name, partition_name
FROM dba_tab_partitions
WHERE table_owner = UPPER('&&user');
BEGIN
FOR r1 IN c1 LOOP
sql_stmt := 'SELECT COUNT(1) FROM &&user..' || r1.table_name
||' PARTITION ( '||r1.partition_name ||' )';
EXECUTE IMMEDIATE sql_stmt INTO counter;
DBMS_OUTPUT.PUT_LINE(RPAD(r1.table_name
||'('||r1.partition_name||')',30) || ' '||TO_CHAR(counter));
END LOOP;
END;
/
SPOOL OFF
```

Showing Primary Key and Foreign Key Relationships

Sometimes when diagnosing constraint issues, it is useful to display data dictionary information regarding what primary key constraint is associated with a foreign key constraint. For example, perhaps you are attempting to insert into a child table, an error is thrown, indicating that the parent key does not exist, and you want to display more information about the parent key constraint.

The following script queries the DBA_CONSTRAINTS data dictionary view to determine the parent primary key constraints related to child foreign key constraints. You need to provide as input to the script the owner of the table and the child table for which you want to display primary key constraints.

```
SQL> select
a.constraint_type cons_type
,a.table_namechild_table
,a.constraint_name child_cons
,b.table_nameparent_table
,b.constraint_name parent_cons
,b.constraint_type cons_type
from dba_constraints a
,dba_constraints b
where a.owner = upper('&owner')
and a.table_name = upper('&table_name')
and a.constraint_type = 'R'
and a.r_owner = b.owner
and a.r_constraint_name = b.constraint_name;
```

The preceding script prompts you for two SQL*Plus ampersand variables (OWNER, TABLE_NAME); if you are not using SQL*Plus, you may need to modify the script with the appropriate values before you run it.

The following output shows that there are two foreign key constraints. It also shows the parent table's primary key constraints.

```
C CHILD_TABLE CHILD_CONS PARENT_TABLE PARENT_CONS C
- --------------- -------------------- --------------- -----
R REG_COMPANIES REG_COMPANIES_FK2 D_COMPANIES D_COMPANIES_PK P
R REG_COMPANIES REG_COMPANIES_FK1 CLUSTER_BUCKETS CLUSTER_BUCKETS_PK P
```

When the CONSTRAINT_TYPE column (of DBA/ALL/USER_CONSTRAINTS) contains an R value, the row describes a referential integrity constraint, meaning the child table constraint references a primary key constraint. You use the technique of joining the same table twice to retrieve the primary key constraint information. The child constraint columns (R_OWNER, R_CONSTRAINT_NAME) match another row in the DBA_CONSTRAINTS view that contains the primary key information.

You can also do the reverse of the prior query in this section; for a primary key constraint, you want to find the foreign key columns (if any) that correlate to it. The next script takes the primary key record and looks to see if it has any child records with a constraint type of R. When you run this script, you are prompted for the primary key table owner and name.

319

```
SQL> select
b.table_name primary_key_table
,a.table_name fk_child_table
,a.constraint_name fk_child_table_constraint
from dba_constraints a
,dba_constraints b
where a.r_constraint_name = b.constraint_name
and a.r_owner = b.owner
and a.constraint_type = 'R'
and b.owner = upper('&table_owner')
and b.table_name = upper('&table_name');
```

Here is some sample output.

PRIMARY_KEY_TABLE	FK_CHILD_TABLE	FK_CHILD_TABLE_CONSTRAINT
CLUSTER_BUCKETS	CB_AD_ASSOC	CB_AD_ASSOC_FK1
CLUSTER_BUCKETS	CLUSTER_CONTACTS	CLUSTER_CONTACTS_FK1
CLUSTER_BUCKETS	CLUSTER_NOTES	CLUSTER_NOTES_FK1

Displaying Object Dependencies

Let's say you need to drop a table, but before you drop it, you want to display any objects that are dependent on it. For example, you may have a table that has synonyms, views, materialized views, functions, procedures, and triggers that rely on it. Before making the change, you want to review what other objects are dependent on the table. You can use the DBA_DEPENDENCIES data dictionary view to display object dependencies. The following query prompts you for a username and an object name.

```
SQL> select '+' || lpad(' ',level*2) || type || ' ' || owner || '.' || name
dep_tree
from dba_dependencies
connect by prior owner = referenced_owner and prior name = referenced_name
and prior type = referenced_type
start with referenced_owner = upper('&object_owner')
and referenced_name = upper('&object_name')
and owner is not null;
```

In the output, each object listed has a dependency on the object you entered. Lines are indented to show the dependency of an object on the object in the preceding line.

```
DEP_TREE
+ TRIGGER STAR2.D_COMPANIES_BU_TR1
+ MATERIALIZED VIEW CIA.CB_RAD_COUNTS
+ SYNONYM STAR1.D_COMPANIES
+ SYNONYM CIA.D_COMPANIES
+ MATERIALIZED VIEW CIA.CB_RAD_COUNTS
```

In this example, the object being analyzed is a table named D_COMPANIES. Several synonyms, materialized views, and one trigger are dependent on this table. For instance, the materialized view CB_RAD_COUNTS, owned by CIA, is dependent on the synonym D_COMPANIES, owned by CIA, which is dependent on the D_COMPANIES synonym, owned by STAR1.

The DBA_DEPENDENCIES view contains a hierarchical relationship between the OWNER, NAME, and TYPE columns and their referenced column names of REFERENCED_OWNER, REFERENCED_NAME, and REFERENCED_TYPE. Oracle provides several constructs to perform hierarchical queries. For instance, START WITH and CONNECT BY allow you to identify a starting point in a tree and walk either up or down the hierarchical relationship.

The previous SQL query in this section operates on only one object. If you want to inspect every object in a schema, you can use SQL to generate SQL to create scripts that display all dependencies for a schema's objects. The piece of code in the next example does that. The code uses some constructs specific to SQL*Plus for formatting and output, such as setting the page sizes and line sizes and spooling the output.

```
UNDEFINE owner
SET LINESIZE 132 PAGESIZE 0 VERIFY OFF FEEDBACK OFF TIMING OFF
SPO dep_dyn_&&owner..sql

SELECT 'SPO dep_dyn_&&owner..txt' FROM DUAL;
 --
SELECT
'PROMPT ' || '_____'|| CHR(10) ||
'PROMPT ' || object_type || ': ' || object_name || CHR(10) ||
'SELECT ' || '"' || '+' || '"' || ' ' || '|| LPAD(' || '"' || ' '
|| '"' || ',level+3)' || CHR(10) || ' || type || ' || '"' || ' ' || '"' ||
```

```
' || owner || ' || '"' || '.' || '"' || ' || name' || CHR(10) ||
' FROM dba_dependencies ' || CHR(10) ||
' CONNECT BY PRIOR owner = referenced_owner AND prior name =
referenced_name '
|| CHR(10) ||
' AND prior type = referenced_type ' || CHR(10) ||
' START WITH referenced_owner = ' || '"' || UPPER('&&owner') || '"' ||
CHR(10) ||
' AND referenced_name = ' || '"' || object_name || '"' || CHR(10) ||
' AND owner IS NOT NULL;'
FROM dba_objects
WHERE owner = UPPER('&&owner')
AND object_type NOT IN ('INDEX','INDEX PARTITION','TABLE PARTITION');
--
SELECT 'SPO OFF' FROM dual;
SPO OFF
SET VERIFY ON LINESIZE 80 FEEDBACK ON
```

You should now have a script named dep_dyn_<owner>.sql, created in the same directory from which you ran the script. This script contains all the SQL required to display dependencies on objects in the owner you entered. Run the script to display object dependencies. In this example, the owner is CIA.

```
SQL> @dep_dyn_cia.sql
```

When the script runs, it spools a file with the format dep_dyn_<owner>.txt. You can open that text file with an OS editor to view its contents. Here is a sample of the output from this example.

```
TABLE: DOMAIN_NAMES
+ FUNCTION STAR2.GET_DERIVED_COMPANY
+ TRIGGER STAR2.DOMAIN_NAMES_BU_TR1
+ SYNONYM CIA_APP.DOMAIN_NAMES
```

This output shows that the DOMAIN_NAMES table has three objects dependent on it: a function, a trigger, and a synonym.

The Dual Table

The DUAL table is part of the data dictionary. This table contains one row and one column and is useful when you want to return exactly one row, and you do not have to retrieve data from a particular table; in other words, you want to return a value. For example, you can perform arithmetic operations.

```
SQL> select 34*.15 from dual;
34*.15
----------
5.1
SQL> select sysdate from dual;
SYSDATE
---------
25-JUN-23
```

With Oracle 23ai, the dual table is still available; however, it is no longer needed for such queries. You can now do a SELECT without a FROM clause.

```
SQL> select 34*.15;

   34*.15
   ----------
        5.1
SQL> select sysdate;

SYSDATE
---------
25-JUN-23
```

Annotations

Annotations are new with 23ai. They can be used on database objects. You can annotate a column, index, and view to describe the use and intent of that object and data. If you needed to define that a column was personal information, you can use annotations to highlight that the data should be hidden in a UI, or if you had columns that were automatically capturing modification dates and users, annotations can be used to say the column is for reads but not for inserts and updates. Also, can you imagine if there was intent on an index or specifically why that index was created? The annotations on an index can cover that it is used for a quarterly report or improved the report that the boss runs daily.

These are part of the data dictionary and why this is being discussed here, but they can provide important information for applications in how the data is to be used. Annotations can be added to objects at creation or added or even removed with an alter statement. Let's look at the inventory and emp table used in previous examples.

```
SQL> create table inventory
(inv_id number generated as identity,
inv_desc varchar2(30),
created_dt date default sysdate annotations(system_generated,
allowed_reads_for_filtering );

SQL> create emp
(emp_id number annotations(private_information 'PII hide in UI'),
ename varchar2(50) annotations(name_format 'Last name'),
department_id number);

--Index detail to remember why it was created
SQL> create index emp_dept_idx on emp(deptment_id) annotations (purpose
'Used for yearly bonus report');

--change annotations on a column
SQL> alter table emp modify ename annotations (drop name_format,
add name_format 'last name, first name');

To view
SQL> select object_type, object_name, column_name, annotation_name,
annotation_value
from user_annotations_usage
where object_name in ('EMP');
```

OBJECT_TYPE	OBJECT_NAME	COLUMN_NAME	ANNOTATION_NAME	ANNOTATION_VALUE
TABLE	EMP	ENAME	PRIVATE_INFORMATION	PII hide in UI
TABLE	EMP	ENAME	NAME_FORMAT	last name

The data dictionary is very useful for viewing the objects and configuration of the database. The static information in the CDB/DBA/ALL/USER views provides a ton of information that can even be used in application information about the objects. The dynamic performance views offer a real-time window into events currently transacting in the database. These views provide information about currently connected users, SQL executing, where resources are consumed, and so on. DBAs use these views extensively to monitor and troubleshoot performance issues.

CHAPTER 11

Large Objects

Organizations often deal with substantial files that need to be stored and viewed by business users. Generally, LOBs are a data type suited to storing large and unstructured data, such as text, log, image, video, sound, and spatial data. Oracle supports the following types of LOBs.

- Character large object (CLOB)

- National character large object (NCLOB)

- Binary large object (BLOB)

- Binary file (BFILE)

Now, with Oracle Database 23ai, the size of LOBs inline for tables is 8,000 bytes, and for previous versions, it was 4,000. But you should not necessarily use a LOB data type because of other datatypes, such as JSON, VARCHAR2, or RAW for binary data.

Before "lobbing" you into implementing LOBs, reviewing each LOB data type and its appropriate use is prudent. After that, examples of creating and working with LOBs and relevant features you should understand are provided.

Describing LOB Types

Since earlier versions of Oracle, the ability to store large files in the database has vastly improved with the CLOB, NCLOB, BLOB, and BFILE data types. These additional LOB data types let you store much more data with greater functionality. Table 11-1 summarizes the types of Oracle LOBs available and their descriptions.

327

Table 11-1. *Oracle Large Object Data Types*

Data Type	Description	Maximum Size
CLOB	Character large object for storing character documents, such as big text files, log files, XML files, and so on	(4GB-1)*block size
NCLOB	National character large object; stores data in national character set format; supports characters with varying widths*	(4GB-1)*block size
BLOB	Binary large object for storing unstructured bitstream data (images, videos, and so on)	(4GB-1)*block size
BFILE	Binary file large object stored on the filesystem outside of database; read-only	2^64-1 bytes (OS may impose a size limit that is less than this)

*NCLOB along with the other national character sets are not needed to store multibyte characters. I normally use CLOB and VARCHAR2 with just making sure the sizing is large enough to handle multibyte character.

As you can see from Table 11-1, the maximum size of a LOB can range from 8 TB to 128 TB, depending on how the database is configured.

A CLOB such as text or XML and JSON can also be stored as a CLOB or JSON data type. Using the JSON data type in 23ai allows you to use the data as designed as JSON. In previous releases, you could migrate the JSON from the CLOB to the JSON data type or the relational table. Because, as you saw in a previous chapter, you can just use the relational data to create a JSON duality view.

BLOBs are not human-readable. Typical uses for a BLOB are spreadsheets, documents, images, and audio and video data.

CLOBs, NCLOBs, and BLOBs are known as internal LOBs. This is because these data types are stored inside the Oracle database in data files. Internal LOBs participate in transactions and are covered by Oracle's database security and backup and recovery features.

BFILEs are known as external LOBs. BFILE columns store a pointer to a file on an OS that is outside the database. You can think of a BFILE as a mechanism for providing read-only access to large binary files outside the database on the OS file system.

Sometimes, the question arises as to whether you should use a BLOB or a BFILE. BLOBs participate in database transactions and can be backed up, restored, and recovered by Oracle. BFILEs do not participate in the database transactions, are read-only, and are not covered by backup and recovery of the database. BFILEs are more appropriate for large binary files that are read-only and that do not change while an application is running. For instance, you may have large binary video files that are referenced by a database application. In this scenario, the business determines that you do not need to create and maintain a 500 TB database when all the application really needs is a pointer (stored in the database) to the locations of the large files on disk.

Illustrating LOBs, Locators, Indexes, and Chunks

Internal LOBs (CLOB, NCLOB, BLOB) store data in pieces called *chunks*. A chunk is the smallest unit of allocation for a LOB and is made up of one or more database blocks. LOB locators are stored in rows containing a LOB column. The LOB locator points to a LOB index. The LOB index stores information regarding the location of LOB chunks. When a table is queried, the database uses the LOB locator and associated LOB index to locate the appropriate LOB chunks. Figure 11-1 shows the relationship between a table, a row, a LOB locator, and a LOB locator's associated index and chunks.

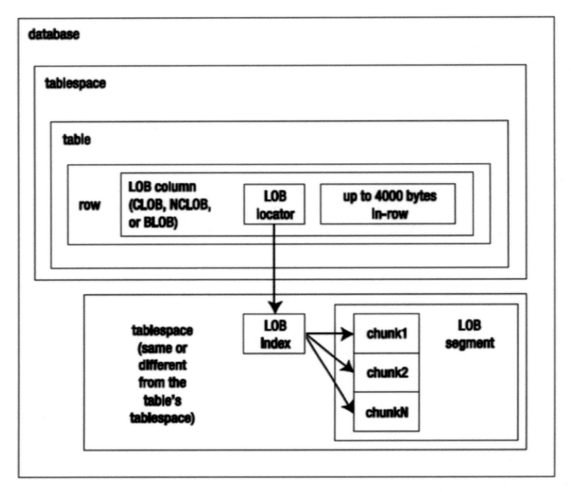

Figure 11-1. *Relationship of table, row, LOB locator, LOB index, and LOB segment*

The LOB locator for a BFILE stores the directory path and filename on the OS. Figure 11-2 shows a BFILE LOB locator that references a file on the OS.

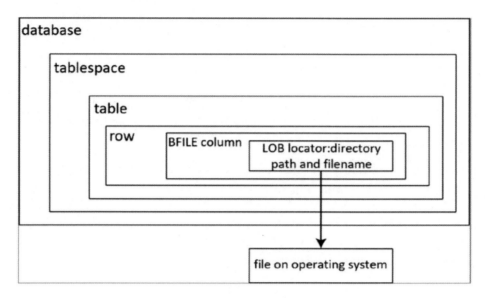

Figure 11-2. *The BFILE LOB locator contains information for locating a file on the OS*

Note   The DBMS_LOB package performs operations on LOBs through the LOB locator.

SecureFiles

LOBs have two storage architectures: the original BasicFiles and the newer SecureFiles. With Oracle 23ai, you need to be using SecureFiles. Unless you are using an ancient version of Oracle, you should always use the SecureFiles architecture, which has better performance and advanced features, including the following.

- Encryption (requires Oracle Advanced Security Option)

- Compression (requires Oracle Advanced Compression Option)

- Deduplication (requires Oracle Advanced Compression Option)

SecureFiles encryption lets you transparently encrypt LOB data (just like other data types). The compression feature allows significant space savings. The deduplication feature eliminates duplicate LOBs that otherwise would be stored multiple times.

You need to do a small amount of planning before using SecureFiles. Specifically, using SecureFiles requires the following.

- A SecureFiles LOB must be stored in a tablespace using ASSM.

- The `DB_SECUREFILE` initialization parameter controls whether a SecureFiles file can be used and defines your database's default LOB architecture.

To create an ASSM-enabled tablespace, specify the `SEGMENT SPACE MANAGEMENT AUTO` clause, which is the default. The following is an example.

```
SOL> create tablespace lob_data
datafile '/uoi/dbfile/db23ai/lob_dataoi.dbf'
size iooom
extent management local
uniform size im
segment space management auto;
```

If you have existing tablespaces, you can verify the use of ASSM by querying the `DBA_TABLESPACES` view. The `SEGMENT_SPACE_MANAGEMENT` column should have AUTO value for any tablespaces you want to use with SecureFiles.

```
SOL> select tablespace_name, segment_space_management from dba_tablespaces;
```

Also, SecureFiles usage is governed by the `DB_SECUREFILE` database parameter. You can use either `ALTER SYSTEM` or `ALTER SESSION` to modify the value of `DB_SECUREFILE`. Table 11-2 describes the valid values for `DB_SECUREFILE`.

Table 11-2. *Description of DB_SECUREFILE Settings*

DB_SECUREFILESetting	Description
NEVER	Creates the LOB as a BasicFiles type, regardless of whether the SECUREFILE option is specified. All SecureFiles LOB-specific options like compress and encrypt will throw an exception.
PERMITTED	Allows creation of SecureFiles LOBs.
PREFERRED	Default value; specifies that all LOBs are created as a SecureFiles type, unless otherwise stated.
ALWAYS	Creates the LOB as a SecureFiles type, unless the underlying tablespace is not using ASSM.
IGNORE	Ignores the SecureFiles option, along with any SecureFiles settings, creates a LOB as a BasicFiles type. All SecureFiles LOB options are ignored.
FORCE	Attempts to create all LOBs as SecureFiles LOBs even if users specify BASICFILE. This option is not recommended, and PREFERRED or ALWAYS should be used.

Creating a Table with a LOB Column

The default underlying LOB architecture is SecureFiles. It is recommended to create a LOB as a SecureFiles. As discussed previously, SecureFiles allows you to use features such as compression and encryption. The DB_SECUREFILE parameter is not required, but you can explicitly state which LOB architecture to implement in the create statement.

```
SQL> create table patchmain (
patch_id number
, patch_desc clob)
lob(patch_desc) store as securefile (tablespace lob_data);
```

If the tablespace is not specified, the LOB segment is stored in the same tablespace as its table.

Before viewing the data dictionary details regarding the LOB columns, insert a record into the table to ensure that segment information is available. The following is an example.

```
SQL> insert into patchmain values(1,'clob text');
```

You can now verify a LOB's architecture by querying the USER_SEGMENTS view.

```
SQL> select segment_name, segment_type, segment_subtype
from user_segments;
```

Figure 11-3 shows some sample output indicating that a LOB segment is a SecureFiles type.

SEGMENT_NAME	SEGMENT_TYPE	SEGMENT_SU
PATCHMAIN	TABLE	ASSM
SYS_IL0000022340C00002$$	LOBINDEX	ASSM
SYS_LOB0000022340C00002$$	LOBSEGMENT	SECUREFILE

You can also query the USER_LOBS view to verify the SecureFiles LOB architecture:

```
SQL> select table_name, segment_name, index_name, securefile, in_row from
user_lobs;
```

Here is the output:

TABLE_NAME	SEGMENT_NAME	INDEX_NAME	SEC	IN_
PATCHMAIN	SYS_LOB0000022340C00002$$	SYS_IL0000022340C00002$$	YES	YES

Figure 11-3. *Sample output*

Implementing a Partitioned LOB

You can create a partitioned table that has a LOB column. Doing so lets you spread a LOB across multiple tablespaces. Such partitioning helps balance I/O, maintenance, and backup and recovery operations.

All partitioning schemes supported by Oracle are fully supported on LOBs. The next example creates a LIST-partitioned table in which LOB column data is stored in tablespaces separate from those of the table data.

```
SQL> CREATE TABLE patchmain(
patch_id NUMBER
,region VARCHAR2(16)
,patch_desc CLOB)
LOB(patch_desc) STORE AS (TABLESPACE patch1)
PARTITION BY LIST (REGION) (
PARTITION p1 VALUES ('EAST')
LOB(patch_desc) STORE AS SECUREFILE
(TABLESPACE patch1 COMPRESS HIGH)
TABLESPACE inv_data1
,
PARTITION p2 VALUES ('WEST')
LOB(patch_desc) STORE AS SECUREFILE
(TABLESPACE patch2 DEDUPLICATE NOCOMPRESS)
TABLESPACE inv_data2
,
PARTITION p3 VALUES (DEFAULT)
LOB(patch_desc) STORE AS SECUREFILE
(TABLESPACE patch3 COMPRESS LOW)
TABLESPACE inv data3
);
```

Note that each LOB partition has its own storage options; again, it is optional, but the default is in the same tablespace as the table. You can view the details about the LOB partitions as shown next.

```
SQL> select table_name, column_name, partition_name, tablespace_name
,compression, deduplication
from user_lob_partitions;
```

Here is some sample output.

TABLE_NAME	COLUMN_NAME	PARTITION_	TABLESPACE_NAME	COMPRE	DEDUPLICATION
PATCHMAIN	PATCH_DESC	P1	PATCH1	HIGH	NO
PATCHMAIN	PATCH_DESC	P2	PATCH2	NO	LOB
PATCHMAIN	PATCH_DESC	P3	PATCH3	LOW	NO

You can also view DBA/ALL/USER_PART_LOBS for information about partitioned LOBs.

You can change the storage characteristics of a partitioned LOB column after it is created. To do so, use the ALTER TABLE ... MODIFY PARTITION statement. You can have compression and deduplication as well.

```
SQL> alter table patchmain modify partition p2 lob(patch_desc) (compress high);
SQL> alter table patchmain modify partition p3 lob(patch_desc)
(deduplicate lob);
```

You can transparently encrypt a SecureFiles LOB column (just like any other column). You can also use tablespace encryption to encrypt the tablespace used for your table and LOBs. The ENCRYPT clause enables Secure Files encryption, using Oracle Transparent Data Encryption (TDE). To do this at the column level or tablespace level, you need to enable a common keystore for the CDB and PDBs using united mode so you can manage the keys in the common keystore.

The Oracle Base Database service creates the keystore when it creates the database for the TDE. The parameters WALLET_ROOT and TDE_CONFIGURATION have the details of the configuration.

```
SQL> show parameter wallet_root
NAME            TYPE        VALUE
-------------   ---------   ------------------------------------------------
wallet_root     string      /opt/oracle/dcs/commonstore/ wallets/db23ai_db23ai
SQL> show parameter tde_configuration
NAME              TYPE            VALUE
-------------   -------------   ------------------------------------------
tde_configuration string                    keystore_configuration=FILE
```

If the database was not created by creating a keystore, you can create the keystore with the following commands.

```
SQL> administer key management create keystore '/opt/oracle/dcs/
commonstore/wallets/db23ai_db23ai/tde' identified by "Cr4zyPa$$word1";
```

Then, the PDB needs to have the keystore enabled and open.

```
SQL> administer key management set keystore open identified by
"Cr4zyPa$$word1";
```

After the TDE wallet configuration is all set up, a table can be created with an encrypted column.

```
SQL> create table patchmain(
patch_id number
, patch_desc clob encrypt)
lob (patch_desc) store as securefile;
```

You can also alter a column to enable encryption.

```
SQL> alter table patchmain modify (patch_desc clob encrypt);
```

The tablespace can be created with encryption.

```
SQL> create tablespace lob_data encryption using 'AES256' encrypt;
```

Note   Partitioning, advanced compression, and advanced security are extra-cost options available only with the Oracle Enterprise Edition.

Maintaining LOB Columns

The following sections describe some common maintenance tasks that are performed on LOB columns or that otherwise involve LOB columns, including moving columns between tablespaces and adding new LOB columns to a table.

Moving a LOB Column

As mentioned previously, if you create a table with a LOB column and do not specify a tablespace, then, by default, the LOB is created in the same tablespace as its table. If the LOB column has started to consume large amounts of disk space and the DBA didn't think about it before, you can use the ALTER TABLE ... MOVE ... STORE AS statement to move a LOB column to a different tablespace.

```
SOL> alter table patchmain
move lob(patch_desc)
store as securefile (tablespace lob_data2);
```

You can verify that the LOB was moved by querying USER_LOBS.

```
SQL> select table_name, column_name, tablespace_name from user_lobs;
```

To summarize, if the LOB column is populated with large amounts of data, you almost always want to store the LOB in a tablespace separate from the rest of the table data. The LOB data has different growth and storage requirements in these scenarios and is best maintained in its own tablespace.

Adding a LOB Column

If you have an existing table to which you want to add a LOB column, use the ALTER TABLE ... ADD statement. The next statement adds the INV_IMAGE column to a table.

```
SQL> alter table patchmain add(inv_image blob);
```

This statement is fine for quickly adding a LOB column to a development environment. For anything else, you should specify the storage characteristics. For instance, this command specifies the LOB tablespace.

```
SQL> alter table patchmain add(inv_image blob) lob(inv_image) store as
securefile(tablespace lob_data);
```

Removing a LOB Column

You may have a scenario where your business requirements change and you no longer need a column. Before you remove a column, consider renaming it so that you can better identify whether any applications or users are still accessing it. LOBs have larger amounts (really, sizes) of data, and restoring can take longer.

```
SQL> alter table patchmain rename column patch_desc to patch_desc_old;
```

After you determine that nobody is using the column, use the ALTER TABLE ... DROP statement to only remove that column.

```
SQL> alter table patchmain drop (patch_desc_old);
```

You can also remove a LOB column by dropping and re-creating a table (without the LOB column). This, of course, permanently removes any data as well.

Also, keep in mind that if your recycle bin is enabled, when you do not drop a table with the PURGE clause, space is still consumed by the dropped table. If you want to remove the space associated with the table, use the PURGE clause or purge the recycle bin after dropping the table.

Caching LOBs

By default, Oracle does not cache LOBs in memory when reading and writing LOB columns. You can change the default behavior by setting the cache-related storage options. This example specifies that Oracle should cache a LOB column in memory.

```
SQL> create table patchmain (
patch_id number
, patch_desc clob)
lob(patch_desc) store as (tablespace lob_data cache);
```

You can verify LOB caching with this query.

```
SQL> select table_name, column_name, cache from user_lobs;
```

Here is some sample output.

TABLE_NAME	COLUMN_NAME	CACHE
PATCHMAIN	PATCH_DESC	YES

Storing LOBs In and Out of a Row

By default, up to 8,000 bytes of a LOB column are stored inline with the table row. Prior to 23ai, it was up to 4,000 bytes. If the LOB is more than 8,000 bytes, then Oracle automatically stores it outside the row data. The main advantage of storing a LOB in a row is that small LOBs require less I/O because Oracle does not have to search out of the row for the LOB data.

However, storing LOB data in a row is not always desirable. The disadvantage of storing LOBs in a row is that the table row sizes are potentially longer. This can affect the performance of full-table scans, range scans, and updates to columns other than the LOB column. In these situations, you may want to disable storage in the row. For example, you explicitly instruct Oracle to store the LOB outside the row with the DISABLE STORAGE IN ROW clause.

```
SQL> create table patchmain(
patch_id number
, patch_desc clob
, lob_file blob)
lob(patch_desc, lob_file)
store as (
tablespace lob_data
disable storage in row);
```

ENABLE STORAGE IN ROW is enabled by default and stores up to 8,000 bytes of a LOB in the table row. The LOB locator is always stored inline with the row, even if you specify DISABLE STORAGE IN ROW.

You cannot modify the LOB storage in a row after the table has been created. The only ways to alter storage in a row are to move the LOB column or drop and re-create the table. This example alters the storage in a row by moving the LOB column.

```
SQL> alter table patchmain
move lob(patch_desc)
store as (enable storage in row);
```

You can verify the in-row storage via the IN_ROW column of USER_LOBS.

```
SQL> select table_name, column_name, tablespace_name, in_row from user_lobs;
TABLE_NAME    COLUMN_NAME    TABLESPACE_NAME    IN_ROW
-----------   ------------   ----------------   ---------------

PATCHMAIN     LOG_FILE       LOB_DATA           YES
PATCHMAIN     PATCH_DESC     LOB_DATA           YES
```

Viewing LOB Metadata

You can use any DBA/ALL/USER_LOBS views to display information about LOBs in your database.

```
SQL> select table_name, column_name, index_name, tablespace_name
from all_lobs
order by table_name;
```

Also, remember that a LOB segment has a corresponding index segment.

```
SQL> select segment_name, segment_type, tablespace_name
from user_segments
where segment_name like 'SYS_LOB%'
or segment_name like 'SYS_IL%';
```

This way, you can query both the segment and the index in the DBA/ALL/USER_SEGMENTS views for LOB information.

You can use the DBA/ALL/USER_SEGMENTS to get the space consumed by the LOB segment. Here is a sample query.

```
SQL> select segment_name, segment_type, segment_subtype, bytes/1024/1024
meg_bytes
from user_segments;
```

You can modify the query to report on only LOBs by joining to the DBA/ALL/USER_LOBS view.

```
SQL> select a.table_name, a.column_name, a.segment_name, a.index_name
,b.bytes/1024/1024 meg_bytes
from user_lobs a, user_segments b
where a.segment_name = b.segment_name;
```

You can also use the `DBMS_SPACE.SPACE_USAGE` package and procedure to report on the blocks being used by a LOB.

Loading LOBs

Loading LOB data is not typically the DBA's job, but you should be familiar with the techniques used to populate LOB columns. Developers may come to you for help with troubleshooting, performance, or space-related issues.

Loading a CLOB

First, create an Oracle database directory object that points to the OS directory in which the CLOB file is stored. This directory object is used when loading the CLOB. In this example, the Oracle directory object is named LOAD_LOB, and the OS directory is / oradata/oracle/lob.

```
SOL> create or replace directory load_lob as '/oradata/oracle/lob';
```

Note   For directories you can also use the same pre-existing directories for DATA_PUMP_DIR.

For reference, listed next is the DDL used to create the table in which the CLOB file is loaded.

```
SOL> create table patchmain(
patch_id number primary key
, patch_desc clob
, patch_file blob)
lob(patch_desc, patch_file)
store as securefile (compress low) tablespace lob_data;
```

This example also uses a sequence named PATCH_SEO. Sequences are one way to manage primary keys, or you can use an IDENTITY column. Here is the sequence creation script.

```
SQL> create sequence patch_seq;
```

The following code uses the DBMS_LOB package to load a text file (patch.txt) into a CLOB column. In this example, the table name is PATCHMAIN, and the CLOB column is PATCH_DESC.

```
SQL> declare
src_clb bfile; -- point to source CLOB on file system
dst_clb clob; -- destination CLOB in table
src_doc_name varchar2(300) := 'patch.txt';
src_offset integer := 1; -- where to start in the source CLOB
dst_offset integer := 1; -- where to start in the target CLOB
lang_ctx integer := dbms_lob.default_lang_ctx;
warning_msg number; -- returns warning value if bad chars
begin
src_clb := bfilename('LOAD_LOB',src_doc_name); -- assign pointer to file
--
insert into patchmain(patch_id, patch_desc) -- create LOB placeholder
values(patch_seq.nextval, empty_clob())
returning patch_desc into dst_clb;
--
dbms_lob.open(src_clb, dbms_lob.lob_readonly); -- open file
--
-- load the file into the LOB
dbms_lob.loadclobfromfile(
dest_lob => dst_clb,
src_bfile => src_clb,
amount => dbms_lob.lobmaxsize,
dest_offset => dst_offset,
src_offset => src_offset,
bfile_csid => dbms_lob.default_csid,
lang_context => lang_ctx,
warning => warning_msg
```

```
);
dbms_lob.close(src_clb); -- close file
--
dbms_output.put_line('Wrote CLOB: ' || src_doc_name);
end;
/
```

You can place this code in a file and execute it from the SQL command prompt. In this example, the file that contains the code is named clob.sql.

```
SQL> set serverout on size 1000000
SQL> @clob.sql
```

Here is the expected output.

```
Wrote CLOB: patch.txt
PL/SQL procedure successfully completed.
```

You can also use SQL*Loader to load the data. Let's examine an example control and parameter file for loading BFILE.

SQL*Loader needs a parfile and control file. The parfile calls the control file. The control file shown next, load_bfile.ctl, has the filename, table name, and details about the file, such as the field separator. The parfile, load_bfile.par, has details about user connection, control file, and log files.

```
$ view load_bfile.ctl
LOAD DATA
INFILE bfile_example.dat
INTO TABLE patchmain
FIELDS TERMINATED BY ','
( patch_id INTEGER EXTERNAL(6),
patch_file BFILE (DirName, FileName),
FileName FILLER CHAR(30), DirName FILLER CHAR(30) )

$ view load_bfile.par
userid=dev1@db23pdb/Pa$$wOrd!
control=load_bfile.ctl
```

```
log=load_bfile.log
bad=load_bfile.bad
data=bfile_example.dat
direct=true
```

After the parfile and control file are set, it is just a command line to call `sqlldr`.

```
$ sqlldr parfile=load_bfile.par
```

Reading BFILEs

As discussed previously, a `BFILE` data type is simply a column in a table that stores a pointer to an OS file. A `BFILE` provides you with read-only access to a binary file on disk. To access a `BFILE`, you must first create a directory object. Next, a table is created that contains a `BFILE` data type.

```
SQL> create table patchmain (patch_id number
, patch_file bfile);
```

For this example, a file named `patch.zip` is located in the directory. You make Oracle aware of the binary file by inserting a record into the table using the directory object and the filename.

```
SQL> insert into patchmain values(1, bfilename('LOAD_LOB','patch.zip'));
```

Now, you can access the `BFILE` via the `DBMS_LOB` package. For instance, if you want to verify that the file exists or display the length of the `LOB`, you can do so as follows.

```
SQL> select dbms_lob.fileexists(bfilename('LOAD_LOB','patch.zip'));
SQL> select dbms_lob.getlength(patch_file) from patchmain;
```

In this manner, the binary file behaves like a `BLOB`. The big difference is that the binary file is not stored within the database.

Oracle lets you store large objects in databases via various `LOB` data types. `LOB`s facilitate storing, managing, and retrieving video clips, images, movies, Word documents, large text files, and so on.

CHAPTER 12

Containers and Pluggables

Oracle Multitenant was introduced in Oracle Database 12c. Now with 23ai it is the only supported architecture. You have already learned how to install Oracle Databases and create pluggable databases with this architecture. A multitenant container database (CDB) can house one or more pluggable databases (PDB). A container is a collection of metadata and data files within a CDB.

A CDB is the container for the resources of the database, and you should view it as the database for the processes, overall memory, and CPU allocation. One set of processes starts with each CDB, and the memory is allocated to the CDB to be used by each PDB. Resource management is discussed later and allows a certain allocation of memory and CPUs to each of the PDBs; otherwise, it is shared as needed across all of the PDBs in the one CDB.

Instead of having multiple database instances on a server, one or a few CDBs can be created to contain all the PDBs. PDBs are separate from each other with data and users so that they do not need their own CDB for isolation.

The Oracle 23ai Database must either contain or be able to be contained; in other words, the database needs to be a container, CDB (or contained in a container, such as a pluggable PDB database), or application container. Oracle 19c was the last database to support noncontainer databases. There are three types of containers.

- A CDB contains one or more PDBs and can contain application containers.

- A PDB is a pluggable, portable group of schemas and objects and, optionally, objects available for an application container.

- An application container is optional but is a way to organize all of the PDBs, data, and metadata for one or more applications.

347

© Michelle Malcher, Darl Kuhn 2024
M. Malcher and D. Kuhn, *Pro Oracle Database 23ai Administration*,
https://doi.org/10.1007/979-8-8688-1038-1_12

As you created a database in 23ai, you created a CDB with one PDB. The CDB had a set of control files, online redo log files, and data files. Every CDB contains a master set of data files and metadata known as the *root container*. Each CDB also contains a seed PDB, which is used as a template for creating other PDBs. Each CDB consists of one master root container, one seed PDB, and one or more PDBs or application containers. Each CDB consists of the following elements.

- One root container, named CDB$ROOT. The root contains the master set of data dictionary views, which have metadata regarding the root and every child PDB with the CDB.

- One static seed container, named PDB$SEED. This container is a template for providing data files and metadata to create new PDBs within CDB.

- One or more PDBs. Each PDB is self-contained and functions like an isolated non-CDB database. Additionally, each PDB contains its own data files and application objects (users, tables, indexes, and so on). When connected to a PDB, there is no visibility to the root container or any other PDBs (unless granted) within the CDB.

Note   In Oracle Database 23ai, you can have three PDBs without additional licensing. You can create up to 4,096 PDBs but need a Multitenant license for PDBs over three.

Everything discussed regarding objects, tables, views, indexes, etc., is all part of the objects contained in the PDB. You also learned about the various dictionary views, including CDB views, which report across all containers (root, seed, and all pluggable databases) in a CDB. In the CDB views, you have a column called CON_ID, which is the unique identifier for each container within the CDB. The root container has a CON_ID of 1. The seed has a CON_ID of 2. Each new PDB created with CDB is assigned a unique sequential container ID.

Take a minute to inspect Figure 12-1.

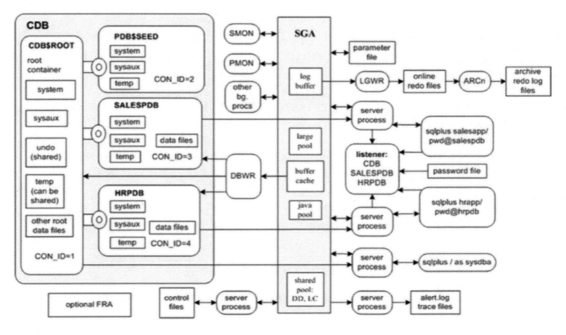

Figure 12-1. *Pluggable database architecture*

If you are a curious DBA, dozens of thoughts immediately come to mind. The following list highlights some key points about the new architecture in Figure 12-1.

- A connection to the CDB is synonymous with connecting to the CDB$ROOT root container. The main purpose of the root container is to provide the resources and house metadata for any associated PDBs.

- You can access the root container via the SYS user, just as in pre-23ai releases of a non-CDB database. In other words, when logged in to the database server, you can use OS authentication to connect directly to the root container, as you have seen in previous chapters.

- The seed PDB (PDB$SEED) exists only as a template for creating new PDBs. You can connect to the seed, but it is read-only, meaning you cannot issue transactions against it.

- Besides the two default containers (root and seed), for this particular CDB in Figure 12-1, two additional PDBs have been manually created, named SALESPDB and HRPDB.

- PDBs exist within individual namespaces. PDB names must be unique within the CDB, but objects within a PDB have to be unique only within the individual PDB but not across other PDBs within the CDB.

- Each PDB has its own SYSTEM and SYSAUX tablespaces and, optionally, a TEMP tablespace.

- If a PDB does not have its own TEMP file, it can consume resources in the root container TEMP file.

- The SYSTEM tablespace of each PDB contains information regarding the PDB metadata, such as its users and objects; this metadata is accessible via the DBA/ALL/USER-level views from the PDB and is visible via CDB-level views from the root container.

- The CDB can house PDBs of different character sets if copied over from another CDB of a different character set.

- You can set the time zones for the CDB and all associated PDBs, or you can set the time zone individually per PDB.

- The CDB instance is started and stopped while connected as SYS to the root container. You cannot start/stop the CDB instance while connected to a PDB (separation of duties from system DBAs and application DBAs).

- One initialization parameter file is read by the instance when starting. A privileged user connected to the root container can modify all initialization parameters. In contrast, a privileged user connected to a PDB can only modify parameters applicable to the currently connected PDB.

- When connected to a PDB and modifying initialization parameters, these modifications apply only to the currently connected PDB and persist for the PDB across database restarts. The ISPDB_MODIFIABLE column in V$PARAMETER shows which parameters are modifiable while connected as a DBA to a PDB. (There are additional security permissions for locking parameters and configurations.)

- Application users can only access the PDBs via a network connection. Therefore, a listener must be running and listening for service names corresponding to associated PDBs. If a listener is not running for PDB service, then there is no way for an application user to connect to a PDB.

- The individual PDBs are not stopped or started per se (not in terms of a database instance like the CDB). You open or close a PDB and are not allocating memory or starting/stopping background processes for a PDB.

- There is one set of control files for the CDB. The control files are managed while connected to the root container as a privileged user.

- UNDO in shared mode means that there is only one UNDO tablespace for the CDB, and the PDBs use the same UNDO tablespace. UNDO works in local mode. Each PDB has its own UNDO tablespace, and if a PDB is cloned, relocated, or plugged into a CDB that is configured to use local undo mode, then the undo tablespace is automatically created for the PDB when opened.

- Flashing back a PDB is possible using the FLASHBACK PLUGGABLE DATABASE statement to return the PDB to a point in time without affecting other PDBs.

- There is one alert log and set of trace files for a CDB. Any applicable database messages for associated PDBs are written to the common CDB alert.

- There is one thread of redo (per instance) that is managed while connected to the root container as a user with appropriate privileges. Only privileged connections to the root can enable archiving or switching online logs. Connections of SYSDBA-privileged users to PDBs cannot alter online redo or archiving settings.

- AWR, ADDM, and ASH reports are issued across all PDBs in the CDB. Resource consumption is identified per PDB.

- When resolving SQL performance issues, queries are associated with a particular PDB via the CON_ID column in views such as V$SQL and V$SQLAREA.

- Security options such as Database Vault can be enabled at a PDB level. The privileges in CDBs and PDBs provide another level of security and separation of duties.

This list is long with a ton of information, but once you digest the nuances of PDB environments, you can effectively implement and manage this technology. One of the main points here is that you can have dozens or more securely isolated PDBs housed within one CDB with only one instance (memory and background processes), one thread of redo, and one set of control files to manage.

Paradigm Shift

It is fairly common for a specific application to request that its database objects (users, tables, indexes, and so on) be placed in a database isolated from other applications. Reasons cited for doing this are often security issues or performance concerns. Before the advent of PDBs, think about how you solved the requirement of separate environments for various applications and development teams. The following are two common solutions employed.

- Create a separate database for each team/application that needs an environment. Sometimes, this approach is implemented with one database per server, which often translates into additional hardware and licensing costs.

- Create separate environments within one database. Usually, this is achieved through separate schemas and distinct tablespaces. This approach requires that there not be any database object naming collisions between applications, for example, with objects such as usernames, tablespace names, and public synonyms.

PDBs provide the security isolation requirement; there is no direct access from one PDB to another. Even a user connected with SYSDBA privileges to a given PDB has no direct SQL access to other PDBs within the CDB. From a security and application perspective, you have totally isolated PDBs within the larger CDB.

As a DBA, instead of having to implement and maintain dozens of individual databases and associated operational tasks (such as provisioning new databases, installs, upgrades, tuning, availability, monitoring, replication, disaster recovery, and backup and recovery), you can manage any number of PDBs as if they were one database from the root container perspective.

Another significant advantage of the pluggable architecture is that a PDB can easily be cloned or transferred from one CDB to another. This allows more options when performing tasks such as provisioning new databases, upgrading databases, load balancing, or moving application data from one environment to another (such as from a development database to a test database). Creating a new environment can be done by cloning another PDB. Moving a PDB from a CDB simply requires that you unplug (via SQL commands) the PDB from the CDB and then associate the metadata and data files (plug-in) with a new CDB.

Moving PDBs also provides additional options for upgrading databases, by creating a new CDB or upgrading an existing one. The upgrade is then performed on the PDBs as they are attached or open. There are fewer databases to patch and upgrade, and you can upgrade one CDB instead of 100 databases.

Because of the consolidation, there is cost reduction along with maintaining the environment. There is hardware consolidation and efficient use of the hardware instead of extra or unused resources by placing several database instances on different servers.

Performance tuning is captured in a consolidated area, and the SGA is available for all PDBs, making it easier to size and tune one instead of all of the individual databases.

Leveraging load balancing and resource management allows meeting SLAs and makes it easier to do migrations and upgrades.

Administrating the Root Container (CDB)

When you manage a CDB, for the most part, you are connecting to the root container as SYS and performing tasks as you would with a non-CDB database. We recommend different users for different tasks, such as backing up, creating new PDBs, and cloning. Even though these are SYSDBA-level tasks, it still makes sense to leave SYSOPER permissions to a different user instead of the risk of shutting down a CDB. Enough of the separation of duties soapbox. However, there are several points to be aware of that are specific to maintaining a CDB. The following tasks can be performed only while connected to the root container with SYSDBA privileges.

- Starting/stopping the instance

- Enabling/disabling archive log mode

- Managing instance settings that affect all databases with the CDB, such as overall memory size

- Backup and recovery of all data files within the database

- Managing control files (adding, restoring, removing, and so on)

- Managing online redo logs

- Managing the root UNDO tablespace

- Managing the root TEMP tablespace

- Creating common users and roles

- Creating PDBs and application containers

Connecting to the Root Container

Connecting to the root container as SYS allows you to perform all the tasks you normally associate with database administration. You can connect as SYS locally from the database server through OS authentication or a network connection (which requires a listener and password file). It is recommended that there are roles set up for CDB administrators to be able to use individual accounts and not log in via SYS. Logins on the server would be needed only when performing the server tasks; otherwise, the connection to the CDB through a network connection should be what is allowed for security and compliance.

Network Connections

If you are initiating a remote connection through the network, you must first set up a listener on the target database server and create a password file (see Chapter 2). Once the listener and password files are established, you can connect remotely over the network, as shown next.

```
$ sqlplus user/password@connection_string
SQL> show user con_id con_name user
USER is "user"
```

```
CON_ID
-----------
3
CON_NAME
---------------MMPDB
USER is "user"
```

For more information on implementing a listener for pluggables, see Chapter 2.

Displaying Currently Connected Container Information

There are some easy techniques for displaying the name of the CDB that you are currently connected to. This example uses the SHOW command to display the container ID, the name, and the user.

```
SQL> show con_id con_name user
```

You can also display the same information via an SQL query.

```
SQL> SELECT SYS_CONTEXT('USERENV', 'CON_ID') AS con_id,
SYS_CONTEXT('USERENV', 'CON_NAME') AS cur_container,
SYS_CONTEXT('USERENV', 'SESSION_USER') AS cur_user
FROM DUAL;
```

Here is some sample output.

```
CON_ID           CUR_CONTAINER     CUR_USER

---------------- ----------------- ------------------

1                CDB$ROOT          USER
```

Starting/Stopping the Root Container

You can start/stop the CDB only while connected as a privileged user to the root container. To start a CDB, connect as SYS or a user with SYSOPER privileges and issue the startup command.

```
$ sqlplus / as sysdba
SQL> startup;
```

Starting the CDB database does not open any associated PDBs unless you have saved the state of the PDB to open automatically. It is recommended to make sure you set the PDBs to start automatically. You can open all PDBs with this command.

```
SQL> alter pluggable database all open;
```

To shut down a CDB database, issue the following command.

```
SQL> shutdown immediate;
```

The prior line shuts down the CDB instance and disconnects any users connected to the database. If any pluggable databases are open, they are closed, and users are disconnected.

For Oracle Restart, the SRVCTL command can be used to start, modify, and stop instances. SRVCTL can be used for CDBs and PDBs, and services need to be created for the PDBs.

```
$ srvctl start database
```

The environment variables are part of the Oracle Restart configuration, and there are several parameters that can be passed in for starting up with different spfiles and parameter files using start options such as mount, restrict, open, and recover.

```
$ srvctl stop database - db mmdb23ai
```

The default option is immediate, but you can specify normal and abort stop options. To create a service for a PDB, use the following.

```
$ srvctl add service -db mmdb23ai -service mmpdbsrv -pdb mmpdb
```

Now, you can use the service to perform commands in a RAC environment or configurations for the PDB. You can modify, stop, and start services, as well as relocate, remove, and get the status of services.

Create Common Users

There are two types of users in a pluggable environment: local and common. A local user is nothing more than a regular user that is created in a PDB. The local type of user in a PDB behaves the same as a user in a non-CDB environment. There is nothing special about administering local users; you learned how to set up users in the first few chapters.

A common user exists in the root container and every PDB. This type of user must be initially created in the root container and is automatically created in all existing PDBs and any PDBs created in the future.

The SYS and SYSTEM accounts are common users that Oracle creates automatically in a pluggable environment.

Common users are created with the string C## or c## at the start of the username. The COMMON_USER_PREFIX parameter lets you change the prefix for the common user. They are easily identifiable with a C## prefix, and no local user can use the prefix C##, which helps enforce that the user is uniquely named across all PDBs. For instance, the following command creates a common user in all PDBs.

```
SQL> create user c##dba identified by "Cr4zyPa$$word!"
```

Common users must be granted privileges from within each pluggable database. In other words, if you grant privileges to a common user while connected to the root container, this does not cascade to the PDBs. If you need to grant a common user a privilege that spans PDBs, then create a common role and assign it to the common user. A common user can log in to any container with the CREATE SESSION privilege.

What use is there for a common user? One situation would be the performance of common DBA maintenance activities across PDBs not requiring SYSDBA-level privileges. For example, you want to set up a DBA account with the privileges to create users, grants, and so on, but you don't want to use an account such as SYS (which has all privileges in all databases). In this scenario, you would create a common DBA user and a DBA common role containing the appropriate privileges. The common role would then be assigned to the common DBA.

Creating Common Roles

Much like you can create a common user that spans all PDBs, you can create a common role in the same manner. Common roles provide a single object to which you can grant privileges that are valid within all pluggable databases associated with the root container.

A common role is created in the root container and is automatically created in all associated PDBs and any PDBs created in the future. Like common users, common roles start with the same prefix string as the user C## or c##. The following is an example.

```
SQL> create role c##dbaprivs container=all;
```

Next, you can assign privileges, as desired, to the common role. Here, the DBA role is assigned to the previously created role.

```
SQL> grant dba to c##dbaprivs container = all;
```

Now, if you assign this common role to a common user, the privileges associated with the role are in effect when the common user connects to any pluggable database associated with the root container.

```
SQL> grant c##dbaprivs to c##dba container = all;
```

Creating Local Users and Roles

A local user is a user that is only for that container and "local" to the container. This is especially used for application users and users that are authorized only in specific PDBs. The PDB may own a schema or can even be a schema-only account.

You can create a local user in a PDB by specifying the CONTAINER clause (or without it). Connect to the PDB for which local users are to be created.

```
SQL> alter session set container=MMPDB;
Session altered.
SQL> create user pdbdba identified by "Cr4zyPa$$word1" container=current;
SQL> create user appuser identified by "Cr4zyPa$$word1";
```

Roles are also common or local. All Oracle-supplied roles are common but can be granted to a local user.

Switching Containers

Once you connect as a common user to any container within the database (either the root or a PDB), you can use the ALTER SESSION command to switch to another container for which you have been granted access. For example, to set the current container to a PDB named SALESPDB, you would do as follows.

```
SQL> alter session set container = salespdb;
```

You can switch back to the root container by specifying the CDB$ROOT.

```
SQL> alter session set container = cdb$root;
```

You do not need a listener to be up and running or a password file to switch containers. As long as the common user has privileges, the user is successfully switched to the new container context. The ability to switch containers is especially useful when you need to connect to a PDB to troubleshoot issues and then connect back to the root container.

PDB Open Modes

PDBs are opened or closed after the CDB is started. It can be opened in one of the following modes.

- Read/write

- Read-only

- Hybrid read-only (new 23ai)

- Migrate mode

The open modes can be viewed in the data dictionary view V$PDBS.

```
SQL> select con_id, name, open_mode from v$pdbs;
CON_ID      NAME              OPEN_MODE
---------   ---------------   --------------------

2           PDB$SEED          READ ONLY
3           MMPDB             READ WRITE
4           HYBRIDPDB         READ WRITE
```

The first two modes make sense, as you can open the database for reading and transactions. Some PDBs can be set to read-only for reporting or snapshots. New in 23 is the hybrid read-only mode, which you can see from v$pdbs shows the database can read and write; however, depending on the user connected to the database, it acts as a read-only PDB. The common user would be permitted to write, and the application or local users would still be able to read. This helps for patching and performing maintenance to still allow access to the PDB as it is in a safe mode for the operations of the common user.

Since the V$PDBS does not show if the pluggable is in hybrid mode, you can use the V$CONTAINER_TOPOLOGY view.

```
SQL> select con_name, open_mode, is_hybrid_read_only
from v$container_topology;
CON_ID      CON_NAME       OPEN_MODE     IS_HYBRID_READ_ONLY
----------  -------------  -----------   -----------------------
1           CDB$ROOT       READ WRITE    NO
2           PDB$SEED       READ ONLY     NO
3           MMPDB          READ WRITE    NO
4           HYBRIDPDB      READ WRITE    YES
```

To modify the PDB open mode, you can use the ALTER PLUGGABLE DATABASE ...
FORCE statement while the database is open. If the database is closed, you do not need
the FORCE.

```
SQL> alter pluggable database HYBRIDPDB open read write force;
SQL> alter pluggable database HYBRIDPDB open hybrid read only force;
```

UPGRADE is another open mode to place the PDB into migration mode. You can run
upgrade scripts or migrate the pluggable database in this mode.

To put a PDB in mounted mode, run the close statement. This shuts down the PDB,
but shutdown is at the CDB level. By closing the PDB, it cannot read from or write to
data files. Any changes made through the CDB are applied when the PDB is opened the
next time.

```
SQL> alter pluggable database MMPDB close;
SQL> select con_id, open_mode from v$pdbs;
CON_ID          OPEN_MODE
----------      --------------------
2               READ ONLY
3               MOUNTED
4               READ WRITE
```

Open Order for PDBs

New in 23ai, you can define an open order for the PDBs. This gives priority to
mission-critical PDBs so that they are started first. The priority is for opening and
upgrades. Priority values are lower to higher values, with the lower values being processed
first. Values can be the same but are processed in any order with the same value. Priorities
are not copied from the source to target PDBs by plug/unplug or refreshable clones.

To change the priority value, use the ALTER PLUGGABLE DATABASE ... PRIORITY statement. Values are between 1 and 4096.

```
SQL> alter pluggable database mmpdb priority 1;
SQL> select con_id, priority from v$pdbs;
CON_ID       PRIORITY
---------    ---------
2            1
3            1
4
```

Starting/Stopping a PDB

From the root container, you can change the open mode of a PDB with the following.

```
SQL> alter pluggable database salespdb open;
```

As discussed in the previous section, you can change the state of the PDB.

```
SQL> startup pluggable database salespdb open read only;
```

You can also open or close all pluggables, which follow the open order with the priority you have set for the PDBs.

```
SQL> alter pluggable database all open;
SQL> alter pluggable database all close immediate;
```

From the pluggable database, connect as SYS, and this look similar to the CDB commands to start and shut down.

```
$ sqlplus pdbsys/Cr4zyPa$$word1@mm23ai:1521/salespdb as
sysdba SQL> startup;
```

To shut down the PDB database when connected to it, use the following command.

```
SQL> shutdown immediate;
```

Creating a Pluggable Database Within a CDB

After you have created a CDB, you can start creating PDBs within it. When you instruct Oracle to create a PDB under the covers, it copies files from an existing database (seed, PDB, or non-CDB, database instance, which is available in previous versions from 19c and lower). Then it builds the new PDB's metadata in the CDB. The key here is to correctly reference which database you want Oracle to use as a template for creating the new PDB.

There are several tools for creating (cloning) a PDB: the CREATE PLUGGABLE DATABASE SQL statement, the DBCA utility, and Enterprise Manager Cloud Control. If you understand how to create PDBs using SQL and DBCA, you should easily be able to use the Enterprise Manager screens to achieve the same objectives.

With the CREATE PLUGGABLE DATABASE statement, you can use any of the following sources to create a PDB.

- Seed database

- Existing PDB (either local or remote)

- Non-CDB database

- Unplugged PDB

With the DBCA, you can create a PDB from any of the following sources.

- Seed database

- RMAN backup

- Unplugged PDB

The following sections cover all the CREATE PLUGGABLE DATABASE variants of creating a PDB. With the DBCA, you can also create the new PDB from the seed database. You should be able to modify that example for your various needs.

Cloning the Seed Database

The CREATE PLUGGABLE DATABASE statement can be used to create a PDB by copying the seed database's data files. First, connect to the root container database as the SYS user (or a common user with create PDB privileges):$ sqlplus sysuser/ Cr4zyPa$$word1@ mmdb23ai as sysdba.

The following SQL statement creates a pluggable database named SALESPDB.

```
SQL> create pluggable database salespdb
admin user salesadm identified by "Cr4zyPa$$word1"
file_name_convert = ('/u01/app/oracle/oradata/mmdb23/pdbseed', '/u01/app/
oracle/oradata/mmdb23/salespdb');
```

After running the prior code, you should see some output similar to the following.

```
Pluggable database created.
```

Here's a simplified statement when using standard files and ASM.

```
SQL> create pluggable database salespdb admin user salesadm identified by
"Cr4zyPa$$word1";
Pluggable database created.
```

Cloning an Existing PDB

You can create a PDB from an existing PDB within the currently connected (local) CDB, or you can create a PDB as a copy of a PDB from a remote CDB. Creating a copy is useful for test environments or troubleshooting problems in production. These two techniques are described in the next two sections.

Local

In this example, an existing PDB (SALESPDB) is used to create a new PDB (SALESPDB2). First, connect to the root container and place the existing source PDB in read-only mode.

```
$ sqlplus sysuser/Cr4zyPa$$word1@mmdb23ai as sysdba
SQL> create pluggable database salespdb2 from salespdb;
```

You can also do this from a snapshot.

```
SQL> alter pluggable database mmpdb snapshot mmpdb1_623;
SQL> create pluggable database mmpdb_copy from mmpdb using snapshot
mmpdb1_623;
```

Remote

You can also create a PDB as a clone of a remote PDB. First, you need to create a database link from the CDB to the PDB that serves as the source for the clone. The local user and the user specified in the database link must have the CREATE PLUGGABLE DATABASE privilege.

This example shows a local connection as SYS to the root container. This is the database in which the new PDB is created.

```
$ sqlplus sysuser/Cr4zyPa$$word1@mmdb23 as sysdba
```

In this database, create a database link to the PDB in the remote CDB. The remote CDB contains a PDB named mmpdb, with a user created with the CREATE PLUGGABLE DATABASE privilege granted to it. This is the user for the database link.

```
SQL> create database link mmpdb_connect
connect to pdbcloneuser identified by "Cr4zyPa$$word1"
using 'mm23ai:1521/mmpdb';
```

Next, connect to the remote database containing the PDB to be cloned.

```
$ sqlplus sysuser/Cr4zyPa$$word1@mm23ai:1521/mmpdb as sysdba
SQL> create pluggable database mmpdb_clone from mmpdb@mmpdb_connect;
```

Refreshable Clone

When creating a clone, it is a copy as of that point in time. A refreshable clone can sync back to the source PDB. This makes this clone useful for testing upgrades, making changes, and switching the roles of a sourcing PDB and its refreshable clone. This can be useful for resources and possible load balancing between CDBs.

The option for this refreshable clone is REFRESH MODE with values of MANUAL or EVERY for minutes. The refreshable clone must be in a closed state or open in read-only mode for refreshes. You need a database link, even if it is in the same CDB. Without setting minutes, the default of 60 minutes is used.

```
SQL> create pluggable database mmpdb_refresh from mmpdb@mmpdb_connect
refresh mode every 120 minutes;
```

Cloning from a Non-CDB Database

When migrating from a database prior to 21c, you might need to create the PDB from a non-CDB if the database was not created as a container. There are three ways of creating a PDB from an existing non-CDB.

- Using the DBMS_PDB package to generate metadata and then create PDB with a CREATE PLUGGABLE DATABASE statement

- Data Pump

- GoldenGate replication

The following example uses the DBMS_PDB package to create a PDB from a non-CDB. See the *Oracle Database Utilities Guide* documentation for more information on Data Pump and GoldenGate.

When using the DBMS_PDB package to convert a non-CDB to a PDB, the non-CDB must be Oracle 12c or higher. To upgrade to a 23ai CDB, the non-CDB needs to be 19c.

```
SQL> startup mount;
SQL> alter database open read only;
```

Then, run the DBMS_PDB package to create an XML file that describes the structure of the non-CDB database.

```
SQL> begin dbms_pdb.describe(pdb_descr_file =>
'/oradata/oracle/ncdb.xml');
end;
/
```

After the XML file is created, shut down the non-CDB database.

```
SQL> shutdown immediate;
```

Next, set your Oracle OS variables and connect to the CDB database that houses the non-CDB as a PDB.

```
$ sqlplus / as sysdba
```

Now, you can optionally check to see if the non-CDB is compatible with the CDB in which it will be plugged. When you run this code, provide the directory and name of the XML file that was created previously.

```
SQL> set serveroutput on
SQL> declare
hold_var boolean;
begin
hold_var :=
dbms_pdb.check_plug_compatibility (pdb_descr_file => '/oradata/oracle/
ncdb.xml');
if hold_var then
dbms_output.put_line ('YES');
else
dbms_output.put_line('NO');
end if;
end;
/
```

If there are no compatibility issues, a YES is displayed by the prior code; a NO is displayed if the PDB is not compatible. You can query the contents of the PDB_PLUG_IN_ VIOLATIONS view for details on why a PDB is not compatible with a CDB.

Next, use the following SQL to create a PDB from the non-CDB. You must specify information such as the name and location of the previously created XML file, the location of the non-CDB data files, and the location where you want the new data files created.

```
SQL> CREATE PLUGGABLE DATABASE pdb23ai
USING '/oradata/oracle/ncdb.xml'
COPY
FILE_NAME_CONVERT = ('/u01/oradb/db19c/',
                     '/u01/oradb/mmdb23/pdb23ai/');
```

If successful, you should see the following.

```
Pluggable database created.
```

Now, connect as SYS to the newly created PDB as SYS.

```
$ sqlplus sys/Cr4zyPa$$word1@'mm23ai:1521/pdb23ai' as sysdba
```

As a last step, run the following script.

```
SQL> @?/rdbms/admin/noncdb_to_pdb.sql
```

You should now be able to open the PDB and begin using it.

Unplugging a PDB from a CDB

Before plugging a PDB into another CDB, it must first be unplugged. Unplugging translates to disassociating a PDB from a CDB and generating an XML file that describes the PDB being unplugged. This XML file can be used in the future to plug the PDB into another CDB. Before going down this path, however, consider the previous section that discussed refreshable clones. This creates another PDB that can be refreshed and switched over. Still, there might be a need to move a PDB offline.

Here are the steps required to unplug a PDB.

1.   Close the PDB (which changes its open mode to MOUNTED).

2.   Unplug the pluggable database via the ALTER PLUGGABLE DATABASE ... UNPLUG command.

First, connect to the root container as the SYS user, and then close the PDB.

```
$ sqlplus sysuser/Cr4zyPa$$word1 as sysdba
SOL> alter pluggable database mmpdb close immediate;
```

Next, unplug the PDB. Make sure you specify a directory in your environment for the location of the XML file.

```
SOL> alter pluggable database mmpdb unplug into '/oradata/oracle/dba/
mmpdb.xml';
```

The XML file contains metadata regarding the PDB, such as its data files. This XML is required to plug the PDB into another CDB.

Note   Once a PDB is unplugged, it must be dropped before it can be plugged back into the original CDB.

Plugging an Unplugged PDB into a CDB

Before a PDB can be plugged into a CDB, it must be compatible with a CDB in terms of data file endianness and compatible database options installed. The character set can differ, which is how you can get a different character set for PDBs in the same CDB. You can verify the compatibility via the DBMS_PDB package. You must provide as input to the package the directory and name of the XML file created when the PDB was unplugged. Here is an example.

```
SQL> set serveroutput on
SQL> declare
hold_var boolean;
begin
hold_var := dbms_pdb.check_plug_compatibility(pdb_descr_file => '/oradata/
oracle/dba/mmpdb.xml');
if hold_var then
dbms_output.put_line('YES');
else
dbms_output.put_line('NO');
end if;
end;
/
```

If there are no compatibility issues, a YES is displayed by the prior code; a NO is displayed if the PDB is not compatible. You can query the contents of the PDB_PLUG_IN_ VIOLATIONS view for the details on why a PDB is not compatible with a CDB.

Plugging in a PDB is done with the CREATE PLUGGABLE DATABASE command. When you plug a PDB into a CDB, you must provide some key information using these two clauses.

- USING clause: This clause specifies the location of the XML file created when the PDB was unplugged.

- COPY FILE_NAME_CONVERT clause: This clause specifies the source of the PDB data files and the location where the PDB data files will be created within the destination CDB.

To plug in a PDB, connect to the CDB as a privileged user and run the following.

```
SQL> create pluggable database mmpdb
using '/oradata/oracle/dba/mmpdb.xml'
copy
file_name_convert = ('/u01/app/oracle/oradata/cdb19/mmpdb',
'/u01/dbfile/mmdb23ai/mmpdb');
```

You can now open the PDB and begin using it.

Relocating a PDB

Relocating a PDB is an online action instead of unplugging and plugging a database. The source can be open for read and write, and there is minimal or no downtime. The files associated with the PDB are moved to a new location, and the PDB is added to the target CDB and then opened.

The change over to the PDB in the target CDB depends on the listener as part of the stages for relocating. If this is a shared listener for the source and target PDB, additional connection handling is not needed, and the new connections are automatically routed to the new locations. If the PDBs use different listeners, there needs to be a cross-registration of their respective listeners through the parameters local_listener and remote_listener.

The following command starts the relocation.

```
SQL> create pluggable database mmpdb_re from mmpdb@mmconnect relocate
availability max;
```

After this is completed, you can open the target PDB for read-write.

This relocation can also be performed in DBCA for an interface, or you can run it in silent mode and code it if you have a list of PDBs that need relocation.

Checking the Status of Pluggable Databases

You may want to check its status after creating, cloning, or moving a PDB. You can view the status of all PDBs within a CDB while connected to the root container. For instance, a user with DBA privileges can report on the status of all PDBs via this query.

```
SQL> select pdb_id, pdb_name, status from cdb_pdbs;
PDB_ID      PDB_NAME            STATUS
----------- ------------------- ----------------
2           PDB$SEED            NORMAL
3           MMPDB               NORMAL
4           SALESPDB            NORMAL
```

It's even easier if you just want to see it in open mode.

```
SQL> show pdbs
CON_ID      NAME        OPEN_MODE    RESTRICTED
----------- ----------- ----------- ----------
2           PDB$SEED    READ ONLY   NO
3           MMPDB       READ WRITE  NO
4           SALESPDB    READ WRITE  NO
```

Examples from previous sections show the containers and PDBs available for the CDB.

If you run the prior queries while connected directly to a PDB, you only get the information for the PDB currently connected to.

Administrating Pluggable Databases

You have already learned many administration tasks for CDBs and PDBs. The PDBs are considered application databases or configured for user objects and data. You still have administrative tasks that must be performed while connected directly to the PDB. You can open/close a PDB, check its status, show currently connected users, and so on. You can administer a PDB as a privileged connection to the root container, or you can perform tasks while connected as a privileged user directly to the PDB itself.

Keep in mind that when you connect as SYS to a PDB within the CDB, you can only perform SYS-privileged operations for the PDB to which you are connected. You cannot start/stop the container instance or view data dictionary information related to other PDBs within the CDB. The multitenant environment provides a separation of duties for an administrator and application administrators. A PDB can be secured to just be specific administrators. You can administer one or more PDBs, and another team or DBAs would be taking care of the CDB administration or the PDB administration of other PDBs.

Connecting to a PDB

You can connect to a PDB as SYS locally or over the network. To make a local connection, first connect to the root container as a common user with privileges on the PDB, and then use the SET CONTAINER command to connect to the desired PDB.

```
SQL> alter session set container = salespdb;
```

The prior connection does not require a listener or password file; a connection over the network requires both. This next example makes a network connection via SQL*Plus and specifies the PDB's host, listener port, and service name when connecting via SQL*Plus.

```
$ sqlplus pdbsys/Cr4zyPa$$word1@mm23ai:1521/salespdb as sysdba
```

If you are unsure how to set up a listener and a password file, see Chapter 2. If you use the DBCA utility to create the PDB, the listener for the PDB is set up. For instructions on how to register a PDB service name with the listener, see the next section.

Managing a Listener in a PDB Environment

Recall from Chapter 2 that a listener is the process that enables remote network connections to a database. Most database environments require a listener to operate. When a client attempts to connect to a remote database, the client provides three key pieces of information: the host the listener is on, the host port the listener is listening on, and a database service name.

Each database has one or more service names assigned to it. By default, there is usually one service name that is derived from the database's unique name and domain. You can manually create one or more service names for a database. DBAs sometimes create more than one service so that resource usage can be controlled or monitored for each service. For example, a service may be created for a sales application, and a service may be created for the HR application. Each application connects to the database via its service name. The service connection information appears in each session's SERVICE_ NAME column of the V$SESSION view.

If you start a default listener with no listener.ora file in place, the PMON background process automatically registers any databases (including any pluggable) as a service.

```
$ lsnrctl start
```

Eventually, you should see the databases (including any PDBs) registered with the default listener.

When starting the listener, if there is a `listener.ora` file present, the listener attempts to statically register any service names that appear in the `listener.ora` file.

By default, the PDBs are registered with a service name that is the same as the PDB name. The default service is typically the one that you would use to make connections.

```
$ sqlplus pdbsys/Cr4zyPa$$word1@mm23ai:1521/salespdb as sysdba
```

You can verify which services are running by connecting as SYS to the root container and querying, as follows.

```
SQL> select name, network_name, pdb from v$services order by pdb, name;
```

You can also verify which services a listener is listing for via the `lsnrctl` utility.

```
$ lsnrctl services
```

Oracle recommends that you configure an additional service (besides the default service) for any applications that need to access a PDB. You can manually configure services using the SRVCTL utility or the DBMS_SERVICE package. This example shows how to configure a service via the DBMS_SERVICE package. First, connect as SYS to the PDB in which you want to create the service via the default service.

```
$ sqlplus pdbsys/Cr4zyPa$$word1@mm23ai:1521/salespdb as sysdba
```

Make sure the PDB is open for read-write mode.

```
SOL> SELECT con_id, name, open_mode FROM v$pdbs;
```

Next, create a service. This code creates and starts a service named SALESWEST.

```
SOL> exec DBMS_SERVICE.CREATE_SERVICE(service_name => 'SALESWEST', network_
name => 'SALESWEST');
SOL> exec DBMS_SERVICE.START_SERVICE(service_name => 'SALESWEST');
```

Now, application users can connect to the SALESPDB pluggable database via the service.

```
$ sqlplus appuser/Cr4zyPas$$word1@mm23ai:1521/saleswest
```

> **Caution**   If you have multiple CDB databases on one server, ensure that the PDB service names are unique across all CDB databases on the server. It is not advisable to register two PDB databases with the same name with one common listener. This leads to confusion as to which PDB you are actually connecting to.

Modifying Initialization Parameters Specific to a PDB

Oracle allows some initialization parameters to be modified while connected as a privileged user to a PDB. You can view these parameters via the following query.

```
SOL> select name
from v$parameter
where ispdb_modifiable='TRUE'
order by name;
```

Here is a snippet of the output.

```
NAME
-----------------------------
sort_area_size
sql_trace
sqltune_category
star_transformation_enabled
statistics_level
```

When you make initialization parameter changes while connected directly to a PDB, these changes affect only the currently connected PDB. The parameter changes do not affect the root container or other PDBs. For example, say you wanted to change the value of OPEN_CURSORS. First, connect directly to the PDB as a privileged user and issue the ALTER SYSTEM statement.

```
$ sqlplus pdbsys/Cr4zyPas$$word1@mm23ai:1521/salespdb as sysdba SQL> alter system set open_cursors=100;
```

The prior change modifies the value of OPEN_CURSORS only for the SALESPDB. Furthermore, the setting of OPEN_CURSORS for SALESPDB persists across database restarts.

Renaming a PDB

Occasionally, you may be required to rename a PDB. For instance, the database may have been originally misnamed, or you may no longer be using it and want to append _OLD to its name. To rename a pluggable database, first connect to it as SYSDBA-privileged account.

```
$ sqlplus pdbsys/Cr4zyPas$$word1@mm23ai:1521/salespdb as sysdba
```

Next, stop the PDB and restart it in restricted mode.

```
SQL> shutdown immediate;
SQL> startup restrict;
```

Now, the pluggable database can be renamed.

```
SQL> alter pluggable database rename global_name to salespdb2022;
```

Limiting the Amount of Space Consumed by PDB

You can place an overall limit on the amount of disk space a PDB can consume. This is not just the max size of the datafiles but the complete set of datafiles for multiple tablespaces. The sizing of the databases should be available through ASM disk groups or filesystem sizing.

In this example, an overall limit of 500 GB is placed on a pluggable database. First, connect to the pluggable database as SYS.

```
$ sqlplus pdbsys/Cr4zyPas$$word1@mm23ai:1521/salespdb as sysdba
```

Next, alter the pluggable database's maximum size limit. This command limits the size of the pluggable database to a maximum of 500 GB.

```
SQL> alter pluggable database salespdb storage (maxsize 500G);
```

The space is not the only resource that PDB can limit. CPU and memory can be limited by using the PDB parameters or resource management plans. As a privileged user in the PDB, you can alter the system to set CPU_COUNT equal to less than the overall CPU_COUNT for the CDB. This does not allow the PDB to use more than those CPU resources. The same is true for memory in setting the memory limit parameters in the PDB, again less than the CDB. Connect to the PDB and use the following alter statements.

```
SQL> alter system set CPU_COUNT = 2 scope = both;
SQL> alter system set SGA_TARGET = 16G scope = both;
```

Restricting Changes to SYSTEM at PDB

In administering the PDB, the parameters can be changed as described at the PDB level. You can also change these parameters for a PDB at the CDB level. The changes can be restricted so that only CDB administrators can modify these settings for the PDB. This allows the CDB DBAs to know how many PDBs are in the CDB. The changes are kept even while the sysdba user in each PDB can have the DBA permissions in the PDB and administer the PDB. This provides another level of security or separation of duties to ensure that the PDB parameters are managed to fit the overall environments. Restrict what makes sense for the environment and other parameters allowed in the PDB by the administrators or DBAs for the PDBs.

This is done with PDB_LOCKDOWN. The lockdown profile is created and set for a PDB, and the commands are added to the profile to restrict PDB DBAs from changing the configurations, such as those set with CPU, memory, etc.

The following is a quick overview of creating PDB_LOCKDOWNs in the CDB.

```
SQL> create lockdown profile pdbprofile1;
SQL> alter lockdown profile pdbprofile1 disable statement=('alter system')
clause=('set') option all;
```

This locks down and disables any alter system set commands for the users, including DBA privileged users, in the PDB and does not allow these types of changes in the PDB where this is enabled.

```
SQL> alter session set container=mmpdb;
SQL> show parameter pdb_lockdown
NAME                    TYPE        VALUE
--------------------    ----------  ---------
pdb_lockdown            string
SQL> alter system set pdb_lockdown=pdbprofile1;
```

You can view the parameters in PDB_LOCKDOWN.

```
SQL> show parameter pdb_lockdown
NAME                     TYPE         VALUE
--------------------     ----------   -------------
pdb_lockdown             string       PDBPROFILE1
```

Oracle has dynamic lockdown profiles that allow additional parameter settings, resource manager plans, and options. They are dynamic because they do not require that the PDB be restarted and take effect immediately.

Viewing PDB History

If you need to view when a PDB was created, you can query the CDB_PDB_HISTORY view, as shown next.

```
SQL> COL db_name FORM A10
SQL> COL con_id FORM 999
SQL> COL pdb_name FORM A15

SQL> COL operation FORM A16
SQL> COL op_timestamp FORM A10
SQL> COL cloned_from_pdb_name FORMAT A15
--
SQL> SELECT db_name, con_id, pdb_name, operation,
        op_timestamp, cloned_from_pdb_name
FROM cdb_pdb_history
WHERE con_id > 2
ORDER BY con_id;
```

Here is some sample output.

```
DB_NAME    CON_ID PDB_NAME     OPERATION    OP_TIMESTA  CLONED_FROM_PDB
---------- ------ -----------  -----------  ----------- -----------------
CDB        3      SALESPDB     CREATE       04-DEC-12   PDB$SEED
CDB        4      HRPDB        CREATE       10-FEB-13   PDB$SEED
```

In this way, you can determine when a PDB was created and from what source.

Dropping a PDB

Occasionally, you may need to drop a PDB. You may want to do so because you do not need the PDB anymore or because you are transferring (unplugging/plugging) to a different CDB and you want to drop the PDB from the original CDB. If you need to remove a PDB, you can do it in two ways.

- Drop the PDB and its data files.

- Drop the PDB and leave its data files in place.

If you never plan on using the PDB again, you can drop it and specify that the data files should also be removed. If you plan on plugging the PDB into a different CDB, then (of course) don't drop the data files, as doing so removes them from disk.

To drop a PDB, first connect to the root container as a privileged account and close the PDB.

```
SQL> alter pluggable database mmpdb close immediate;
```

This example drops the PDB and its data files.

```
SQL> drop pluggable database mmpdb including datafiles;
```

If successful, you should see this message.

```
Pluggable database dropped.
```

This next example drops a PDB without removing the data files. You may want to do this if you're moving the pluggable database to a different CDB.

```
SQL> drop pluggable database mmpdb;
```

In this manner, the PDB is disassociated from the CDB, but its data files remain intact on disk in the file system.

CHAPTER 13

RMAN Backups and Reporting

Oracle Recovery Manager (RMAN) is provided by default when you install the Oracle software (for both the Standard Edition and Enterprise Edition). RMAN offers a robust and flexible set of backups and restore features. The following list highlights some of the most salient qualities.

- Easy-to-use commands for backup, restore, and recovery

- Ability to track which files have been backed up and where to

- Manages the deletion of obsolete backups and archivelogs

- Through parallelization can use multiple processes for backup, restore, and recovery

- Incremental backups that back up only the changes since the previous backup

- Ability to apply incremental backups to an image copy

- Recovery at the database, tablespace, data file, table, or block level

- Advanced compression and encryption features

- Integration with media managers for tape backups

- Backup validation and testing; restore validation and testing

- Cross-platform data conversion

© Michelle Malcher, Darl Kuhn 2024
M. Malcher and D. Kuhn, *Pro Oracle Database 23ai Administration*,
https://doi.org/10.1007/979-8-8688-1038-1_13

- Data Recovery Advisor, which assists with diagnosing failures and proposing solutions

- Ability to detect corrupt blocks in data files

- Advanced reporting capabilities from the RMAN command line

The goal of this chapter is to present enough information about RMAN so you can make reasonable decisions about how to implement a solid backup strategy. The basic RMAN components are described first. Afterward, let's walk through many of the decision points involved in implementing RMAN.

Note   The RMAN-related chapters in this book are not intended to be a complete reference on all aspects of backup and restore. That would take an entire book. These chapters contain the basic information you need to use RMAN successfully. If you require advanced RMAN information regarding backup, restore, and recovery, see *Backup and Recovery Reference* in the Oracle documentation.

Understanding RMAN

The RMAN ecosystem consists of many different components. Figure 13-1 shows the interactions of the main RMAN pieces. Refer to this diagram when reading this section.

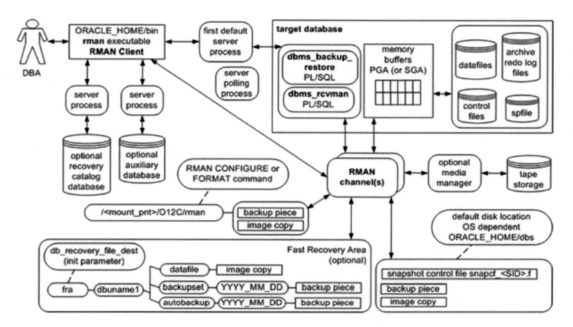

Figure 13-1. *RMAN architectural components*

The following list describes the RMAN architectural components and definitions.

- *DBA*: This is the human interaction to ensure successful backups and restores.

- *Target database*: This is the database that RMAN is backing up. You connect to the target database with the RMAN command line's TARGET parameter (see the next section for more information).

- *RMAN client*: This is the rman utility from which you issue BACKUP, RESTORE, and RECOVER commands. On most database servers, the rman utility is located in the ORACLE_HOME/bin directory (along with all the other Oracle utilities, such as sqlplus and expdp).

- *Oracle server processes*: When you execute the rman client and connect to the target database, two Oracle server background processes are started. The first default server process interacts with the PL/SQL packages to coordinate the backup activities. The secondary polling process occasionally updates Oracle data dictionary structures.

- *Channels*: This is the Oracle server process for handling I/O between files backed up (or restored) and the backup device (disk or tape).

- *PL/SQL packages*: RMAN uses two internal PL/SQL packages (owned by SYS) to perform backup and restore tasks: DBMS_RCVMAN and DBMS_BACKUP_RESTORE. DBMS_RCVMAN accesses information in the control file and passes that to the RMAN server processes. The DBMS_BACKUP_ RESTORE package performs most of RMAN's work. For example, this package creates the system calls that direct the channel processes to perform B&R operations.

- *Memory buffers* (PGA or SGA): RMAN uses a memory area in the PGA (and sometimes in the SGA) as a buffer when reading from data files and copying subsequent blocks to back up files.

- *Auxiliary database*: RMAN restores target database data files to this database to duplicate a database, create a Data Guard standby database, or perform a database point-in-time recovery (DBPITR).

- *Backup/back up*: This word can be a noun or a verb. The physical files (*backup*) store the backed-up files; copying and archiving files is *backing up*. Backups can consist of backup sets and backup pieces or image copies.

- *Backup set*: When you run an RMAN BACKUP command, it creates one or more backup sets by default. A backup set is a logical RMAN construct that groups backup piece files. You can think of the relationship of a backup set to a backup piece as similar to the relationship between a tablespace and a data file: one is a logical construct, and the other is a physical file.

- *Backup piece file*: This is an RMAN binary backup file. Each logical backup set consists of one or more backup piece files. These are the physical files that RMAN creates on disk or tape. They are binary, proprietary format files that only RMAN can read or write to. A backup piece can contain blocks from many different data files. Backup piece files are typically smaller than data files, because backup pieces contain only blocks used in the data files.

- *Image copy*: This is initiated with the BACKUP AS COPY command. It is a type of backup in which RMAN creates identical copies of a data file, archivelog file, or control file. Image copies can be operated on by OS utilities such as the Linux cp and mv commands. Image copies are used as part of incrementally updated image backups. Sometimes, it is preferable to use image copies rather than backup sets if you need to be able to restore quickly.

- *Recovery catalog*: This optional database schema contains tables used to store metadata information regarding RMAN backup operations. Oracle strongly recommends using a recovery catalog because it provides more options for backup and restore. The catalog is normally remote and does not have to be in each database.

- *Media manager*: This third-party software allows RMAN to back up files directly to tape. Backing up to tape is desirable when you do not have enough room to back up directly to disk or when disaster recovery requirements necessitate a backup to storage that can be easily moved offsite.

- *Fast recovery area* (FRA): This is a disk area that RMAN can use for backups. You can also use the FRA to multiplex control files and online redo logs. You instantiate a fast recovery with the database initialization parameters DB_RECOVERY_FILE_DEST_SIZE and DB_RECOVERY_FILE_DEST.

- *Snapshot control file*: RMAN requires a read-consistent view of the control file when either backing up the control file or synchronizing with the recovery catalog (if it is being used). In these situations, RMAN first creates a temporary copy (snapshot) of the control file. This allows RMAN to use a version of the control file that is guaranteed not to change while backing up the control file or synchronizing with the recovery catalog being used).

Types of Backups with RMAN

There are the different types of backups.

- *Full backup*: All modified blocks associated with the data file are backed up. A full backup is not a backup of the entire database. For example, you can make a full backup of one data file.

- *Incremental level 0 backup*: This backs up the same blocks as a full backup. The only difference between a level 0 backup and a full backup is that you can use a level 0 backup with other incremental backups but not a full backup.

- *Incremental level 1 backup*: This backs up only blocks that have been modified since the previous backup. Level 1 incremental backups can be either differential or cumulative. A differential level 1 backup is the default and backs up all blocks modified since the last level 0 or level 1 backup. A cumulative level 1 backup backs up all blocks that have changed since the last level 0 backup.

- *Incrementally updated backup*: This first creates an image copy of the data files, after which subsequent backups are incremental backups that are merged with the image copy. This is an efficient way to use image copies for backups. Media recoveries using incrementally updated backups are fast because the image copy of the data file is used during the restore.

- *Block change tracking*: This is a database feature that keeps track of blocks that have changed in the database. A record of the changed blocks is kept in a binary file. RMAN can use the binary file's contents to improve incremental backups' performance. Instead of scanning all modified blocks in a data file, RMAN can determine which blocks have changed from the binary block change tracking.

- *Archivelog backups*: This performs the backup of the archivelogs and allows freeing up space in the archivelog directory. Archivelog backups are normally included as part of the data files but can also be run separately to manage the disk space for the archivelogs.

Now that you understand the RMAN architectural components and the types of backups you can make, you are ready to start up RMAN and configure it for your environment.

Starting RMAN

There are several components and terms to understand; however, running the backup using RMAN is fairly straightforward. With this understanding, you have all of these options depending on your database. If you are maintaining a database that has 24/7 requirements, you need to be able to back up and restore the database effectively.

To connect to RMAN, you need to establish the following.

- OS environment variables

- Access to a privileged OS account or a database user with SYSBACKUP privileges

The easiest way to connect to RMAN is to log in to the server on which the target database resides as the owner of the Oracle software (usually named oracle, on Linux/Unix boxes). When you log in as oracle, you need to establish several OS variables before you can use utilities such as rman and sqlplus. Setting these required OS variables is covered in Chapter 2. RMAN can be run from another server with the Oracle software installed. The service or SID name is needed to connect to the target database to perform the backup.

At a minimum, you need to set ORACLE_HOME and ORACLE_SID. Additionally, it is convenient if the PATH variable includes the ORACLE_HOME/bin directory. This is the directory that contains the Oracle utilities.

After establishing your OS variables, you can invoke RMAN from the OS, as shown next.

```
$ rman target /
```

You can also use the following.

```
$ rman target backupuser@mmdb23ai
```

When connecting to RMAN, you do not have to specify the AS SYSDBA clause (as you do when connecting to a database as a privileged user in SQL*Plus). This is because RMAN always requires that you connect as a database user with SYSDBA privileges. Any user needs to have the SYSBACKUP role granted to perform the backups.

The SYSBACKUP privilege allows you to assign privileges to a user that include only the permissions needed to perform backup and restore operations. The SYSBACKUP privilege contains the subset of SYSDBA privileges required for carrying out such operations. SYSBACKUP is needed to perform backups.

The previous example of logging in to RMAN uses OS authentication. This type of authentication means that if you can log in to an authorized OS account (such as the owner of the Oracle software, usually oracle), you are allowed to connect to the database without having to provide a username and password. You administer OS authentication by assigning special groups to OS accounts. When you install the Oracle binaries in a Linux/Unix environment, you are required to specify at the time of installation the names of the OS groups that are assigned the database privileges of SYSDBA, SYSOPER, and SYSBACKUP—typically, the dba, oper, and backupdba groups, respectively (see Chapter 1). As part of an enterprise backup solution, creating a separate user for backups to perform the backups to disk or tape and schedule to run automatically is recommended.

Note   It is typical to be in a SQL*Plus session and accidentally attempt an RMAN command or try running RMAN from SQL*Plus. Well, that does not work.

```
SOL> rmanSP2-0042: unknown command "rman" - rest of line ignored.
```

The reason is that the rman client is an OS utility, not a SQL*Plus function. You must invoke the rman client from the OS prompt.

RMAN Architectural Decisions

Archiving should be enabled for your production database; otherwise, you cannot do a point-in-time recovery. You can use RMAN out of the box to run commands like this to back up your entire target database.

```
$ rman target /
RMAN> backup database;
```

If you run this command at the CDB level, it back up your container database and all pluggable databases in the container.

If you only want to back up the CDB, use the following.

```
$ rman target /
RMAN> backup database root;
```

From the CDB you can also back up just the pluggable databases by listing them.

```
$ rman target /
RMAN> backup pluggable database mmpdb, salespdb;
```

You can also back up a database from any of the pluggable databases and just back up the PDB you use as the target.

If you experience a media failure, you can restore all data files as follows.

```
RMAN> shutdown immediate;
RMAN> startup mount;
RMAN> restore database;
```

After your database is restored, you can fully recover it.

```
RMAN> recover database;
RMAN> alter database open;
```

You are good to go, right? No, not quite. RMAN's default attributes are reasonably set for simple backup requirements. The out-of-the-box RMAN settings may be appropriate for small development or test databases. But, for any business-critical database, you must consider where the backups are stored, how long to store backups on disk or tape, which RMAN features are appropriate for the database, and so on. The following sections in this chapter walk you through many backup and recovery architectural decisions necessary for implementing RMAN in a production environment. RMAN has a vast and robust variety of options for customizing backups, managing backup files, and performing restores; typically, you do not need to implement many of RMAN's features. However, each time you implement RMAN to back up a production database, you should think through each decision point and decide whether you require an attribute.

Run RMAN Remotely or Locally

If you run RMAN remotely, make sure you are using the same version of RMAN. It needs to be compatible with the Oracle database. If you run RMAN locally, you use the same version as the database.

Running remotely allows backups from one central location, even if the backup files are created on the target database server.

Specify the Backup User

As discussed previously, RMAN requires that you use a database user with SYSBACKUP privileges. Whether running RMAN from the command line or invoking RMAN in a script, using a backup user is appropriate. For example, here is how to connect to RMAN from the command line.

```
$ rman target BACKUPUSER/$password
```

Use Online Backups

Most production databases have 24/7 availability requirements. Therefore, you need to take online RMAN backups. Your database must be in archivelog mode for online backups and to recover to a point in time. You must carefully consider how to place archivelogs, how to format them, how often to back them up, and how long to retain them before deletion.

Set the Archivelog Destination and File Format

Oracle writes the archivelogs to one or more of the following locations.

- Default location

- FRA

- Location specified via the LOG_ARCHIVE_DEST_N initialization parameters

If you do not use an FRA and if you do not explicitly set the archivelog destination via a `LOG_ARCHIVE_DEST_N` initialization parameter, then the archivelogs are written to an OS-dependent location with the format `%t_%s_%r.dbf` (`%t` is the timestamp, `%s` is the log sequence number, and `%r` is the log ID).

With FRA, the archivelogs are written to a directory in the FRA by default. The default filename format of the archivelog files created in the FRA is Oracle Managed File (OMF). It is better to set the parameters and choose a format.

```
log_archive_dest_1 = 'LOCATION=/oraarch1/mmdb23ai'
log_archive_format = '%t_%s_%r.arc'
```

The `.arc` extension avoids the potentially confusing task of identifying a file as an archivelog file or a live database data file.

Configure Channel Format

When writing to multiple disk locations, it is easier to specify the directories using `CONFIGURE CHANNEL ... FORMAT`. Here is a typical configuration specifying the following.

```
RMAN> configure device type disk parallelism 3;
RMAN> configure channel 1 device type disk format '/u01/db23ai/rman/
rman1_%U.bk';

RMAN> configure channel 2 device type disk format '/u02/db23ai/rman/
rman2_%U.bk'; RMAN> configure channel 3 device type disk format '/u03/
db23ai/rman/rman3_%U.bk';
```

In these lines of code, you should configure the device-type parallelism degree to match the number of channels you allocated. RMAN allocates the number of channels specified by the degree of parallelism; other configured channels are ignored. For instance, if you specify a degree of parallelism of 2, RMAN allocates only two channels, regardless of the number of channels you configured via the `CONFIGURE CHANNEL` command.

In this example of configuring three channels, suppose the `BACKUP` command is issued as follows.

```
RMAN> backup database;
```

RMAN allocates three channels, all on separate mount points (/u01, /u02, /u03), and writes in parallel to the specified locations. RMAN creates as many backup pieces in the three locations as it deems necessary to create a backup of the database.

If you need to unconfigure a channel after running the backup, do so as follows.

```
RMAN> configure channel 3 device type disk clear;
```

Set the Autobackup of the Control File

You should always configure RMAN to back up the control file automatically after running any RMAN BACKUP or COPY command or after you make physical changes to the database that result in updates to the control file (such as adding/removing a data file). Use the SHOW command to display the current setting of the control file autobackup.

```
RMAN> show controlfile autobackup;
```

Here is some sample output.

```
RMAN configuration parameters for database with db_unique_name db23ai are:
CONFIGURE CONTROLFILE AUTOBACKUP ON;
```

The following line of code shows how to enable automatic backup of the control file feature.

```
RMAN> configure controlfile autobackup on;
```

The automatic control file backup always goes into its own backup set. When autobackup of the control file is enabled, if you use an spfile, it is automatically backed up along with the control file.

Back up Archivelogs

You should back up your archivelogs regularly. The archivelog files should not be removed from disk until you have backed them up at least once. We usually like to keep on disk any archivelogs generated since the last good RMAN backup.

Generally, we instruct RMAN to back up the archivelogs while the data files are backed up. This is a sufficient strategy in most situations. Here is the command to back up the archivelogs along with the data files.

```
RMAN> backup database plus archivelog;
```

Sometimes, if your database generates a great deal of redo, you may need to back up your archivelogs at a frequency different from that of the data files. DBAs may back up the archivelogs two or three times a day; after the logs are backed up, the DBAs delete them to make room for more current archivelog files.

In most situations, you do not need any archivelogs generated before your last good backup. For example, if a data file has experienced media failure, you need to restore the data file from a backup and then apply any archivelogs that were generated during and after the backup of the data file.

On some occasions, you may need archivelogs that were generated before the last backup. For instance, you may experience a media failure, attempt to restore your database from the last good backup, find corruption in that backup, and therefore need to restore from an older backup. At that point, you need a copy of all archivelogs that have been generated since that older backup was made.

Retention policies are part of this, too. How far back do you need to be able to restore? If there are failures of media when restoring, having the archivelogs allow you to recover.

Determine the Location for the Snapshot Control File

RMAN requires a read-consistent view of the control file for the following tasks.

- Synchronizing with the recovery catalog

- Backing up the current control file

RMAN creates a snapshot copy of the current control file used as a read-consistent copy while performing these tasks. This ensures that RMAN is working from a copy of the control file that is not being modified.

The default location of the snapshot control file is OS-specific. The default location/ format on Linux platforms is `$ORACLE_HOME/dbs/snapcf_@.f`. Note that the default location is not in the FRA.

You can display the current snapshot control file details using the SHOW command.

```
RMAN> show snapshot controlfile name;
CONFIGURE SNAPSHOT CONTROLFILE NAME TO
   '/ora01/app/oracle/product/23.1.0.1/db23ai/dbs/snapcf_db23ai.f'; # default
```

Use a Recovery Catalog

RMAN always stores its latest backup operations in the target database control file. You can set up an optional recovery catalog to store metadata regarding RMAN backups. The recovery catalog is a separate schema (usually in a database different from that of the target database) that contains database objects (tables, indexes, and so on) that store the RMAN backup information. The recovery catalog does not store RMAN backup pieces, only backup metadata.

The following are the main advantages of using a recovery catalog.

- It provides a secondary repository for RMAN metadata. If you lose all your control files and backups of your control files, you can still retrieve RMAN metadata from the recovery catalog.

- It stores RMAN metadata for a much longer than possible when using a control file for the repository.

- It offers access to all RMAN features. Some restore and recovery features are simpler when using a recovery catalog.

The disadvantage of using a recovery catalog is that this is another database you have to set up, maintain, and back up. Additionally, when you start a backup and attempt to connect to the recovery catalog, if the recovery catalog is not available for any reason (server down, network issues, and so on), you can continue with the backup without a recovery catalog.

You must also be aware of versioning aspects when using a recovery catalog. Make sure the version of the database you use to store the recovery catalog is compatible with the version of the target database. When you upgrade a target database, be sure the recovery catalog is upgraded (if necessary).

Configure RMAN's Backup Retention Policy

RMAN retention policies allow you to specify how long you want to retain backups. RMAN has two mutually exclusive methods of specifying a retention policy.

- Recovery window

- Number of backups (redundancy)

With a recovery window, you specify the number of days in the past for which you want to recover to any point in that window. For example, if you specify a retention policy window of five days, then RMAN does not mark as obsolete backups of data files and archivelogs that are required to be able to restore to any point in that five-day window.

```
RMAN> configure retention policy to recovery window of 5 days;
```

You can also specify that RMAN keeps a minimum number of backups. For instance, if redundancy is set to 2, then RMAN does not mark the latest two backups of data files and archivelog files as obsolete.

```
RMAN> configure retention policy to redundancy 2;
```

Delete Backups, Based on Retention Policy

You can report on backups that RMAN has determined to be obsolete per the retention policy, as follows.

```
RMAN> report obsolete;
```

To delete obsolete backups, run the DELETE OBSOLETE command.

```
RMAN> delete obsolete;
```

You are prompted with the following.

```
Do you really want to delete the above objects (enter YES or NO)?
```

If you are scripting the procedure, you can specify the delete not to prompt for input.

```
RMAN> delete noprompt obsolete;
```

To have RMAN delete obsolete archivelogs.

```
RMAN> crosscheck archivelog all;
RMAN> delete archivelog all;
```

Run the CROSSCHECK command before running the DELETE command. Doing so ensures that RMAN knows whether a file is on disk.

Use Backup Sets or Image Copies

When you issue an RMAN BACKUP command, you can specify that the backup is one of the following.

- Backup set
- Image copy

A backup set is the default type of RMAN backup. A backup set contains backup pieces, which are binary files that only RMAN can write to or read from. Backup sets are desirable because they are generally smaller than the data files being backed up. RMAN automatically attempts to create backup pieces with unused block compression. In this mode, RMAN reads a bitmap to determine which blocks are allocated and reads only from those blocks in the data files.

Contrast the backup set with an image copy. An image copy creates a byte-for-byte identical copy of each data file. The advantage of creating an image copy is that (if necessary) you can manipulate the image copy without using RMAN (as with an OS copy utility). Additionally, in the event of a media failure, an image copy is a fast method of restoring data files because RMAN has only to copy the file back from the backup location (there is no reconstructing of the data file because it is an exact copy).

The size of the backup to disk is almost always a concern. Backup sets are more efficient regarding disk space consumption. Because backup sets can take advantage of RMAN compression, there is also less I/O involved compared with an image copy. In many environments, reducing the I/O so as not to impact other applications is a concern.

However, if you feel that you need direct control over the backup files that RMAN creates, or you are in an environment where the speed of the restore process is paramount, consider using image copies.

Use Incremental Backups

Incremental backup strategies are appropriate for large databases in which only a small portion of the database blocks change from one backup to the next. If you are in a data warehouse environment, you may want to consider an incremental backup strategy because it can greatly reduce the size of your backups. For example, you may want to run a weekly level 0 backup and then run a daily level 1 incremental backup.

The term RMAN level 0 incremental backup doesn't exactly describe itself very well, either. A level 0 incremental backup backs up the same blocks as a full backup. In other words, the following two commands back up the same blocks in a database.

```
RMAN> backup as backupset full database;
RMAN> backup as backupset incremental level=0 database;
```

The only difference between the prior two commands is that an incremental level 0 backup can be used with other incremental backups. In contrast, a full backup cannot participate in an incremental backup strategy. Therefore, we almost always prefer to use the INCREMENTAL LEVEL=0 syntax (as opposed to a full backup); it gives you the flexibility to use the level 0 incremental backup along with subsequent incremental level 1 backups.

Use Block Change Tracking

This feature keeps track of when a database block changes. If you use an incremental backup strategy, you can enhance performance because by implementing this feature, RMAN does not have to scan each block (under the high-water mark) in the data files to determine whether it needs to be backed up. Rather, RMAN only has to access the block change tracking file to find which blocks have changed since the last backup and directly access those blocks. If you work in a large data warehouse environment and use an incremental backup strategy, consider enabling block change tracking to enhance performance.

```
SQL> alter database enable block change tracking;
```

Configure Informational Output

A good practice is to always set the NLS_DATE_FORMAT variable at the OS level (before running RMAN) so that the date and time information are displayed in the RMAN log instead of just the date, which is the default.

```
$ export NLS_DATE_FORMAT='dd-mon-yyyy hh24:mi:ss'
```

This is useful during troubleshooting, especially when RMAN fails because you can use the exact date/time information for the RMAN error and compare it with the alert. log and OS/XML logs to verify what other events occurred in the database/server.

Also, consider executing SET ECHO ON to ensure that RMAN commands are displayed within the log before the command is executed. Execute SHOW ALL as well to display the current settings of RMAN variables. These settings are useful when troubleshooting and tuning.

Put It Together in a Script

An RMAN script can pull these configurations together and automate the backup job. The following is an instructional script that shows how these components work together.

```
 1 #!/bin/bash
 2 HOLDSID=${1} # SID name
 3 PRG=`basename $0`
 4 USAGE="Usage: ${PRG} <database name> "
 5 if [ -z "${HOLDSID}" ]; then
 6 echo "${USAGE}"
 7 exit 1
 8 fi
 9 #-----------------------------------------------------------------------
10 # source environment variables (see Chapter 2 for details on oraset)
11 . /etc/oraset $HOLDSID
12 BOX=`uname -a | awk '{print$2}'`
13 MAILX='/bin/mailx'
14 MAIL_LIST='dba@company.com'
15 export NLS_DATE_FORMAT='dd-mon-yyyy hh24:mi:ss'
16 date
17 #-----------------------------------------------------------------------
18 LOCKFILE=/tmp/$PRG.lock
19 if [ -f $LOCKFILE ]; then
20   echo "lock file exists, exiting..."
21   exit 1
22 else
23echo "DO NOT REMOVE, $LOCKFILE" > $LOCKFILE
24 fi
25 #
26 rman nocatalog <<EOF
```

```
27 connect target /
28 set echo on;
29 show all;
30 crosscheck backup;
31 crosscheck copy;
32 configure controlfile autobackup on;
33 configure controlfile autobackup format for device type disk to '/u01/
   db23ai/rman/db23ai_ctl_%F.bk';
34 configure retention policy to redundancy 1;
35 configuredevice type disk parallelism 2;
36 configure channel 1 device type disk format '/u01/db23ai/rman/
   db23ai_%U.bk';
37 configure channel 2 device type disk format '/u02/db23ai/rman/
   db23ai_%U.bk';
38 backup as compressed backupset incremental level=0 database plus
   archivelog;
39 delete noprompt obsolete;
40 EOF
41 #-------------------------------------------------------------------------
42 if [ $? -ne 0 ]; then
43   echo "RMAN problem..."
44   echo "Check RMAN backups" | $MAILX -s "RMAN issue: $ORACLE_SID on
     $BOX" $MAIL_LIST
45 else
46 echo "RMAN ran okay..."
47 fi
48 #-------------------------------------------------------------------------
49 if [ -f $LOCKFILE ]; then
50   rm $LOCKFILE
51 fi
52 #-------------------------------------------------------------------------
53 date
54 exit 0
```

This gives a basic script for a starting point to understanding the RMAN recommendations and being able to implement them. There is also a good chance that a script has already been configured for your environment, which helps understand it.

Check for Corruption

A backup file is only good if you can restore it. You can use RMAN to check for corruption in data files, archivelogs, and control files. You can also verify whether a backup set is restorable. The RMAN VALIDATE command is used to perform these types of integrity checks. There are three ways you can run the VALIDATE command.

- VALIDATE

- BACKUP ... VALIDATE

- RESTORE ... VALIDATE

Using VALIDATE

The VALIDATE command can be used to check for missing files or physical corruption in database data files, archivelog files, control files, spfiles, and backup set pieces. For example, this command validates all data files and the control files.

```
RMAN> validate database;
```

You can also validate just the control file, as follows.

```
RMAN> validate current controlfile;
```

You can validate the archivelog files, as follows.

```
RMAN> validate archivelog all;
```

You may want to combine all the prior integrity checks into one command, as follows.

```
RMAN> validate database include current controlfile plus archivelog;
```

Under normal conditions, the VALIDATE command checks only for physical corruption. You can specify that you also want to check for logical corruption using the CHECK LOGICAL clause.

```
RMAN> validate check logical database include current controlfile plus
archivelog;
```

VALIDATE has a variety of uses. Here are a few more examples.

```
RMAN> validate database skip offline;
RMAN> validate copy of database;
RMAN> validate tablespace system;
RMAN> validate datafile 3 block 20 to 30;
RMAN> validate spfile;
RMAN> validate backupset <primary_key_value>;
RMAN> validate recovery area;
RMAN> validate pluggable database pdbname;
```

If RMAN detects any corrupt blocks, the V$DATABASE_BLOCK_CORRUPTION is populated. This view contains information on the file number, block number, and number of blocks affected. You can use this information to perform a block-level recovery.

Physical corruption is a change to a block such that its contents do not match the physical format that Oracle expects. By default, RMAN checks for physical corruption when backing up, restoring, and validating data files. With logical corruption, a block is in the correct format, but the contents are not consistent with what Oracle expects, such as in a row piece or an index entry.

Using BACKUP ... VALIDATE

The BACKUP ... VALIDATE command is very similar to the VALIDATE command in that it can check to see if data files are available and if the data files contain any corrupt blocks. The following is an example.

```
RMAN> backup validate database;
```

This command does not actually create any backup files. It only reads the data files and checks for corruption. Like the VALIDATE command, BACKUP VALIDATE, by default, checks only for physical corruption. You can instruct it to check as well for logical corruption, as shown next.

```
RMAN> backup validate check logical database;
```

Here are some variations of the BACKUP ... VALIDATE command.

```
RMAN> backup validate database current controlfile;
RMAN> backup validate check logical database current controlfile plus
archivelog;
```

Also, like the VALIDATE command, BACKUP ... VALIDATE populate V$DATABASE_BLOCK_CORRUPTION if it detects any corrupt blocks. The information in this view can be used to determine which blocks can potentially be restored by block-level recovery.

Using RESTORE ... VALIDATE

The RESTORE ... VALIDATE command is used to verify backup files used in a restore operation. This command validates backup sets, data file copies, and archivelog files.

```
RMAN> restore validate database;
```

No actual files are restored when using RESTORE ... VALIDATE. This means you can run the command while the database is online and available.

Using a Recovery Catalog

When you use a recovery catalog, it is possible to create the recovery catalog user in the same database, on the same server, as your target database. However, that approach is not recommended because you do not want the availability of your target database or of the server on which the target database resides to affect the recovery catalog. Therefore, you should create the recovery catalog database on a server different from your target databases. The recovery catalog can be used for the whole database environment depending on sizing, but remember it normally stores the information stored in control files.

Creating a Recovery Catalog

When we use a recovery catalog, we prefer to have a dedicated database that is used only for the recovery catalog. This ensures that the recovery catalog is not affected by any maintenance or downtime required by another application (and vice versa).

Listed next are the steps for creating a recovery catalog.

1. Create a database on a server different from your target database, to be used for the recovery catalog. Make sure the database is adequately sized. We have found that Oracle's recommended sizes are usually much too small. Here are some adequate recommendations for initial sizing.

   SYSTEM tablespace: 500 MB

   SYSAUX tablespace: 500 MB

   TEMP tablespace: 500 MB

   UNDO tablespace: 500 MB

   Online redo logs: 25 MB each; three groups, multiplexed with two members per group

   RECCAT tablespace: 500 MB

2. Create a tablespace to be used by the recovery catalog user. We recommend giving the tablespace a name such as RECCAT so that it is readily identifiable as the tablespace that contains the recovery catalog metadata.

   ```
   SQL> CREATE TABLESPACE reccat
   DATAFILE '/u01/dbfile/O12C/reccat01.dbf' SIZE 500M
   EXTENT MANAGEMENT LOCAL UNIFORM SIZE 128k
   SEGMENT SPACE MANAGEMENT AUTO;
   ```

3. Create a user that own the tables and other objects used to store the target database metadata. We recommend giving the recovery catalog user a name such as RCAT so that it is readily identifiable as the user that owns the recovery catalog objects. Also, grant the RECOVERY_CATALOG_OWNER role to the RCAT user and CREATE SESSION.

```
SQL> CREATE USER rcat IDENTIFIED BY Pa33word1
TEMPORARY TABLESPACE temp
DEFAULT TABLESPACE reccat
QUOTA UNLIMITED ON reccat;
--
GRANT RECOVERY_CATALOG_OWNER TO rcat;
GRANT CREATE SESSION TO rcat;
```

4. Connect through RMAN as RCAT and create the recovery catalog objects.

```
$ rman catalog rcat/Pa33word1
```

5. Now, run the CREATE CATALOG command.

```
RMAN> create catalog
RMAN> exit;
```

6. This command may take a few minutes to run. When finished, you can verify that the tables were created with the following query.

```
$ sqlplus rcat/Pa33word1
SQL> select table_name from user_tables;
```

7. Here is a small sample of the output.

```
TABLE_NAME

------------------------------

DB
NODE
CONF
DBINC
```

Registering a Target Database

Now, you can register a target database with the recovery catalog. Log in to the target database server. Ensure that you can establish connectivity to the recovery catalog database. For instance, one approach is to populate the TNS_ADMIN/tnsnames.ora file with an entry that points to the remote database. On the target database server, register the recovery catalog as follows.

```
$ rman target / catalog rcat/Pa33word1@rcat
```

When you connect, you should see verification that you are connecting to both the target and the recovery catalog.

```
connected to target database: DB23AI (DBID=3423216220)
connected to recovery catalog database
```

Next, run the REGISTER DATABASE command.

```
RMAN> register database;
```

Now, you can run backup operations and have the metadata about the backup tasks written to both the control file and the recovery catalog. Make sure you connect to the recovery catalog and target database each time you run RMAN commands.

```
$ rman target / catalog rcat/Pa33word1@rcat
RMAN> backup database;
```

Backing Up the Recovery Catalog

Make certain you include a strategy for backing up and recovering the recovery catalog database. For the most protection, be sure the recovery catalog database is in archivelog mode and use RMAN to back up the database.

You can also use a tool such as Data Pump to take a snapshot of the database. The downside to using Data Pump is that you can potentially lose some information in the recovery catalog that was created after the Data Pump export.

Keep in mind that if you experience a complete failure on your recovery catalog database server, you can still use RMAN to back up your target databases. But you cannot connect to the recovery catalog. Therefore, any scripts that instruct RMAN to connect to the target and the recovery catalog must be modified.

Also, if you completely lose a recovery catalog and do not have a backup, one option is to re-create it from scratch. When you re-create it, you reregister the target databases with the recovery catalog. You lose any long-term historical recovery catalog metadata.

Synchronizing the Recovery Catalog

You may have an issue with the network that renders the recovery catalog inaccessible. In the meantime, you connect to your target database and perform backup operations. The network issues are resolved sometime later, and you can again connect to the recovery catalog.

In this situation, you need to resynchronize the recovery catalog with the target database so that the recovery catalog is aware of any backup operations that are not stored in it. Run the following command to ensure that the recovery catalog has the most recent backup information.

```
$ rman target / catalog rcat/Pa33word1@rcat
RMAN> resync catalog;
```

Keep in mind that you have to resynchronize the catalog only if, for some reason, you are performing backup operations without connecting to the catalog. Under normal conditions, you do not have to run the RESYNC command.

Recovery Catalog Versions

We recommend that you create a recovery catalog for each version of the target databases that you are backing up. Doing so saves you some headaches with compatibility issues and upgrades. We have found it easier to use a recovery catalog when the database version of the rman client is the same version used when creating the catalog.

Yes, having multiple versions of the recovery catalog can cause some confusion. However, if you are in an environment with several different versions of the Oracle database, then multiple recovery catalogs may be more convenient.

Dropping a Recovery Catalog

If you are not using a recovery catalog and no longer need the data, you can drop it. To do so, connect to the recovery catalog database as the catalog owner and issue the DROP CATALOG command.

```
$ rman catalog rcat/Pa33word1@rcat
RMAN> drop catalog;
```

You are prompted as follows.

```
recovery catalog owner is RCAT
enter DROP CATALOG command again to confirm catalog removal
```

If you enter the DROP CATALOG command again, all the objects in the recovery catalog are removed from the recovery catalog database. It is recommended you make a backup of the catalog before performing any drop commands or after registering databases.

The other way to drop a catalog is to drop the owner. To do so, connect to the recovery catalog as a user with DBA privileges and issue the DROP USER statement.

```
$ sqlplus / as sysdba
SQL> drop user rcat cascade;
```

SQL*Plus does not prompt you twice; it does as you instructed and drops the user and its objects. Again, the only reason to do this is when you are certain you do not need the recovery catalog or its data any longer. Use caution when dropping a user or the recovery catalog: another good practice is that you take a Data Pump export of the recovery catalog owner before dropping it.

Querying for Output in the Data Dictionary

You can still view the most recent RMAN output by querying the data dictionary if you do not capture any RMAN output. The V$RMAN_OUTPUT view contains messages recently reported by RMAN.

```
SQL> select sid, recid, output
from v$rman_output
order by recid;
```

The V$RMAN_OUTPUT view is an in-memory object that holds up to 32,768 rows. Information in this view is cleared out when you stop and start your database. The view is handy when you are using the RMAN SPOOL LOG command to spool output to a file and cannot view what is happening at your terminal.

RMAN Reporting

There are several different methods for reporting on the RMAN environment.

- LIST command
- REPORT command
- Query metadata via data dictionary views

When first learning RMAN, the difference between the LIST and REPORT commands may seem confusing because the distinction between the two is not clear-cut. In general, we use the LIST command to view information about existing backups and use the REPORT command to determine which files need to be backed or to display information on obsolete or expired backups.

SQL queries can provide details for specialized reports (not available via LIST or REPORT) or for automating reports, for example, generally implementing an automated check via a shell script and SQL that reports whether the RMAN backups have run within the last day.

Using LIST

When investigating issues with RMAN backups, one of the first tasks we usually undertake is connecting to the target database and running the LIST BACKUP command. This command allows you to view backup sets, backup pieces, and the files included in the backup.

```
RMAN> list backup;
```

The command shows all RMAN backups recorded in the repository. You may want to spool the backups to an output file so that you can save the output and then use an OS editor to search through and look for specific strings in the output.

To get a summarized view of backup information, use the LIST BACKUP SUMARY command.

```
RMAN> list backup summary;
```

You can also use the LIST command to report just image copy information.

```
RMAN> list copy;
```

To list all files that have been backed up and the associated backup set, issue the following command.

```
RMAN> list backup by file;
```

These commands display archivelogs on disk.

```
RMAN> list archivelog all;
RMAN> list copy of archivelog all;
```

Also, this command lists the backups of the archivelogs (and which archivelogs are contained in which backup pieces).

```
RMAN> list backup of archivelog all;
```

There are many ways you can run the LIST command (and, likewise, the REPORT command, covered in the next section). The prior methods are the ones you run most of the time. See the *Oracle Database Backup and Recovery Reference Guide* documentation for a complete list of options.

Using REPORT

The RMAN REPORT command is useful for reporting on a variety of details. You can quickly view all the data files associated with a database as follows.

```
RMAN> report schema;
```

The REPORT command provides information about backups marked obsolete via the RMAN retention policy. The following is an example.

```
RMAN> report obsolete;
```

You can report on data files that need to be backed up, as defined by the retention policy, as follows.

```
RMAN> report need backup;
```

Several ways to report on data files need to be backed up. Here are some other examples.

```
RMAN> report need backup redundancy 2;
RMAN> report need backup redundancy 2 datafile 2;
```

The REPORT command may also be used for data files that have never been backed up, or that may contain data created from a NOLOGGING operation. For example, say you have direct-path loaded data into a table, and the data file in which the table resides has not been backed up. The following command detects these conditions.

```
RMAN> report unrecoverable;
```

Using SQL

There are several data dictionary views available for querying backup information. Table 13-1 describes RMAN-related data dictionary views. These views are available regardless of your use of a recovery catalog (the information in these views is derived from the control file).

Table 13-1. *Description of RMAN Backup Data Dictionary Views*

View Name	Information Provided
V$RMAN_BACKUP_ JOB_DETAILS	RMAN backup jobs
V$BACKUP	Backup status of online datafiles placed in backup mode
V$BACKUP_ARCHIVELOG_ DETAILS	Archive logs backed up
V$BACKUP_CONTROLFILE_ DETAILS	Control files backed up
V$BACKUP_COPY_DETAILS	Control file and data files copies
V$BACKUP_DATAFILE	Control files and data files backed up
V$BACKUP_DATAFILE_ DETAILS	Data files backed up in backup sets, image copies, and proxy copies
V$BACKUP_FILES	Data files, control files, spfiles, and archivelogs backed up
V$BACKUP_PIECE	Backup piece files
V$BACKUP_PIECE_DETAILS	Backup piece details
V$BACKUP_SET	Backup sets
V$BACKUP_SET_DETAILS	Backup set details

Sometimes, DBAs new to RMAN have a hard time grasping the concept of backups, backup sets, backup pieces, and data files and how they relate. We find the following query useful when discussing RMAN backup components. This query displays backup sets, the backup pieces with the set, and the data files that are backed up within the backup pieces.

```
SQL> SET LINES 132 PAGESIZE 100
SQL> BREAK ON REPORT ON bs_key ON completion_time ON bp_name ON file_name
SQL> COL bs_key         FORM 99999 HEAD "BS Key"
SQL> COL bp_name FORM a40 HEAD "BP Name"
SQL> COL file_name FORM a40 HEAD "Datafile"
SQL> --
SQL> SELECT
 s.recid bs_key
,TRUNC(s.completion_time) completion_time
,p.handle bp_name
```

The output here has been shortened to fit on the page.

```
BS Key COMPLETIO BP Name                              Datafile
------ --------- ------------------------------------ ------------------------
159    11-JUN-23 /u01/DB23AI/rman/r16qnv59jj_1_1.bk /u01/dbfile/db23ai/
                                                         inv_data2.dbf
                                      /u01/dbfile/db23ai/lob_data01.dbf
                                       /u01/dbfile/db23ai/p14_tbsp.dbf
                                       /u01/dbfile/db23ai/p15_tbsp.dbf
                                       /u01/dbfile/db23ai/p16_tbsp.dbf
```

Sometimes, it is useful to report on the performance of RMAN backups. The following query reports the time taken for an RMAN backup per session.

```
SQL> COL hoursFORM 9999.99
SQL> COL time_taken_display FORM a20
SQL> SET LINESIZE 132
SQL> --
SQL> SELECT
session_recid
```

```
,compression_ratio
,time_taken_display
,(end_time - start_time) * 24 as hours
,TO_CHAR(end_time,'dd-mon-yy hh24:mi') as end_time
FROM v$rman_backup_job_details
ORDER BY end_time;
```

Here is some sample output.

SESSION_RECID	COMPRESSION_RATIO	TIME_TAKEN_DISPLAY	HOURS	END_TIME
15	1	00:05:08	.09	11-jun-23 13:41
27	3.79407176	00:00:09	.00	11-jun-23 13:52
33	1.19992137	00:05:01	.08	11-jun-23 14:07

A session connection to RMAN summarizes the contents of V$RMAN_BACKUP_ JOB_DETAILS. Therefore, the report output is more accurate if you connect to RMAN (establishing a session) and then exit after the backup job is complete. If you remain connected to RMAN while running multiple backup jobs, the query output reports all backup activity while connected (for that session).

You should have an automated method of detecting whether RMAN backups are running and if data files are being backed up. One reliable method of automating such a task is to embed SQL into a shell script and then run the script periodically from a scheduling utility such as cron.

We typically run two basic types of checks regarding the RMAN backups.

- Have the RMAN backups run recently?

- Are there any data files that have not been backed up recently?

The following shell script checks for these conditions. You need to modify the script and provide it with a username and password for a user that can query the data dictionary objects referenced in the script and change the email address of where messages are sent. When running the script, you need to pass in two variables: the Oracle SID and the threshold number of past days you want to check for the last time the backups ran or when a data file was backed up.

```
#!/bin/bash
#
if [ $# -ne 2 ]; then
```

```
    echo "Usage: $0 SID threshold"
    exit 1
fi
# source oracle OS variables
. /var/opt/oracle/oraset $1
crit_var=$(sqlplus -s <<EOF
/ as sysdba
SET HEAD OFF FEEDBACK OFF
SELECT COUNT(*) FROM
(SELECT (sysdate - MAX(end_time)) delta
FROM v\$rman_backup_job_details) a
WHERE a.delta > $2;
EOF)
#
if [ $crit_var -ne 0 ]; then
    echo "rman backups not running on $1" | mailx -s "rman problem" dkuhn@
    gmail.com
else
    echo "rman backups ran ok"
fi
#-----------------------------------------------------------------------------
crit_var2=$(sqlplus -s <<EOF
/ as sysdba
SET HEAD OFF FEEDBACK OFF
SELECT COUNT(*)
FROM
(
SELECT name
FROM v\$datafile

MINUS

SELECT DISTINCT
f.name
FROM v\$backup_datafile d
    ,v\$datafilef
```

```
WHERE d.file#= f.file#
ANDd.completion_time > sysdate - $2);
EOF)
#
if [ $crit_var2 -ne 0 ]; then
  echo "datafile not backed up on $1" | mailx -s "backup problem" dba@
  company.com
else
  echo "datafiles are backed up..."
fi
#
exit 0
```

For example, to check if backups have been running successfully within the past two days, run the script (named rman_chk.bsh).

```
$ rman_chk.bsh INVPRD 2
```

The prior script is basic but effective. You can enhance it as required for your RMAN environment.

Migration using RMAN

RMAN can be used to migrate databases across different operating system platforms and cloud platforms. The backup set can also have the XML file used for creating Pluggable Databases, and you can plug in the database from this backup set and help with migration to other Oracle Databases.

To do this, create a full backup of the Pluggable Database, including the archived redo logs.

```
RMAN> backup database plug archivelog all tag for_migration;
```

If you are in the container database.

```
RMAN> backup pluggable database pdb23ai plus archivelog all tag
for_migration;
```

With Oracle Database 23ai, you can copy the SBT backups to other locations. You might be asking *SBT backups*? These are tape backups and even if you are not using physical tape for backup copies, the commands are the same to go to cloud destinations. It is just a different device type for your backups. This is useful to copy the backups across different applications for migrations. You might want to copy from one cloud to another, like from AWS to OCI.

The previous way to do this was to restore the backup to disk and then copy it to another media, but now you can copy from one device to another. Here is an example run command for the RMAN script.

```
Run { allocate channel t1 device type sbt parms = 'SBT_LIBRARY=oracle.oci';
input device parms = 'SBT_LIBRARY=oracle.osbws'; backupset all; }
```

It is important to have good backups and verify that the correct files are being backed up regularly, but these files do not matter much unless you can actually use them to restore a database that has been corrupted or had some disaster occur. The next chapter shows you how to handle restore and recovery.

CHAPTER 14

RMAN Restore and Recovery

We said it in the previous chapter and will say it again: a backup is good only if you can use it to restore. Ideally, you will never need it, but a restore process needs to be documented, tested, and practiced. Practicing allows errors to occur and for you to document strange things that can happen so that you can remain calm when needing to complete the restore under pressure. It also helps verify that there are good backups available. Another benefit is that it allows you to think through ways to get up and running very quickly.

We have heard so many stories of tape backups not being available or that the previous night's backups failed, so a day of data loss is the minimum. Practicing restoring allows other solutions to be put into place to protect from these horror stories of being unable to recover or get the data back from a disaster or even errors. Files can get corrupted, areas can be flooded, and hardware failures can happen.

Most situations in which you need to restore and recover will not be as bad as that. Even in places where there are safeguards and few natural disasters, something always seems to occur to make you want to test the recovery and validate the backups. With this in mind, there is a need for the following.

- A backup strategy

- A DBA with backup and recovery skills

- A restore and recovery strategy, including a requirement to test the restore and recovery periodically

This chapter walks you through the restore and recovery process and the common tasks you must perform when dealing with media failures.

© Michelle Malcher, Darl Kuhn 2024
M. Malcher and D. Kuhn, *Pro Oracle Database 23ai Administration*,
https://doi.org/10.1007/979-8-8688-1038-1_14

Determining Whether Media Recovery Is Required

The term *media recovery* means the restoration of files that have been lost or damaged, owing to the failure of the underlying storage media (usually a disk of some sort) or accidental removal of files. Usually, you know that media recovery is required through an error such as the following.

```
ORA-01157: cannot identify/lock data file 1 - see DBWR trace file
ORA-01110: data file 1: '/u01/dbfile/db23ai/system01.dbf'
```

The error may be displayed on your screen when performing DBA tasks, such as stopping and starting the database. Or, you might see such an error in a trace file or the alert.log file. It is also possible that the error might be delayed in appearing since the file has not been written to or because of the OS. If you do not notice the issue immediately, the database stops processing transactions with a severe media failure, and users start calling you.

To understand how Oracle determines that media recovery is required, you must first understand how Oracle determines that everything is OK. When Oracle shuts down normally, part of the shutdown process is to flush all modified blocks in memory to disk, mark the header of each data file with the current SCN, and update the control file with the current SCN information.

On startup, Oracle checks to see if the SCN in the control file matches the SCN in the header of the data files. If there is a match, Oracle attempts to open the data files and online redo log files. If all files are available and can be opened, Oracle starts normally. This also means while Oracle is running and available, there is a possibility for corruption or a file to be removed that will not be noticed until that file is read or written to or Oracle is stopped and started. The following query compares the SCN in the control file for each data file with the SCN in the data file headers.

```
SQL> SET LINES 132
SQL> COL nameFORM a40
SQL> COL statusFORM A8
SQL> COL file#FORM 9999
SQL> COL control_file_SCN FORM 999999999999999
SQL> COL datafile_SCNFORM 999999999999999
--
SQL> SELECT
```

```
a.name
,a.status
,a.file#
,a.checkpoint_change# control_file_SCN
,b.checkpoint_change# datafile_SCN
,CASE
    WHEN ((a.checkpoint_change# - b.checkpoint_change#) = 0) THEN
    'Startup Normal'
    WHEN ((b.checkpoint_change#) = 0)THEN 'File Missing?'
    WHEN ((a.checkpoint_change# - b.checkpoint_change#) > 0) THEN
    'Media Rec. Req.'
    WHEN ((a.checkpoint_change# - b.checkpoint_change#) < 0) THEN
    'Old Control File'
    ELSE 'what the ?'
  END datafile_status
FROM v$datafilea -- control file SCN for datafile
    ,v$datafile_header b -- datafile header SCN
WHERE a.file# = b.file#
ORDER BY a.file#;
```

If the control file SCN values are greater than the data file SCN values, then media recovery is most likely required. This would be the case if you restored a data file from a backup and the SCN in the restored data file had an SCN less than the data file in the current control file.

The V$DATAFILE_HEADER view uses the physical data file on disk as its source. The V$DATAFILE view uses the control file as its source.

You can also directly query the V$DATABASE_HEADER for more information. The ERROR and RECOVER columns report any potential problems. For example, a YES or NULL value in the RECOVER column indicates that there is a problem.

```
SQL> select file#, status, error, recover from v$datafile_header;
```

Here is some sample output.

```
FILE#      STATUS  ERROR                 REC
---------- ------- --------------------- ---
1          ONLINE                        FILE NOT FOUND
2          ONLINE                        NO
3          ONLINE                        NO
```

Determining What to Restore

Media recovery requires that you perform manual tasks to get your database back in one piece. These tasks usually involve a combination of RESTORE and RECOVER commands. You have to issue an RMAN RESTORE command if, for some reason (accidental deleting of files, disk failure, and so on), your data files have experienced media failure.

How the Process Works

When you issue the RESTORE command, RMAN automatically decides how to extract the data files from any of the following available backups.

- Full database backup

- Incremental level-0 backup

- Image copy backup generated by the BACKUP AS COPY command

After the files are restored from a backup, you are required to apply redo to them via the RECOVER command. When you issue the RECOVER command, Oracle examines the SCNs in the affected data files and determines whether any need to be recovered. Media recovery is required if the SCN in the data file is less than the corresponding SCN in the control file.

Oracle retrieves the data file SCN and then looks for the corresponding SCN in the redo stream to establish where to start the recovery process. If the starting recovery SCN is in the online redo log files, the archivelog files are not required for recovery.

During a recovery, RMAN automatically determines how to apply redo. First, RMAN applies any incremental backups that are greater than level 0, such as the incremental level 1. Next, any archivelog files on disk are applied. If the archivelog files do not exist on disk, RMAN attempts to retrieve them from a backup set.

To be able to perform a complete recovery, all the following conditions need to be true.

- Your database is in archivelog mode.

- You have a good baseline backup of your database.

- You have any required redo generated since the backup (archivelog files, online redo log files, or incremental backup that RMAN can use for recovery instead of applying redo).

There are a wide variety of restore-and-recovery scenarios. How you restore and recover depends directly on your backup strategy and which files have been damaged. Listed next are the general steps to follow when facing a media failure.

1. Determine which files need to be restored.

2. Set your database mode to nomount, mount, or open—depending on the damage.

3. Use the RESTORE command to retrieve files from RMAN backups.

4. Use the RECOVER command for data files requiring recovery.

5. Open your database.

Your particular restore-and-recovery scenario may not require that all the previous steps be performed. For instance, you may want to restore your spfile, which does not require a recovery step.

The first step in the restore-and-recovery process is to determine which files have experienced media failure. You can usually determine which files must be restored from the following sources.

- Error messages displayed on your screen, either from RMAN or from SQL*Plus

- Alert.log file and corresponding trace files

- Data dictionary views

Additionally, to the previously listed methods, you should consider the Data Recovery Advisor to obtain information about the failure's extent and corresponding corrective action.

Using Data Recovery Advisor

The Data Recovery Advisor tool was introduced in Oracle Database 11g. In the event of a media failure, this tool displays the failure details, recommends corrective actions, and performs the recommended actions if you specify that it do so. It is like having another set of eyes to provide feedback when in a restore-and-recovery situation. There are four modes of Data Recovery Advisor.

- Listing failures

- Suggesting corrective action

- Running commands to repair failures

- Changing the status of a failure

The Data Recovery Advisor is invoked from RMAN. You can think of the Data Recovery Advisor as a set of RMAN commands to assist you when dealing with media failure.

Listing Failures

When using the Data Recovery Advisor, the LIST FAILURE command displays any issues with the data files, control files, or online redo logs.

```
RMAN> list failure;
```

If there are no detected failures, you see a message indicating no failures. Here is some sample output indicating that there may be an issue with a data file.

```
Failure ID Priority Status    Time Detected Summary
---------- -------- --------- ------------- -------
6222       CRITICAL OPEN      12-JUN-23     System datafile 1:
 '/u01/dbfile/db23ai/system01.dbf' is missing
```

To display more information about the failure, use the DETAIL clause.

```
RMAN> list failure 6222 detail;
```

Here is the additional output for this example.

```
Impact: Database cannot be opened
```

With this type of failure, the prior output indicates that the database cannot be opened.

If you suspect a media failure, yet the Data Recovery Advisor is not reporting any issues, run the VALIDATE DATABASE command to verify that the database is intact.

Suggesting Corrective Action

The ADVISE FAILURE command advises how to recover from potential problems the Data Recovery Advisor detects. If you have multiple failures with your database, you can directly specify the failure ID to get advice on a given failure, as follows.

```
RMAN> advise failure 6222;
```

Here is a snippet of the output for this particular issue.

```
Optional Manual Actions
=======================
1. If file /u01/dbfile/db23ai/system01.dbf was unintentionally renamed
or moved,
restore it
Automated Repair Options
========================
Option Repair Description
------ ------------------
1      Restore and recover datafile 1
       Strategy: The repair includes complete media recovery with no
data loss Repair script: /ora01/app/oracle/diag/rdbms/db23ai/db23ai/hm/
reco_4116328280.hm
```

In this case, the Data Recovery Advisor created a script that can be used to potentially fix the problem. The contents of the repair script can be viewed with an OS utility. The following is an example.

```
$ cat /ora01/app/oracle/diag/rdbms/db23ai/db23ai/hm/reco_4116328280.hm
```

Here are the contents of the script for this example.

```
# restore and recover datafile
restore ( datafile 1 );
recover datafile 1;
sql 'alter database datafile 1 online';
```

After reviewing the script, you can run the suggested commands manually or have the Data Recovery Advisor run the script via the REPAIR command (see the next section for more information).

Repairing Failures

If you have identified a failure and viewed the recommended advice, you can proceed to the repair work. If you want to inspect what the REPAIR FAILURE command does without actually running the commands, use the PREVIEW clause.

```
RMAN> repair failure preview;
```

Before you run the REPAIR FAILURE command, ensure that you first run the LIST FAILURE and ADVISE FAILURE commands from the same connected session. In other words, the RMAN session you are in must run the LIST and ADVISE commands within the same session before running the REPAIR command.

If you are satisfied with the repair suggestions, run the REPAIR FAILURE command.

```
RMAN> repair failure;
```

You are prompted at this point for confirmation.

```
Do you really want to execute the above repair (enter YES or NO)?
```

Type YES to proceed.

```
YES
```

If all goes well, you should see a final message like the following in the output.

```
repair failure complete
```

Changing the Status of a Failure

One last note on the Data Recovery Advisor: if you know that you have had a failure and that it is not critical (e.g., a data file missing from a tablespace that is no longer used), then use the CHANGE FAILURE command to alter the priority of a failure. In this example, a missing data file belongs to a noncritical tablespace. First, obtain the failure priority via the LIST FAILURE command.

```
RMAN> list failure;
```

Here is some sample output.

```
Failure ID Priority Status    Time Detected Summary
---------- -------- --------- ------------- -------
5          HIGH     OPEN      12-JUN-28     One or more
non-system datafiles are missing
```

Next, change the priority from HIGH to LOW with the CHANGE FAILURE command.

```
RMAN> change failure 5 priority low;
```

You are prompted to confirm that you really do want to change the priority.

```
Do you really want to change the above failures (enter YES or NO)?
```

If you do want to change the priority, then type YES, and press the Enter key. If you run the LIST FAILURE command again, you will see that the priority has now been changed to LOW.

```
RMAN> list failure low;
```

Complete Recovery

The term *complete recovery* means you can restore all transactions that were committed before a failure occurred. Complete recovery does not mean you are restoring and recovering all data files in your database. For instance, you are performing a complete recovery if you have a media failure with one data file or even one data block, and you restore and recover the one data file or block. For complete recovery, the following conditions must be true.

- Your database is in archivelog mode.

- You have a good baseline backup of the data files that have experienced media failure.

- You have any required redo that has been generated since the last backup.

- All archive redo logs start from the point at which the last backup began.

- Any incremental backups that RMAN can use for recovery are available.

- Online redo logs containing transactions that have not been archived are available.

If you have experienced a media failure and have the required files to perform a complete recovery, you can restore and recover your database.

You can determine which files RMAN uses for restore and recovery before you perform the restore and recovery. You can also instruct RMAN to verify the integrity of the backup files used to restore and recover.

Previewing Backups Used for Recovery

Use the RESTORE ... PREVIEW command to list the backups and archive redo log files that RMAN uses to restore and recover database data files. The RESTORE ... PREVIEW command does not actually restore any files. Rather, it lists the backup files that will be used for a restore operation. This example previews the backups required to restore and recover the entire database.

```
RMAN> restore database preview;
```

You can also preview required backup files at a summarized level of detail.

```
RMAN> restore database preview summary;
```

You can also preview required backup files at a summarized level of detail.

```
RMAN> restore database preview summary;
```

Here is a snippet of the output.

```
List of Backups
===============
Key    TY LV S Device Type Completion Time #Pieces #Copies Compressed  Tag
----   -- -- - ----------- --------------- ------- ------- ---------- ---
9207   B F A DISK      05-JUL-23 1 1 NO         TAG20230705T010705
9232   B 1 A SBT_TAPE 05-JUL-23 1 1 YES         DBTREGULAR-L11688534102946HLS
9359   B 1 A SBT_TAPE 06-JUL-23 1 1 YES         DBTREGULAR-L11688620533112ORN
...
```

```
List of Archived Log Copies for database with db_unique_name
MMDB23AI_MMDB23AI
=====================================================KeyThrd
Seq S Low Time
------- ---- ------- - ---------
1778 1 1779 A 05-JUL-23
    Name: +RECO/MMDB23AI_MMDB23AI/ARCHIVELOG/2023_07_05/thread_1_
    seq_1779.1254.11413512471779 1 1780 A 05-JUL-23
    Name: +RECO/MMDB23AI_MMDB23AI/ARCHIVELOG/2023_07_05/thread_1_
    seq_1780.1255.1141354861
...
recovery will be done up to SCN 42403694
Media recovery start SCN is 39020785
Recovery must be done beyond SCN 40884072 to clear datafile fuzziness
validation succeeded for backup piece
Finished restore at 08-JUL-23
```

Here are some more examples of how to preview backups required for restore and recovery.

```
RMAN> restore tablespace system preview;
RMAN> restore pluggable database mmpdb preview;
RMAN> restore archivelog from time 'sysdate -1' preview;
RMAN> restore datafile 1, 2, 3 preview;
```

Validating Backup Files Before Restoring

There are several levels of verification that you can perform on backup files without actually restoring anything. If you only want RMAN to verify that the files exist and check the file headers, use the RESTORE ... VALIDATE HEADER command, as shown next.

```
RMAN> restore database validate header;
```

The command only validates the existence of backup files and checks the file headers. You can further instruct RMAN to verify the integrity of blocks within backup files required to restore the database data files via the RESTORE ... VALIDATE command without the HEADER clause. Again, RMAN does not restore any data files in this mode.

```
RMAN> restore database validate;
```

This command checks only for physical corruption within the backup files. You can also check for logical corruption as follows.

```
RMAN> restore database validate check logical;
```

Here are some other examples of using RESTORE … VALIDATE.

```
RMAN> restore datafile 1, 2, 3 validate;
RMAN> restore pluggable database mmpdb validate;
RMAN> restore controlfile validate;
```

This first step in restoring and recovering is important to ensure the files are available for the complete restore. The command does not take long to run and allows you to make sure with the preview command you know what needs to be restored and validated so you know you have files that are available.

Testing Media Recovery

The prior sections covered reporting and verifying the restore operations. You can also instruct RMAN to verify the recovery process via the RECOVER...TEST command. Before performing a test recovery, you need to ensure that the data files being recovered are offline. Oracle throws an error for any online data files being recovered in test mode. In this example, the tablespace USERS is restored first, and then a trial recovery is performed.

```
RMAN> connect target /
RMAN> startup mount;
RMAN> restore tablespace users;
RMAN> recover tablespace users test;
```

If there are any missing archive redo logs that are required for recovery, the following error is thrown.

```
RMAN-06053: unable to perform media recovery because of missing log
RMAN-06025: no backup of archived log for thread 1 with sequence 6 ...
```

If the testing of the recovery succeeded, you see messages such as the following, indicating that the application of redo was tested but not applied.

```
ORA-10574: Test recovery did not corrupt any data block
ORA-10573: Test recovery tested redo from change 4586939 to 4588462
ORA-10572: Test recovery canceled due to errors
ORA-10585: Test recovery can not apply redo that may modify control file
```

Here are some other examples of testing the recovery process.

```
RMAN> recover database test;
RMAN> recover tablespace users, tools test;
RMAN> recover datafile 1,2,3 test;
```

Restoring and Recovering the Entire Database

The RESTORE DATABASE command restores every data file in your database. The exception to this is when RMAN detects that data files have already been restored; in that case, it does not restore them. If you want to override that behavior, use the FORCE command.

When you issue the RECOVER DATABASE command, RMAN automatically applies redo to any data files that need recovery. The recovery process includes applying changes found in the following files.

- Incremental backup pieces (applicable only if using incremental backups)

- Archivelog files (generated since the last backup or incremental backup applied)

- Online redo log files (current and unarchived)

You can open your database after the restore-and-recovery process is complete. Complete database recovery works only if you have good backups of your database and access to all redo generated after the backup was taken. You need all the redo required to recover the database data files. If you do not have all the required redo, you most likely have to perform an incomplete recovery (see the "Incomplete Recovery" section later in this chapter).

Your database has to be at least mounted to restore data files using RMAN. This is because RMAN reads information from the control file during the restore-and-recovery process.

You can perform a complete database-level recovery with either the current control file or a backup control file.

Using the Backup Control File

This technique uses an autobackup of the control file retrieved from the FRA. This situation works for having to restore a control or in case of media loss when the control file is no longer available. In this scenario, the control file is retrieved from a backup before restoring and recovering the database.

```
$ rman target /
RMAN> startup nomount;
RMAN> restore controlfile from autobackup;
RMAN> alter database mount;
RMAN> restore database;
RMAN> recover database;
RMAN> alter database open resetlogs;
```

If successful, the following is the last message you should see.

```
Statement processed
```

Restoring and Recovering Tablespaces

Sometimes, you have a media failure that is localized to a particular tablespace or set of tablespaces. In this situation, it is appropriate to restore and recover at the tablespace level of granularity. The RMAN RESTORE TABLESPACE and RECOVER TABLESPACE commands restore and recover all data files associated with the specified tablespace(s).

Restoring Tablespaces While the Database Is Open

It has been our experience that we need a data file, a tablespace, or even a block of data restored because of a failure. In that case, you do not need to restore the entire database, and the rest of the database can be up and running. If your database is open, you must take offline the tablespace you want to restore and recover. You can do this for any tablespace except SYSTEM and UNDO. This example restores and recovers the USERS tablespace while the database is open.

```
$ rman target /
RMAN> alter tablespace users offline immediate;
RMAN> restore tablespace users;
RMAN> recover tablespace users;
RMAN> alter tablespace users online;
```

After the tablespace is brought online, you should see a message like the following.

```
Statement processed
```

Restoring Tablespaces While the Database Is in Mount Mode

Usually, when performing a restore and recovery, DBAs shut down the database and restart it in mount mode in preparation for performing the recovery. Placing a database in mount mode ensures that no users are connecting to the database and that no transactions are transpiring.

Also, if you are restoring and recovering the SYSTEM tablespace, then you must start the database in mount mode. Oracle does not allow restoring and recovering the SYSTEM tablespace data files while the database is open. This next example restores the SYSTEM tablespace while the database is in mount mode.

```
$ rman target /
RMAN> shutdown immediate;
RMAN> startup mount;
RMAN> restore tablespace system;
RMAN> recover tablespace system;
RMAN> alter database open;
```

If successful, the following is the last message you should see.

```
Statement processed
```

Notice that you can do startup and shutdown commands in RMAN. This is useful for the recovery process and not having to switch tools and stay in one tool.

Restoring Read-Only Tablespaces

RMAN restores read-only tablespaces along with the rest of the database when you issue a RESTORE DATDABASE command. For example, the following command restore all data files (including those in read-only mode).

```
RMAN> restore database;
```

If you are using a backup that was created after the read-only tablespace was placed in read-only mode, then no recovery is necessary for the read-only data files. In this situation, no redo has been generated for the read-only tablespace since it was backed up.

Restoring Temporary Tablespaces

You do not have to restore or re-create missing locally managed temporary tablespace temp files. When you open your database for use, Oracle automatically detects and re-creates locally managed temporary tablespace temp files.

When Oracle automatically re-creates a temporary tablespace, it log a message to your target database alert.log such as the following.

```
Re-creating tempfile <your temporary tablespace filename>
```

If, for any reason, your temporary tablespace becomes unavailable, you can also re-create it yourself. Because there are never any permanent objects in temporary tablespaces, you can simply re-create them as needed. Here is an example of how to create a locally managed temporary tablespace.

```
SQL> CREATE TEMPORARY TABLESPACE temp TEMPFILE;
```

If your temporary tablespace exists but the temporary data files are missing, you can just add them, as shown.

```
SQL> alter tablespace temp add tempfile;
```

Restoring and Recovering Data Files

A data file–level restore and recovery works well when a media failure is confined to a small set of data files. With data file–level recoveries, you can instruct RMAN to restore and recover either with a data filename or with a data file number. For data files not associated with the SYSTEM or UNDO tablespaces, you have the option of restoring and recovering while the database remains open. While the database is open, however, you must first take offline any data files being restored and recovered. Recovering data files works at the container and pluggable database level.

Restoring and Recovering Data Files While the Database Is Open

Use the RESTORE DATAFILE and RECOVER DATAFILE commands to restore and recover at the data file level. When your database is open, you are required to take offline any data files that you are attempting to restore and recover. This example restores and recovers data files while the database is open.

```
RMAN> alter database datafile 4, 5 offline;
RMAN> restore datafile 4, 5;
RMAN> recover datafile 4, 5;
RMAN> alter database datafile 4, 5 online;
```

Use the RMAN REPORT SCHEMA command to list data filenames and file numbers. You can also query the NAME and FILE# columns of V$DATAFILE to take names and numbers.

You can also specify the name of the data file you want to restore and recover. The following is an example.

```
RMAN> alter database datafile '/u01/dbfile/db23ai/users01.dbf' offline;
RMAN> restore datafile '/u01/dbfile/db23ai/users01.dbf';
RMAN> recover datafile '/u01/dbfile/db23ai/users01.dbf';
RMAN> alter database datafile '/u01/dbfile/db23ai/users01.dbf' online;
```

Restoring and Recovering Data Files While the Database Is Not Open

In this scenario, the database is first shut down and then started in mount mode. You can restore and recover any data file in your database while the database is not open. This example shows the restoring of data file 1, which is associated with the SYSTEM tablespace of the container database (CDB).

```
$ rman target /
RMAN> shutdown abort;
RMAN> startup mount;
RMAN> restore datafile 1;
RMAN> recover datafile 1;
RMAN> alter database open;
```

You can also specify the filename when performing a data file recovery.

```
$ rman target /
RMAN> shutdown abort;
RMAN> startup mount;
RMAN> restore datafile '/u01/dbfile/db23ai/system01.dbf';
RMAN> recover datafile '/u01/dbfile/db23ai/system01.dbf';
RMAN> alter database open;
```

Restoring Data Files to Nondefault Locations

Sometimes, a failure occurs that renders the disks associated with a mount point inoperable. In these situations, you need to restore and recover the data files to a location different from the one where they originally resided. Another typical need for restoring data files to nondefault locations is for files that you are restoring to a different database server, on which the mount points are completely different from those of the server on which the backup originated.

Use the SET NEWNAME and SWITCH commands to restore data files to nondefault locations. Both of these commands must be run from within an RMAN run{} block. You can think of using SET NEWNAME and SWITCH as a way to rename data files (similar to the SQL ALTER DATABASE RENAME FILE statement).

This example changes the location of data files when doing a restore and recover. First, place the database in mount mode.

```
$ rman target /
RMAN> startup mount;
```

Then, run the following block of RMAN code.

```
run{
set newname for datafile 4 to '/u02/dbfile/db23ai/users01.dbf';
set newname for datafile 5 to '/u02/dbfile/db23ai/users02.dbf';
restore datafile 4, 5;
switch datafile all; # Updates repository with new datafile location.
recover datafile 4, 5;
alter database open;
}
```

This is a partial listing of the output.

```
datafile 4 switched to datafile copy
input datafile copy RECID=79 STAMP=8045The33148 file name=/u02/dbfile/
db23ai/users01.dbf
datafile 5 switched to datafile copy
input datafile copy RECID=80 STAMP=804533148 file name=/u02/dbfile/db23ai/
users02.dbf
```

If the database is open, you can place the data files offline and then set their new names for restore and recovery, as follows.

```
run{
alter database datafile 4, 5 offline;
set newname for datafile 4 to '/u02/dbfile/db23ai/users01.dbf';
set newname for datafile 5 to '/u02/dbfile/db23ai/users02.dbf';
restore datafile 4, 5;
switch datafile all; # Updates repository with new datafile location.
recover datafile 4, 5;
alter database datafile 4, 5 online;
}
```

Here is the same example using ASM; the newname is just referring to the disk group.

```
run{
set newname for datafile 4 to '+DATA';
set newname for datafile 5 to '+DATA';
restore datafile 4, 5;
```

```
switch datafile all; # Updates repository with new datafile location.
recover datafile 4, 5;
alter database open;
}
```

Performing Block-Level Recovery

Block-level corruption is rare and is usually caused by some sort of I/O error. It can rescue you from having to do a complete restore of a data file with recovery. However, if you do have an isolated corrupt block within a large data file, it is nice to have the option of performing a block-level recovery. Block-level recovery is useful when a small number of blocks are corrupt within a data file. Block recovery is not appropriate if the entire data file needs media recovery. We have actually had to use this a few times; however, now, with ASM, this type of issue has been significantly reduced.

RMAN automatically detects corrupt blocks whenever a BACKUP, VALIDATE, or BACKUP VALIDATE command is run. Details on corrupt blocks can be viewed in the V$DATABASE_BLOCK_CORRUPTION view. In the following example, the regular backup job has reported a corrupt block in the output.

```
ORA-19566: exceeded limit of 0 corrupt blocks for file...
```

Querying the V$DATABASE_BLOCK_CORRUPTION view indicates which file contains corruption.

```
SQL> select * from v$database_block_corruption;
FILE#   BLOCK# BLOCKS CORRUPTION_CHANGE#   CORRUPTIO CON_ID
------  ------ ------ -----------  ------- --------- -------
4       20     1      0                    ALL ZERO  0
```

Your database can be either mounted or open when performing block-level recovery. You do not have to take offline the data file being recovered. You can instruct RMAN to recover all blocks reported in V$DATABASE_BLOCK_CORRUPTION, as follows.

```
RMAN> recover corruption list;
```

If successful, the following message is displayed.

```
media recovery complete...
```

Another way to recover the block is to specify the data file and block number, like so.

```
RMAN> recover datafile 4 block 20;
```

It is preferable to use the RECOVER CORRUPTION LIST syntax because it clears out any blocks recovered from the V$DATABASE_BLOCK_CORRUPTION view.

RMAN cannot perform block-level recovery on block 1 (data file header) of the data file.

Block-level media recovery allows you to keep your database available and reduces the mean time to recovery, as only the corrupt blocks are offline during the recovery. Your database must be in archivelog mode for performing block-level recoveries. RMAN can restore the block from the flashback logs (if available). If the flashback logs are not available, then RMAN attempts to restore the block from a full backup, a level 0 backup, or an image copy backup generated by the BACKUP AS COPY command. After the block has been restored, any required archivelogs must be available to recover the block. RMAN cannot perform block media recovery using incremental level 1 (or higher) backups.

Restoring a Container Database and Its Pluggable Databases

You saw the commands to recover the database, including all the data files for the root and pluggables. Also, the examples showed how to validate just the pluggable databases with RESTORE DATABASE and RECOVER DATABASE. This restores and recovers the root container, seed, and all associated pluggable databases.

```
$ rman target /
RMAN> startup mount;
RMAN> restore database;
RMAN> recover database;
RMAN> alter database open;
RMAN> alter pluggable database all open;
```

Restoring and Recovering Root Container Data Files

If just data files associated with the root container have been damaged, then you can restore and recover at the root level. In this example, the root container's system data file is being restored, so the database must not be open. The following commands instruct RMAN to restore only the data files associated with the root container database via the keyword root.

```
$ rman target /
RMAN> startup mount;
RMAN> restore database root;
RMAN> recover database root;
RMAN> alter database open;
```

In the prior code, the restore database root command instructs RMAN to restore only data files associated with the root container database. After the container database is opened, you must open any associated pluggable databases. You can do so from the root container, as shown next.

```
RMAN> alter pluggable database all open;
```

You can check the status of your pluggable databases via this query.

```
SQL> select name, open_mode from v$pdbs;
```

Restoring and Recovering a Pluggable Database

You have two options for restoring and recovering a pluggable database.

- Connect as the container root user, and specify the pluggable database to be restored and recovered.

- Connect directly to the pluggable database as a privileged pluggable-level user and issue RESTORE and RECOVER commands.

This first example connects to the root container and restores and recovers the data files associated with the salespdb pluggable database. For this to work, the pluggable database must not be open (because the pluggable database's system data files are also being restored and recovered).

```
$ rman target /
RMAN> alter pluggable database salespdb close;
RMAN> restore pluggable database salespdb;
RMAN> recover pluggable database salespdb;
RMAN> alter pluggable database salespdb open;
```

You can also connect directly to a pluggable database and perform restore and recovery operations. When connected directly to the pluggable database, the user only has access to the data files associated with the pluggable database.

```
$ rman target sys/Pa$$word1@salespdb
RMAN> shutdown immediate;
RMAN> restore database;
RMAN> recover database;
RMAN> alter database open;
```

The prior code affects only data files associated with the pluggable database to which you are connected. The pluggable database needs to be closed for this to work. However, the root container database can be opened or mounted. Also, you must use a backup that was taken while connected to the pluggable database as a privileged user. The privileged pluggable database user cannot access backups of data files initiated by the root container database privileged user.

Restoring Archivelog Files

RMAN automatically restores any archivelog files that it needs during a recovery process. You normally do not need to restore archivelog files manually. However, you may want to do so if any of the following situations apply.

- You need to restore archivelog files in anticipation of later performing a recovery; the idea is that if the archivelog files are already restored, it speeds up the recovery operation.

- You are required to restore the archivelog files to a nondefault location, either because of media failure or because of storage space issues.

- You need to restore specific archivelog files to inspect them via LogMiner.

If you have enabled an FRA, then RMAN will, by default, restore archivelog files to the destination defined by the initialization parameter DB_RECOVERY_FILE_ DEST. Otherwise, RMAN uses the LOG_ARCHIVE_DEST_N initialization parameter (where N is usually 1) to determine where to restore the archivelog files.

If you restore archivelog files to a nondefault location, RMAN knows the location they were restored to and automatically finds these files when you issue any subsequent RECOVER commands. RMAN will not restore archivelog files that it determines are already on disk. Even if you specify a nondefault location, RMAN will not restore an archivelog file to disk if the file already exists. In this situation, RMAN simply returns a message stating that the archivelog file has already been restored. Use the FORCE option to override this behavior.

If you are uncertain of the sequence numbers to use during a restore of log files, you can query the V$LOG_HISTORY view.

Keep in mind that you cannot restore an archivelog that you never backed up. Also, you cannot restore an archivelog if the backup file containing the archivelog is no longer available. Run the LIST ARCHIVELOG ALL command to view archivelogs currently on disk, and run LIST BACKUP OF ARCHIVELOG ALL to verify which archivelog files are in available RMAN backups.

Restoring to the Default Location

The following command restores all archivelog files that RMAN has backed up.

```
RMAN> restore archivelog all;
```

If you want to restore from a specified sequence, use the FROM SEQUENCE clause. You may want to run this query first to establish the most recent log files and sequence numbers that have been generated.

```
SQL> select sequence#, first_time from v$log_history order by 2;
```

This example restores all archivelog files from sequence 68.

```
RMAN> restore archivelog from sequence 68;
```

If you want to restore a range of archivelog files, use the FROM SEQUENCE and UNTIL SEQUENCE clauses or the SEQUENCE BETWEEN clause, as shown. The following commands restore archivelog files from sequence 68 through sequence 78 using thread 1.

```
RMAN> restore archivelog from sequence 68 until sequence 78 thread 1;
RMAN> restore archivelog sequence between 68 and 78 thread 1;
```

By default, RMAN will not restore an archivelog file if it is already on disk. You can override this behavior if you use the FORCE, like so.

```
RMAN> restore archivelog from sequence 1 force;
```

Restoring to a Nondefault Location

Use the SET ARCHIVELOG DESTINATION clause to restore archivelog files to a location different from the default. The following example restores to the nondefault location /u01/archtemp. The option of the SET command must be executed from within an RMAN run{} block.

```
run{
set archivelog destination to '/u01/archtemp';
restore archivelog from sequence 8 force;
}
```

Space is the main reason for having to do this, but these types of restores are great test and practice cases to work through to experience this behavior and document for the "just in case" scenario.

Restoring a Control File

If you are missing one control file and you have multiple copies, then you can shut down your database and simply restore the missing or damaged control file by copying a good control file to the correct location and name of the missing control file. This works if all except one file are corrupted and the multiple copies are truly on separate disks. If there is a disk or controller failure, it is possible that at least one of the control files is still available. Part of the RMAN strategy is to take the backup of the control file for these issues.

Listed next are three typical scenarios when restoring a control file.

- Using a recovery catalog

- Using an autobackup

- Specifying a backup filename

When you are connected to the recovery catalog, you can view backup information about your control files even while your target database is in nomount mode. To list backups of your control files, use the LIST command, as shown next.

```
$ rman target / catalog rcat/Pa$$word1@rcat
RMAN> startup nomount;
RMAN> list backup of controlfile;
```

If you are missing all your control files and you are using a recovery catalog, then issue the STARTUP NOMOUNT and RESTORE CONTROLFILE commands.

```
RMAN> startup nomount;
RMAN> restore controlfile;
```

RMAN restores the control files to the location defined by your CONTROL_FILES initialization parameter. You should see a message indicating that your control files have been successfully copied from an RMAN backup piece. You can now alter your database into mount mode and perform any additional restore-and-recovery commands required for your database.

Note   When you restore a control file from a backup, you must perform media recovery on your entire database and open your database with the OPEN RESETLOGS command, even if you did not restore any data files. You can determine whether your control file is a backup by querying the CONTROLFILE_ TYPE column of the V$DATABASE view.

Using an Autobackup

When you enable the autobackup of your control file and are using an FRA, restoring your control file is fairly simple. First, connect to your target database and then issue a STARTUP NOMOUNT command, followed by the RESTORE CONTROLFILE FROM AUTOBACKUP command, as shown next.

```
$ rman target /
RMAN> startup nomount;
RMAN> restore controlfile from autobackup;
```

RMAN restores the control files to the location defined by your `CONTROL_FILES` initialization parameter. You should see a message indicating that your control files have been successfully copied back from an RMAN backup piece. Here is a snippet of the output.

```
channel ORA_DISK_1: control file restore from AUTOBACKUP complete
```

You can now alter your database into mount mode and perform any additional restore-and-recovery commands required for your database. Practicing this example would be to move your control files off to another directory in a TEST environment and walk through the restore options. Copying off the files allows you to quickly get back up and running by moving them back, but it does give you practice with these restores.

Specifying a Backup Filename

When restoring a database to a different server, these are generally the first few steps in the process: take a backup of the target database, copy to the remote server, and then restore the control file from the RMAN backup. In these scenarios, the name of the backup piece is known that contains the control file. Here is an example in which you instruct RMAN to restore a control file from a specific backup piece file.

```
RMAN> startup nomount;
RMAN> restore controlfile from
'/u01/db23ai/rman/rman_ctl_c-3423216220-20130113-01.bk';
```

The control file is restored to the location defined by the `CONTROL_FILES` initialization parameter.

Restoring the Spfile

You might want to restore an `spfile` for several different reasons.

- You accidentally set a value in the `spfile` that keeps your instance from starting.

- You accidentally deleted the `spfile`.

- You are required to see what the `spfile` looked like at some point in time in the past.

One scenario (this has happened to us more than once) is that you are using an spfile, and one of the DBAs on your team does something inexplicable, such as the following.

```
SQL> alter system set processes=1000000 scope=spfile;
```

The parameter is changed in the spfile on disk but not in memory. Sometime later, the database is stopped for some maintenance. When attempting to start the database, you cannot even get the instance to start in a nomount state. This is because a parameter has been set to a ridiculous value that consumes all the memory on the box. In this scenario, the instance may hang, or you may see one or more of the following messages.

```
ORA-01078: failure in processing system parameters
ORA-00838: Specified value of ... is too
```

If you have an RMAN backup available that has a copy of the spfile as it was before it was modified, you can simply restore the spfile. If you are using a recovery catalog, here is the procedure for restoring the spfile.

```
$ rman target / catalog rcat/Pa$$word1@rcat
RMAN> startup nomount;
RMAN> restore spfile;
```

- If you are not using a recovery catalog, there are a number of ways to restore your spfile. Your approach depends on several variables, such as whether you are using an FRA.

- You have configured a channel backup location for the autobackup.

- You are using the default location for autobackups.

This is a general overview of these scenarios to show steps that need to be taken, but not every detail is listed here. Determine the location of the backup piece that contains the backup of the spfile and do the restore, as follows.

```
RMAN> startup nomount force;
RMAN> restore spfile to '/tmp/spfile.ora'
    from '/u01/db23ai/rman/rman_ctl_c-3423216220-20130113-00.bk';
```

You should see a message like the following.

```
channel ORA_DISK_1: SPFILE restore from AUTOBACKUP complete
```

In this example, the spfile is restored to the /tmp directory. Once restored, you can copy the spfile to ORACLE_HOME/dbs, with the proper name. For our environment (database name: db23ai), it would be as follows.

```
$ cp /tmp/spfile.ora $ORACLE_HOME/dbs/spfiledb23ai.ora
```

It is also possible to create a new spfile from a parameter file called init.ora. We like to schedule regular copies of the spfile to an init.ora file.

Incomplete Recovery

The term *incomplete database recovery* means you cannot recover all committed transactions. *Incomplete* means you do not apply all redo to restore up to the point of the last committed transaction in your database. In other words, you are restoring and recovering to a point in time in the past. For this reason, incomplete database recovery is also called *database point-in-time recovery* (DBPITR). Typically, you perform incomplete database recovery for one of the following reasons.

- You do not have all the redo required to perform a complete recovery. You are missing either the archivelog files or the online redo log files that are required for complete recovery. This situation could arise because the required redo files are damaged or missing.

- You purposely want to roll back the database to a point in time in the past. For example, you would do this if somebody accidentally truncated a table and you intentionally wanted to roll back the database just before the truncate table command was issued.

Incomplete database recovery consists of two steps: restore and recovery. The restore step re-creates data files, and the recover step applies the redo up to the specified point in time. The restore process can be initiated from RMAN in two ways.

- RESTORE DATABASE UNTIL

- FLASHBACK DATABASE (may not need the restore depending on the UNDO information)

For most incomplete database recovery circumstances, you use the `RESTORE DATABASE UNTIL` command to instruct RMAN to retrieve data files from the RMAN backup files. This type of incomplete database recovery is the main focus of this section of the chapter. The Flashback Database feature is covered in the "Flashing Back a Database" section later in this chapter.

The `UNTIL` portion of the `RESTORE DATABASE` command instructs RMAN to retrieve data files from a point in time in the past based on one of the following methods.

- Time

- SCN

- Log sequence number

- Restore point

The RMAN `RESTORE DATABASE UNTIL` command retrieves all data files from the most recent backup set or image copy. RMAN automatically determines from the `UNTIL` clause which backup set contains the required data files. If you omit the `UNTIL` clause of the R command, RMAN retrieves data files from the latest available backup set or image copy. In some situations, this may be the behavior you desire. It is recommended you use the `UNTIL` clause to ensure that RMAN restores from the correct backup set. When you issue the `RESTORE DATABASE UNTIL` command, RMAN establishes how to extract the data files from any of the following types of backups.

- Full database backup

- Incremental level 0 backup

- Image copy backup generated by the `BACKUP AS COPY` command

You cannot perform an incomplete database recovery on a subset of your database's online data files. When performing incomplete database recovery, all the checkpoint SCNs for all online data files must be synchronized before you can open your database with the `ALTER DATABASE OPEN RESETLOGS` command. You can view the data file header SCNs and the status of each data file via this SQL query.

```
SQL> select file#, status, fuzzy,
error, checkpoint_change#,
to_char(checkpoint_time,'dd-mon-rrrr hh24:mi:ss') as checkpoint_time
from v$datafile_header;
```

The FUZZY column V$DATAFILE_HEADER contains data files with one or more blocks with an SCN value greater than or equal to the checkpoint SCN in the data file header. If a data file is restored and has a FUZZY value of YES, then media recovery is required.

The only exception to this rule of not performing an incomplete recovery on a subset of online database files is a tablespace point-in-time recovery (TSPITR), which uses the RECOVER TABLESPACE UNTIL command. TSPITR is used in rare situations; it restores and recovers only the tablespace(s) you specify.

The recovery portion of an incomplete database recovery is always initiated with the RECOVER DATABASE UNTIL command. RMAN automatically recovers your database up to the point specified with the UNTIL clause. Like the RESTORE command, you can recover up to the time, change/SCN, log sequence number, or restore point. When RMAN reaches the specified point, it automatically terminates the recovery process.

Note   Regardless of what you specify in the UNTIL clause, RMAN converts that into a corresponding UNTIL SCN clause and assigns the appropriate SCN. This avoids timing issues, particularly those caused by daylight saving time.

During a recovery, RMAN automatically determines how to apply redo. First, RMAN applies any incremental backups available. Next, any archivelog files on disk are applied. If the archivelog files do not exist on disk, then RMAN attempts to retrieve them from a backup set. The following conditions must be true if you want to apply redo as part of an incomplete database recovery.

- Your database is in archivelog mode.

- You have a good backup of all data files.

- You have all redo required to restore up to the specified point.

When performing an incomplete database recovery with RMAN, you must have your database in mount mode. RMAN needs the database in mount mode to read and write to the control file. Also, with an incomplete database recovery, any SYSTEM tablespace data files are always recovered. Oracle does not allow your database to be open while restoring the SYSTEM tablespace data file(s).

After incomplete database recovery is performed, you are required to open your database with the ALTER DATABASE OPEN RESETLOGS command. Any time after issuing an ALTER DATABASE OPEN RESETLOGS, make sure a new backup is taken after this point, as other backups may become invalid if trying to restore after the resetlogs.

Depending on the scenario, you can use RMAN to perform a variety of incomplete recovery methods. The next section discusses how to determine what type of incomplete recovery to perform.

Determining the Type of Incomplete Recovery

Time-based restore and recovery are commonly used when you know the approximate date and time to which you want to recover your database. For instance, you may know approximately the time you want to stop the recovery process but not a particular SCN.

Log sequence-based and cancel-based recovery work well when you have missing or damaged log files. In such scenarios, you can recover only up to your last good archivelog file.

SCN-based recovery works well if you can pinpoint the SCN at which you want to stop the recovery process. You can retrieve SCN information from views such as V$LOG and V$LOG_HISTORY. You can also use tools such as LogMiner to retrieve the SCN of a particular SQL statement.

Restore point recoveries work only if you have established restore points. In these situations, you restore and recover up to the SCN associated with the specified restore point.

TSPITR is used in situations in which you need to restore and recover just a few tablespaces. You can use RMAN to automate many of the tasks associated with this type of incomplete recovery.

Performing Time-Based Recovery

To restore and recover your database back to a point in time in the past, you can use either the UNTIL TIME clause of the RESTORE and RECOVER commands or the SET UNTIL TIME clause within a run{} block. It is useful to have run{} blocks of code with the correct syntax available to replace a TIME to perform the restores without having to search for the syntax. Using these examples in the book and running test and practice restores give you the blocks of code needed to have ready to use. RMAN restores and recovers the database up to, but not including, the specified time. In other words, RMAN restores any transactions committed prior to the time specified. RMAN automatically stops the recovery process when it reaches the time you specified.

The default date format that RMAN expects is YYYY-MM-DD:HH24:MI:SS. However, it is recommended to use the TO_DATE function and specify a format mask. This eliminates ambiguities with different national date formats and having to set the OS NLS_DATE_FORMAT variable. The following example specifies a time when issuing the restore and recover commands.

```
$ rman target /
RMAN> startup mount;
RMAN> restore database until time
            "to_date('15-jun-2018 12:20:00', 'dd-mon-rrrr hh24:mi:ss')";
RMAN> recover database until time
            "to_date('15-jun-2018 12:20:00', 'dd-mon-rrrr hh24:mi:ss')";
RMAN> alter database open resetlogs;
```

If everything goes well, you should see output like the following.

```
Statement processed
```

Performing Log Sequence–Based Recovery

Usually, this type of incomplete database recovery is initiated because you have a missing or damaged archivelog file. If that is the case, you can recover only up to your last good archivelog file because you cannot skip a missing archivelog.

How you determine which archivelog file to restore up to (but not including) varies. For example, if you are physically missing an archivelog file and RMAN cannot find it in a backup set, you receive a message such as this when trying to apply the missing file.

```
RMAN-06053: unable to perform media recovery because of missing log
RMAN-06025: no backup of archived log for thread 1 with sequence 19...
```

Based on the previous error message, you would restore up to (but not including) log sequence 19.

```
$ rman target /
RMAN> startup mount;
RMAN> restore database until sequence 19;
RMAN> recover database until sequence 19;
RMAN> alter database open resetlogs;
```

If successful, you should see output like the following.

```
Statement processed
```

Performing SCN-Based Recovery

SCN-based incomplete database recovery works in situations in which you know the SCN value at which you want to end the restore-and-recovery session. RMAN recovers up to, but not including, the specified SCN. RMAN automatically terminates the restore process when it reaches the specified SCN.

You can view your database SCN information in several ways.

- Using LogMiner to determine an SCN associated with a DDL or DML statement

- Looking in the `alert.log` file

- Looking in your trace files

- Querying the `FIRST_CHANGE#` column of `V$LOG`, `V$LOG_HISTORY`, and `V$ARCHIVED_LOG`

After establishing the SCN to which you want to restore, use the `UNTIL SCN` clause to restore up to, but not including, the SCN specified. The following example restores all transactions that have an SCN that is less than 95019865425.

```
$ rman target /
RMAN> startup mount;
RMAN> restore database until scn 95019865425;
RMAN> recover database until scn 95019865425;
RMAN> alter database open resetlogs;
```

If everything goes well, you should see output like the following.

```
Statement processed
```

Restoring to a Restore Point

There are two types of restore points: normal and guaranteed. The main difference between a guaranteed restore point and a normal restore point is that a guaranteed restore point does not eventually age out of the control file; a guaranteed restore point persists until you drop it. Guaranteed restore points do require an FRA. However, for incomplete recovery using a guaranteed restore point, you do not need to have the flashback database enabled.

You can create a normal restore point using SQL*Plus as follows.

```
SQL> create restore point MY_RP;
```

This command creates a restore point named MY_RP, which is associated with the SCN of the database at the time the command was issued. You can view the current SCN of your database, as shown next.

```
SQL> select current_scn from v$database;
```

You can view restore point information in the V$RESTORE_POINT view, as follows.

```
SQL> select name, scn from v$restore_point;
```

The restore point acts as a synonym for the particular SCN. The restore point allows you to restore and recover to an SCN without having to specify a number. RMAN restores and recovers up to, but not including, the SCN associated with the restore point.

This example restores and recovers to the MY_RP restore point.

```
$ rman target /
RMAN> startup mount;
RMAN> restore database until restore point MY_RP;
RMAN> recover database until restore point MY_RP;
RMAN> alter database open resetlogs;
```

Restoring Tables to a Previous Point

You can restore individual tables from RMAN backups via the RECOVER TABLE command. This gives you the ability to restore and recover a table back to a point in time in the past.

The table-level restore feature uses a temporary auxiliary instance and the Data Pump utility. Both the auxiliary instance and Data Pump create temporary files when restoring the table. Before initiating a table-level restore, first create two directories: one to hold files used by the auxiliary instance and one to store a Data Pump dump file.

```
$ mkdir /tmp/oracle
$ mkdir /tmp/recover
```

The prior two directories are referenced within the RECOVER TABLE command via the AUXILIARY DESTINATION and DATAPUMP DESTINATION clauses. In the following bit of code, the INV table, owned by MV_MAINT, is restored as it was at a prior SCN.

```
RMAN> recover table mv_maint.inv of pluggable database salepdb
until scn 4689805
auxiliary destination '/tmp/oracle'
datapump destination '/tmp/recover';
```

Providing that RMAN backups are available that contain the state of the table at the specified SCN, a table-level restore and recovery is performed. You can also restore a table to an SCN, a point in time, or a log sequence number.

When RMAN performs a table-level recovery, it automatically creates a temporary auxiliary database, uses Data Pump to export the table, and then imports the table back into the target database as it was at the specified restore point. After the restore is finished, the auxiliary database is dropped, and the Data Pump dump file is removed.

Flashback

Although the RECOVER TABLE command is a nice enhancement, we recommend that if you have an accidentally dropped table, you first explore using the recycle bin or Flashback Table to Before Drop feature to restore the table. Or, if the table was erroneously deleted, then use the Flashback Table feature to restore the table to a point in time in the past. It might even be possible to restore from a FLASHBACK QUERY using CTAS (create table as). If neither of the prior options is viable, then consider using the RMAN Recover Table feature.

Using FLASHBACK QUERY has saved us from several issues, and it really is our first point to go to with any application or data issue where something has been changed or deleted. Saving the table at that point in time allows validation and getting the system back to where it needs to be.

Flashing Back a Table

To simplify the recovery of an accidentally dropped table, Oracle introduced the Flashback Table feature. Oracle offers two different types of Flashback Table operations.

- FLASHBACK TABLE TO BEFORE DROP quickly undrops a previously dropped table. This feature uses a logical container named the recycle bin.

- FLASHBACK TABLE flashes back to a recent point in time to undo the effects of undesired DML statements. You can flash back to an SCN, a timestamp, or a restore point.

Oracle introduced FLASHBACK TABLE TO BEFORE DROP to allow you to quickly recover a dropped table. When you drop a table, if you do not specify the PURGE clause, Oracle does not drop the table—instead, the table is renamed. Any tables you drop (that Oracle renames) are placed in the recycle bin. The recycle bin provides you with an efficient way to view and manage dropped objects.

To use the Flashback Table feature, you do not need to implement an FRA, nor do you need Flashback Database to be enabled.

The FLASHBACK TABLE TO BEFORE DROP operation works only if your database has the recycle bin feature enabled (which it is by default). You can check the status of the recycle bin as follows.

```
SQL> show parameter recyclebin
NAME                                 TYPE        VALUE
------------------------------------ ----------- ----------
recyclebin                           string      on
```

FLASHBACK TABLE TO BEFORE DROP

Here is an example. Suppose the INV table is accidentally dropped.

```
SQL> drop table inv;
```

Verify that the table has been renamed by viewing the contents of the recycle bin.

```
SQL> show recyclebin;

ORIGINAL NAME   RECYCLEBIN NAME                   OBJECT TYPE  DROP TIME
--------------- -------------------------------- ------------------------
INV             BIN$0zIqhEFlcprgQ4TQTwq2uA==$0 TABLE          2023-01-11:
                                                               12:16:49
```

The SHOW RECYCLEBIN statement shows only tables that have been dropped. To get a more complete picture of renamed objects, query the RECYCLEBIN view.

```
SQL> select object_name, original_name, type
from recyclebin;
```

Here is the output.

```
OBJECT_NAME                          ORIGINAL_NAM TYPE
----------------------------------   ------------ --------
BIN$OzIqhEFjcprgQ4TQTwq2uA==$0       INV_PK       INDEX
BIN$OzIqhEFkcprgQ4TQTwq2uA==$0       INV_TRIG     TRIGGER
BIN$OzIqhEFlcprgQ4TQTwq2uA==$0       INV          TABLE
```

In this output, the table also has a primary key that was renamed when the object was dropped. To undrop the table, do the following.

```
SQL> flashback table inv to before drop;
```

The prior command restores the table to its original name. This statement, however, does not restore the index to its original name.

```
SQL> select index_name from user_indexes where table_name='INV';
INDEX_NAME
--------------------------------------------------
BIN$OzIqhEFjcprgQ4TQTwq2uA==$0
```

In this scenario, you have to rename the index.

```
SQL> alter index "BIN$OzIqhEFjcprgQ4TQTwq2uA==$0" rename to inv_pk;
```

You also have to rename any trigger objects in the same manner. If referential constraints were in place before the table was dropped, you must manually re-create them.

If, for some reason, you need to flash back a table to a name different from the original name, you can do so as follows.

```
SQL> flashback table inv to before drop rename to inv_bef;
```

Flashing Back a Table to a Previous Point in Time

If a table was erroneously deleted from, you have the option of flashing back the table to a previous point in time. The Flashback Table feature uses information in the undo tablespace to restore the table. The point in time in the past depends on your undo tablespace retention period, which specifies the minimum time that undo information is kept.

If the required flashback information is not in the undo tablespace, you receive an error like the following.

```
ORA-01555: snapshot too old
```

In other words, to be able to flash back to a point in time in the past, the required information in the undo tablespace must not have been overwritten.

FLASHBACK TABLE TO SCN

Suppose you are testing an application feature, and you want to quickly restore a table back to a specific SCN. As part of the application testing, you record the SCN before testing begins.

```
SQL> select current_scn from v$database;
CURRENT_SCN
-------------
4760099
```

You perform some testing and then want to flash back the table to the SCN previously recorded. First, ensure that row movement is enabled for the table.

```
SQL> alter table inv enable row movement;
SQL> flashback table inv to scn 4760089;
```

The table should now reflect transactions that were committed as of the historical SCN value specified in the FLASHBACK statement.

FLASHBACK TABLE TO TIMESTAMP

You can also flash back a table to a prior point in time. For example, to flash back a table to 15 minutes in the past, first enable row movement and then use FLASHBACK TABLE.

```
SQL> alter table inv enable row movement;
SQL> flashback table inv to timestamp(sysdate-1/96);
```

The timestamp you provide must evaluate to a valid format for an Oracle timestamp. You can also explicitly specify a time, as follows.

```
SQL> flashback table inv to timestamp
     to_timestamp('14-jun-23 12:07:33','dd-mon-yy hh24:mi:ss');
```

FLASHBACK TABLE TO RESTORE POINT

A restore point is a name associated with a timestamp or an SCN in the database. You can create a restore point that contains the current SCN of the database, as follows.

```
SQL> create restore point point_a;
```

Later, if you flash back a table to that restore point, first enable row movement.

```
SQL> alter table inv enable row movement;
SQL> flashback table inv to restore point point_a;
```

The table should now contain transactions at the SCN associated with the specified restore point.

FLASHBACK DATABASE

The Flashback Database brings the database back to a point in time in the past. Flashback Database uses information stored in flashback logs; it does not rely on restoring database files (as do cold backup, hot backup, and RMAN).

Flashback Database is not a substitute for a backup of your database. If you experience a media failure with a data file, you cannot use Flashback Database to flash back to before the failure. If a data file is damaged, you must restore and recover it using a physical backup (hot, cold, or RMAN).

The Flashback Database feature may be desirable in situations in which you want to consistently reset your database back to a point in time in the past. For instance, you may periodically want to set a test or training database back to a known baseline. Or, you may be upgrading an application and, before making large-scale changes to the application database objects, mark the starting point. After the upgrade, if things do not go well, you want the ability to quickly reset the database back to the point in time before the upgrade took place.

There are several prerequisites for Flashback Database.

- The database must be in archivelog mode.

- You must be using an FRA.

- The Flashback Database feature must be enabled.

You can verify the status of these features using the following SQL*Plus statements.

```
SQL> archive log list;
SQL> show parameter db_recovery_file_dest;
```

To enable the Flashback Database feature, alter your database into flashback mode, as shown next.

```
SQL> alter database flashback on;
```

You can verify the flashback status as follows.

```
SQL> select flashback_on from v$database;
```

After you enable Flashback Database, you can view the flashback logs in your FRA with this query.

```
SQL> select name, log#, thread#, sequence#, bytes
from v$flashback_database_logfile;
```

The range of time in which you can flash back is determined by the DB_FLASHBACK_ RETENTION_TARGET parameter. This specifies the upper limit, in minutes, of how far your database can be flashed back.

You can view the oldest SCN and time you can flash back your database to by running the following SQL.

```
SQL> select
 oldest_flashback_scn
 ,to_char(oldest_flashback_time,'dd-mon-yy hh24:mi:ss')
from v$flashback_database_log;
```

If, for any reason, you need to disable Flashback Database, you can turn it off as follows.

```
SQL> alter database flashback off;
```

You can use either RMAN or SQL*Plus to flash back a database. You can specify a point in time in the past using one of the following.

- SCN

- Timestamp

- Restore point

- Last RESETLOGS operation (works from RMAN only)

This example creates a restore point.

```
SQL> create restore point flash_1;
```

Next, the application performs some testing, after which the database is flashed back to the restore point so that a new round of testing can begin.

```
SQL> shutdown immediate;
SQL> startup mount;
SQL> flashback database to restore point flash_1;
SQL> alter database open resetlogs;
```

At this point, your database should be transactionally consistent with how it was at the SCN associated with the restore point.

Restoring and Recovering to a Different Server

When you think about architecting your backup strategy, as part of the process, you must also consider how you will restore and recover. Your backups are only as good as when you tested a restore and recovery. A backup strategy can be rendered worthless without a good restore-and-recovery strategy. The last thing you want to happen is to have a media failure, go to restore your database, and then find out you are missing critical pieces, you do not have enough space to restore, something is corrupt, and so on.

One of the best ways to test an RMAN backup is to restore and recover it to a different database server. This exercises all your backup, restore, and recovery DBA skills. If you can restore and recover an RMAN backup on a different server, it gives you confidence when a real disaster hits. You can think of all the prior material in this book as the building blocks of how backup and recovery work.

Note   RMAN does have a DUPLICATE DATABASE command, which works well for copying a database from one server to another. If you are going to be performing this type of task often, we recommend that you use RMAN's duplicate database functionality. However, you may still have to copy a backup of a database manually from one server to another, especially when the security is such that you cannot directly connect a production server to a development environment. You can use RMAN to duplicate a database based on backups you copy from the target to the auxiliary server. See MOS note 874352.1 for more on targetless duplication.

In this example, the originating server and destination server have different mount points. Listed next are the high-level steps required to take an RMAN backup and use it to re-create a database on a separate server.

1. Create an RMAN backup on the originating database.

2. Copy the RMAN backup to the destination server. All steps that follow are performed on the destination database server.

3. Ensure that Oracle is installed.

4. Source the required OS variables.

5. Create an `init.ora` file for the database to be restored.

6. Create any required directories for data files, control files, and dump/trace files.

7. Start up the database in nomount mode.

8. Restore the control file from the RMAN backup.

9. Start up the database in mount mode.

10. Make the control file aware of the location of the RMAN backups.

11. Rename and restore the data files to reflect new directory locations.

12. Recover the database.

13. Set the new location for the online redo logs.

14. Open the database.

15. Add the temp file.

16. Rename the database (optional).

This chapter and previous ones explained how to do all these steps. The difference here is that steps 3 to 16 are performed on the new destination server, providing you the checklist to restore on a different server.

If the originating server and destination server have different mount point names, you need to rename the files.

RMAN can be used for any type of restore-and-recovery scenario. If you need to restore, take a breath, remember your practice, and think through your options. It might be instinctive to restore the entire database, but a FLASHBACK QUERY might be all that is needed. Be sure to validate and preview the restore; this ensures you have the files you need and sets you up for a successful restore. Testing and practicing ensure you have good backup files and strategy and lets you think through the best way to restore and recover your database.

CHAPTER 15

External Tables

External tables are an easy way to use files to load data, run queries against to provide transformations, load only needed data, or use the files as reference data without even loading it to the database tables.

The Oracle external table feature enables you to perform a few operations.

- Transparently select information from OS files that have been delimited or from fixed fields into the database.

- Create platform-independent dump files that can be used to transfer data. You can also create the files as compressed and encrypt them for efficient and secure data transportation.

- Allow SQL to be run inline against the file data without creating an external table in the database.

- Use cloud storage to store your files and access the data using external tables.

One common use of an external table is selecting data from an OS file via SQL statements. Simply put, external tables allow reading data in the database from a file without having to load the data into a table first. This allows transformations to be done against the files while loading the needed data into the database. Using the external table can simplify or enhance extract/transform/load (ETL) processes.

You can also use an external table feature to select data from the database and write that information to a binary dump file. The definition of the external table determines what tables and columns are used to unload data. Using an external table in this mode provides a method for extracting large amounts of data to a platform-independent file that you can later load into a different database.

© Michelle Malcher, Darl Kuhn 2024
M. Malcher and D. Kuhn, *Pro Oracle Database 23ai Administration*,
https://doi.org/10.1007/979-8-8688-1038-1_15

All that is required to enable external tables is to first create a database directory object that specifies the location of the OS file. Then, you use the CREATE TABLE... ORGANIZATION EXTERNAL statement to make the database aware of the OS files that can be used as sources or targets of data.

Note   Oracle Cloud databases can use the DBMS_CLOUD package to create external tables for files you have a URI for in cloud storage.

This chapter covers ways of loading data by comparing SQL*Loader and Data Pump with external tables. Several examples illustrate the flexibility and power of using external tables as a loading and data transformation tool.

SQL*Loader vs. External Tables

One general use of an external table is to employ SQL to load data from an OS file into a regular database table. This facilitates loading large amounts of data from files into the database. Almost anything you can do with SQL*Loader, you can achieve with external tables. An important difference is that SQL*Loader loads data into a table; external tables do not need to do this. Another important difference is that SQL*Loader can work with files accessible on any database user's local computer, whereas external tables work only with files accessible directly from the database server. External tables are more flexible and intuitive than SQL*Loader. Additionally, you can obtain very good performance when loading data with external tables by using direct path and parallel features, and you can even partition external tables.

A quick comparison of how data is loaded into the database via SQL*Loader and external tables highlights the usage. You can use the following steps to load and transform data with SQL*Loader.

1. Create a parameter file that SQL*Loader uses to interpret the format of the data in the OS file.

2. Create a regular database table into which SQL*Loader inserts records. The data is staged here until they can be further processed.

3. Run the SQL*Loader `sqlldr` utility to load data from the OS file into the database table (created in step 2). When loading data, SQL*Loader has features that allow you to transform data. This step requires you to correctly map the parameter file to the table and corresponding columns and may take a few attempts.

4. Create another table that contains the completely transformed data.

5. Run SQL to extract the data from the staging table from step 2, and then transform and insert the data into the production table from step 4.

Compare the previous SQL*Loader list to the following steps for loading and transforming data using external tables.

1. Execute a `CREATE TABLE...ORGANIZATION EXTERNAL` script that maps the structure of the OS file to table columns. After this script is run, you can directly use SQL to query the contents of the OS file.

2. Create a regular table to hold the completely transformed data or insert it into an existing table.

3. Run SQL statements to load and fully transform the data from the external table from step 1 into the table created in step 2.

For many companies, SQL*Loader underpins large data-loading operations. It continues to be a good tool for that task. However, you may want to investigate using external tables. External tables have the following advantages.

- Loading data with external tables is more straightforward and requires fewer steps.

- The interface for creating and loading from external tables is SQL*Plus or your favorite SQL tool.

- You can view data (via SQL) in an external table before they're loaded into a database table.

- You can load, transform, and aggregate the data without an intermediate staging table. For large amounts of data, this can be a huge space savings.

External Table Types

You've learned about the SQL*Loader type of external tables, which is used by default. However, other types of external tables have their own access drivers and help you work with the different data types you might be using.

The following are types of external tables.

- ORACLE_LOADER

- ORACLE_DATAPUMP

- ORACLE_HDFS

- ORACLE_HIVE

The default is ORACLE_LOADER, as discussed. It can load data or be used in SQL statements to join against internal tables to do transformations and then load. It cannot unload data.

ORACLE_DATAPUMP can perform both loads and unloads of data in binary dump files. Even the files that are written can be read back into the database.

ORACLE_HDFS extracts data in a Hadoop Distributed File System (HDFS), and ORACLE_HIVE extracts data from Apache Hive. Both of these are useful for big data platforms and working to pull data into your Oracle internal tables for further analytics and machine learning.

Creating External Tables

There are setup steps needed for external tables. You need a directory. The directory object defines the location of the files. The location is the data files for ORACLE_LOADER and ORACLE_DATAPUMP types. Access parameters are also needed, which are related to the type of external table. Each of the types has its own types of access drivers.

Loading CSV Files into the Database

You can load small or very large CSV files into the database using external tables and SQL. You can also use other file types, but based on the use case and need, there might be other ways to load data more efficiently, such as JSON or other data. It also depends if this is a one-time load or a regular process that is being automated with external tables.

Figure 15-1 shows the architectural components of using an external table to view and load data from an OS file. The CREATE TABLE...ORGANIZATION EXTERNAL statement creates a database object that SQL statements can use to directly select from the OS file.

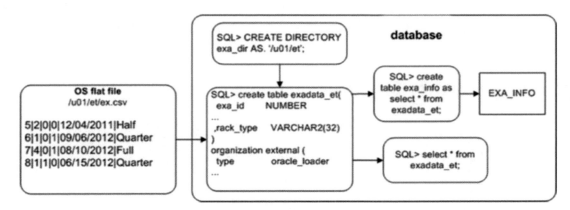

Figure 15-1. *Architectural components of an external table used to read a file*

The following are the steps for using an external table to access an OS file.

1. Create a database directory object that points to the location of the CSV file.

2. Grant read and write privileges on the directory object to the user creating the external table. (Even though it is easier to use a DBA-privileged account with various security options, access to the tables and data might not be available to the account. Permissions need to be verified and granted as needed, as this is probably a load process that should not have DBA privileges.)

3. Run the CREATE TABLE...ORGANIZATION EXTERNAL statement.

4. Use SQL*Plus or other SQL tools to access the contents of the CSV file.

In this example, the file is named example_sales.csv and is located in the /oradata/sales directory. It contains the following data.

```
4|19|1097578|iphone|discover|1/19/2023|2.99
9|2670|1212876|mac|amex|1/11/2023|3.99
8|1037|1164794|galaxy|mastercard|1/21/2023|2.99
```

Wasn't this supposed to be a CSV example? Of course, but that is just a delimited file, and some of the delimiters can be different from commas and separated by characters like a pipe (|). The character depends on the data and the user supplying the file. A comma is not always useful as the delimiter, as the data being loaded may contain commas as valid characters within the data. A fixed field length can also be used instead of using a delimiter.

Create a Directory Object and Granting Access

First, create a directory object that points to the location of the file on disk.

```
SQL> create directory example_dir as '/oradata/sales';
```

Grant READ and WRITE on the directory object to the user (your account or application account) that is accessing the directory object.

```
SQL> grant read, write on directory example_dir to app_user;
```

Create Table

Then, fashion the script that creates the external table that references the file. The CREATE TABLE...ORGANIZATION EXTERNAL statement provides the database with the following information.

- How to interpret data in the file and mapping of the data in the file to column definitions in the database

- A DEFAULT DIRECTORY clause that identifies the directory object, which in turn specifies the directory of the file on disk

- The LOCATION clause, which identifies the name of the file

The next statement creates a database object that looks like a table but can retrieve data directly from the file.

```
SQL> create table example_salesdata (
sale_id number
, sale_type number
, customer_id number
, device varchar2(30)
, payment_type varchar2(30)
```

```
, sale_date date
, sale_price number
)
organization external (
type oracle_loader
default directory example_dir
access parameters
(records delimited by newline
        Fields terminated by '|'
missing field values are null
(sale_id
, sale_type
, customer_id
, device
, payment_type
, sale_date char date_format date mask "mm/dd/yyyy"
, sale_price)
)
location ('example_sales.csv')
)
reject limit unlimited;
```

An external table named example_salesdata is created when you execute this script. Now, use SQL*Plus to view the contents of the file.

```
SQL> select sale_id,customer_id,payment_type, sale_date, sale_price from
example_salesdata;
SALE_ID    CUSTOMER_ID PAYMENT_TYPE      SALE_DATE   SALE_PRICE
---------- ----------- ----------------- ----------- ----------
4          1097578     discover          1/19/2023   2.99
9          1212876     amex              1/11/2023   3.99
8          1164794     mastercard        1/21/2023   2.99
```

Generating SQL to Create an External Table

If you are currently working with SQL*Loader and want to convert to using external tables, you can use the SQL*Loader to generate the SQL required to create the external table using the EXTERNAL_TABLE option. A small example can demonstrate this process. Suppose you have the following table DDL.

```
SQL> create table books
(book_id number,
book_desc varchar2(30));
```

In this situation, you want to load the following data from a CSV file into the BOOKS table. The data is in a file named books.dat and is as follows.

```
1|RMAN Recipes
2|Linux for DBAs
3|SQL Recipes
```

You also have a books.ctl SQL*Loader control file that contains the following data.

```
load data
INFILE 'books.dat'
INTO TABLE books
APPEND
FIELDS TERMINATED BY '|'
(book_id,
book_desc)
```

You can use SQL*Loader with the EXTERNAL_TABLE=GENERATE_ONLY clause to generate the SQL required to create an external table. The following is an example.

```
$ sqlldr dk/f00 control=books.ctl log=books.log external_
table=generate_only
```

The prior line of code does not load any data. Rather, it creates a file named books. log that contains the SQL required to create an external table. Here is a partial listing of the code generated.

```
CREATE TABLE "SYS_SQLLDR_X_EXT_BOOKS"
(
```

```
"BOOK_ID" NUMBER,
"BOOK_DESC" VARCHAR2(30)
)
ORGANIZATION external
(
TYPE oracle_loader
DEFAULT DIRECTORY SYS_SQLLDR_XT_TMPDIR_00000
ACCESS PARAMETERS
(
RECORDS DELIMITED BY NEWLINE CHARACTERSET US7ASCII
BADFILE 'SYS_SQLLDR_XT_TMPDIR_00000':'books.bad'
LOGFILE 'books.log_xt'
READSIZE 1048576
FIELDS TERMINATED BY "|" LDRTRIM
REJECT ROWS WITH ALL NULL FIELDS
(
"BOOK_ID" CHAR(255)
TERMINATED BY "|",
"BOOK_DESC" CHAR(255)
TERMINATED BY "|"
)
)
location
(
'books.dat'
)
)REJECT LIMIT UNLIMITED;
```

Before you run the prior code, create a directory that points to the location of the books.dat file. The following is an example.

```
SQL> create or replace directory SYS_SQLLDR_XT_TMPDIR_00000 as '/u01/
sqlldr';
```

Now, if you run the SQL code generated by SQL*Loader, you should be able to view the data in the SYS_SQLLDR_X_EXT_BOOKS table.

```
SQL> select * from SYS_SQLLDR_X_EXT_BOOKS;
```

Here is the expected output.

```
BOOK_ID  BOOK_DESC
-------- -------------------
1        RMAN Recipes
2        Linux for DBAs
3        SQL Recipes
```

This is a powerful technique, especially if you already have existing SQL*Loader control files and want to ensure that you have the correct syntax when converting to external tables.

Viewing External Table Metadata

At this point, you can also view metadata regarding the external table. Query the DBA_EXTERNAL_TABLES view for details.

```
SQL> select
owner
,table_name
,default_directory_name
,access_parameters
from dba_external_tables;
```

Here is a partial listing of the output.

```
OWNER    TABLE_NAME    DEFAULT_DIRECTORY_NA ACCESS_PARAMETERS

-------  ------------  -------------------- ---------------------

SYS      EXADATA_ET    EXA_DIR                  records delimited ...
```

Additionally, you can select from the DBA_EXTERNAL_LOCATIONS table for information regarding any flat files referenced in an external table.

```
SQL> select
owner
,table_name
,location
from dba_external_locations;
```

Here is some sample output.

```
OWNER        TABLE_NAME        LOCATION
----------   ---------------   ---------------
SYS          EXADATA_ET        ex.csv
```

Loading a Regular Table from the External Table

Now, you can load data contained in the external table into a regular database table. When you do this, you can take advantage of Oracle's direct-path loading and parallel features. This example creates a regular database table that is loaded with data from the external table.

```
SQL> create table exa_info(
exa_idNUMBER
,machine_count NUMBER
,hide_flagNUMBER
,oracleNUMBER
,ship_dateDATE
,rack_typeVARCHAR2(32)
) nologging parallel 2;
```

You can direct-path load this regular table (via the APPEND hint) from the contents of the external table listed in the dba_external_tables view, as follows.

```
SQL> insert /*+ APPEND */ into exa_info select * from exadata_et;
```

You can verify that the table was direct-path loaded by attempting to select from it before you commit the data.

```
SQL> select * from exa_info;
```

After you commit the data, you can select from the table.

```
SQL> commit;
SQL> select * from exa_info;
```

Conversion errors may appear when reading or writing data with external tables. Conversion of numbers to dates or character fields should be recognized, but when receiving these errors, it is possible to explicitly create the conversion in the statements. Using TO_NUMBER, TO_DATE, and TO_CHAR helps to avoid these issues if the conversion is not made implicitly.

The other way to direct-path load a table is to use the CREATE TABLE AS SELECT (CTAS) statement. A CTAS statement automatically attempts to do a direct-path load. In this example, the EXA_INFO table is created and loaded in one statement.

```
SQL> create table exa_info nologging parallel 2 as select * from
exadata_et;
```

By using direct-path loading and parallelism, you can achieve loading performance similar to that of SQL*Loader. The advantage of using SQL to create a table from an external table is that you can perform complex data transformations using standard SQL features when building your regular database table (EXA_INFO, in this example).

CTAS statements automatically process with the degree of parallelism defined for the underlying table. However, when you use INSERT AS SELECT statements, you may need to either use the statement-level hint ENABLE_PARALLEL_DML or enable parallelism for the session.

```
SQL> alter session enable parallel dml;
```

As a last step, you should generate statistics for any table loaded with a large amount of data. Here is an example.

```
SQL> exec dbms_stats.gather_table_stats(ownname => 'SYS', tabname => 'EXA_
INFO', cascade => true);
```

External Tables with Oracle Cloud Database

Cloud databases let you easily use files from cloud storage, and this is just a quick example of leveraging files in your cloud environment with your database.

You don't have to have a directory created to use external tables, but you need to know the URI for the file, that is, the namespace and tenancy information, along with the filename.

DBMS_CLOUD is a package that allows you to load data. It also provides ways to do the following.

- Access management

- Objects and files

- Bulk file management

- REST APIs

We realize this is a little detour of just talking about external tables, but this provides a powerful package to help you manage data with your cloud environment. As you can see, it has some useful REST APIs for management and ways to manage files. It also allows you to set and manage credentials. The next couple of chapters cover more ways to administer cloud databases, but let's look at how DBMS_CLOUD external tables are created.

DBMS_CLOUD Create Table

You can leverage your JSON and CSV files in your cloud storage to perform SQL statements against external tables.

The following is an example of creating an external table for a CSV file. You see, the location is now file_uri_list, and the type of the file is CSV.

```
begin
dbms_cloud.create_external_table (table_name => 'salesdata_ext'
, file_uri_list => 'https://objectstorage.us-ashburn-1.oraclecloud.com/n/
ten_namespace/b/bucket_name/o/example_sales_2023.csv'
, format => json_object ('type' value 'csv', 'skipheaders' value '1')
, column_list => 'sale_id number
, sale_type number
, customer_id number
, device varchar2(30)
, payment_type varchar2(30)
, sale_date date
, sale_price number');
end;
```

After creating the table, you can use the data in SQL statements or load data from the file.

Here is one more quick example with a JSON file.

```
begin
dbms_cloud.create_external_table ( table_name => 'json_salesdata_ext'
, file_uri_list => 'https://objectstorage.us-ashburn-1.oraclecloud.
com/n/ten_namespace/b/bucket_name/o/customersales.json', column_list =>
'json_document clob', field_list => 'json_document', format => json_object
('delimiter' value '\n') );
end;
```

Inline SQL from External Table

It is possible to select directly from the file with the use of EXTERNAL without actually creating an external table in the data dictionary. This allows external data to be part of a subquery, virtual view, or another transformation type of process.

The following is an example of how this works.

```
SELECT columns FROM EXTERNAL ((column definitions) TYPE [ access_driver_
type] external_table_properties [REJECT LIMIT clause])
SQL> select first_name, last_name, hiredate, department_name from external
( (first _name varchar2(50),
last_name varchar2(50),
hiredate date,
department_name varchar2(50))
type oracle_loader
default directory ext_data
access parameters (
records delimited by newline nobadfile nologfile
fields date_format date mask "mm/dd/yyyy")
location ('empbydep.csv') reject limit unlimited)
empbydep_external
where department='HR';
```

The empbydep_external table is not actually created as an external table, and this data is available to query and specify any of the columns or filter by a different selection in the WHERE CLAUSE. This is also possible with JSON and useful when accessing data APIs provided in the JSON format. This does not load the data into the table but can be queried and used in several different methods for views and reference data that is available by API to complete data sets in data integrations.

Unloading and Loading Data Using an External Table

External tables can also select data from a regular database table and create a binary dump file. This is known as *unloading data*. The advantage of this technique is that the dump file is platform-independent and can be used to move large amounts of data between servers of different platforms.

You can also encrypt or compress data, or both when creating the dump file. Doing so provides an efficient and secure way of transporting databases between database servers.

A small example here illustrates the technique of using an external table to unload data. Here are the steps required.

1. Create a directory object that specifies where you want the dump file placed on disk. Again, grant read and write access to the directory object for the user that needs access.

2. Use the CREATE TABLE...ORGANIZATION EXTERNAL...AS SELECT statement to unload data from the database into the dump file.

First, create a directory object. The next bit of code creates a directory object named DP that points to the /oradump directory.

```
SQL> create directory dp as '/oradump';
SQL> grant read, write on directory dp to larry;
```

This example depends on a table named INV; for reference, the following is the DDL for the INV table.

```
SQL> create table inv
(inv_id number,
inv_desc varchar2(30));
```

To create a dump file, use the ORACLE_DATAPUMP access driver of the CREATE TABLE...ORGANIZATION EXTERNAL statement. This example unloads the INV table's contents into the inv.dmp file.

```
SQL> create table inv_ext
Organization external (
Type oracle_datapump
Default directory dp
Location ('inv.dmp')
) as select * from inv;
```

The previous command creates two things.

- An external table name INV_EXT, based on the structure and data within the INV table

- A platform-independent dump file named inv.dmp

Now, you can copy the inv.dmp file to a separate database server and base an external table on this dump file. The remote server (to which you copy the dump file) can be a platform different from the server on which you created the file. For example, you can create a dump file on a Windows server, copy it to a Linux server, and select from the dump file via an external table.

In this example, the external table is named INV_DW.

```
SQL> create table inv_dw
(inv_id number
, inv_desc varchar2(30))
organization external (
type oracle_datapump
default directory dp
location ('inv.dmp'));
```

After it's created, you can access the external table data from SQL*Plus.

```
SQL> select * from inv_dw;
```

You can also create and load data into regular tables using the dump file.

```
SQL> create table inv as select * from inv_dw;
```

This provides a simple and efficient mechanism for transporting data from one platform to another.

Oracle Data Pump

Let's take a bit of time to look at Data Pump. This is a utility to unload and load data into the database. It can also provide a quick backup, replicating, and securing copy of your data and metadata. You can use Data Pump in a variety of ways.

- Perform point-in-time logical backups of the entire database or subsets of data

- Replicate entire databases or subsets of data for testing or development

- Quickly generate DDL required to re-create objects

- Upgrade a database by exporting from the old version and importing it into the new version

When considering ways of uploading, unloading data, and using the different utilities or external tables, you can look at this list of the functionality of Data Pump to help decide what tool works best for the job.

- Performance with large data sets, allowing efficient export and import of data

- Interactive command-line utility, which lets you disconnect and then later attach to active Data Pump jobs along with monitoring job progress

- Ability to export large amounts of data from a remote database and import them directly into a local database without creating a dump file

- Ability to make on-the-fly changes to schemas, tablespaces, data files, and storage settings from export to import

- Sophisticated filtering of objects and data

- Use to perform transportable tablespace export

- Security-controlled (via database) directory objects and data directories

- Advanced features, such as compression and encryption

There are additional ways to move data between databases, as discussed in this chapter, but also with pluggable databases, cloning, backup and restores, and other functionality.

Data Pump Architecture

Data Pump consists of the following components.

- Expdp (Data Pump export utility)

- Impdp (Data Pump import utility)

- DBMS_DATAPUMP PL/SQL package (Data Pump application programming interface [API])

- DBMS_METADATA PL/SQL package (Data Pump Metadata API)

The expdp and impdp utilities use the DBMS_DATAPUMP and DBMS_METADATA built-in PL/SQL packages when exporting and importing data and metadata. The DBMS_DATAPUMP and DBMS_METADATA packages can also be used outside the Data Pump jobs, useful in monitoring and retrieving DDL statements.

When you start a Data Pump export or import job, a master OS process is initiated, and a database status table is created for the duration of the Data Pump job. There are different modes of the Data Pump job.

- FULL

- SCHEMA

- TABLE

- TABLESPACE

- TRANSPORTABLE

For example, if you export a schema, a table is created in your account with the name SYS_EXPORT_SCHEMA_NN, where NN is a number that makes the table name unique in the user's schema. This status table contains information such as the objects' exported/ imported, start time, elapsed time, rows, and error count. The status table has more than 80 columns.

A Data Pump export creates an export file and a log file. The export file contains the objects being exported. The log file contains a record of the job activities. Export writes data out of the database, and import brings information into the database.

Taking an Export

A small amount of setup is required when you run a Data Pump export job. The following explains the steps.

1. Create a database directory object that points to an OS directory that you want to write/read Data Pump files to/from. (The directory object was used with the external tables.)

2. Grant read and write privileges on the directory object to the database user running the export.

3. From the OS prompt, run the expdp utility.

The following are the first two steps since the directory object with the external tables has been discussed.

```
SQL> create directory dp_dir as '/oradump';
SQL> grant read, write on directory dp_dir to mv_maint;
```

You can now use Data Pump to export data from the database. The simple example in this section shows how to export a table. Previous examples in this book used tables such as INV and EMP that you can use as tables for export.

```
$ expdp mv_maint/Pa$$w0rd123! Directory=dp_dir tables=inv dumpfile=exp_inv.
dmp logfile=exp_inv.log
```

The expdp utility creates a file named exp_inv.dmp in the /oradump directory, containing the information required to re-create the INV table and populate it with data as it was at the time the export was started. Additionally, a log file named exp_inv.log is created in the /oradump directory, containing logging information associated with this export job.

If you do not specify a dump file name, Data Pump creates a file named expdat.dmp. If a file named expdat.dmp already exists in the directory, Data Pump throws an error. If you do not specify a log file name, then Data Pump creates one named export. log. If a log file named export.log already exists, then Data Pump overwrites it.

Tip   Although it is possible to execute Data Pump as the SYS user, it is better to use a different user. First, SYS is required to connect to the database with the AS SYSDBA clause. This requires a Data Pump parameter file with the USERID parameter and quotes around the associated connect string. This is unwieldy. Second, most tables owned by SYS cannot be exported (there are a few exceptions, such as AUD$). If you attempt to export a table owned by SYS, Data Pump throws an ORA-39166 error and indicate that the table doesn't exist. This is confusing. Even when exporting a FULL database, the SYS, ORDSYS, and MDSYS system schemas are not exported, even if exporting using an SYS account.

Import a Table

One of the key reasons to export data is so that you can re-create database objects. You may want to do this as part of a backup strategy or to replicate data to a different database. Data Pump import uses an export dump file as its input and re-creates database objects contained in the export file. The procedure for importing is similar to exporting.

1. Create a database directory object where you want to read/write Data Pump files.

2. Grant read and write privileges on the directory object.

3. From the OS prompt, run the impdp command.

Before running the import job, drop the INV table that was created previously.

```
SOL> drop table inv purge;
```

Next, re-create the INV table from the export taken with the import.

```
$ impdp mv_maint/Pa$$wOrd123! Directory=dp_dir dumpfile=exp_inv.dmp
logfile=imp_inv.log
```

You should now have the INV table re-created and populated with data as it was at the time of the export. Instead of dropping the table, you can also append the data to the table with the TABLE_EXISTS_ACTION parameter. Options are SKIP, APPEND, REPLACE, or TRUNCATE, with APPEND being the default.

```
$ impdp mv_maint/Pa$$wOrd123! directory=dp_dir dumpfile=exp_inv.dmp table_
exists_action=append content=data_only
```

Use a Parameter File

Instead of typing commands on the command line, in many situations, it is better to store the commands in a file and then reference the file when executing Data Pump export or import. Using parameter files makes tasks more repeatable and less prone to error. You can place the commands in a file once and then reference that file multiple times.

Additionally, some Data Pump commands (such as FLASHBACK_TIME) require quotation marks; in these situations, it is sometimes hard to predict how the OS interprets them. Whenever a command requires quotation marks, it is highly preferable to use a parameter file.

To use a parameter file, first create an OS text file that contains the commands you want to use to control the behavior of your job. This example uses the Linux vi command to create a text file named exp.par.

```
$ vi exp.par
```

Now, place the following commands in the exp.par file.

```
userid=mv_maint/Pa$$wOrd123!
directory=dp_dir
dumpfile=exp.dmp
logfile=exp.log
tables=inv
reuse_dumpfiles=y
```

Next, the export operation references the parameter file via the PARFILE command-line option.

```
$ expdp parfile=exp.par
```

Data Pump processes the parameters in the file as if they were typed on the command line. If you find yourself repeatedly typing the same commands or using commands that require quotation marks or both, then consider using a parameter file to increase your efficiency.

Export and Import an Entire Database

When you export an entire database, this is referred to as a *full export*, and the resultant export file contains everything required to make a copy of your database. Unless restricted by filtering parameters, a full export consists of the following.

- All DDL required to re-create tablespaces, users, user tables, indexes, constraints, triggers, sequences, stored PL/SQL, and so on

- All table data (except the SYS schemas SYS, ORDSYS, or MDSYS)

A full export is initiated with the FULL parameter set to Y and must be done with a user with DBA privileges or the DATAPUMP_EXP_FULL_DATABASE role granted to it. Here is an example of taking a full export of a database.

```
$ expdp mv_maint/Pa$$Ord123! directory=dp_dir dumpfile=full.dmp
logfile=full.log full=y
```

Once you have a full export, you can use its contents to re-create objects in the original database (e.g., if a table is accidentally dropped) or replicate the entire database or subsets of users/tables to a different database. This next example assumes that the dump file has been copied to a different database server and is now used to import all objects into the destination database.

```
$ impdb mv_maint/Pa$$wOrd123! directory=dp_dir dumpfile=full.dmp
logfile=fullimp.log full=y
```

Schema Level

When you initiate an export, unless otherwise specified, Data Pump starts a schema-level export for the user running the export job. User-level exports are frequently used to copy a schema or set of schemas from one environment to another. The following command starts a schema-level export for the MV_MAINT user.

```
$ expdp mv_maint/Pa$$wOrd123! directory=dp_dir dumpfile=mv_maint.dmp
logfile=mv_maint.log
```

You can initiate a schema-level export for users other than those running the export job with the SCHEMAS parameter. The following command shows a schema-level export for multiple users.

```
$ expdp mv_maint/Pa$$wOrd123! directory=dp_dir dumpfile=mv_maint.dmp
logfile=mv_maint.log schemas=hsolo,hr
```

With the schema-level import, there are things to be aware of.

- No tablespaces are included in a schema-level export.

- The import job attempts to re-create any users in the dump file. An error is thrown if a user already exists, and the import job continues.

- Tables owned by the user are imported and populated. If a table already exists, you must instruct Data Pump on how to handle this with the TABLE_EXISTS_ACTION parameter.

Table Level

You can instruct Data Pump to operate on specific tables via the TABLES parameter. For example, say you want to export the following.

```
$ expdp mv_maint/Pa$$wOrd123! directory=dp_dir dumpfile=tab.dmp
tables=sales.inv, sales.inv_items
```

Similarly, you can initiate a table-level import by specifying a table-level-created dump file.

```
$ impdp mv_maint/Pa$$wOrd123! directory=dp_dir dumpfile=tab.dmp
```

You can also initiate a table-level import using a full-export dump file or a schema-level export. To do this, specify which tables you want extracted from the full- or schema-level export.

```
$ impdp mv_maint/Pa$$wOrd123! directory=dp_dir dumpfile=full.dmp
tables=sales.inv
```

Tablespace Level

A tablespace-level export/import operates on objects contained within specific tablespaces. This example exports all objects contained in the USERS tablespace.

```
$ expdp mv_maint/Pa$$w0rd123! directory=dp_dir dumpfile=tbsp.dmp
tablespaces=users
```

You can initiate a tablespace-level import by using a full export but specifying the TABLESPACES parameter.

```
$ impdp mv_maint/Pa$$w0rd123! directory=dp_dir dumpfile=full.dmp
tablespaces=users
```

A tablespace-level import attempts to create any tables and indexes within the tablespace. The import doesn't try to re-create the tablespaces themselves. Since PDB databases have their own tablespaces, so this might be an easy level for PDB exports.

Export Tablespace Metadata

Sometimes, you may be required to replicate an environment, replicating a production environment into a testing environment. One of the first tasks is to replicate the tablespaces. To this end, you can use Data Pump to pull out the DDL required to re-create the tablespaces for an environment.

```
$ expdp mv_maint/Pa$$w0rd123! directory=dp_dir dumpfile=inv.dmp full=y
include=tablespace
```

The FULL parameter instructs Data Pump to export everything in the database. However, when used with INCLUDE, Data Pump exports only the objects specified with that command. In this combination, only metadata regarding tablespaces are exported; no data within the data files is included with the export. You could add the parameter and value of CONTENT=METADATA_ONLY to the INCLUDE command, but this would be redundant. Now, you can use the SQLFILE parameter to view the DDL associated with the tablespaces that were exported.

```
$ impdp mv_maint/Pa$$w0rd123! directory=dp_dir dumpfile=inv.dmp
sqlfile=tbsp.sql
```

When you use the SQLFILE parameter, nothing is imported. In this example, the prior command only creates a file named tbsp.sql, containing SQL statements pertaining to tablespaces. You can modify the DDL and run it in the destination database environment, or if nothing needs to change, you can directly use the dump file by importing tablespaces into the destination database.

Specifying a Query

You can use the QUERY parameter to instruct Data Pump to write to a dump file only rows that meet a certain criterion. You may want to do this if you're re-creating a test environment and only need subsets of the data. Keep in mind that this technique is unaware of any foreign key constraints that may be in place, so you can't blindly restrict the data sets without considering parent-child relationships.

The QUERY parameter has this general syntax for including a query.

```
QUERY = [schema.][table_name:] query_clause
```

The query clause can be any valid WHERE clause. The query must be enclosed by either double or single quotation marks. We recommend using double quotation marks because you may need to have single quotation marks embedded in the query to handle VACHAR2 data. Also, you should use a parameter file to avoid confusion about how the OS interprets the quotation marks.

This example uses a parameter file and limits the rows exported for two tables. Here is the parameter file used when exporting.

```
userid=mv_maint/Pa$$wOrd123!
directory=dp_dir
dumpfile=inv.dmp
tables=inv
query=inv:"WHERE inv_desc='Book'"
```

The previous lines are in the inv.par parameter file. The export job references the parameter file as follows.

```
$ expdp parfile=inv.par
```

The resulting dump file only contains rows filtered by the QUERY parameters. Again, be mindful of any parent-child relationship and ensure that what gets exported does not violate any constraints on the import.

You can also specify a query when importing data. The following is a parameter file that limits the rows imported into the INV table based on the INV_ID column.

```
userid=mv_maint/Pa$$w0rd123!
directory=dp_dir
dumpfile=inv.dmp
tables=inv
query=inv:"WHERE inv_id > 10"
```

The import job references the parameter file as follows.

```
$ impdp parfile=inv2.par
```

Exclude Objects from Export or Import

For export, the EXCLUDE parameter instructs Data Pump not to export specified objects (whereas the INCLUDE parameter instructs Data Pump to include only specific objects in the export file). The EXCLUDE parameter has this general syntax.

```
EXCLUDE=object_typ [:name_cluase][, ...]
```

The OBJECT_TYPE is a database object, such as TABLE or INDEX. To see which object types can be filtered, view the OBJECT_PATH column of DATABASE_EXPORT_OBJECTS, SCHEMA_EXPORT_OBJECTS, or TABLE_EXPORT_OBJECTS. For example, run this query if you want to view what schema-level objects can be filtered.

```
select object_path
from schema_export_objects
where object_path not like '%/%';
```

Here is a snippet of the output.

```
OBJECT_PATH
--------------
STATISTICS
SYNONYM
```

```
SYSTEM_GRANT
TABLE
TABLESPACE_QUOTA
TRIGGER
```

This EXCLUDE parameter example says that you are exporting a table but want to exclude the indexes and grants.

```
$ expdp mv_maint/Pa$$w0rd123! directory=dp_dir dumpfile=inv.dmp tables=inv
exclude=index,grant
```

You can filter at a more granular level by using NAME_CLAUSE. The NAME_CLAUSE option of EXCLUDE allows you to specify a SQL filter.

List Contents of Dump Files

Data Pump has a robust method of creating a file that contains all the SQL that is executed when an import job runs. Data Pump uses the DBMS_METADATA package to create the DDL that you can use to re-create objects in the Data Pump dump file.

Use the SQLFILE option of Data Pump import to list the contents of a Data Pump export file. This example creates a file named expfull.sql, containing the SQL statements that the import process calls (the file is placed in the directory defined by the DPUMP_DIR2 directory object).

```
$ impdp hr/Pa$$w0rd123! directory=dpump_dir1 dumpfile=expfull.dmp
SQLFILE=dpump_dir2:expfull.sql
```

If you do not specify a separate directory, such as dpump_dir2, in the previous example, the SQL file is written to the location specified in the DIRECTORY option.

When you use the SQLFILE option with an import, the impdp process does not import any data; it only creates a file that contains the SQL commands that the import process would run. It is sometimes handy to generate a SQL file for the following reasons.

- Preview and verify the SQL statements before running the import.

- Run the SQL manually to pre-create database objects.

- Capture the SQL required to re-create database objects (users, tables, indexes, and so on).

In regard to the last bulleted item, sometimes what is checked into the source code control repository does not match what has really been applied to the production database. This procedure can be handy for troubleshooting or documenting the state of the database at a point in time.

Monitoring Data Pump Jobs

When you have long-running Data Pump jobs, you should occasionally check the job status to ensure it has not failed, become suspended, and so on. There are several ways to monitor the status of Data Pump jobs.

- Screen output

- Data Pump log file

- Querying data dictionary views

- Database alert log

- Querying the status table

- Interactive command mode status

- Using the process status (ps) OS utility

- Oracle Enterprise Manager

The most obvious way to monitor a job is to view the status that Data Pump displays on the screen as the job is running. If you disconnected from the command mode, the status is no longer displayed on your screen. In this situation, you must use another technique to monitor a Data Pump job.

This chapter has covered different ways of loading and unloading data by using external tables in the database, SQL*Loader, and Data Pump options. This helps manage the data and the metadata of the database objects.

CHAPTER 16

Automation and Troubleshooting

In almost any type of database environment, from development to testing to production, DBAs rely heavily on SQL statements, blocks of code, and scripts to perform tasks. The following are some typical jobs that DBAs automate.

- Shutdown and startup of databases and listeners

- Backups

- Validating the integrity of backups

- Checking for errors

- Removing old trace or log files

- Checking for errant processes

- Checking for abnormal conditions

- Performance tuning

With 23ai, performance tuning is being added to this list, as you can do this with automatic indexing, partitioning, and materialized views. This is not all the performance tuning and configurations you would do, but it takes a step to provide the needed actions for tuning the frequent SQL. We investigate the automation of this shortly, but first, let's look at the other scripts we can automate.

Automation comes into play when these scripts, which are blocks of code, become part of a process that does not require DBA intervention to run. The tasks are performed regularly by scheduled processes or workflows that execute the necessary scripts without direct interaction. Routine maintenance jobs are normally the easiest to automate and

© Michelle Malcher, Darl Kuhn 2024
M. Malcher and D. Kuhn, *Pro Oracle Database 23ai Administration*,
https://doi.org/10.1007/979-8-8688-1038-1_16

produce a check that a task completed successfully or possibly failed for verification. What sometimes gets complicated are the jobs that require a change or understanding of a failure to correct and continue without human interaction in the process. Allowing a database for self-healing, tuning, and patching is what the Oracle database has become. Oracle Autonomous Database is an example of this, and these tasks happen as expected so that the DBA can work in other areas and provide consulting in data integrations, development, and data strategies.

Automating routine tasks allows DBAs to be much more effective and productive. Automated environments are inherently smoother running and more efficient than manually administered systems. DBA jobs that run automatically from scripts consistently execute the same set of commands each time and are less prone to human error and mistakes. There are many tasks to be automated and a handful of scripts that are needed for applications and other maintenance jobs.

Oracle Database has a scheduler to schedule jobs, tasks, and scripts to run against the database. Enterprise Manager provides some centralized management of the jobs. There needs to be an enterprise solution that is provided instead of the cron utility on every server. The jobs can either be scripted to deploy with the database, such as backup jobs, or have a scheduling process to manage several databases. Looking at the Oracle Scheduler utility, you can deploy the schedule with the database creation for the needed tasks and automation. Oracle Scheduler can be used to schedule jobs in a wide variety of configurations.

Automating Jobs with Oracle Scheduler

Oracle Scheduler is a tool that provides a way of automating the scheduling of jobs. Oracle Scheduler is implemented via the DBMS_SCHEDULER internal PL/SQL package. Oracle Scheduler offers sophisticated features for scheduling jobs, such as detailed scheduling, privileged-based models, and storing schedules. More than 70 procedures and functions are available within the DBMS_SCHEDULER package. For more information, see the *Oracle Database PL/SQL Reference Guide* documentation.

Note   In earlier releases, DBMS_JOBS was the package for scheduling. DBMS_JOBS has been deprecated, and DBMS_SCHEDULER should now be used.

Creating and Scheduling a Job

The example in this section shows how to use DBMS_SCHEDULER to run an OS shell script on a daily basis. First, a shell script is created that contains an RMAN backup command. For this example, the shell script is named rmanback.bsh and is located in the /orahome/oracle/bin directory. The shell script also assumes that there is an /orahome/oracle/bin/log directory available. Here is the shell script.

```
#!/bin/bash
# source oracle OS variables;
. /etc/oraset db23ai
rman target / << EOF
spool log to '/orahome/oracle/bin/log/rmanback.log'
backup database;
spool log off;
EOF
exit 0
```

Next, the CREATE_JOB procedure of the DBMS_SCHEDULER package is used to create a daily job. Next, connect as SYS or as the SYSBACKUP user with CREATE and ALTER JOB permissions, and execute the following command.

```
SQL> begin
dbms_scheduler.create_job(
job_name => 'rman_backup',
job_type => 'executable',
job_action => '/orahome/oracle/bin/rmanback.bsh',
repeat_interval => 'freq=daily;byhour=9;byminute=35',
start_date => to_date('18-01-2023','dd-mm-yyyy'),
job_class => 'default_job_class',
auto_drop => false,
comments => 'rman backup job',
enabled => true);
end;
```

In the prior code, the JOB_TYPE parameter can be one of the following types: STORED_ PROCEDURE, PLSQL_BLOCK, EXTERNAL_SCRIPT, SQL_SCRIPT, or EXECUTABLE. In this example, an external shell script is executed, so the job is of type EXTERNAL.

The REPEAT_INTERVAL parameter is set to FREQ=DAILY;BYHOUR=9;BYMINUTE=35. This instructs the job to run daily at 9:35 a.m. The REPEAT_INTERVAL parameter of the CREATE_JOB is capable of implementing sophisticated calendaring frequencies. For instance, it supports a variety of yearly, monthly, weekly, daily, hourly, by-the-minute, and by-the- second schedules. The *Oracle Database PL/SQL Packages and Types Reference Guide* contains several pages of syntax details for just the REPEAT_INTERVAL parameter.

The JOB_CLASS parameter specifies which job class to assign the job to. Typically, you would create a job class and assign a job to that class, whereby the job would inherit the attributes of that particular class. For example, you may want all jobs in a particular class to have the same logging level or to purge log files in the same manner. A default job class can be used if you have not created any job classes. The previous example uses the default job class.

Credentials should be set up for local and remote external jobs. Oracle can use default users, but for security policies and capturing the execution of the job, it is better to create a user for authenticating the external jobs. DBMS_CREDENTIAL stores the user details and can store a Windows domain user, such as a service account, to execute these jobs. Credentials are owned by SYS and can also be managed using DBMS_CREDENTIAL.

The AUTO_DROP parameter is set to FALSE in this example. This instructs the Oracle Scheduler not to automatically drop the job after it completes. (The default is TRUE, although TRUE does not drop jobs set to repeat forever since they never "complete.")

Viewing Job Details

To view details about how a job is configured, query the DBA_SCHEDULER_JOBS view. This query selects information for the RMAN_BACKUP job.

```
SQL> select job_name
 ,last_start_date
 ,last_run_duration
 ,next_run_date
 ,repeat_interval
from dba_scheduler_jobs
where job_name='RMAN_BACKUP';
```

Each time a job runs, a record of the job execution is logged in the data dictionary. To check the status of a job execution, query the DBA_SCHEDULER_JOB_LOG view. There should be one entry for every time a job has run.

```
SQL> select job_name
,log_date
,operation
,status
from dba_scheduler_job_log
where job_name='RMAN_BACKUP';
```

Modifying Job Logging History

By default, the Oracle Scheduler keeps 30 days' worth of log history. You can modify the default retention period via the SET_SCHEDULER_ATTRIBUTE procedure. For example, this command changes the default number of days to 15.

```
SQL> exec dbms_scheduler.set_scheduler_attribute('log_history',15);
```

To remove the contents of the log history completely, use the PURGE_LOG procedure.

```
SQL> exec dbms_scheduler.purge_log();
```

Modifying a Job

You can modify various attributes of a job via the SET_ATTRIBUTE procedure. This example modifies the RMAN_BACKUP job to run weekly, on Mondays.

```
SQL> begin
  dbms_scheduler.set_attribute(
    name=>'rman_backup'
    ,attribute=>'repeat_interval'
    ,value=>'freq=weekly; byday=mon');
end;
```

You can verify the change by selecting the REPEAT_INTERVAL column from the DBA_SCHEDULER_JOBS view. The following is what the REPEAT_INTERVAL column now shows for the RMAN_BACKUP job.

```
freq=weekly; byday=mon
```

From the prior output, you can see that the job runs the following Monday, and because no BYHOUR and BYMINUTE options were specified (when modifying the job), the job is scheduled to run at the default time of 12 a.m.

Stopping a Job

If you have a job that has been running for an abnormally long period of time, you may want to abort it. Use the STOP_JOB procedure to stop a currently running job. This example stops the RMAN_BACKUP job while it is running.

```
SQL> exec dbms_scheduler.stop_job(job_name=>'rman_backup');
```

The STATUS column of DBA_SCHEDULER_JOB_LOG shows STOPPED for jobs stopped using the STOP_JOB procedure.

Disabling a Job

You may want to temporarily disable a job because it is not running correctly. You need to ensure that the job does not run while troubleshooting the issue. Use the DISABLE procedure to disable a job.

```
SQL> exec dbms_scheduler.disable('rman_backup');
```

If the job is running, consider stopping the job first or using the FORCE option of the DISABLE procedure.

```
SQL> exec dbms_scheduler.disable(name=>'rman_backup',force=>true);
```

Enabling a Job

You can enable a previously disabled job via the ENABLE procedure of the DBMS_ SCHEDULER package. This example re-enables the RMAN_BACKUP job.

```
SQL> exec dbms_scheduler.enable(name=>'rman_backup');
```

Tip   You can check to see if a job has been disabled or enabled by selecting the ENABLED column from the DBA_SCHEDULER_JOBS view.

Copying a Job

If you have a current job that you want to clone, you can use the COPY_JOB procedure to accomplish this. The procedure takes two arguments: the old job name and the new job name. Here is an example of copying a job where RMAN_BACKUP is a previously created job, and RMAN_NEW_BACK is the new job that is created.

```
SOL> begin
   dbms_scheduler.copy_job('rman_backup','rman_new_back');
end;
/
```

The copied job is created but not enabled. You must enable the job first (see the previous section for an example) before it runs.

Running a Job Manually

You can manually run a job outside its regular schedule. You might want to do this to test the job to ensure that it is working correctly. Use the RUN_JOB procedure to initiate a job manually. This example manually runs the previously created RMAN_BACKUP job.

```
SOL> begin
dbms_scheduler.run_job(
job_name => 'rman_backup',
use_current_session => false);
end;
/
```

The USE_CURRENT_SESSION parameter instructs Oracle Scheduler to run the job as the current user (or not). A value of FALSE instructs the scheduler to run the job as the user who originally created and scheduled the job.

Deleting a Job

If you no longer require a job, you should delete it from the scheduler. Use the DOP_JOB procedure to permanently remove a job. This example removes the RMAN_BACKUP job.

```
SQL> begin
  dbms_scheduler.drop_job(job_name=>'rman_backup');
end;
/
```

The code drops the job and removes any information regarding the dropped job from the DBA_SCHEDULER_JOBS view.

Examples of Automated DBA Jobs

In today's often chaotic business environment, it is almost mandatory to automate jobs. If you do not automate, you may forget to do a task, or if performing a job manually, you may introduce an error in the procedure. If you do not automate, you could find yourself replaced by a more efficient or cheaper set of DBAs.

Even if you look at Oracle's Autonomous, it is being automated to take care of necessary tasks, patching, scaling, and tuning. This shows the need to automate to manage environments.

When a script fails, it makes sense to receive an email, but too many successful job emails can cause noise and miss a failure. However, not receiving an email in success or failure is really a failure since it is in a state of uncertainty. A way to report on scripts that run for databases is a centralized report that shows success or failure from the consolidated logs or queries from an output table. Reviewing a daily email or having a dashboard validates that all jobs are running properly.

DBAs automate a wide variety of tasks and jobs. Almost any type of environment requires you to create an OS script that encapsulates a combination of OS commands, SQL statements, and PL/SQL blocks. Besides scripts, there are now configurations in the database that do some of the checks or process restarts.

The following scripts in this chapter are a sample of the wide variety of different types of tasks that DBAs automate. This set of scripts is by no means complete. Many of these scripts may not be needed in your environment. The point is to give you a good sampling of the types of automated jobs and the techniques used to accomplish a task.

Tip   Use `catcon.pl`, an Oracle-provided Perl script, to run SQL statements on all PDBs in a CDB. `catcon.pl` is found in `$ORACLE_HOME/rdbms/admin`, and the usage details are in MOS Note 1932340.1.

Run the following from the OS prompt from the `$ORACLE_HOME/rdbms/admin` directory.

```
catcon: $ORACLE_HOME/perl/bin/perl catcon.pl -d /u01/oradata -l / home/
oracle/script_logs -b script_name script_name.sql
```

Starting and Stopping the Database and Listener

If a database server is to reboot or restart, it is desirable to have the Oracle databases and listener automatically restart with the server. This process used to be part of a parameter in the `/etc/oratab` file for the database to automatically restart. It would be called in the `dbstart` and `dbshut` commands and was Y for restart and N for manual intervention.

Now, there is Oracle Restart, which is especially useful for a multicomponent environment with RAC and ASM, but adding databases as part of the restart is simple. When the database is created using `dbca`, the database is added to the Oracle Restart configuration. The same is true when you remove the database using `dbca`: the database is removed from Oracle Restart. If you use Oracle Net Configuration Assistant (`netca`) to create or delete a listener, `netca` adds or removes from Oracle Restart.

There are a few ways to add a database and listener to Oracle Restart if using a different method from `dbca`, either scripted or manual, with `creatdb` steps. With the database software installation, there is a version of Enterprise Manager Database Control that can only add databases and listeners to the Oracle Restart configuration. The `srvctl` utility allows adding, modifying, and deleting databases and listeners with the commands. The commands can become part of the scripted creation of databases, so this task becomes part of the steps and not a manual task that is done afterward.

For the listener, the `GRID_HOME` or `ORACLE_HOME` needs to be set, depending on if the listener is started in the `GRID` or `ORACLE_HOME`. The default listener is added with the following.

```
$ cd $GRID_HOME/bin
$ ./ srvctl add listener
```

To add another listener, the name of the listener would be provided.

To add a database, do this.

```
$ cd $ORACLE_HOME/bin
$ ./ srvctl add service -d db23ai -o /u01/app/oracle/product/23.1.0/db_1
```

- -o is the ORACLE_HOME directory.

- -d is the database name.

To remove a database, use this.

```
$ srvctl remove database -d db23ai
```

A service can also be disabled to still be available but not run with the automatic restart. To disable or enable a database, do this.

```
$ srvctl disable database -d db23ai
```

The srvctl utility is part of the Oracle software and available in the ORACLE_HOME, so the grid infrastructure does not need to be installed to add databases and services to Oracle Restart. Oracle Restart ensures the databases are automatically restarted with a server restart as long as they are enabled in the restart configuration.

Checking for Archivelog Destination Fullness

Sometimes DBAs and SAs do not adequately plan and implement a location for storing archivelog files on disk, or there is more growth and activity than expected. In these scenarios, it is sometimes convenient to have a script that checks for space in the primary location and that sends out warnings before the archivelog destination becomes full. Additionally, you may want to implement within the script that the archivelog location automatically starts an RMAN job to back up and delete the archivelogs to free up space.

Scripts such as this prove useful in chaotic environments with issues with the archivelog destination filling up at unpredictable frequencies. If the archivelog destination fills up, the database hangs. In some environments, this is highly unacceptable. You could argue that you should never let yourself get into this type of situation. Therefore, if you are brought in to maintain an unpredictable environment and get the phone calls at 2 a.m., you may want to consider implementing a script such as the one provided in this section.

Before using the following script, change the variables within the script to match your environment. The script sends a warning email when the threshold goes below the amount of space specified by the THRESH_GET_WORRIED variable and runs an RMAN backup of the archivelogs.

```
#!/bin/bash
PRG='basename $0'
DB=$1
USAGE="Usage: ${PRG} <sid>"
if [ -z "$DB" ]; then
  echo "${USAGE}"
  exit 1
fi
# source OS variables
. /var/opt/oracle/oraset ${DB}
# Set thresholds for getting concerned.
THRESH_GET_WORRIED=2000000 # 2Gig from df -k
MAILX="/bin/mailx"
MAIL_LIST="dba@company.com "
BOX='uname -a | awk '{print$2}''
#
loc='sqlplus -s <<EOF
CONNECT / AS sysdba
SET HEAD OFF FEEDBACK OFF
SELECT SUBSTR(destination,1,INSTR(destination,'/',1,2)-1)
FROM v\\$archive_dest WHERE dest_name='LOG_ARCHIVE_DEST_1';
EOF'
# The output of df depends on your version of Linux/Unix,
# you may need to tweak the next line based on that output.
Free_space='df -k | grep ${loc} | awk '{print $4}''
echo box = ${BOX}, sid = ${DB}, Arch Log Mnt Pnt = ${loc}
echo "free_space= ${free_space} K"
echo "THRESH_GET_WORRIED= ${THRESH_GET_WORRIED} K"
#
if [ $free_space -le $THRESH_GET_WORRIED ]; then
$MAILX -s "Arch Redo Space Low ${DB} on $BOX" $MAIL_LIST <<EOF
```

```
Archive log dest space low running backup now,
box: $BOX, sid: ${DB}, free space: $free_space
EOF
# Run RMAN backup of archivelogs and delete after backed up
rman nocatalog <<EOF
connect target /
backup archivelog all delete input;
EOF
else
  echo no need to backup and delete, ${free_space} KB free on ${loc}
fi
#
exit 0
```

If you are using an FRA for the location of your archivelog files, you can derive the archive location from the V$ARCHIVED_LOG view. The following is an example.

```
SQL> select
  substr(name,1,instr(name,'/',1,2)-1)
from v$archived_log
where first_time =
  (select max(first_time) from v$archived_log);
```

There are also a few other ways to manage this space when using FRA, and it is definitely another reason to use FRA instead of just setting a directory. The threshold can be determined using SQL from v$recovery_file_dest instead of looking at the file system.

```
SQL> select name, space_limit, space_used from v$recovery_file_dest;
NAME SPACE LIMIT SPACE USED/u02/oradata/FRA 104857648576
```

The FRA size can be increased to accommodate more archivelogs until the space is freed up by a backup and delete or purge of old backups. The FRA destination can also be changed. It is easier to automate the process of increasing the FRA size and running a backup to ensure the archivelog directory does not fill up. The following can be inserted into the previous script before the RMAN script.

```
SQL> alter system set DB_RECOVERY_FILE_DEST_SIZE=20G scope=both;
```

Enhanced Error Messages

23ai adds enhanced error messages to the alert logs and in response to queries. For example, in a query where one of the columns should have been included in a group by clause, you would have received an error, NOT A GROUP BY EXPRESSION. However, in 23ai you would receive more information about what column needs to be included and even help reference in the Oracle documentation.

```
ERROR at line 1:
ORA-00979: "PRODUCT_ID": must appear in the GROUP BY clause or be used in
an aggregate function
Help: https://docs.oracle.com/error-help/db/ora-00979
```

Instead of trying to figure out which column is causing the problem, this helps to resolve the issue quickly. Knowing more information about the error and maybe what constraint or specifics on the columns to be used and even a link to get more information about the error message is a valuable resource for troubleshooting.

Checking for Locked Production Accounts

Usually, a database profile should specify that a database account becomes locked after a designated number of failed login attempts. For example, set the DEFAULT profile FAILED_LOGIN_ATTEMPTS to 5. Sometimes, however, a rogue user or developer attempts to guess the production account password and, after five attempts, locks the production account. When this happens, an alert is needed to know about it as soon as possible so that it can be investigated for either a security incident or an issue for the user and then unlock the account.

Schema-only accounts help with this issue, as the application account is not used for logging in and cannot lock users out.

The following shell script checks the LOCK_DATE value in DBA_USERS for a list of production database accounts.

```
#!/bin/bash
if [ $# -ne 1 ]; then
  echo "Usage: $0 SID"
  exit 1
fi
```

```
# source oracle OS variables
. /etc/oraset $1
#
crit_var=$(sqlplus -s <<EOF
/ as sysdba
SET HEAD OFF FEED OFF
SELECT count(*)
FROM dba_users
WHERE lock_date IS NOT NULL
AND username in ('CIAP','REPV','CIAL','STARPROD');
EOF
#
if [ $crit_var -ne 0 ]; then
  echo $crit_var
    echo "locked acct. issue with $1" | mailx -s "locked acct. issue"
dba@company.com
else
  echo $crit_var
  echo "no locked accounts"
fi
exit 0
```

This shell script is called from a scheduling tool, such as cron. For example, this cron entry instructs the job to run every 10 minutes (this entry should actually be a single line of code but has been placed on two lines to fit on the page).

```
0,10,20,30,40,50 * * * * /home/oracle/bin/lock.bsh DWREP
   1>/home/oracle/bin/log/lock.log 2>&1
```

This way, an email notification goes out when one of the production database accounts becomes locked. If the risk level is acceptable, as part of this script, there should be a step to unlock the account after a set amount of time, and it is recorded that there were failed login attempts.

Checking for Too Many Processes

On some database servers, you may have many background SQL*Plus jobs. These batch jobs may perform tasks such as copying data from remote databases and large daily update jobs. In these environments, it is useful to know if, at any given time, there is an abnormal number of shell scripts or SQL*Plus processes running on the database server. An abnormal number of jobs could indicate that something is broken or hung.

The next shell script has two checks: one to determine the number of shell scripts that are named with the extension of bsh and one to determine the number of processes that contain the string of sqlplus.

```
#!/bin/bash
#
if [ $# -ne 0 ]; then
  echo "Usage: $0"
  exit 1
fi
#
crit_var=$(ps -ef | grep -v grep | grep bsh | wc -l)CHAPTER
if [ $crit_var -lt 20 ]; then
  echo $crit_var
  echo "processes running normal"
else
  echo "too many processes"
    echo $crit_var | mailx -s "too many bsh procs: $1" dba@company.com
fi
#
crit_var=$(ps -ef | grep -v grep | grep sqlplus | wc -l)
if [ $crit_var -lt 30 ]; then
  echo $crit_var
  echo "processes running normal"
else
  echo "too many processes"
    echo $crit_var | mailx -s "too many sql procs: $1" dba@company.com
fi
#
exit 0
```

The prior shell script, proc_count.bsh, is run once an hour from a cron job (this entry should be a single line of code but is placed on two lines to fit on the page).

```
33 * * * * /home/oracle/bin/proc_count.bsh
  1>/home/oracle/bin/log/proc_count.log 2>&1
```

Verifying the Integrity of RMAN Backups

As part of your backup-and-recovery strategy, you should periodically validate the integrity of the backup files. This is also included in using RMAN to back up the database, but a separate job can run against them to validate for restore. RMAN provides a RESTORE...VALIDATE command that checks for physical corruption within the backup files. The following script starts RMAN and spools a log file. The log file is subsequently searched for the keyword error. An email is sent if there are any errors in the log file.

```
#!/bin/bash
#
if [ $# -ne 1 ]; then
  echo "Usage: $0 SID"
  exit 1
fi
# source oracle OS variables
. /etc/oraset $1
#
date
BOX='uname -a | awk '{print$2}''
rman nocatalog <<EOF
connect target /
spool log to $HOME/bin/log/rman_val.log
set echo on;
restore database validate;
EOF
grep -i error $HOME/bin/log/rman_val.log
if [ $? -eq 0 ]; then
  echo "RMAN verify issue $BOX, $1" | \
  mailx -s "RMAN verify issue $BOX, $1" dba@company.com
```

```
else
  echo "no problem..."
fi
#
date
exit 0
```

The `RESTORE...VALIDATE` does not actually restore any files; it validates only that the files required to restore the database are available and checks for physical corruption.

If you need to check for logical corruption, specify the `CHECK LOGICAL` clause. For example, the prior shell script would have this line in it to check for logical corruption.

```
restore database validate check logical;
```

For large databases, the validation process can take a great deal of time (because the script checks each block in the backup file for corruption). If you only want to verify that the backup files exist, specify the `VALIDATE HEADER` clause as follows.

```
restore database validate header;
```

This command checks only for valid information in the header of each file that would be required for a restore and recovery.

Autonomous Database

The previous scripts and tasks, when scheduled, are just scratching the surface of automating jobs for the Oracle database. Processes that start to take the results of these scripts, apply the fixes, and perform the next actions are getting closer to automation. Oracle 23ai Database has many processes and hooks, allowing environments to configure even more automation. Oracle Autonomous Database is a service available in the Oracle Cloud environment (OCI) and is available for serverless or dedicated implementations. Oracle Exadata Cloud@Customer can provide on-premises Autonomous Database. This database is a self-healing, self-patching, and self-driving database. This allows you to focus on the data and application development and let Autonomous maintenance be handled by the automation built into the environment.

Autonomous databases are managed and backed up by automated processes, and if needed, they perform failover and basic troubleshooting to handle issues. Issues can be an increase in processing power that is needed or additional storage. If the database is not heavily utilized, it can shrink back down to save costs. The database has information about when activities occur, and through learning, it can monitor performance issues and take measures to remediate them.

A secure configuration and security options are implemented by default in the Oracle Cloud. The Autonomous Database has enabled threat detection and encryption, which protect the data that it is storing. Patching is also automated so that the process can apply the fix when there is a vulnerability. These steps happen without manual intervention, and with a highly available environment, the database experiences no downtime.

In this cloud environment, what is a DBA to do? There are plenty of opportunities with development, data integrations, quality, and other areas of security and business intelligence that add value to the enterprise.

There are plenty of features of the database that can be used to manage other areas of the business, and even new features of the database should be built into applications. The DBAs can be the ones to help drive this. The Oracle Cloud and Oracle Cloud@ Customer (in your data center) provide the monitoring, support, and automation of the processes for provisioning and patching databases for backup.

The Oracle Cloud databases (Autonomous Databases, Oracle Base Database Service) can even be managed with the same tools as an on-premises database with tools that DBAs are already familiar with, such as SQL Developer, DB Actions, and Cloud Control. Figure 16-1 shows the interface for DB Actions. This tool provides options for SQL, Data Modeler, REST, Graph, and Data Load. This tool is similar to using SQL Developer. Users are managed through the cloud services, and DBAs can help manage these resources and provide input for migrations to the cloud environments. Not all the pieces need to be managed, such as the file system; backups are scheduled, and database activity and performance are monitored.

Figure 16-1. *Database Actions interface*

As the Autonomous Database continues to gather information about the activity for performance and security, it changes query plans and indexes to improve and detect anomalies for security prevention controls. Oracle 23ai Database is being used to transform how database environments are implemented. Even if not using Autonomous, you can leverage the information about how Autonomous is being managed to your on-prem environment to deploy some of the automated tuning. There are autoupgrades that help with patching, but because Autonomous lives on Oracle Exadata and in the Oracle Cloud, there are plenty of ways for the environment to be automated and tuned. Even though you can copy some of the processes and tuning, there are additional jobs and tasks that allow Autonomous to run more efficiently and leave the management to Oracle systems.

The databases are services that can be supplied on demand for business needs. The processes and steps to make that service available need fewer manual steps and more automated processes along with remediation.

Database Troubleshooting

So far, scripts have been provided to help avoid issues with the database. Even in the brief discussion about Autonomous Database, self-repairing was discussed as there are tasks that can be done automatically to fix and have the database up and available.

But some things might need to be investigated, such as connectivity issues, performance or ways to load data faster. The overall health of the database environment needs to be monitored and then quickly assessed if something is not quite right or errors are being thrown.

We have already described many tools for troubleshooting the data dictionary views and verifying that the monitoring and maintenance scripts are working. Error messages can be in the database logs but also captured in the regular scripts run against the database that help with the investigation.

Quickly Triaging

When getting the call that there is an issue with the database, it is critical to be able to ask questions and know the right questions to ask. Understanding the issue is the first step and must be done quickly to get to the other troubleshooting steps. DBAs will be called upon to troubleshoot database and non-database issues, such as server, connection, and network issues because these are all part of the database system. Or maybe the data is not being returned quickly enough.

The following are a handful of questions that are useful to understand the issue.

- Is this in the application or with a direct connection to the database?

- Is this a new process, query, or application code?

- How long has this been slow? Has it happened before, or is this the first time?

- Is anything (such as an error message or hanging) being returned?

- Do you have any error messages that you are receiving?

As the answers are coming in, you can check the alert logs and the script output from the regular jobs, ping the database and database server, and see if you can log in. This should give you a good start for troubleshooting the issue.

As you have been automating jobs that perform tasks such as verifying the database availability, you should already know of some issues. Automated jobs help you proactively handle issues so that they do not turn into database downtime.

Checking Database Availability

The first few checks do not require logging in to the database server. Rather, they can be performed remotely via SQL*Plus or SQLcl and OS commands. Performing the initial checks remotely over the network establishes whether all the system components are working.

One quick check to determine whether the remote server is available, the database is up, the network is working, and the listener is accepting incoming connections is to connect via an SQL*Plus client to a remote database over the network. The initial testing could use a non-DBA account. Here is an example of connecting over the network by providing the user, password, port, host, and service name.

```
$ sqlplus michelle/Pa$$wOrd123@'mmsrv1:1521/mmdb23ai'
```

The remote server is available if a connection can be made and the database and listener are up and working. At this point and with the questions that were asked, we can verify the connectivity issue has to do with the application or with something other than the database.

If the prior SQL command does not work, establish whether the remote server is available. This can be done with a `ping` command issued to the host.

```
$ ping mmsrv1
```

You can also try the IP address in case the Domain Name System (DNS) server is not available.

If the ping works, you should see output such as the following.

```
64 bytesfrom mmsrv1 (192.168.254.215): icmp_seq=1 ttl=64 time=0.044 ms
```

If the ping does not work, there is probably an issue with the network or the database server. If the database server is not available, it is time to contact a system administrator or network administrator.

If the ping works, check to see if the remote server is reachable via the port the listener is listening on. The `telnet` command can accomplish this.

```
$ telnet IP <port>
```

In this example, a network connection is attempted to the server's IP address on the 1521 port.

```
$ telnet 192.168.254.215 1521
```

If the IP address is reachable on the specified port, you should see "Connected to . . ." in the output, like so.

```
Trying 192.168.254.216...
Connected to ora04.
Escape character is '^]'.
```

If the `telnet` command does not work, contact the SA or the network administrator.

If the `telnet` command does work and there is network connectivity to the server on the specified port, then use the `tnsping` command to test network connectivity to the remote server and database using Oracle Net. This example attempts to reach the `mmdb23ai` remote service.

```
$ tnsping mmdb23ai
```

If successful, the output should contain the `OK` string, as follows.

```
Attempting to contact (DESCRIPTION = (ADDRESS = (PROTOCOL = TCP)(HOST =
MMSRV1) (PORT = 1521)) (CONNECT_DATA = (SERVICE_NAME = mmdb23)))
OK (20 msec)
```

If `tnsping` works, the remote listener is up and working. It does not necessarily mean the database is up, so you may need to log in to the database server to investigate further. If `tnsping` does not work, the listener or the database is down or hung.

Pluggable databases would work the same with `tnsping`, and if there are issues, double-check the listener that all the expected database, container, and pluggable databases were added as needed.

To further investigate issues, log in directly to the server to perform additional checks, such as a mount point filling up. Ideally, if there was another issue, one of the logs or monitoring scripts reported it; however, the checks on the server might be necessary at this point.

Locating the Alert Log and Trace Files

The default alert log directory path has this structure.

```
$ORACLE_HOME/rdbms/log
```

Or find it easily with the show parameter command.

```
SQL> show parameter background
```

You can override the default directory path for the alert log by setting the DIAGNOSTIC_DEST initialization parameter. Usually, the db_unique_name is the same as the instance_name, but it depends on the environment. In RAC and Data Guard environments, however, the db_unique_name is often different from the instance_name. You can verify the directory path with this query.

```
SQL> select value from v$diag_info where name = 'Diag Trace';
```

The name of the alert log follows this format.

```
Alert_<ORACLE_SID>.log
```

You can also locate the alert log from the OS (whether the database is started via these OS commands).

```
$ cd $ORACLE_HOME
$ find . -iname alert_<ORACLE_SID>.log
$ find . -iname alert_mmdb23ai.log
```

Check the alert log for any messages, errors, and activity that might help troubleshoot the issue. As discussed with the sizing of redo, there might be too frequent checkpoints and other details that show up in the alert log. Scan or search the alert log for error messages and warnings.

Tip   Trace and log files might also need to be cleared out, and setting up an automated job to remove these older files helps keep the ORACLE_HOME directories at a good size to keep this file system from filling up and causing issues. Consider using the Automatic Diagnostic Repository Command Interpreter (ADRCI) utility to purge old trace files.

Inspecting the Alert Log

When dealing with database issues, the `alert.log` file should be one of the first files you check for relevant error messages. You can use OS tools or the ADRCI utility to view the `alert.log` file and corresponding trace files.

Viewing the Alert Log via OS Tools

After navigating to the directory that contains the `alert.log`, you can see the most current messages by viewing the end (furthest down) of the file (in other words, the most current messages are written to the end of the file). To view the last 50 lines, use the `tail` command.

```
$ tail -50 alert_<ORACLE_SID>.log
```

You can continuously view the most current entries by using the f switch.

```
$ tail -f alert_<ORACLE_SID>.log
```

You can also directly open the `alert.log` with an OS editor (such as `vi`).

```
$ vi alert_<ORACLE_SID>.log
```

Sometimes, it is handy to define a function that allows you to open the `alert.log`, regardless of your current working directory.

When inspecting the end of the `alert.log`, look for errors that indicate these types of issues.

- The archiver process hung owing to inadequate disk space

- File system out of space

- Tablespace out of space

- ORA- 600 or 7445 errors

- Running out of memory in the buffer cache or shared pool

- Media error indicating that a data file is missing or damaged

- An error indicating an issue with writing an archivelog

There is almost always a corresponding trace file for a serious error message listed in the alert.log file. For example, the following is the accompanying message for the prior error message.

```
Errors in file $ORACLE_HOME/rdbms/mmdb23ai/trace/mmdb23ai_ora_5272.trc
```

Inspecting the trace file often (but not always) provides additional insight into the issue.

Identifying Bottlenecks via OS Utilities

Normally, after checking the database and details in the logs and still not finding an issue, it is good to bring in server admins, but you can first check for additional bottlenecks and problems with the server.

With the Oracle environment, there is a tendency to assume that you have a dedicated machine for one Oracle database. However, that might always be the case. Other databases and applications may also be running on the server. There might also be other versions of the Oracle database running.

In the Linux environments, several tools are available for monitoring resource usage. Table 16-1 summarizes the most commonly used OS utilities for diagnosing performance issues. Being familiar with how these OS commands work and how to interpret the output allows you to better diagnose server performance issues, especially when it is a non-Oracle or even a non-database process that is hindering performance for everything on the server.

Table 16-1. *Performance and Monitoring Utilities*

Tool	Purpose
vmstat	Monitors processes, CPU, memory, and disk I/O bottlenecks
top	Identifies sessions consuming the most resources
watch	Periodically runs another command
ps	Identifies highest CPU- and memory-consuming sessions; used to identify Oracle sessions consuming the most system resources (normally `ps -ef` for a list of processes)
mpstat	Reports CPU statistics
sar	Displays CPU, memory, disk I/O, and network usage, both current and historical
free	Displays free and used memory
df	Reports on disk usage
iostat	Displays disk I/O statistics
netstat	Reports on network statistics

When diagnosing performance issues, it is useful to determine where the OS is constrained. For instance, try to identify whether the issue is related to CPU, memory, I/O, or a combination of these.

Tip   With all these commands, you can use the command with the `--help` parameter to get usage and additional parameters.

Identifying System Bottlenecks

Whenever there are application performance issues or availability problems, seemingly (from the DBA's perspective), the first question is, "What is wrong with the database?" Regardless of the source of the problem, the DBA is often required to see if the database is behaving well. Approaching these issues when looking at the database and system-wide resources is an important part of the research and troubleshooting. The following are useful tools for displaying system-wide resource usage.

- vmstat

- top

The vmstat (virtual memory statistics) tool is intended to help you quickly identify bottlenecks on your server. The top utility provides a dynamic, real-time view of system resource usage.

Using vmstat

The vmstat utility displays real-time performance information about processes, memory, paging, disk I/O, and CPU usage. Now, you only need to know what to look for in the output. The following are some suggestions.

- If the wa (time waiting for I/O) column is high, this usually indicates that the storage subsystem is overloaded.

- If b (processes blocked) is consistently greater than 0, you may not have enough CPU processing power.

- If so (memory swapped out to disk) and si (memory swapped in from disk) are consistently greater than 0, you may have a memory bottleneck.

One line of the server statistics is returned and gives the average statistics calculated from the last time the system was rebooted. You can also gather vmstat over a period of time with parameters <interval in seconds> and <number of intervals>.

```
$ vmstat 2 10
```

Or you can use the watch tool to run the vmstat command regularly on the screen to capture the differences between each snapshot. This is useful only if you are working on finding the root cause of the issue because, in a large database environment, you will not be able to watch the screen for one database server. This is also why it is good to work with the server administrators and leverage the tools they might be using. Being a DBA means understanding the server configuration and databases, but working with other teams and using tools for monitoring is essential in large environments.

```
$ watch -n 5 -d vmstat
```

513

To see the memory statistics in megabytes, use the S m parameters.

```
$ vmstat -S m
```

Using top

Another quick utility for identifying resource-intensive processes is the top command. Use this tool to quickly identify which processes are the highest consumers of resources on the server. By default, the top command repeatedly refreshes every three seconds with information regarding the most CPU-intensive processes.

```
$ top
```

You can run it in batch mode and send the output to a file for later analysis.

```
$ top -b > tophat.out
```

Stop the batch job so a very large output file is not created, causing another issue.

The top-consuming sessions are listed in the first column. This doesn't necessarily show a bottleneck, but you can see the processes using the resources on the server.

Mapping an Operating System Process to a SQL Statement

When identifying OS processes, it is useful to view which processes consume the greatest amount of CPU. If the resource hog is a database process, mapping the OS process to a database job or query is also useful. To determine the ID of the processes consuming the most CPU resources, use a command such as ps, as follows.

```
$ ps -ef -o pcpu,pid,user,tty,args | sort -n -k 1 -r | head
```

Here is a snippet of the output.

```
14.6 24875 oracle ?    oracledb23ai(DESCRIPTION=(LOCAL=YES)(ADDRESS=...
 0.8 21613 oracle ?    ora_vktm_db23ai
 0.1 21679 oracle ?    ora_mmon_db23ai
```

You can see that session 24875 is the top consumer of CPU resources and is associated with the db23ai database. With that information, log in to the database and use the SQL statement to determine what type of program is associated with OS process 24875.

```
SQL> select
  'USERNAME : ' || s.username|| chr(10) ||
  'OSUSER   : ' || s.osuser  || chr(10) ||
  'PROGRAM  : ' || s.program || chr(10) ||
  'SPID     : ' || p.spid    || chr(10) ||
  'SID      : ' || s.sid     || chr(10) ||
  'SERIAL#  : ' || s.serial# || chr(10) ||
  'MACHINE  : ' || s.machine || chr(10) ||
  'TERMINAL : ' || s.terminal
from v$session s,
  v$process p
where s.paddr = p.addr
and p.spid = &PID_FROM_OS;
```

Here is the relevant output.

```
USERNAME : MV_MAINT
OSUSER   : oracle
PROGRAM  : sqlplus@mmpdb (TNS V1-V3)
SPID     : 24875
SID      : 111
SERIAL#  : 899
MACHINE  : mmsrv1
TERMINAL : pts/4
```

Once you have identified a top-consuming process associated with a database, you can query the data dictionary views based on the SPID to identify what the database process is executing.

Finding Resource-Intensive SQL Statements

One of the best ways to isolate a poorly performing query is to have a user or developer complain about a specific SQL statement. In this situation, there is no detective work involved. You can directly pinpoint the SQL query that needs tuning.

However, you do not often have the luxury of a human telling you where to look when investigating performance issues. Even Oracle 23ai Database utilizes machine learning to gather statistics to help with performance and anticipate when query plans change and detect regressions in SQL statements. Real-time statistics use a regression model that predicts the current statistics. This keeps the impact of gathering statistics low and refreshing stats fast to avoid bad optimizer query plans.

Before leveraging SQL plan management in Oracle Database, the optimizer needs information about the data and statistics of the tables to help with tuning. You can also use performance reporting to determine which SQL is consuming the most resources in a database. The following lists what is used to feed into the SQL plans.

- Real-time execution statistics with machine learning

- Near real-time statistics

- Oracle performance reports

Now, let's query V$SQL_MONITOR to monitor the near real-time resource consumption of SQL queries.

```
SQL> select * from (
select a.sid session_id, a.sql_id
,a.status
,a.cpu_time/1000000 cpu_sec
,a.buffer_gets, a.disk_reads
,b.sql_text sql_text
from v$sql_monitor a
     ,v$sql b
where a.sql_id = b.sql_id
order by a.cpu_time desc)
where rownum <=20;
```

In the SQL statement, we retrieve all records with an inline view to organize the statements by CPU_TIME, in descending order. This query can be modified to order the results by the statistics of your choice or to display only the queries that are currently executing; for example, change the order by clause to disk_reads.

The statistics in V$SQL_MONITOR are updated every second, so you can view resource consumption as it changes. These statistics are gathered by default if an SQL statement runs in parallel or consumes more than five seconds of CPU or I/O time.

You can also query views such as V$SQLSTATS to determine which SQL statements consume an inordinate number of resources. For example, use the following query to identify the ten most resource-intensive queries based on CPU time.

```
SQL> select * from(
select s.sid, s.username, s.sql_id
,sa.elapsed_time/1000000, sa.cpu_time/1000000
,sa.buffer_gets, sa.sql_text
from v$sqlarea sa
    ,v$session s
where s.sql_hash_value = sa.hash_value
ands.sql_address= sa.address
ands.username is not null
order by sa.cpu_time desc)
where rownum <= 10;
```

> **Note**   Keep in mind that V$SQLAREA contains statistics that are cumulative for the duration of a given session. If a session runs an identical query several times, the statistics for that connection are the total for all the query runs. In contrast, V$SQL_MONITOR shows the statistics accumulated for the current run of a given SQL statement. Therefore, each time a query runs, new statistics are reported for that query in V$SQL_MONITOR.

SQL Analysis Report

The SQL Analysis Report is a new section in a SQL execution plan. This appears at the end of the plan to provide additional information about joins, indexes, and data type mismatches to help diagnose common problems. For example, the new report points out situations.

- Query missing a join condition and causing a Cartesian product

- A WHERE clause predicate that prevents an index from being used

- A WHERE clause with a data type mismatch

- Use of UNION instead of a UNION ALL

This report is available when you use DBMS_XPLAN.

```
SQL> select * from table(DBMS_XPLAN.DISPLAY_CURSOR(FORMAT=>'typical'));
--After the plan there is a section with more details
SQL Analysis Report (identified by operation id/Query Block Name/
Object Alias):
```

This additional information helps with SQL tuning and troubleshooting. It might also be useful information to see why indexes are not being used or what information might be useful in indexes and WHERE clauses.

SQL Plan Management

SQL execution plans come in the form of SQL plan baselines for comparing and testing for regressions in SQL statements. SQL plans are captured, and with 23ai, plan changes are detected at parse time and validated if the plan has changed. If you think machine learning is taking away the DBA's performance tuning job, you are wrong; it is actually making it better. There is reduced risk in plans changing, and with all the statements running against the database, it is great to leverage the real-time SQL plan management in 23ai.

Errors can be intercepted and changed with alternative solutions that return the expected results without issues in the application. The OPTIMIZER_CAPTURE_SOL_PLAN_ BASELINES and OPTIMIZER_USE_SOL_PLAN_BASELINES parameters control the SQL plan capture and baselines. Execution plans can be captured automatically on a running system, but you can also import a plan from a staging table or a tuning set. It helps with application changes, upgrades, and migrations to be able to use consistent plans.

Here is an example of loading from a SQL tuning set.

```
SOL> declare
v_result pls_integer;
begin
v_result := dbms_spm.load_plans_from_sqlset(sqlset_name => 'MM_STS', basic
filter => 'sql text like ''select%orders%''');
end;
/
```

If there are no SQL plan regressions when a plan changes, the plan can evolve and improve the plan. This can be done automatically or after review by the DBA. The capture is done by turning on the parameter, and when the capture is completed, it can be set to false.

```
SOL> alter session set optimizer_capture_sql_plan_baselines=TRUE;
```

After capturing information and researching the resource-intensive SQL statements, you can use the SQL plan management evolve advisor to see different plans.

Note   Oracle 23ai has automatic indexing, partitioning, and materialized views to improve statements and allow the SQL plan to evolve and improve performance.

The following test alternative plans of SQL you want to repair.

```
SQL> exec dbms_spm.set_evolve_task_parameter( task_name => 'mmsqltask',
parameter => 'ALTERNATE_PLAN_SOURCE', value => 'CURSOR_CACHE+AUTOMATIC_
WORKOAD_REPOSITORY+SQL_TUNING_SET');
```

SQL plan management, along with real-time statistics, allows DBAs to effectively tune repeatable SQL statements in the database.

Running Oracle Diagnostic Utilities

Oracle provides several utilities for diagnosing database performance issues.

- Automatic workload repository (AWR)

- Automatic database diagnostic monitor (ADDM)

- Active session history (ASH)

- Statspack

AWR, ADDM, and ASH tools provide advanced reporting capabilities that allow you to troubleshoot and resolve performance issues and are available through the Diagnostics and Tuning pack as an extra license from Oracle. Statspack is a free utility and requires no license. But with a multitenant environment, you need to deploy Statspack in the pluggable database for tuning statements in the pluggable database, and the jobs need to be configured using dbms_scheduler.

All these tools rely heavily on the underlying v$ dynamic performance views. Oracle maintains a vast collection of these views, which track and accumulate database performance metrics. For example, if you run the following query, you notice that Oracle Database 23ai has about 875 v$ views and gv$ has almost the same.

```
SQL> select substr(name,1,2) view_name, count(*)
from v$fixed_table

group by view_name;

VIEW_NAM COUNT(*)
-------- ----------
X$          1523
GV           834
V$           876
```

V$FIXED_TABLE provides information about the dynamic performance views, including the underlying X$ tables and GV$ views for RAC environments.

The Oracle performance utilities rely on periodic snapshots from these internal performance views. Two of the most useful views regarding performance statistics are the v$sysstat and v$sesstat views. The v$sysstat view offers more than 800 types of database statistics. This v$sysstat view contains information about the entire database, whereas the v$sesstat view contains statistics on individual sessions. A few of the values in the v$sysstat and v$sesstat views represent the current usage of the resource. These values are as follows.

- Opened cursors current

- Logins current

- Session cursor cache current

- Work area memory allocated

The rest of the values are cumulative. The values in v$sysstat are cumulative for the entire container from the time the instance was started or pluggable opened. The values in the v$sesstat are cumulative per session from the time the session was started. Some of the more important performance-related cumulative values are these.

- CPU used

- Consistent gets

- Physical reads

- Physical writes

For cumulative statistics, the way to measure periodic usage is to note the value of a statistic at a starting point and then note the value again at a later point in time and capture the delta. This is the approach used by the Oracle performance utilities, such as AWR and Statspack. Periodically, Oracle takes snapshots of the dynamic wait interface views and stores them in a repository. You can also manually capture a snapshot.

Tip You can access AWR, ADDM, and ASH from Enterprise Manager. If you can access Enterprise Manager, you will find the interface fairly intuitive and visually helpful. Statspack is only available as text.

Using AWR

An AWR report is good for viewing the entire system's performance and identifying the top resource-consuming SQL queries. Run the following script to generate an AWR report.

```
SQL> @?/rdbms/admin/awrrpt
```

You can run the AWR reports from the PDB or CDB root container. The reports are from PDB using AWR_PDB views in that PDB, or if you use AWR_ROOT views (like the DBA_HIST views), they show the AWR data stored only on a CDB root.

From the AWR output, you can identify top resource-consuming statements by examining the "SQL Ordered by Elapsed Time" or "SQL Ordered by CPU Time" section of the report.

Oracle automatically takes a snapshot of your database once an hour and populates the underlying AWR tables that store the statistics. By default, seven days of statistics are retained.

You can also generate an AWR report for a specific SQL statement by running the awrsqrpt.sql report. When you run the following script, you are prompted for the SQL_ID of the query of interest.

```
SQL> @?/rdbms/admin/awrsqrpt.sql
```

Using ADDM

The ADDM report provides useful information on which SQL statements are candidates for tuning. Use the following SQL script to generate an ADDM report.

```
SQL> @?/rdbms/admin/addmrpt
```

The report recognizes that the database is pluggable if run inside the PDB container.

Look for the section of the report labeled "SQL Statements Consuming Significant Database Time." Here is some sample output.

```
FINDING 2: 29% impact (65043 seconds)
-------------------------------------
SQL statements consuming significant database time were found.
   RECOMMENDATION 1: SQL Tuning, 6.7% benefit (14843 seconds)
   ACTION: Investigate the SQL statement with SQL_ID "46cc3t7ym5sx0" for
```

The ADDM report analyzes data in the AWR tables to identify potential bottlenecks and high resource-consuming SQL queries.

Using ASH

The ASH report allows you to focus on short-lived SQL statements that have been recently run and that may have executed only briefly. Run the following script to generate an ASH report.

```
SQL> @?/rdbms/admin/ashrpt
```

Search the output for the section labeled "Top SQL." Here is some sample output.

```
Top SQL with Top Events    DB/Inst: MMDB23AI/mmdb23ai (Jul 29 22:27
to 22:42)
SQL ID                     FullPlanhash         Planhash
---------------------      ------------------   ----------------
Sampled #                  of Executions%       Activity Event
---------------------      ------------------   ----------------
% Event Top Row Source      % RwSrc
-------  ---------------------------------
Container Name
---------------------------------------------
2651cv0dd1yb9    308129442       1388734953
         1 14.29 CPU + Wait for CPU
  14.29 SELECT STATEMENT       14.29
```

The previous output indicates that the query is waiting for CPU resources. In this scenario, the problem may be that another query is consuming the CPU resources.

When is the ASH report more useful than the AWR or ADDM report? The AWR and ADDM output shows top-consuming SQL in terms of total database time. If the SQL performance problem is transient and short-lived, it may not appear on the AWR and ADDM reports. In these situations, an ASH report is more useful.

Using Statspack

If you do not have a license to use the AWR, ADDM, and ASH reports, the free Statspack utility can help you identify poorly performing SQL statements. Run the following script as SYS to install Statspack in the PDB.

```
SQL> @?/rdbms/admin/spcreate.sql
SQL> grant create job to PERFSTAT;
```

The prior script creates a PERFSTAT user that owns the Statspack repository. Once crated, then connect as the PERFSTAT user, and run this script to enable the automatic gathering of Statspack statistics.

```
SOL> @ ?/rdbms/admin/spauto.sql
```

After gathering some snapshots, you can run the following script as the PERFSTAT user to create a Statspack report.

```
SOL> @?/rdbms/admin/spreport.sql
```

Tip   See the `$ORACLE_HOME/rdbms/admin/spdoc.txt` file for the Statspack documentation.

Detecting and Resolving Locking Issues

Sometimes, a developer or application user reports that a process that normally takes seconds to run now takes several minutes and does not appear to be doing anything. The problem is usually a space-related issue (e.g., the archive redo destination is full and has suspended all transactions).

A process has a lock on a table row and is not committing or rolling back, thus preventing another session from modifying the same row.

Oracle 23ai has automated aborting a low-priority transaction that holds a row lock and blocks higher-priority transactions. The priority is set to high, medium, or low for a user transaction. Users can also configure a maximum time a transaction waits.

First, check the alert log to see if any obvious issues have occurred recently, such as a wait on tablespace to extend. If there is nothing obvious in the alert log file, run a SQL query to look for locking issues.

```
SOL> set lines 80
SOL> col blkg_user form a10
SOL> col blkg_machine form a10
SOL> col blkg_sid form 99999999
SOL> col wait_user form a10
SQL> col wait_machine form a10
```

```
SQL> col wait_sid form 9999999
SQL> col obj_own form a10
SQL> col obj_name form a10
SQL> col blkg_sql form a50
SQL> col wait_sql form a50
--
SQL> select
 s1.username      blkg_user, s1.machine      blkg_machine
,s1.sid           blkg_sid, s1.serial#       blkg_serialnum
,s1.process       blkg_OS_PID
,substr(b1.sql_text,1,50) blkg_sql
,chr(10)
,s2.username      wait_user, s2.machine      wait_machine
,s2.sid           wait_sid, s2.serial#       wait_serialnum
,s2.process       wait_OS_PID
,substr(w1.sql_text,1,50) wait_sql
,lo.object_id     blkd_obj_id
,do.owner         obj_own, do.object_name obj_name
from v$lock             l1
    ,v$session         s1
    ,v$lock            l2
    ,v$session         s2
    ,v$locked_object   lo
    ,v$sqlarea         b1
    ,v$sqlarea         w1
    ,dba_objects       do
where s1.sid = l1.sid
and s2.sid = l2.sid
and l1.id1 = l2.id1
and s1.sid = lo.session_id
and lo.object_id = do.object_id
and l1.block = 1
and s1.prev_sql_addr = b1.address
and s2.sql_address = w1.address
and l2.request > 0;
```

This situation is typical when applications do not explicitly issue a commit or rollback at appropriate times in the code. Oracle 23ai provides a way to prioritize the transactions to know how long a transaction waits before the lock is released before aborting the lower-priority transaction.

You can also manually kill one of the sessions. Keep in mind that terminating a session may have unforeseen effects, and using the new features allows the transactions to roll back.

Resolving Open-Cursor Issues

The OPEN_CURSORS initialization parameter determines the maximum number of cursors a session can have open. This setting is per session. The default value of 50 is usually too low for any application. When an application exceeds the number of open cursors allowed, the following error is thrown.

ORA-01000: maximum open cursors exceeded

Usually, the prior error is encountered when

- OPEN_CURSORS initialization parameter is set too low

- Developers write code that does not close cursors properly

To investigate this issue, first determine the current setting of the parameter.

```
SQL> show parameter open_cursors;
```

If the value is less than 300, consider setting it higher. It is typical to set this value to 1,000 for busy OLTP systems. As shown here, you can dynamically modify the value while your database is open.

```
SQL> alter system set open_cursors=1000;
```

If you are using an spfile, consider making the change both in memory and in the spfile, at the same time.

```
SQL> alter system set open_cursors=1000 scope=both;
```

After setting OPEN_CURSORS to a higher value, if the application continues to exceed the maximum value, you probably have an issue with code that is not properly closing cursors.

If you work in an environment that has thousands of connections to the database, you may want to view only the top cursor-consuming sessions. The following query uses an inline view and the ROWNUM pseudocolumn to display the top 20 values.

```
SOL> select * from (
select a.value, c.username, c.machine, c.sid, c.serial#
from v$sesstat a
    ,v$statname b
    ,v$session c
Where a.statistic# = b.statistic#
And    c.sid        = a.sid
And    b.name        = 'opened cursors current'
And    a.value       != 0
And    c.username IS NOT NULL
order by 1 desc,2)
where rownum < 21;
```

If a single session has more than 1,000 open cursors, the code is probably written so the cursors are not closing. When the limit is reached, somebody should inspect the application code to determine whether a cursor is not being closed.

Tip It is recommended that you query V$SESSION instead of V$OPEN_CURSOR to determine the number of open cursors. V$SESSION provides a more accurate count of the cursors currently open.

Troubleshooting Undo Tablespace Issues

Problems with the undo tablespace are usually of the following nature.

```
ORA-01555: snapshot too old
ORA-30036: unable to extend segment by ... in undo tablespace 'UNDOTBS1'
```

The prior errors can be caused by many different issues, such as incorrect sizing of the undo tablespace or poorly written SQL or PL/SQL code. A snapshot that is too old can also occur during exports because of updates to very large tables and is normally seen when either the undo retention or the size is not properly set. For an export, it is an easy fix to rerun at a quieter time. So, sometimes it is just rerunning the job or transaction on the database. If these happen too often, it might be because of the undo tablespace size. Or, if the system is sharing the undo tablespace in the CDB, you can create the undo tablespace in each of the PDBs.

Determining Whether the Undo Is Correctly Sized

Suppose you have a long-running SQL statement that is throwing an ORA-01555: snapshot too old error, and you want to determine whether adding space to the undo tablespace might help alleviate the issue. Run this next query to identify potential issues with your undo tablespace. Make sure you are in the PDB that you are checking the undo tablespace. The following query checks for issues that have occurred within the last day.

```
SQL> select to_char(begin_time,'MM-DD-YYYY HH24:MI') begin_time
,ssolderrcnt    ORA_01555_cnt, nospaceerrcnt   no_space_cnt
,txncount       max_num_txns, maxquerylen      max_query_len
,expiredblks    blck_in_expired
from v$undostat
where begin_time > sysdate - 1
order by begin_time;
```

The ORA_01555_CNT column indicates the number of times your database has encountered the ORA-01555: snapshot too old error. If this column reports a nonzero value, you need to do one or more of the following tasks.

- Ensure that code does not contain COMMIT statements within cursor loops

- Tune the SQL statement throwing the error so that it runs faster

- Ensure that you have good statistics (so that your SQL runs efficiently)

- Increase the UNDO_RETENTION initialization parameter

The NO_SPACE_CNT column displays the number of times space was requested in the undo tablespace. In this example, there were no such requests. If the NO_SPACE_CNT reports a nonzero value, however, you may need to add more space to your undo tablespace.

A maximum of four days worth of information is stored in the V$UNDOSTAT view. The statistics are gathered every 10 minutes for a maximum of 576 rows in the table. If you have stopped and started your database within the last four days, this view only contains information from when you last started your database.

Another way to get advice on the undo tablespace sizing is to use the Oracle Undo Advisor, which you can invoke by querying the PL/SQL DBMS_UNDO_ADV package from a SELECT statement. The following query displays the current undo size and the recommended size for an undo retention setting of 900 seconds.

```
SQL> select
    sum(bytes)/1024/1024 cur_mb_size
  ,dbms_undo_adv.required_undo_size(900) req_mb_size
from dba_data_files
where tablespace_name =
    (select
    value
    from v$parameter
    where name = 'undo tablespace');
```

Here is some sample output.

```
CUR_MB_SIZE REQ_MB_SIZE
----------- -----------
36864         20897
```

The output shows that the undo tablespace currently has 36 GB allocated to it. In the prior query, you used 900 seconds as the amount of time to retain information in the undo tablespace. To retain undo information for 900 seconds, the Oracle Undo Advisor estimates that the undo tablespace should be 20.4 GB. In this example, the undo tablespace is sized adequately. If it were not sized adequately, you would have to either add space to an existing data file or add a data file to the undo tablespace.

Handling Temporary Tablespace Issues

Issues with temporary tablespaces are somewhat easy to spot. For example, the following error is thrown when the temporary tablespace runs out of space.

```
ORA-01652: unable to extend temp segment by 128 in tablespace TEMP
```

When you see this error, you need to determine whether there is not enough space in the temporary tablespace or if a rare runaway SQL query has temporarily consumed an inordinate amount of temporary space. Both issues are discussed in the following sections. Multiple temporary tablespaces can be created in a PDB. You can allocate an isolated temporary tablespace to a user to avoid causing issues with other users or applications.

Determining Whether Temporary Tablespace Is Sized Correctly

The temporary tablespace is used as a sorting area on disk when a process has consumed the available memory and needs more space. Operations that require a sorting area include the following.

- Index creation

- SQL sorting and hashing operations

- Temporary tables and indexes

- Temporary LOBs

- Temporary B-trees

There is no exact formula for determining whether your temporary tablespace is sized correctly. It depends on the number and types of queries, index build operations, parallel operations, and the size of your memory sort space (PGA). You must monitor your temporary tablespace while there is a load on your database to establish its usage patterns. Since TEMP tablespaces are temporary files, they are handled differently than the data files, and details are found in a different view. Run the following query to show the allocated and free space within the temporary tablespace.

```
SQL> select tablespace_name
,tablespace_size/1024/1024 mb_size
,allocated_space/1024/1024 mb_alloc
,free_space/1024/1024      mb_free
from dba_temp_free_space;
```

The topics covered in this chapter went from automating jobs to troubleshooting, which was definitely on purpose. The automated scripts and tuning make it easier to determine the cause of issues and problems. If you are using the tools available, you know where to look when the pressure is on to fix an issue and troubleshoot a problem.

Diagnosing issues sometimes requires some system and network administrator skills. An effective DBA must know how to leverage the Oracle data dictionary to identify problems and know what jobs are being handled by the database and where to look to determine the actual issues.

Even though there are whole books devoted to troubleshooting and performance tuning, all topics and activities are difficult to cover. However, this hits some of the top topics as you support your environment.

Migration to Multitenant and Fleet Management

Oracle Database 23ai supports only a multitenant architecture. You saw this during the installation of the database software and the creation of databases as a container database was created with a pluggable database. If you are using a noncontainer database in 19c or earlier release of the Oracle Database, the upgrade process includes migration to multitenant and then upgrading to 23ai.

There are several advantages to this architecture.

- Secure separation of DBA duties

- Separation of data and code

- Easier management and monitoring

- Easier movement of data and code

- Performance tuning

- Fewer database patches and upgrades

The management of the different containers (CDB, PDB, and application) can be separated into different teams or administrators. A common user manages the CDB and performs the tasks at that level without data access in the PDB. The PDB administrator has a local account to manage the PDB or PDBs but limited access to the whole environment and access to the CDB. And because the PDB holds the user data, actions available in the PDB do not interrupt the CDB and other PDBs. You can perform point-in-time recovery and flashback at the PDB level because it acts almost like a separate database.

© Michelle Malcher, Darl Kuhn 2024
M. Malcher and D. Kuhn, *Pro Oracle Database 23ai Administration*,
https://doi.org/10.1007/979-8-8688-1038-1_17

This book has discussed running jobs in the PDBs or CDBs and all the data dictionary views that now start with CDB_ along with the DBA_/ALL_/USER_ views. This demonstrates the different privileges and responsibilities of the DBAs.

PDBs can be plugged into a CDB, which helps with the movement of data and code within the PDB. Cloning is also available with PDBs for managing different environments, such as development and production.

Performance and tuning metrics are gathered and collected to one host, and the resources are managed in place for memory, CPU, and processes. Instead of all the individual database instances, the metrics can be managed in the CDB and fine-tuned if necessary in PDBs.

Ease of management begins with the CDB managing the environment with a single operation. This simplifies patching and backup strategies. It also leads us to the discussion of fleet management. This chapter covers what a fleet is and how you can manage, provision, and patch them.

Upgrades to new versions get easier with a multitenant architecture, and there are options to leverage moving PDBs to an already upgraded CDB. It is also easier to patch one CDB instead of 100 database instances, and it is easier to do upgrades.

Migration to Multitenant

When creating new databases in 23ai, you get multitenant CDBs and PDBs. However, there are databases that need to be upgraded to 23ai, and many of them can be noncontainer, single-instance databases. This is the chance to consolidate and leverage all the advantages discussed, but there are a few steps and choices you have when migrating.

The settings always depend on database size, availability requirements, and backup strategies that are needed. Data Pump jobs can migrate data to a newly built 23ai database. Exporting and importing the data move the data, but there will be an outage when importing the data, and how big the database is matters.

As discussed with the backup and recovery processes, there are strategies for upgrading and migrating and plenty of options. The main things to consider are the following.

- Repeatable process

- Easy way to back out or downgrade

- Database size

- Downtime window

Simplicity is another piece to consider, especially when maintaining a large environment. It is important to have steps to validate the process, execute it, and verify that the migration was successful.

Plug-In Method

Let's use an example to walk through the steps to migrate to multitenant.

First, check the compatibility of the database. This is performed on the source.

```
SQL> exec dbms_pdb.describe('/tmp/salesdb.xml');
```

This creates a manifest XML file with information about services and data files of the database to be migrated.

Next, check the compatibility of the CDB, which is the target.

```
SQL> set serveroutput on
begin
if dbms_pdb.check_plug_compatibility('/tmp/salesdb.xml') THEN
dbms_output.put_line('PDB compatible? ==> Yes');
else
dbms_output.put_line('PDB compatible? ==> No');
end if;
end;
/
```

This checks for any issues that appear when plugging in the database instance to the CDB. There is valuable information in the PDB_PLUG_IN_VIOLATIONS view after running the check_plug_compatibility script. There might be errors and warning messages that can be resolved before plugging the database in. For example, the version might be the same, so you can upgrade first or let the upgrade occur after plugging the database in. Also, there are possible informational warnings, such as requiring noncdb_to_pdb.sql to run after it is plugged into the CDB.

```
SQL> select type, message
from pdb_plug_in_violations
where name='SALESDB' and status <> 'RESOLVED';
```

Next, you need to create the manifest file of the source single-instance database. The database needs to be in read-only mode.

Restart the source database in read-only mode.

```
SQL> shutdown immediate
SQL> startup mount
SQL> alter database open read only;
```

The manifest file needs to be generated.

```
SQL> exec dbms_pdb.describe('/tmp/salesdb.xml');
SQL> shutdown immediate;
```

This is the same command that ran on the source to validate the manifest file, but now the database was in read-only mode.

In the target CDB, the next step is to create the PDB from the manifest file just created.

```
SQL> create pluggable database salesdb using '/tmp/salesdb.xml' nocopy
tempfile reuse;
```

Some steps are still needed to complete the migration to a container PDB. Convert to a PDB by running noncdb_to_pdb.sql.

```
SQL> alter pluggable database salesdb open;
SQL> alter session set container = salesdb;
SQL> @?/rdbms/admin/noncdb_to_pdb.sql
SQL> alter pluggable database salesdb close;
SQL> alter pluggable database salesdb open;
```

Once again, check any plug-in violations from the target CDB.

```
SQL> select type, message
from pdb_plug_in_violations
where name='SALESDB' and status <> 'RESOLVED';
```

Verify that the PDB is open so you can save the state of the PDB to have it set to auto-start.

```
SQL> select open_mode, restricted from v$pdbs;
SQL> alter pluggable database salesdb save state;
```

Once you plug the database in, it cannot revert to a noncontainer, single-instance database. There are other recoverability options, but it should be considered to troubleshoot the issues in the container and give you another reason to check those error and warning messages before migrating.

When you plug in a database, you can use AutoUpgrade to upgrade the database with the new CDB. The target CDB is part of the config file, so the database is upgraded.

Here is the config file.

```
$ cat db19to23.cfg
Upgl.source_home=/u01/app/oracle/product/19
upgl.target_home=/u01/app/oracle/product/23
upgl.sid=salesdb
upgl.target_cdb_cdb=cdb23ai
```

Run the autoupgrade command with the config file.

```
$ java -jar autoupgrade.jar -config db19to23.cfg -mode deploy
```

No-Copy or Copy Options

The options that let you migrate to a multitenant architecture reuse the data files. The failback option uses Data Pump to return to a non-CDB, single-instance database. The recovery option is not necessarily faster, but the migration option is a simple and faster method.

If the recovery plan needed to be faster, then it might make more sense to copy the data files instead of reusing them. This includes copying and renaming the files with FILE_NAME_CONVERT. It takes longer to migrate because there is a copy of the files before plugging in the database and migrating, but it is a quicker rollback plan. You create the manifest file and shut down the database. Copy the data files to a new location or a new name.

In the target CDB, the next step is to create a PDB from the manifest file just created.

```
SQL> create pluggable database salesdb using '/tmp/salesdb.xml' copy file_
name_convert=('SALES19C','SALESDB');
```

One more migration to mention for plugging in a database is to clone the database over a database link. This consists of cloning a non-CDB single-instance database to a pluggable database in a CDB. The autoupgrade command and the config file make it easier to set up the options, and the database link makes it possible.

Here is the config file.

```
$ cat db19_to_23.cfg
upgl.source_home=/uo1/app/oracle/product/19
upgl.target_home=/uo1/app/oracle/product/db23ai
upgl.sid=salesdb
upgl.target_cdb=cdb23ai
upgl.target_pdb_name=salesdb
upgl.target_pdb_copy_option=file_name_convert=('SALES19C','SALESDB')
```

Run the following command.

```
$ java -jar autoupgrade.jar -config db19_to23.cgf -mode deploy
```

Other migration options are some of the typical options for upgrade migrations, not just from a non-CDB to a container.

- Data Pump

- Goldengate

- Transportable tablespaces

These options keep the original database for a rollback plan, like copying the data files. Goldengate does allow zero downtime, while the other migration options require some downtime to copy, move, and upgrade.

Tip There is a great resource for upgrades and migrations with Mike Dietrich's blog, "Upgrade your Database – NOW!" He gives more information on these options and helps plan the migration.

Multitenant migration in 19c is a good first step to getting to 23ai. You can upgrade and migrate at the same time if you are going from 19c. The upgrade path to 23ai is from 19c or 21c. If you are using a non-CDB, single-instance database in 19c, then it makes sense to migrate it to a pluggable one.

Fleet Management

As a DBA, you probably take care of several databases. Your job involves managing the environment, servers, software, storage, and more. Patching large environments is a difficult task, and you also want to be able to provision new databases quickly and easily. When talking numbers like that, there needs to be a way to manage multiple databases as a group, also called a *fleet*. This includes upgrading and patching with repeatable processes, making it easier to roll through and minimize downtime.

Oracle's Fleet Patching and Provisioning (FPP) tool helps maintain the life cycle of a large environment. This is one way to think of fleet management, which is discussed in the next couple of sections. After that, let's look at fleet administrators. Not only do they do the patching and provisioning tasks, but this has developed into a new role for Autonomous Databases on dedicated systems. It's a slightly different way of looking at fleet management and administration, but it's an important responsibility for DBAs transitioning to multitenant and cloud environments.

Oracle Fleet Patching and Provisioning

FPP provides a standard method to patch, upgrade, and provision databases, and it is a service in the grid infrastructure. It applies to both the grid and database homes across all environments. The software is installed once and stored on the FPP server, which maintains a gold image of the software and patches for patching and upgrades. Commands can be run against hundreds of targets at the same time. This allows you to do quarterly patches and implements the much-needed automation for these large environments.

New database patches and updates are images, and each image for the database version is new. This includes quarterly security patches and release updates. The images are not just the database but also the grid home.

FPP can be configured as a central server to deploy gold images to any number of nodes and database and grid homes across the environment. Clients of FPP would be configured to retrieve the gold images from the FPP server and, based on policies, upload and apply operations to the server where the client is configured. Since this is part of the grid infrastructure, it can run locally without any central server. The local Oracle homes can be patched, and additional nodes can be provisioned locally with this option.

Types of Patching

Patching in place requires a longer downtime as you apply the patch in the current environment. This requires stopping instances, patching and starting the database again, and running the additional patching or upgrade steps. This way, you must install or run the patch each time.

FPP uses out-of-place patching because it deploys a new working copy, and then databases are moved to the Oracle home. This might be something you already do. Install new patched binaries in the new Oracle grid or database home. After that, the process consists of a stop, a move, and a start. The outage includes the time to restart in a new home with the newly installed binaries.

With multitenant, you can also patch a CDB and the PDBs together. PDBs can be patched separately by moving them to a new CDB running in the patched or upgraded Oracle home.

FPP Steps

The FPP server is a repository for four types of data.

- Gold images

- Working copies

- Client information

- Metadata related to users, roles, and permissions

An FPP server can use ASM to store the images and the file system. Let's walk through the steps to set up an FPP server in a grid home, which assumes the grid infrastructure is installed with ASM.

First, create a disk group in ASM for images using the configuration assistance or log into the ASM instance and use SQL to create the disk group.

```
$ $GRID_HOME/bin/asmca
```

Or do the following.

```
$ . oraenv +ASM
SQL> create diskgroup fppimage disk '/dev/oracleasm/disk/disk_fpp01';
```

A mount point is needed on the nodes of the closer.

```
$ mkdir -p /u03/fppstorage/images
```

Check to see whether the Grid Infrastructure Management Repository is configured.

```
$ srvctl status mgmtdb
```

If not configured and running, it can be in the grid home with the following.

```
$ mgmtca createGIMRContainer -storageDiskLocation fppimage
```

Create the FPP server resource.

```
$ srvctl add rhpserver -storage /u03/fppstorage/images -diskgroup fppimage
$ srvctl start rhpserver
```

The following overviews the steps for fleet patching and provisioning.

1. Create reference environments with the required set of patches.

2. Create gold images and set the version.

3. Subscribe the database and grid homes to a gold image.

4. Deploy the image to a new Oracle home.

5. Switch targets from the old to the new Oracle home.

To create a gold image, you can import or add an image with `rhpctl` commands. Here is an example.

```
$ rhpctl import -image DB23_1
```

The parameters would include the type of image, so if it is Oracle Database or grid, you can create your own image types along with the built-in image types. By default, the type of image is the Oracle Database, but other types would need to be specified using the parameter -`imagetype`.

The built-in base image types are as follows.

- ORACLEDBSOFTWARE

- ORACLEGISOFTWARE

- ORACLEGGSOFTWARE

- EXAPATCHSOFTWARE

- SOFTWARE

Provisioning the gold image is done with the same `rhpctl` command but using the `workingcopy` parameter. This is an example of how to do this on a local client.

```
$ rhpctl add workingcopy -workingcopy DB_HOME_231 -image DB23_1
- storagetype LOCAL
```

Or for client.

```
$ rhpctl add workingcopy -image DB23_1 -path /u01/app/oracle/
product/23.1.00/db23ai -workingcopy DB_HOME_23AI -client client_042
-oraclebase /u01/app/oracle
```

Note   Enterprise Manager software is another way to implement fleet patching and provisioning. It can assist in these steps and configuration. It provides information for the reference environment with the available patches. By using the `emcli` command, you can create the gold image.

There are requirements to set up the FPP server and Enterprise Manager, but you can see some of the commands that help create and manage images with this example. This creates a new version.

```
$ emcli db_software_maintenance -createSoftwareImage -input_file="data:/
home/user/input_file"
```

The following is an example to get a list of images in production.

```
$ emcli db_software_maintenance -getImages
```

In creating images, you must apply the patches to sources, create another image with the patched version, and verify the image.

Once the images have been added to the FPP server, they can be queried.

```
$ rhpctl query image
```

Then, get the specific details from one of the images.

```
$ rhpctl query image -image DB23_1
```

User Groups

You know the different groups available to manage the Oracle software and processes. This is important when you are looking at upgrading and patching. The same user groups are needed to own the software on the servers and deploy them.

Groups are managed as part of the provisioning. They are not inherited in the images. The groups can be set using the -groups parameter on the rhpctl command. FPP uses the group of the user that is running the command to copy the image to the working copy.

Methods of Patching

Rolling through patches without too much downtime is important for most environments. Databases need to be up and available, so planning a strategy to keep it consistent, minimize downtime, and automate is important.

By default, rolling patching of the grid infrastructure is the method for FPP. When not using FPP, you can have two installed homes that basically use the same method, but this requires more manual intervention. The following are different methods for the grid infrastructure.

- *Rolling*: Moves the grid infrastructure home sequentially through each node in the clusters

- *Nonrolling*: Done in parallel to patch all of the nodes at the same time

- *Batch*: Patches the Oracle grid and database homes at the same time

- *Zero downtime*: Does not bring down the databases that are part of the cluster while patching; this method automates the database upgrades without interrupting the service

With fleet patching and provisioning, the idea here is to provide another solution for large environments and manage a patching system to roll out patched versions of the Oracle home consistently and efficiently. So, where you might have spent time patching and not even the ability to patch the whole environment, management tasks can focus on working with the gold images, testing the releases, and implementing the most effective solution for the environment.

Fleet Management with Autonomous

Shifting gears slightly, let's look at another type of fleet management. This is not completely different from patching and provisioning, but it does include some of these tasks. This is also not a tool to help you manage large environments but defines the responsibilities of an administrator of databases in the cloud on dedicated Exadata Infrastructure and Exadata Cloud@Customer.

Autonomous Database – Serverless (ADB-S) is a quick database creation through the Oracle Cloud Infrastructure console. It doesn't appear much is needed from a database administrator; however, Autonomous Database Dedicated has administrative tasks and responsibilities. This includes managing and monitoring the container databases for the environment.

The fleet administrators create and manage the Autonomous Container Database resources. They need the appropriate permissions in the Oracle Cloud to administer the Autonomous Exadata VM Clusters and the container database. The fleet administrators must also set up the networking resources needed for the database environment and connections.

The beginning of this book discussed the different roles that DBAs do and the different default roles that are part of the configuration to have a separation of duties. This includes managing the grid environment vs. the databases and backups. The same applies here. The infrastructure side of Autonomous Dedicated is very similar to managing the container databases and servers in multitenant. Both of these are for the administration of the fleet of databases.

Autonomous Database – Serverless is doing these same tasks to provide the self-service databases managed by Oracle. The fleet administration is responsible for these components in the dedicated architecture: the Exadata components, container databases, and security.

Provisioning

The ADB Dedicated architecture consists of the following.

- Exadata infrastructure

- Autonomous VM cluster

- Autonomous Container Database

- Autonomous Database

The Exadata infrastructure can be in an Oracle Cloud Infrastructure (OCI) region or Exadata Cloud@Customer (so in your data center). This includes the compute nodes, storage, and networking.

The VM cluster is the virtual machines set up for the Autonomous Container Databases to run on, and it provides high availability with all nodes. The VMs allocate all the resources of the Exadata infrastructure.

The Autonomous Container Database is the CDB set up to manage the pluggable databases. Autonomous Databases are pluggable databases that can be configured to be transactional or configured for data warehouse workloads.

Provisioning includes all these components. Fleet administrators need the right policies and permissions at the cloud tenancy level and then need system DBA permissions to create CDBs and PDBs. The architecture should use a compartment in the tenancy to properly allocate resources and policies at the right level. In the OCI tenancy, create a compartment for the users, VMs, databases, and other resources.

Policies

After creating a compartment in the tenancy, let's call it fleetdatabases in our examples. A group should be created to manage the fleet administrators, fleetDBA. The policies and users should be added to the group. The following is a list of policies that can be manually edited in the OCI console under Policies for the compartment.

```
Allow group fleetDBA to manage cloud-exadata-infrastructures in compartment
fleetdatabases
Allow group fleetDBA to manage autonomous-database-family in compartment
fleetdatabases
Allow group fleetDBA to use virtual-network-family in compartment
fleetdatabases
Allow group fleetDBA to use tag-namespaces in compartment fleetdatabases
Allow group fleetDBA to use tag-defaults in compartment fleetdatabase
```

Note Compartments, groups, and policies are all created through the OCI console. If you want to automate this process and use either the command line or scripts, you can do this by creating Terraform scripts for consistent provisioning in the environments.

Fleet administrators can either have permission to give database users the permissions for Autonomous Databases or have the policies created for the database user groups. These would be users managing and using the Autonomous Databases in their own compartment in the tenancy. Policies can depend on the environment and what the users are allowed to do. Additional policies might be allowed, or different users might be allowed only certain policies. Here are some additional examples.

```
Allow group ADBusers to manage autonomous-databases in compartment
ADBuserscompartment
Allow group ADBusers to manage autonomous-backups in compartment
ADBuserscompartment
Allow group ADBusers to use virtual-network-family in compartment
ADBuserscompartment
Allow group ADBusers to manage instance-family in compartment
ADBuserscompartment
Allow group ADBusers to manage buckets in compartment
ADBuserscompartment
```

Users can be added to the groups with the policies for permissions. The fleet administrators would be in the fleetDBA group, and those just using ADBs would be in the ADBusers group.

Network

Fleet administrators are not necessarily responsible for the network configuration but can provide some input and guidelines. The network is configured with similar policies for on-prem databases. For example, databases should be in a private subnet without Internet access, subnets have their own security lists, and ingress ports should be opened only as needed.

It is important here to include network administrators to configure the network configurations and ensure the database servers comply with policies. With databases, you need to confirm that the TCP traffic allows port 1521. If using APEX and SQLDeveloper and Database Actions, port 443 would be allowed. Additional ports would be 2484 and 6200 for encrypted traffic and application continuity.

If access is needed to the Internet, an Internet gateway can be created in the virtual cloud network (VCN). Bastion hosts can also be configured for SSH access and developer client machines.

Exadata Infrastructure

From the OCI console, under Autonomous Database, there are two choices: Autonomous Database and Dedicated Infrastructure. Autonomous Database is a serverless option typically used for creating ADBs in the OCI environment. Dedicated Infrastructure is where you would be setting up the components of the dedicated environment.

It is important to make sure you are creating the Exadata infrastructure in the right compartment, as this has the policies granted and keeps the database components in the same area.

Let's walk through some screenshots from the OCI console to show the steps for the components and discuss the responsibilities of the fleet administrator. Figure 17-1 shows the starting point for creating the Exadata infrastructure.

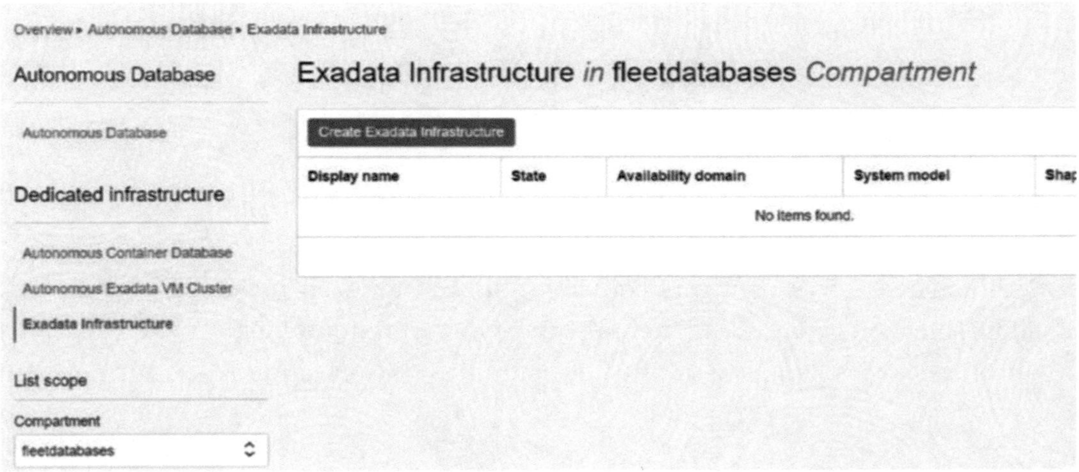

Figure 17-1. *Creating Exadata infrastructure*

In Figure 17-2, the compartment is the first choice and should be prepopulated if already working in that compartment. Name the infrastructure, and refer to your company standards and guidelines for naming conventions. There is a choice of availability domain that depends on the tenancy you are working in and another choice on the system model for Exadata. The default is the latest and greatest model available.

Create Exadata Infrastructure

Provide basic information for the Exadata infrastructure

Choose a compartment

| fleetdatabases | ⇕ |

oreopengiun (root)/fleetdatabases

Display name

Exadata-Infra-company

A user-friendly name to help you easily identify the resource. Display name can be changed at any time.

Select an availability domain

| AD-1 | ✓ | AD-2 | AD-3 |
| SrUC:PHX-AD-1 | | SrUC:PHX-AD-2 | SrUC:PHX-AD-3 |

Select the Exadata system model ⓘ

X9M-2

Compute and storage configuration

Database servers

2

Storage servers

3

Resource totals

OCPUs: 252
Storage: 192 TB

Create Exadata Infrastructure   Save as stack   Cancel

Figure 17-2. *Exadata infrastructure form*

Maintenance can be configured differently and customized, including on the schedule shown in Figure 17-3. Patching can be rolling or nonrolling.

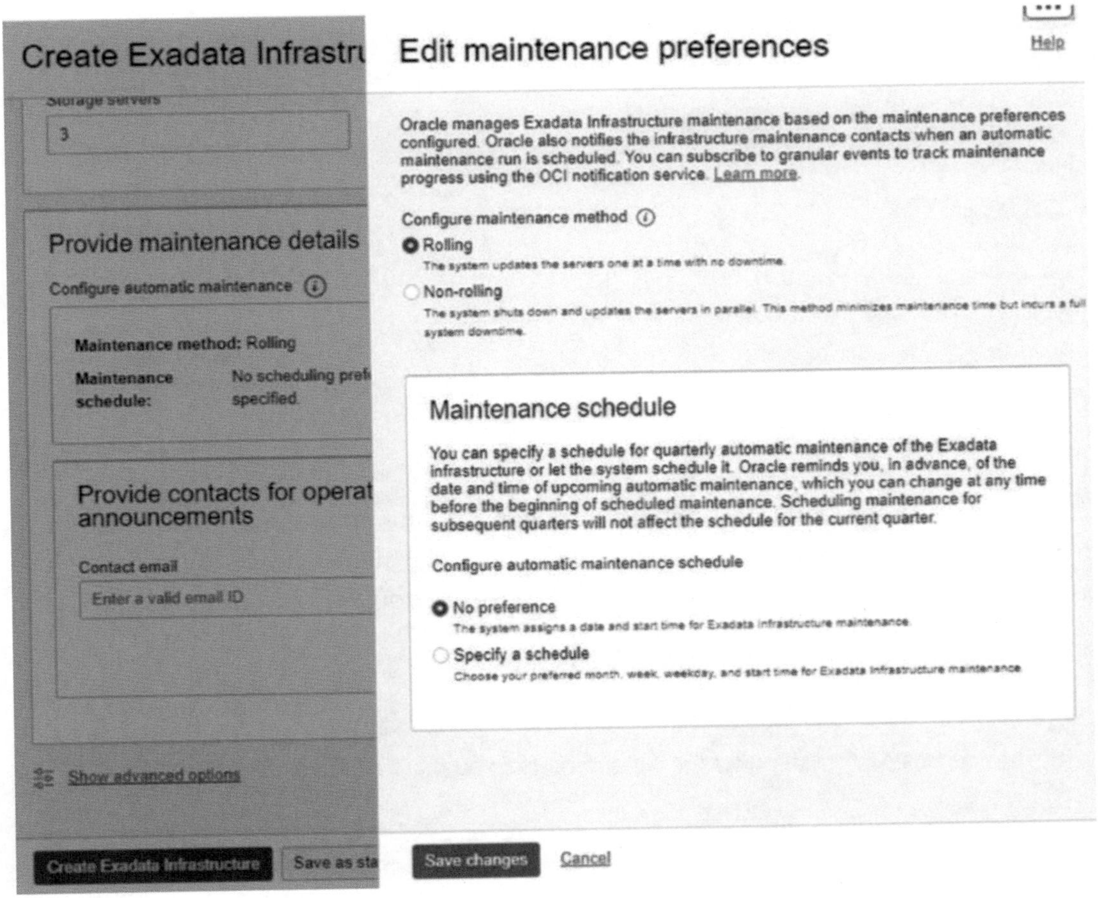

Create Exadata Infrastru

Storage servers

3

Provide maintenance details

Configure automatic maintenance (i)

Maintenance method: Rolling

Maintenance   No scheduling pref
schedule: specified.

Provide contacts for operat announcements

Contact email

Enter a valid email ID

Show advanced options

Create Exadata Infrastructure   Save as sta

Edit maintenance preferences   Help

Oracle manages Exadata Infrastructure maintenance based on the maintenance preferences configured. Oracle also notifies the infrastructure maintenance contacts when an automatic maintenance run is scheduled. You can subscribe to granular events to track maintenance progress using the OCI notification service. Learn more.

Configure maintenance method (i)

● Rolling
   The system updates the servers one at a time with no downtime.

○ Non-rolling
   The system shuts down and updates the servers in parallel. This method minimizes maintenance time but incurs a full system downtime.

Maintenance schedule

You can specify a schedule for quarterly automatic maintenance of the Exadata infrastructure or let the system schedule it. Oracle reminds you, in advance, of the date and time of upcoming automatic maintenance, which you can change at any time before the beginning of scheduled maintenance. Scheduling maintenance for subsequent quarters will not affect the schedule for the current quarter.

Configure automatic maintenance schedule

● No preference
   The system assigns a date and start time for Exadata infrastructure maintenance.

○ Specify a schedule
   Choose your preferred month, week, weekday, and start time for Exadata infrastructure maintenance.

Save changes   Cancel

Figure 17-3. Advance options maintenance

Once the Exadata infrastructure is created, the VM clusters can be created. Figure 17-4 shows this as the next choice, working the way up from the Exadata infrastructure.

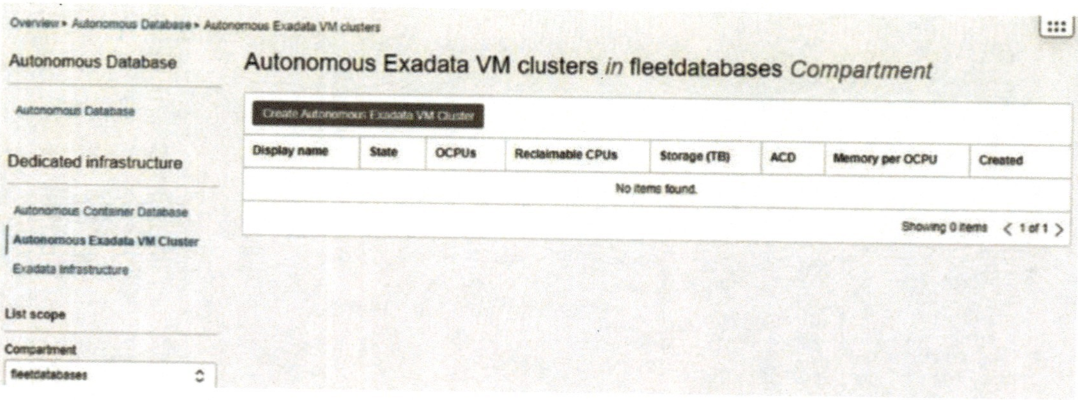

Figure 17-4. *Creating VM clusters*

Figure 17-5 shows that the previously created Exadata infrastructure is included to create the VMs on the right infrastructure. The display name should follow your company standards or guidelines for this database environment.

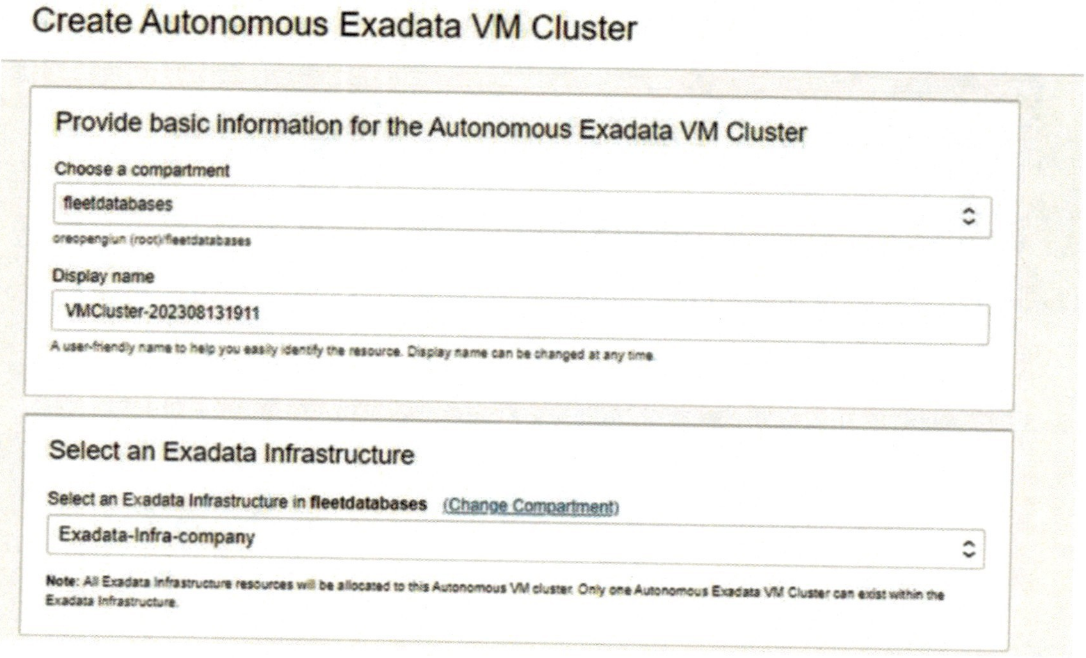

Figure 17-5. *Information for autonomous VM cluster*

ECPUs are the elastic cores for Autonomous Database. Figure 17-6 shows not just the ECPUs to adjust but other resources on the VM to put limits on containers. Setting the details on the number of Autonomous Container Databases doesn't limit the number of pluggables or Autonomous Databases in the container. But the memory and storage limits might do that.

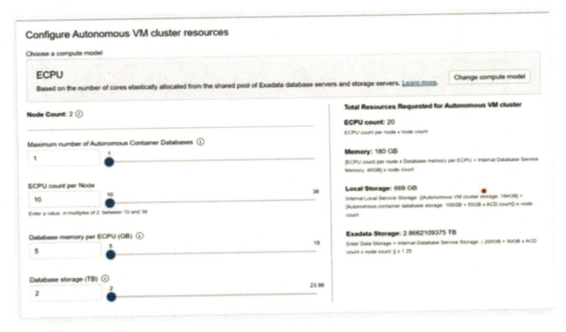

Figure 17-6. *Setting VM resources for containers*

The last component to examine here is the Autonomous Container Database, as shown in Figure 17-7.

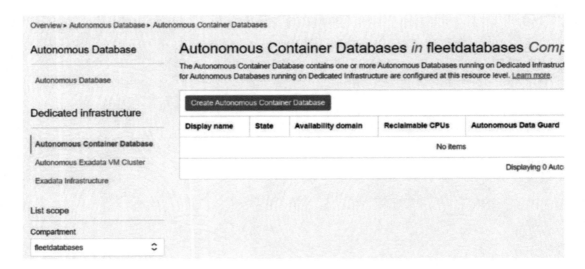

Figure 17-7. *Creating the Autonomous Container Database*

The create information requires the compartment, the Exadata infrastructure, and the VM Cluster, as shown in Figure 17-8. Also, here you see that the version of the Autonomous Container Database is available for the base image.

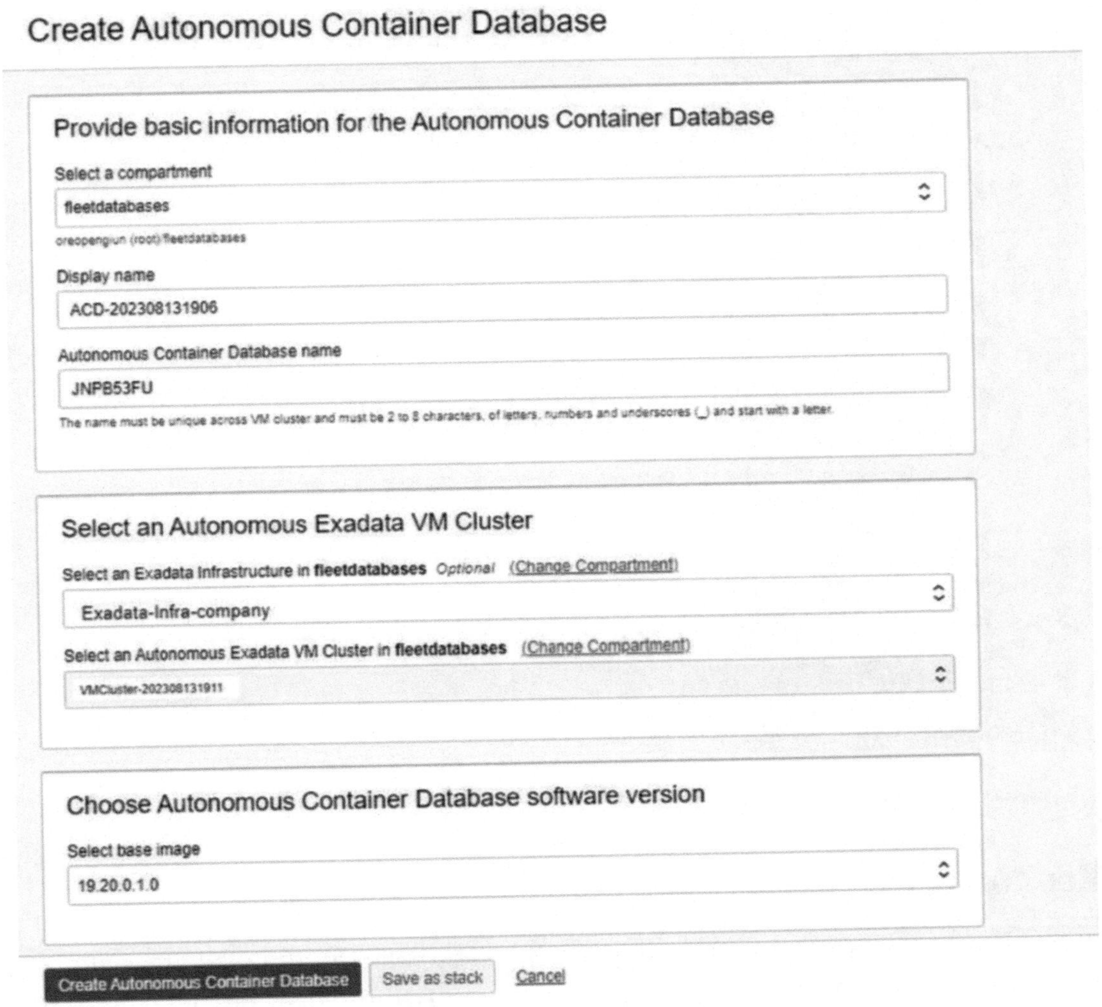

Create Autonomous Container Database

Provide basic information for the Autonomous Container Database

Select a compartment

fleetdatabases

oreopengiun (root)/fleetdatabases

Display name

ACD-202308131906

Autonomous Container Database name

JNPB53FU

The name must be unique across VM cluster and must be 2 to 8 characters, of letters, numbers and underscores (_) and start with a letter.

Select an Autonomous Exadata VM Cluster

Select an Exadata Infrastructure in **fleetdatabases** *Optional*   (Change Compartment)

Exadata-Infra-company

Select an Autonomous Exadata VM Cluster in **fleetdatabases**   (Change Compartment)

VMCluster-202308131911

Choose Autonomous Container Database software version

Select base image

19.20.0.1.0

Create Autonomous Container Database   Save as stack   Cancel

Figure 17-8. *Providing information for the Autonomous Container Database*

The last step in creating the container is editing the automatic maintenance.
Figure 17-9 shows the choices for the schedule and patching.

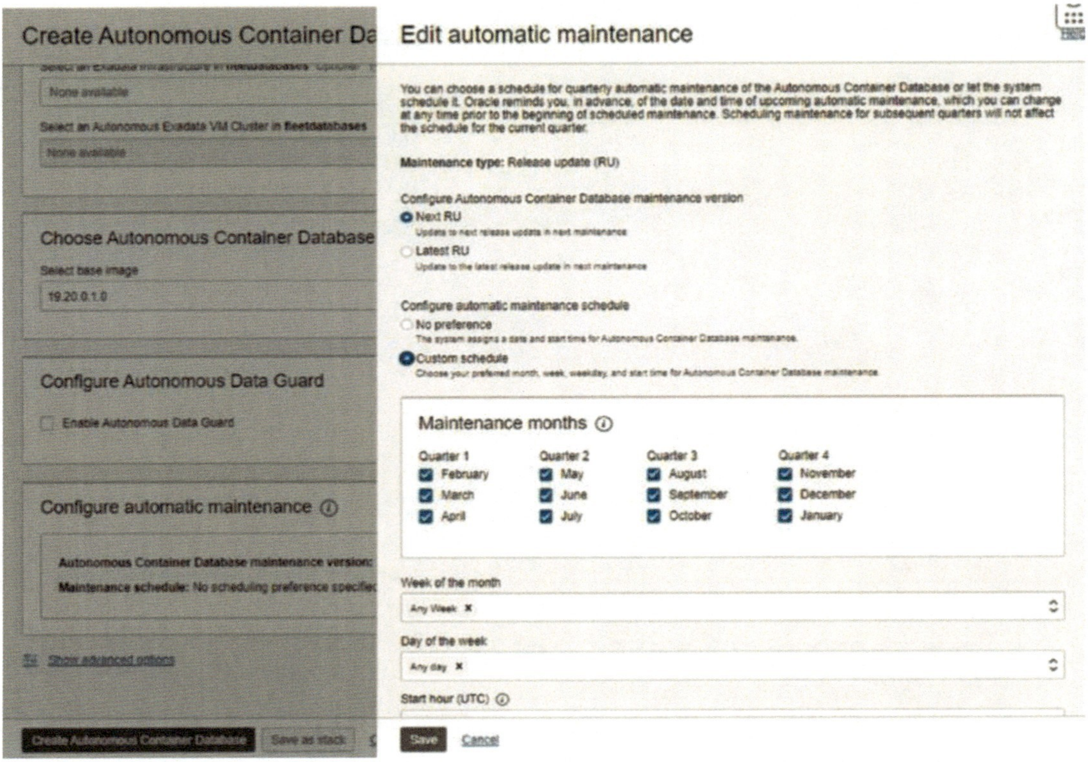

Figure 17-9. *Configuring maintenance*

Monitoring

Ideally, you are seeing that there are opportunities for database administrators with fleet management. Whether patching or Autonomous Dedicated, the architecture and infrastructure need to be configured and managed, even if the Autonomous Database is then provided on demand. The health of the environment also needs to be monitored.

The dedicated environment has similar choices as database creation, but notice that the software and patching are automated. Even with automation, there are different areas of management and policies that can be inserted to ensure you meet your company's requirements.

It is also important for the fleet administrator to monitor the ADBs and tune them. Different configurations might be needed for VMs or the Autonomous Container Database. Like migrating pluggable databases, the fleet administration can relocate databases in different containers to help with performance or redistribute resources as needed. This is part of the monitoring and migration tasks needed for the dedicated system.

Restoring and availability come into play here, too. Most of the information from the previous chapters can be leveraged to manage large and cloud databases.

A dedicated environment also lets you set the different options in the maintenance schedule and types of patching. There are no choices with ADB-S, but with dedicated, it can meet your company's needs and maintenance windows and backup strategies. This also includes deciding on the VM clusters, the number of Autonomous Container Databases created, and the resources allocated.

When migrating to multitenant and cloud, the database administrator's job changes. There are options for fleet administration and FPP server management. The administration tasks here are infrastructure system administration responsibilities. The next chapter looks at other ways the administration role is changing with the management of the data.

CHAPTER 18

Data Management

This book has covered what you need to do to build, create, secure, and tune database environments. DBAs need to know how to administer databases and make them available for all the applications the company needs to run the business. There is quite a bit to do because it includes architecting the environment for security and performance and making it easy to use and access. The data is a critical asset for a company. The data has a ton of value beyond merely capturing it for processes and transactions. It provides the information needed to make intelligent decisions and predicts how best to do something or change processes for efficiency. Even the forward-thinking of artificial intelligence (AI) is based on the volumes of data available.

It might seem with all the details of administering and managing the environment, there is enough for a DBA to do without having to worry about data management. That might be true in some environments, which is a reason to separate system DBAs, fleet DBAs, and application DBAs. But as automation is implemented and more questions arise about how to leverage data, you should dive into some data management concepts and know at least some of the tools that Oracle Database offers.

Oracle Database 23ai has several new features that simplify application development and data management. It is also converging the relational model of the database with other models to use structured and unstructured data, JSON documents, graphs, and vectors. This provides an opportunity to use data to innovate and drive business outcomes. Let's use that data, capital, and assets to work for the company and not just store data.

© Michelle Malcher, Darl Kuhn 2024
M. Malcher and D. Kuhn, *Pro Oracle Database 23ai Administration*,
https://doi.org/10.1007/979-8-8688-1038-1_18

Models

Data modeling is an important part of application development, so you understand how to structure the data. Decisions are made based on the application requirements, what information is needed, and how it is needed. I could probably discuss the value of normalization vs. denormalization of the data model for another couple of chapters. Whether to use surrogate or natural keys on tables, but those topics are not necessarily the point of the data management and model discussion here. During application development, decisions are made to use data in a particular way based on the requirements. This might even influence the database that is being used. Therefore, it is important to understand the capabilities of the database and tools to support these types of decisions and requirements. There is a need to understand if something limits the use of the data or creates a need for complex data integrations if the data will be leveraged in other places.

It is good to recognize that the data requirements for one application might not be the same for another. Being a database administrator, there are opportunities here to help develop a data architecture or plan to be able to reuse data, leverage the information in other analysis and calculations where it makes sense, or even use the data in other formats, making it easy to create specific applications that might be different from relational models. So, if you need to use different models of the data, such as hierarchical, graph, and object, are there ways you can do that in the Oracle Database? Of course! The purpose of this discussion is to look at different ways of using the same data sets and leveraging a relational model for graph models, hierarchical for machine learning, and all the relational models for several different uses and applications.

Workloads also play a part in how you model your data. Is this transactional data? Warehouse data? Normally, we find there are different hybrid approaches to this as well. All these factors come into play when designing systems and wanting to make the applications perform well. There are parameters and configurations to tune the database based on workloads and types of data being used, but the database doesn't limit the workloads or types. The database architect and administrator are responsible for creating a robust system and data model for these applications and tuning them along the way.

After the applications run and you've collected all kinds of data and information, shouldn't this data be harnessed for business decisions and other applications? Absolutely. Even after all the model decisions are made and applications have been running, there are reasons to use data in different ways because of the importance of the information that has been collected.

Oracle 23ai has several new features focused on easier data management, using different data types and capabilities with different workloads. This is to help leverage the existing data and gather new information while simplifying development.

JSON

Let's look again at the JSON data type. JSON documents for applications make it easier to view and pull in custom information, such as their properties and attributes, as a JSON document. JSON is an easy-to-parse data format and doesn't need the complete schema defined. JSON is a text format and the components are identified within the document. It is also easy to send JSON as an API and validate the format. JSON documents are popular with developers for temporarily storing data.

Oracle 23ai introduced JSON Relational Duality Views and the JSON data type, along with the functions to verify and format JSON documents using SQL. Talking about JSON in this way, instead of a data type or different type of view in the database, highlights more of how applications are using the data or how development teams are accessing the data. You can provide them with data in a format that uses the existing relational tables in the database, and they can access the JSON documents.

Let's use customer, items, and orders tables for example purposes, as shown next.

```
SQL> create table customer
 (customer_id number primary key,
 customer_name varchar2(80),
 address1 varchar2(80),
 city varchar2(80),
 state varchar2(20),
 zipcode number,
 geo_location sdo_geometry,
 customer_begin_date date);
Table created.
SQL> create table items
 (item_id number primary key,
 item_name varchar2(80),
 item_description varchar2(4000),
 item_price number);
```

```
Table created.
SQL> create table orders
 (order_id number primary key,
 customer_id number,
    item_id number,
order_date date);
Table created.
SQL> alter table orders add constraint fk_customer foreign key
(customer_id)
references customer(customer_id);
SQL> alter table orders add constraint fk_items foreign key (item_id)
references items(item_id);
--need to have foreign key references for creating duality views.
```

These tables were created for taking orders, and then the data needs to be passed off to print invoices, ship products, or other processes for these orders. The different systems can take the data in JSON documents, so all the information is provided at once to give the needed details. If the transaction data was not stored as relational tables, and only as JSON, we might have duplicate data that would need to be kept regarding items and customers. Changes to items would have to update different documents for orders, which might cause data consistency issues. The relational tables handle this. The JSON Relational Duality View on top of these tables provides the JSON document with real-time consistent data. Updates, inserts, and deletes can also be handled through these views.

Here is a sample JSON Relational Duality View, and you can create several other views depending on the needed attributes and uses. Since it does not store the data, just the metadata, creating a view designed for the use case is easy.

```
SQL> create json relational duality view cust_orders_dv as
select JSON {'customer_id' is c.customer_id,
'customer_name' is c.customer_name,
'order' is [select JSON {'order_id' is o.order_id,
'order_date' is o.order_date,
'item_id' is o.item_id }
from orders o
where c.customer_id=o.customer_id]}
from customer c;
```

Maybe there was a shipped column that allows changes through the view to update that the order has been shipped. This topic was discussed with views, but it is important to mention it again when discussing data management. There is flexibility here in these schemas as well. If you need another JSON view, creating one is simple since the data is not being stored again. Also, you can include only the columns you want to use or only allow updates to specific parts of the document when using JSON Relational Duality. This is to start to get the ideas flowing and recognize when the development teams are looking for the JSON format, there are ways to do just that.

Besides the relational tables and JSON views, you can do analytics on the data and include JSON in machine learning and graph algorithms.

Graph

Relational data seems like enough to make connections in data; however, some connections may require recursive queries and multiple joins that might be difficult to do with straight SQL. Even if you look at the previous example of tables and compare customers connected by location, when they became customers, and the items they ordered, traversing through a graph structure might be easier.

Oracle 23ai has native support for property graph data structures, and you can use a GRAPH_TABLE function and MATCH clause to write the queries. There are more than 60 built-in algorithms for graph analytics. The following are some areas for these analytics.

- Detecting components and communities
- Evaluating structures
- Predicting links
- Ranking and walking
- Path-finding
- Machine learning

Now, you can start thinking of the questions you can ask of the data, such as making product recommendations, identifying dependencies and relationships, and detecting fraud. You can even think of the operational data where this can help with workflows and dependencies of assets and systems.

Let's look at a quick example using the same tables of customers and orders. You can have the customer table be a vertex, and items as a vertex. Orders are the edges because this shows the connections. The graph shows items the customers have ordered and allows you to see additional related orders.

```
SQL> create property graph cust_orders
vertex tables(
customer key (customer_id) properties (customer_name, city,state),
items key (item_id) properties (item_name, item_price)
)
edge tables (
orders
source key (item_id) references items (item_id)
 destination key (customer_id) references customer (customer_id)
properties (item_id,customer_id,order_id, order_date)
);
```

After creating the graph, let's query it for matches and count the items ordered.

```
SQL> select item_name, count(1)
from graph_table (cust_orders
match (src)-[is orders] -> (dst)
columns (dst.item_name)) group by item_name;
```

The () are for the vertex's customer or items, and [ ] are for the edges that are the orders.

The match clause specifies the pattern from the graph_table, which is the path pattern for the graph. As you can see, the same data is used without moving it to another graph database or a separate system; this allows us to perform the analytics or use the graph algorithms against the data.

These simple examples might not give you the big picture of the data possibilities, but knowing you have different ways of viewing, connecting, and analyzing the data with queries on existing data will be useful. This allows you to leverage the data assets and use a single source of truth with all the other security, performance, and reliability of the database that has been configured.

Machine Learning and AI

Like graph algorithms, Oracle 23ai has more than 30 algorithms ready for machine learning models. Did anyone ask for AI? Machine learning is AI, and of course, there is more AI beyond just machine learning, but these are the interesting pieces you can perform in the Oracle Database. The Oracle Database statistic collection is now leveraging machine learning algorithms to make real-time statistics more efficient and predict information about data changes and growth. Machine learning is there to answer additional questions and can analyze large volumes of data. What questions are being asked of your data? Have you been able to answer the business needs with reports and queries? If not, it is time to investigate implementing graph and machine learning and using the data for business value.

There are plenty of use cases for AI for helping customers, providing chatbots, making operations more efficient, generating code for applications and even helping with the business's bottom line.

Also, there is a large amount of unstructured data with photos, videos, documents and more that the Oracle Database 23ai can now combine with structured data to do similarity searches with AI Vector Search. This capability with leveraging the AI models of choice to create vector embeddings, store them in the database, and seamlessly combine semantic and traditional search to gain even better insights. Think about being able to search a product photo with the description or even the instruction manual to bring back the right information for the customer based on a question the customer asked or searched for. It might be for comparisons or be based on a specific product that has that filter first to search for additional information, which uses photo details or descriptions for the similarity search.

Different models are available to create data vectors, and storing that data with other business data allows filtering and semantic searches and leverages business data to augment the data. Vectors and business data can power retrieval Augmented Generation (RAG) to bring additional context to the LLMs and this can augment the user prompts. Oracle Database 23ai allows you to use models of your choice, and you can import models using ONNX, an open source format for the models. You can use either DBMS_VECTOR.LOAD_ONNX_MODEL or DBMS_DATA_MINING.IMPORT_ONNX_MODEL.

```
SQL> execute DBMS_VECTOR.load_onnx_model(
        'MiniLM','all-MiniLM-L6-v2.onnx','doc_model');
```

The Oracle Database can also use other models outside of the database through services and API calls so that you can create the embeddings or just load embeddings. Along with the new vector data type in Oracle 23ai, new functions and procedures generate embeddings and do the vector distance searches. Let's look back at the example of creating a table with a vector.

```
SQL> create table product (
product_id number,
product_name varchar2(80),
product_description varchar2(1000),
product_vector vector,
product_photo_vector vector);
SQL> insert into product (product_id,product_name,product_photo_vector)
Values (1,'Test1','[0.4342485,0.6134194,-0.44895060,...,...]');
SQL> update product set product_vector= vector_embedding(MiniLM using
product_description);
SQL> select product_id, product_name, product_description
from product
order by vector_distance(product_photo_vector, :QUERY_VEC)
fetch approximate first 10 rows only;
```

Business use cases continue with machine learning, such as predictive maintenance, or focus on customers and have churn and acquisition or even look at employee retention. Marketing cases with product bundling and financial industries might focus on fraud detection, and with these different business problems, different algorithms are available to work with the data. Machine learning can automatically discover patterns and create actionable information. Machine learning models can be built quickly using the DBMS_DATA_MINING PL/SQL package. You need to understand the types of algorithms such as classification, which can be used for predictions about customers. In Autonomous Database, Oracle AutoML is available and can help you select the right types of algorithms. AutoML helps nonexpert users leverage machine learning in the Oracle Database. Here is the process for AutoML.

- *Auto algorithm selection*: Finds the best algorithm from in-database algorithms

- *Adaptive sampling*: Identifies and adjusts the right sample size

- *Auto feature selection*: Improves accuracy and performance

- *Auto model tuning*: Improves models with automated tuning

AutoML provides a quick way to get started with machine learning, test the built-in algorithms, and build models without completely understanding all the science. However, with the different skill sets, the packages are available.

For example, let's take our customer list and, based on a customer's start date, figure out if the customer is at risk of not purchasing additional items.

```
SQL> create or replace view vw_customer_longterm as
select c.customer_id, c.customer_name, decode(to_char(customer_begin_
date,'YYYY','2023',1,0) cust_date_value,decode(nvl(o.order_id,0),0,0,1)
order_value
from customer c left outer join orders o on o.customer_id=c.customer_id;
View created.
SQL> declare
v_setlst dbms_data_mining.setting_list;
begin
v_setlst(dbms_data_mining.algo_name) := dbms_data_mining.algo_support_
vector_machines;
v_setlst(dbms_data_mining.prep_auto) := dbms_data_mining.prep_auto_on;
dbms_data_mining.create_model2(
model_name => 'FIND_LONGTERM',
mining_function => 'CLASSIFICATION',
data_query => 'select * from mmtest.customer_longterm',
set_list => v_setlst,
case_id_column_name => 'CUSTOMER_ID',
target_column_name => 'CUST_DATE_VALUE');
end;
/
SQL> create table customer_longterm
as select customer_id,
prediction(FIND_LONGTERM usering *) cust_likely_to_leave,
prediction_details(FIND_LONGTERM using *) PD
from vw_customer_longterm;
```

Machine learning can confirm observations and find new patterns. Discovery and predictive relationships are ways to start harnessing the data by pulling information out of the data.

Before looking at some tools available for machine learning, let's look at Database Actions for Oracle Database in the cloud, as shown in Figure 18-1. There are several different tools here. Under Development, there is a SQL Worksheet, Data Modeler, JSON Collections, REST APIs, APEX, Liquibase, and other tools. As you can see, there is quite a bit to explore. Many of these tools are also on-premises but need to be installed or enabled. For on-premises tools, SQL Developer is a good starting point to download and use with all the Oracle databases on-prem and in the cloud. Another tool is SQLcl, which is a command-line interface to the databases. SQLcl comes with SQL Developer and provides a command-line tool instead of installing the Oracle client to use SQLPlus.

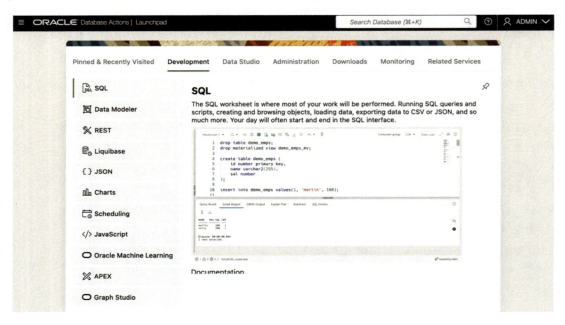

Figure 18-1. *Database actions*

From Database Actions, you can launch the Oracle Machine Learning user interface. Figure 18-2 shows how to get started with Oracle Machine Learning with Autonomous Database.

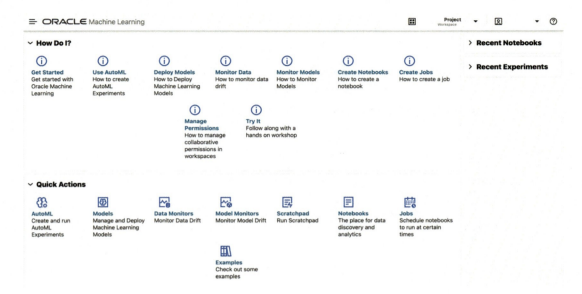

Figure 18-2. *Machine learning user interface*

You can get to this user interface from Database Actions, and as you can see in Figure 18-2, you can create notebooks for data discovery and analytics. There are also plenty of examples to browse through. Again, you can leverage AutoML and the machine learning UI in OCI to familiarize yourself with the provided algorithms. The same algorithms are available in the Oracle Database on-premises and by using SQL as the example provided to create the model. The platform that you use might have different tools but still provides the same standard SQL and capabilities in the database.

Selecting examples gives you several examples to explore and see the built-in algorithms at work. Figure 18-3 demonstrates the "OML4SQL Anomaly Detection SVM" template, which includes a model using the 1-Class SVM algorithm to detect anomalies in the data.

≡ **ORACLE** Machine Learning

Build anomaly detection model using the 1-Class SVM algorithm   FINISHED

```
%script

BEGIN DBMS_DATA_MINING.DROP_MODEL('CUSTOMERS360MODEL');
EXCEPTION WHEN OTHERS THEN NULL; END;
/
DECLARE
    v_setlst DBMS_DATA_MINING.SETTING_LIST;
BEGIN
    v_setlst('ALGO_NAME')    := 'ALGO_SUPPORT_VECTOR_MACHINES';
    V_setlst('PREP_AUTO')    := 'ON';

    DBMS_DATA_MINING.CREATE_MODEL2(
        MODEL_NAME             => 'CUSTOMERS360MODEL',
        MINING_FUNCTION        => 'CLASSIFICATION',
        DATA_QUERY             => 'select * from CUSTOMERS360_V',
        SET_LIST               => v_setlst,
        CASE_ID_COLUMN_NAME    => 'CUST_ID',
        TARGET_COLUMN_NAME     => NULL);
END;


PL/SQL procedure successfully completed.


----------------------------


PL/SQL procedure successfully completed.
```

Figure 18-3. *Machine learning example*

After reviewing the examples, new notebooks can be created with scripts, SQL, or other languages such as R or Python to create the machine learning models.

As a database administrator, you are providing ways to work with the data in the Oracle Database and gaining insight into the workloads that can be coming your way. Additional resources might be needed, but it goes back to monitoring the databases. It depends on how much data and which algorithms will be used, and you can capture workloads on the system and tune them accordingly. Besides just application and transaction code running on the database, there are analytic workloads that include machine learning that use the different data types and leverage all kinds of data.

Data Studio

Data Studio is one of the tools under Database Actions in OCI for Autonomous Database, as shown in Figure 18-1. You have learned about Data Pump, external tables, and SQL*Loader; it is also good to know about Data Studio. Even with Autonomous, if you do not have to take care of the patching and some of the administration, there are opportunities with data. The data management discussed so far can all be done in Autonomous or on-premises. The opportunities with data, various workloads, and different analytics provide answers, possibilities, and other insights derived from the data. With Oracle Autonomous Database from Database Actions, if you select the Data Studio overview, you see four options for loading, analyzing, gaining insights, and cataloging data. Figure 18-4 shows these main areas and how to get started using Data Studio.

Figure 18-4. *Data Studio Overview*

Figure 18-5 walks you through what you want to do, such as loading, linking, or feeding data, as well as where the source of the data is, which can be another database, local file, or cloud storage, including other clouds (AWS, Azure, OCI). You simply select Load Data and provide details about the data, CSV file or database connection, or connection to cloud storage. Then it is a drag and drop of the data to load. These can be set up as jobs or a one-time process. This is a simple way to load data into an Autonomous Database. You can load from CSV, Excel, Parquet, JSON, and other files by just dragging and dropping the file and watching the data loading jobs that have been configured.

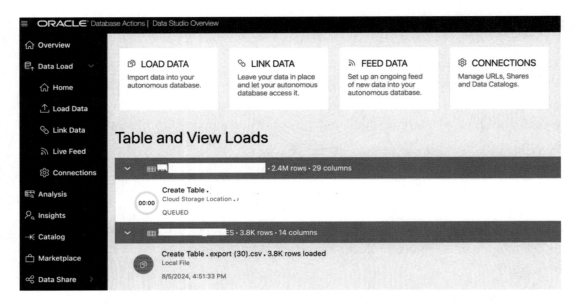

Figure 18-5. *Data loader options*

Depending on how you want to work with JSON files, there are ways to create JSON collections under the Development section of Database Actions with JSON. This is a UI that works for managing JSON data. There are several ways of working with JSON through the tools and SQL in the database.

DBMS_CLOUD

DBMS_CLOUD is a package that manages several Autonomous Database processes and routines, especially when working with all the cloud resources that are part of this database system. The cloud console provides an interface, but behind the scenes, many of these activities use the DBMS_CLOUD package. Instead of using the user interface, there is a package that you can use to do several of these tasks, from loading data to setting up credentials.

DBMS_CLOUD offers subprograms for the following areas.

- Access management

- Object and file storage

- Bulk file management

- REST APIs

Credentials are set up for the management within the package and allow setting up the least privileges for loading data and for querying external data in cloud resources, including in other clouds besides OCI.

Permissions on the package are needed. When you create a user in Database Actions, there are options to allow setting the permissions, but you can also grant the following through SQL.

```
SQL> grant execute on dbms_cloud to mmalcher;
```

Credentials are stored in the DBA/ALL/USER_CREDENTIALS view, which grants access to OCI users managing resources external to the Autonomous Database and allowing data to be exported and loaded or processed for various sources. To run these procedures, you can be connected through SQL in Database Actions or SQL Developer connections to the Autonomous Database.

```
SQL> begin
dbms_cloud.create_credential(
credential_name => 'OCI_ADB_DATAMGMT',
username => 'mmalcher@company.com',
password => 'Cr4zyPa$$wOrd!');
end;
```

Objects and files can be in object storage in the cloud and other clouds, and instead of having a local file, you need to access these files for external tables to work with the data in data lakes and other formats.

Here is an example of creating an external table in Autonomous using object storage files (assuming the customer name, dates, and totals are in the file).

```
SQL> begin
dbms_cloud.create_external_table (
table_name => 'CUSTOMER_SALES_JULY',
credential_name => 'OCI_ADB_DATAMGMT',
file_uri_list => 'https://objectstorage.us-ashburn-1.oracelcloud.com/n/
namespace1/b/customer_sales/cust_sales_0723.csv',
format => json_object('type' value 'csv', 'skipheaders' value '1'),
   field_list => 'CUSTOMER_ID,
CUSTOMER_NAME,
CUSTOMER_TOTAL,
```

```
SALE_DATE DATE ''mm/dd/yyyy''',
column_list => 'CUSTOMER_ID NUMBER,
CUSTOMER_NAME VARCHAR2(100),
CUSTOMER_TOTAL NUMBER,
SALE_DATE DATE');
end;
```

The format for the external tables can be CSV, JSON, ORC, Avro, or Parquet and is not limited to CSV files. Indexes can also be created on the external files with `dbms_cloud.create_external_text_index` to search through the files and find values.

Here is an example of copying a file as one more example for objects and files.

```
SQL> begin
dbms_cloud.copy_object (
source_credential_name => 'OCI_ADB_DATAMGMT',
source_object_uri => 'https://objectstorage.us-ashburn-1.oraclecloud.com/n/
namespace1/b/customer_sales/o/cust_sales_june.csv',
target_object_uri => 'https://objectstorage.us-ashburn-1.oraclecloud.com/n/
namespace1/b/ext_tables_bucket/o/cust_sales_june.csv');
end;
```

You can also use the `dbms_cloud.list_files` function to get a list of the files in directories. As you saw for `data_pump`, a directory is needed, and in Autonomous, there isn't a file system; however, object storage can serve as these directories. You can query using this function to get the details of the files listed in the `data_pump_dir` directory.

```
SQL> select * from dbms_cloud.list_files('DATA_PUMP_DIR');
```

And if you want to see the objects in one of the locations, you can list the objects in a bucket.

```
SOL> select * from dbms_cloud.list_objects('OCI_ADB_DATAMGMT',
'https://objectstorage.us-ashburn-1.oraclecloud.com/n/namspace1 /b/
customer_sales/o/');
```

Just like individual files, there are procedures to handle bulk moves, uploads, and copies.

Another area for DBMS_CLOUD is the Cloud REST API procedures and functions. These procedures can get details about the Cloud REST APIs and can be used in PL/SQL and application code to get API requests and results. Since these are some of the various cloud APIs, you can create buckets in object storage to store the files and manage these types of resources.

Tip   There are several procedures and functions available in DBMS_CLOUD, and reviewing the documentation is very useful here. It is important to understand that the capabilities are there for managing the data and files in the cloud for Autonomous environments.

DBMS_CLOUD_AI

Oracle Autonomous Database 23ai provides a way to use generative AI with a large language model (LLM) to take plain text and convert it into Oracle SQL. This allows you to either generate the SQL code or run the SQL to return a result set. The steps are to configure a profile containing information about the LLM and the database objects/schema you want to include. The DBMS_CLOUD_AI package uses CREATE_PROFILE for the configuration and SET_PROFILE for the current session. This means you can have different profiles with different models, depending on the models you want to use. The AI prompt is SELECT AI action text; it is your natural language prompt. Different actions include runsql, showsql, narrate, chat, and explainsql. It could be very useful to simply query the database with a prompt and have it return SQL without needing to know the tables or columns. It could efficiently answer more questions, and it might even be fun to ask.

REST and ORDS

Oracle REST Data Services provides a way to manage APIs for the data in the database without direct access to the database. The credentials and privileges are all managed in the configuration of enabling the API. This is not just a cloud service; this is available in on-premises databases and a fantastic tool for providing the needed data to applications.

To configure ORDS in the database, you install ORDS and enable it on the database system. Then, you manage the views or tables where you enable ORDS and the REST APIs. ORDS is available for download on the same site where you can get SQL Developer Web and other useful tools for REST services and database management APIs (oracle. com/ords). You can also use yum to install it.

```
$ sudo yum install ords
$ ords -config /etc/ords/config install
```

REST endpoints start with http://localhost:8080/ords normally followed by the schema name and objects. Tables and views need to be enabled.

```
SQL> begin
ords.enable_object(
p_enabled => TRUE,
p_schema => 'MMALCHER',
p_object => 'ITEMS',
p_object_type => 'TABLE',
p_object_alias => 'items');
commit;
end;
```

The various tools also let you use options to enable REST on a database object. Figure 18-6 shows how to use the menu to right-click an object to REST enable a table.

Figure 18-6. *Enabling REST on table*

Figure 18-7 provides the URL to configure authentication for the API and the configured roles.

Figure 18-7. *Configuring REST*

Some credentials are needed if configured to access the data, and then you can test the REST endpoint with the URL `http://localhost:8080/ords/ mmalcher/items/`.

It seems simple enough and is a powerful data management tool to use data for applications. We are just highlighting the ways to get started here with your databases, and there are more ways to configure the services on-premises and in the cloud.

Since this chapter looks at Autonomous as a tool for data management, let's go back to Database Actions and look at the REST tool provided. Figure 18-8 shows the REST overview from Database Actions.

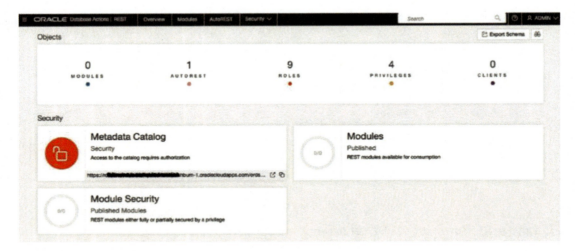

Figure 18-8. *REST Overview*

After enabling an object, you can access the API with the REST endpoint URL. You can also pull up the menu on the table or view, which allows you to edit, get a `curl` command, and open the data, as shown in Figure 18-9.

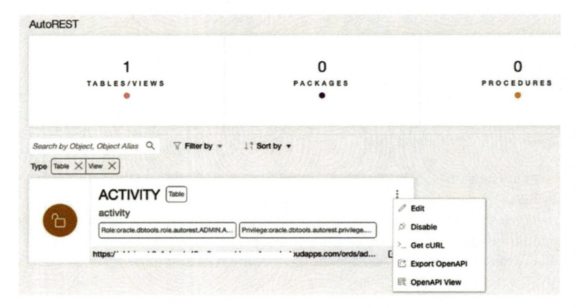

Figure 18-9. *AutoREST, edit*

Security is another REST tool option to examine. As shown in Figure 18-10, you can manage the privileges of the REST APIs and OAuth clients and roles. This allows the separation of administrators and managers of the REST services to grant the needed roles and access.

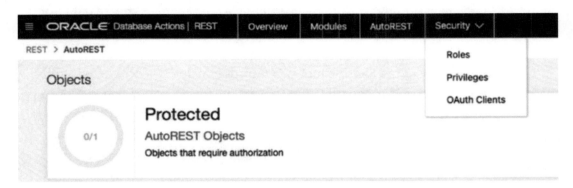

Figure 18-10. *Security for REST*

ORDS is an easy way to provide a data service to access data for applications, integrations, and data management needs. There are tools that allow you to configure ORDS in Autonomous and SQL Developer for on-premises databases. Database Actions is a tool set in the cloud to manage data services. The **DBMS_CLOUD** package is also available without the interface to perform these steps and configurations for data loading, privileges, and data services.

Tip   Oracle offers a great way to try these tools and experiment. It is called Oracle LiveLabs, and there are workshops that you can do for free for each of these areas. Be sure to check it out at `https://developer.oracle.com/livelabs`.

Data Sharing

Data sharing is needed because we always need the data in different places. Systems share data across databases and leverage information in one place to provide important details and facts in another system. We spend plenty of time moving data around and managing it in services so that access to the data is available when and where needed. The database administrator makes sure all these database systems can provide the data as needed, and the systems are highly available and secure, just for data to be used in ways we might not even consider. Database administrators can assist in integrations; however, new business cases always come up that want additional data from different sources, such as files, to be combined and used with the data from the customer database. There are various reasons to relate reference data or other source data from other sources; for example, the data in the inventory systems gets additional information from logs, and so on.

The idea around the Data Sharing tool is to improve business access to data and open these innovations and uses of data. You have done this in reports when sending files, keeping spreadsheets on our laptops, and so on. However, many of these ways to share data require extra work and processing, and make copies and redundant data extractions. You need to handle the security and make sure sensitive data stays that way.

Through the Data Sharing tool, a delta sharing protocol allows you to share data without copying it to another system. A user can consume the data that is made available and request access to the data by providing valid tokens, and the user then accesses the shared data.

The Data Share providers can make the data available to users through the Data Share tool. Figure 18-11 shows the provider and consumer data shares of Data Sharing in Database Actions for Autonomous Database.

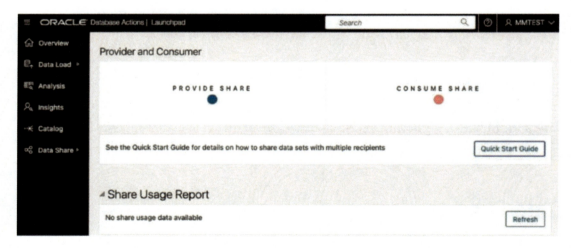

Figure 18-11. *Data Share tool*

When you create users for Autonomous Database, you can give them permissions to use Data Share, along with the other tools, or you can enable a schema for sharing in a SQL session.

```
SQL> begin
dbms_share.enable_schema (
schema_name => 'MMALCHER',
enabled => TRUE);
end;
```

As a data provider, you would start by providing a share, and you can share using object storage. Consumers of the share see the changes to the data only when new versions are published. The tables or objects are added to the data share, and you can define who will receive the share or create the share and add the consumers or recipients later.

The recipients need to subscribe and access the data shares, as shown in Figure 18-12. This also provides them with a personal authorization profile, which allows tracking of how the shares are being used and by which consumers. You can create external tables on top of the data shares to use with SQL, and you can see the data objects that are available to you.

Figure 18-12. *Subscribing to a share*

The data share becomes another tool in building out data lakes, and it can be made available with authentication and authorizations for consumers inside and outside your company. The cloud links provide an approach for sharing data from Autonomous Database and between Autonomous Databases. Now, instead of squirreling away data files, spreadsheets, reports, and so on, a data asset can be shared in a secure way to allow the business to gain access to the needed data and leverage the data for even more valuable insights.

Why are all these data management tools important? As the database administrator, you know where most of the company's data can be found. These tools leverage the same skills in securing the data and enabling the right service for the job. The administrators taking care of the database systems can really dive into ways to make data available in all kinds of formats that are easy to consume.

You can dive into supporting the Oracle Database with system tasks, installations, provisioning, patching, and migrations. This also includes ensuring the database system is highly available and secure and provides business continuity with disaster recovery and database restoration. In large environments, there is plenty to do with tuning and architecting the databases, but data management is expanding to allow businesses to innovate and leverage their data. A professional database administrator can support and manage the environment to allow data services and growth while making sure the database system is reliable and secure. This is an excellent opportunity to add value and manage an extremely important company asset: data!

Index

A

D

E

M

P, Q

W, X, Y, Z

Printed in the United States
by Baker & Taylor Publisher Services